The Sciences Po Series in International Relations and Political Economy

Series Editor, Christian Lequesne

This series consists of works emanating from the foremost French researchers from Sciences Po, Paris. Sciences Po was founded in 1872 and is today one of the most prestigious universities for teaching and research in social sciences in France, recognized worldwide.

This series focuses on the transformations of the international arena, in a world where the state, though its sovereignty is questioned, reinvents itself. The series explores the effects on international relations and the world economy of regionalization, globalization (not only of trade and finance but also of culture), and transnational flows at large. This evolution in world affairs sustains a variety of networks from the ideological to the criminal or terrorist. Besides the geopolitical transformations of the globalized planet, the new political economy of the world has a decided impact on its destiny as well, and this series hopes to uncover what that is.

Published by Palgrave Macmillan:

Politics In China: Moving Frontiers
    edited by Françoise Mengin and Jean-Louis Rocca
Tropical Forests, International Jungle: The Underside of Global Ecopolitics
    by Marie-Claude Smouts, translated by Cynthia Schoch
The Political Economy of Emerging Markets: Actors, Institutions and Financial Crises in Latin America
    by Javier Santiso
Cyber China: Reshaping National Identities in the Age of Information
    edited by Françoise Mengin
With Us or Against Us: Studies in Global Anti-Americanism
    edited by Denis Lacorne and Tony Judt
Vietnam's New Order: International Perspectives on the State and Reform in Vietnam
    edited by Stéphanie Balme and Mark Sidel
Equality and Transparency: A Strategic Perspective on Affirmative Action in American Law
    by Daniel Sabbagh, translation by Cynthia Schoch and John Atherton
Moralizing International Relations: Called to Account
    by Ariel Colonomos, translated by Chris Turner
Norms over Force: The Enigma of European Power
    by Zaki Laidi, translated from the French by Cynthia Schoch
Democracies at War against Terrorism: A Comparative Perspective
    edited by Samy Cohen, translated by John Atherton, Roger Leverdier, Leslie Piquemal, and Cynthia Schoch
Justifying War? From Humanitarian Intervention to Counterterrorism
    edited by Gilles Andréani and Pierre Hassner, translated by John Hulsey, Leslie Piquemal, Ros Schwartz, and Chris Turner
An Identity for Europe: The Relevance of Multiculturalism in EU Construction
    edited by Riva Kastoryano, translated by Susan Emanuel

The Politics of Regional Integration in Latin America: Theoretical and Comparative Explorations
  by Olivier Dabène
Central and Eastern Europe: Europeanization and Social Change
  by François Bafoil, translated by Chris Turner

Central and Eastern Europe

Europeanization and Social Change

François Bafoil

Translated by
Chris Turner

CENTRAL AND EASTERN EUROPE
Copyright © François Bafoil, 2009.

First published in 2009 by
PALGRAVE MACMILLAN®
in the United States—a division of St. Martin's Press LLC,
175 Fifth Avenue, New York, NY 10010.

Where this book is distributed in the UK, Europe and the rest of the world,
this is by Palgrave Macmillan, a division of Macmillan Publishers Limited,
registered in England, company number 785998, of Houndmills,
Basingstoke, Hampshire RG21 6XS.

Palgrave Macmillan is the global academic imprint of the above companies
and has companies and representatives throughout the world.

Palgrave® and Macmillan® are registered trademarks in the United States,
the United Kingdom, Europe and other countries.

ISBN: 978–0–230–60771–2

Library of Congress Cataloging-in-Publication Data

Bafoil, François.
    [Europe centrale et l'Europe de l'Est. English]
    Central and Eastern Europe : europeanization and social change /
François Bafoil ; translated by Chris Turner.
        p. cm.—(Sciences Po series in international relations and
            political economy.)
    Includes bibliographical references and index.
    ISBN-13: 978–0–230–60771–2 (alk. paper)
    ISBN-10: 0–230–60771–3 (alk. paper)
    1. Europe, Eastern—Politics and government—1989– 2. Europe,
Eastern—Economic conditions—1989– 3. Europe, Eastern—Economic
policy—1989– 4. Post-communism—Europe, Eastern. 5. Europe,
Central—Politics and government—1989– 6. Europe, Central—
Economic conditions—1989– 7. Europe, Central—Economic policy—
1989– 8. Post-communism—Europe, Central. I. Turner, Chris. II. Title.

JN96.A58B345 2009
320.947—dc22   2009002716

A catalogue record of the book is available from the British Library.

This book is printed on paper suitable for recycling and made from fully
managed and sustained forest sources. Logging, pulping and manufacturing
processes are expected to conform to the environmental regulations of the
country of origin.

Design by Newgen Imaging Systems (P) Ltd., Chennai, India.

First edition: October 2009

10 9 8 7 6 5 4 3 2 1

CONTENTS

TABLES

INTRODUCTION

Modernization, Europeanization, and Path Dependency

The collapse of the Soviet-type regimes in Central and Eastern Europe in 1989 imposed a twofold set of constraints on the new East European states. The first of these relates to Western modernization, given the extent to which these countries had fallen behind over the preceding decades, if not centuries.[1] The need to "catch up with" the West was all the more crucial since these new states were subject, from the outset, to the globalization of trade that resulted from the opening up of national borders. This dynamic has been interpreted in the sociological literature using the Weberian concepts of legal rules, the rule of law, regulated capitalist economy, and autonomy of fields of action. The second series of constraints relates to the European Union, which most of these countries very quickly sought to join, as much on account of a sense of belonging to a common geopolitical and cultural entity as of the inherent attractiveness of the EU (European Union). The concept of "Europeanization" has become the norm for analyzing Union regulation and the adaptation pressure exerted on the new countries, particularly in the form of—mainly political—conditionality.[2] It so happens that this dual series of constraints, specific to globalization and Europeanization, pressed itself upon the East European states at precisely the point when they were recovering their national sovereignty. For countries that had all been deprived of it for long periods of history—and not only under Communism—this demand for sovereignty imposed itself as the fundamental variable of the post-Communist transformation. This is why systemic change in Central and Eastern Europe should first be understood endogenously—that is to say, as a function of national trajectories. It cannot simply be reduced to the impacts of globalization and Europeanization. More exactly, these constraints can be grasped only through national prisms that have their origins in particular relations of force created before and after 1989 and within reconstructed institutions. The recasting of societal equilibria in fact took place on the basis of the recomposition of resources accumulated before 1989, on contact with opportunities linked to the opening of 1989 and in accordance with the places occupied or acquired by the various actors. The learning processes involved fitted into historical national contexts and the alliances between the different actors were formed against a background of reasserted sovereignty.

This is the basic argument of this work, the aim of which is to analyze the joint effects of the "catch-up revolution" (*die nachholende Revolution*[3]) and the "return to Europe"[4] on the basis of the national shaping of European constraints, starting out from the actors of social change situated in particular, conflictual historical trajectories. In the following pages, we shall not, then, be analyzing the process of the extension of EU regulation to the candidate states from the standpoint of the EU actors. We shall be attempting, rather, to understand how, in the formerly Communist states, and by isolating certain sectors, the various groups submitted themselves to that European regulation and how they adapted it as a function of their collective representations, interest, and different strategies of alliance formation within recomposed institutions. Also, to an extent, we shall be attempting to say how the actors were able to escape this adaptive pressure by bringing other resources to bear. Hence the need to stress the historical starting point, which relates to the legacies deriving from the Communist period, by asking ourselves what remains of these legacies once Communist regulation has disappeared (chapter one). From here we develop a two-pronged analysis of the processes of political and social change after 1989 in Central and Eastern Europe. The first analysis is one that takes the reconstruction of the central states as its object, taking three public policy areas into account: the redefinition of property rights (chapter two), the reform of welfare systems (chapter three), and regionalization (chapter four). The second analyzes the formal and informal capacities for the recomposition of the resources accumulated by several occupational groups. These are employees in industrial enterprises (chapter five), farmers (chapter six), labor unions (chapter seven), the voluntary and community sector (chapter eight) and, finally, parties (chapter nine).

The space designated in these pages by the term Central and Eastern Europe (or simply Eastern Europe) includes the 10 new member states of the EU that joined in 2004 and 2007. The countries of the former Yugoslavia (with the exception of Slovenia) are not included, though the former GDR (German Democratic Republic) is, since the various developments there since 1990 can justifiably be compared with those in Central and Eastern Europe, given the extent to which they represent a typical case of post-Communist transformation leading to integration into the European Union.

Catch-Up and Modernization. The Return to Weber

Economic Rationality and Historical Rationalization

Why begin with Max Weber? First, because the process of change accomplished after 1989 in Central Europe related to issues of the modernization of its societies, economies, and political regimes: though it was clearly cultural in nature, the "catch-up" required was, of course, also economic, with the West operating here as a benchmark. Second, because Communism always had the declared aim of bringing about another type of modernization, the basic features of which the German sociologist lived long enough to grasp.[5] Finally, because, in the Weberian interpretation, this process of modernization involves the basic categories of Europeanization with which this work is concerned: representations, interests, and institutions.[6]

Max Weber identified modernization as the single moment when, in industrial enterprises in the West, actors displayed the highest degree of efficiency, thanks to the implementation of technical and material procedures—calculation—for achieving a goal that had its own logic or *Eigengesetzlichkeit*. The rationality inherent in this dynamic Weber termed "formal purposive rationality" (*Zweckrationalität*), to distinguish it from other behaviors guided by different motivations, of the order of values or feelings. The latter underlie the various orders of life, underpin various forms of exchange, and provide the basis for different types of legitimacy. Formal purposive rationality referred, on the one hand, to the action orientation of the agent and, on the other, to the autonomy of the goal pursued. Moreover, the concept of rationality accounted for a historical process, the process of rationalization that saw the rationally managed enterprise extract itself from the domestic space to occupy a distinct site where the producers were concentrated and the separation between owner and manager was effected. Between these different actors—the employees, shareholders, and managers—contractual rather than personal relations applied. In this way, the enterprise reflected, at the micro level, and for particular equilibria, the combination of different general processes of rationalization specific to distinct areas—technical, legal, scientific, economic, and so on. This process of rationalization extended itself to the working of all organizations in the form of bureaucratization, to modes of life in the form of individualization and the contractualization of relations, and to types of domination in the guise of rational legal domination. The form of political economy specific to the West was thus characterized by a type of (technical or bureaucratic) rationality specific to a type of (waged) work in a given space (the large-scale enterprise) directed toward a goal, profit, under the domination of rational rules and a legitimate authority. In this context, the state has the role of ultimate procedural arbiter in the various different spheres.

This ideal-typical approach to modernization has been equated with rationalization and bureaucratization, since it is these that are involved through the domination of impersonal rules imposing themselves upon individualized actors. Many sociologists have described twentieth-century developments as belonging to Western rationalization. Talcott Parsons created the term "universals" to designate the necessary elements of this process, which saw democracy and individualization prevail and welfare states and affluent societies develop.[7] The German sociologist Wolfgang Zapf has contributed greatly to further disseminating this approach, both in 1989 and since.[8] From a practical point of view, modernization has been analyzed as a set of economic dynamics promoting successively the reduction of agricultural activities, the growth—and subsequently decline—of industrial activities and the growth—eventually reaching exponential proportions—in services. This dynamic of transformation that has, without exception, characterized all the developed economies, has been accompanied by the elimination, to a greater or lesser extent, of illiteracy. It has enabled levels of education and occupational skills to rise. It has intensified urbanization and subsequently spread welfare systems. Finally, modernization has been conceived in terms of the secular transformation of ways of life, thanks to the break-up of the traditional family and its narrowing to the parental unit, female liberation, and the secularization of behavior. All these elements have played a part in increased individualization.

Seen from this angle, is Communism a product of Western modernization? It is definitely so, in so far as it has been possible to see it as the last product of the eighteenth-century wave of rationalism, the wave of the Enlightenment ranged against religious obscurantism. However, rather than extending individualism, which triumphed in the West in the nineteenth century and beyond, Communism may be said to have set itself the task, according to this interpretation, of eliminating the anomic trend, the better to replace it with a collective feeling. It may be said to have been the last attempt to confer a meaning on modernization by basing modern society on community and sharing, rather than on the anomic individual deriving from individualization. In other words, arising out of the same common core as capitalism—that of the Enlightenment against religious obscurantism—Communism can be said to have aspired to reconcile what capitalism had torn asunder: material progress and community or, alternatively, technical knowledge and the faith of the political militant. Irrespective of the assessment that may be made of this endeavor, which Weber for his part denounced as the very basis of Communist irrationality, the Communist societies underwent a vast modernization, as we shall attempt to show in chapter one. They were, in fact, able to point to clear successes in the battle against illiteracy, the creation of a vast education system, and the establishment of a diversified network of technical training and cultural institutions, all of which was designed to provide industrialization with its indispensable material base. In many fields, decades of extreme backwardness were overcome.[9] Modernization extended to modes of life through the generalized spread of wage labor and of very extensive social provision, and the improvement in the situation of women. In short, the legitimacy of the Communist regimes was based largely on the assertion of the modernity of the economies and the generosity of the welfare systems that provided the sole route to social advancement and well-being.

Communist Irrationality

Yet, the radical failure of Communism derived from the confusion it spread in the political, economic, and social orders, as a result of the supremacy of one actor—the Communist Party—over all other organizations and in all fields of action. Because the party was regarded as the highest authority, over which no other institution could exert control, its authority was based on a confusion of ends. It substituted the value of altruism for the pursuit of profit. It commanded that enterprises create not profit, but social bonds. It prevented lawyers from interpreting the law and forced them to apply party law. For artists it laid down the underlying purposes of their art and it decreed what scientists were to study and which theories were outlawed. In short, by depriving every field of action of autonomy, it introduced a heteronomy that led to a generalized despecialization. This generated individual disengagement and, ultimately, a loss of collective bearings. Such a situation could arise only after the imposition of violence on a very large scale. This spread fear and atomized society. Weber used the concept "patrimonial bureaucracy" to describe this confused state, in which both the rational order of a tentacular bureaucracy and a type of domination that was not legal rule but the rule of a particular political party predominated (Weber, 1918). In place of rational legality, the pattern of patrimonialism actually predominated; this borrowed its underpinnings from tradition and hence depended on the loyalty of individuals. For Weber, the thoroughgoing irrationality of this political order consisted in its having rational economic action depend on a value instead of a formal purpose. That value was altruism, fraternity, the social bond, the nation, or the glory of the working class. The terms were all the more loaded for the fact that they were massively travestied by a minority that would never agree to put at risk again a power they had without exception acquired through extortion, violence, and lying (Weber, 1918 [1994]). Because it had perverted the rationality of the actor in its most radical expression—the pursuit of ends and the combination of the means relevant for attaining them—Communism was fundamentally irrational. Several sociologists, writing in the wake of Max Weber, have spoken of economic brigandage[10] and, more recently, of "demodernization."[11]

On the basis of this conclusion that Communism operated irrationally, the first obligation reformers had in 1990 was to reestablish the autonomy of each field, allowing each to set its own rules. For some, on the basis of the recognition of formal legality, this meant the right to stipulate contracts, together with formal rules, technical specialization, procedures, calculations, and respect for measures; for others, particularly noneconomic groups and networks, it meant the right to have the order of values, of affective relations, and sentiment prevail. On this basis, legitimate orders may be distinguished in two ways: either on the basis of legal rationality, which involves contractualization and the measurement of effects, or on the basis of traditional rationality, which involves the primacy of trust and individual relations. Now in 1990 and later, the East European situations displayed a number of discrepancies in this regard. These related mainly to the legacies of the previous period. No immediate adjustment occurred, as should have done according to an ideal-typical approach. On the contrary, maladjustments between the ideal type and reality prevailed. For this reason, the modernization approach was widely criticized;[12] it was objected that it favored a model of—largely North-American—development and, most importantly, that it neglected the deficiencies and failings that went along with Western-style modernization, beginning with unemployment and social exclusion. To seek to designate a final state aimed at from the outset was, said these critics, to yield to the temptation of teleology.[13] It meant a return to the "one best way" and predetermining historical change. Several authors (mainly from East Germany) stressed, rather, the complex aspect of modernization. They pointed out discrepancies and maladjustments in economic progress, with dissociated instances of backwardness and advance. Other writers stressed the power of interest groups or the ability of certain local groups to resist change.[14] All emphasized the resonance of historical continuity over the notion of the break or rupture, and the weight of history over the pretension to force the whole of Central Europe into a single mould.

Europeanization. National Sovereignties and European Regulation

The Stakes of National Sovereignty

For countries that have all been wiped from the map of Europe over periods of varying duration, history is of fundamental significance. They were all, without exception, incorporated at some point into the empires that shaped this part of the continent: the Baltic states were part of the Russian and Prussian empires; Poland was included in the three—Russian, Prussian, and Austro-Hungarian—empires; the Czech Republic, Slovakia, Hungary, and part of Romania were in the Austro-Hungarian empire, while Bulgaria, another part of Romania and part of Hungary were included in the Ottoman empire. Thus, in the modern era, Bulgaria regained its independence in 1878 after more than five centuries beneath the Ottoman yoke. The Baltic States, split between the Teutonic and Russian cultures, existed only during the interwar period. The two regions of Bohemia and Moravia gave rise in 1918, after the addition of Slovakia, to Czechoslovakia, bringing to an end almost three centuries of absence of the State. Finally, Poland reemerged in 1918 after 123 years. Having enjoyed sovereignty for less than 20 years after the First World War, between 1919 and 1939, all these countries saw their national autonomy purely and simply abolished after 1945, when the Soviet-type system was imposed on them. In the case of the Baltic States, this occurred after 1940, while the fateful date for Czechoslovakia was 1948. This first basic requirement to revive a sovereignty annihilated by their "big" neighbors was further intensified by the question raised by the presence of minorities within these countries and by changes of border over the past two centuries. The minorities issue had fuelled extremisms before the Second World War, leading to the catastrophic alliances with Nazism.[15] Once Communism collapsed in 1989, the demand for sovereignty came back on to the agenda with great urgency, in connection both with relations between ethnic majorities and minorities and the transformation of the centralized state architectures. On each occasion, the European Union sought to referee this question, linking respect for minorities and the establishment of regionalization as essential preconditions for membership. On each occasion, change was introduced in a centralized manner, without any concession whatever to potentially centrifugal forces. The constraint of the European rule was adapted on the basis of the fundamental dimension of historical sovereignty.

For this reason, the question of the state after 1989 in central Europe, which is at the center of our concerns in this book, is posed at the point where the demands of national sovereignty intersect with the need to integrate into international trade. The examination of the interconnections between the two is part of a research program on the nature of the state that is one of the most productive in the social sciences.[16] The first aspect of state autonomy connects with the work of Weber, who, in what has become the classic definition, referred to the state as a body holding a monopoly of legitimate violence over a given territory. It is seen both as an arena of conflict, in which groups with divergent interests confront each other, and as the site of autonomy (by way of public policies). The second aspect refers to interstate relations to the international context, which determine the way states develop. In this approach, transnational actors play a major role, on account of the dependencies they create within the states on which they impose themselves. The notion of dependency does not refer here to a one-way process, by which the rich countries would strengthen their position in direct proportion to the dwindling of the receiving countries, regarded for this purpose as peripheral, as the so-called dependency school has long asserted. It refers, rather, to the capacity accorded to the receiving states to strengthen their position thanks to external contributions, whether these are material or financial flows or influxes of ideas. Enquiry into the processes of emergence and forms of consolidation of the post-Communist states fits very precisely into this theoretical framework, with the—fundamental—proviso that the primary dimension of the self-assertion of states after 1989 is colored by the demand for national sovereignty. Hence the very great tension that has characterized the relation between these new states and the European Union, which has represented the focus of action of practically all the governments since 1989. However, far from being perceived only in terms of an "enforced transference of norms"[17]—an interpretation reflecting the experience of Eastern Germany—the exchanges between the EU and the new states deserve primarily to be evaluated as a massive negotiation that has led to a wide-scale redistribution of powers and a constant reconstruction of social consensuses.

Europeanization. An Interpretive Schema

While it underpins a very rich school of analysis in Western European political science,[18] the notion of Europeanization is only just beginning to be applied to the study of Eastern European processes. In this case, attention has mainly been paid to institutional processes,[19] some public policies,[20] and, to a lesser extent, behavioral rather than policy-related matters. In the same way, in fact, as the concept is often misinterpreted in Western Europe as describing the processes of convergence, integration, or formation of the union,[21] its use in connection with Central and Eastern Europe often suffers from an enormous confusion: it is often interpreted to mean "institutional mimicry," if not, indeed, equated with the transformation process that has been under way since 1990. Within this framework, Europeanization might be said to equate to adoption of the EU rules initiated with the first agreements of 1991 or those of the international institutions (the World Bank). All in all, it might be said to equate to adjustment to the constraints of the market and the EU.

What Europeanization Is and Is Not

This is not the perspective of this study, which aims, with respect to the concept of Europeanization, to answer three questions: How does this process operate? When does it take place? And with whom? If the use of this concept is pertinent in the examination of the transformations in Eastern Europe, that is because it enables us, in part, to interpret the strategies of the various actors who adapt the constraints they are faced with—those of globalization and the EU. How do they do this? By bringing into play various registers of resources and alliances that lead to the reformulation of social consensuses. Precisely when did they do it? From 1997 onward, when EU constraints became unavoidable for the candidate countries. In other words, when the European Union made respect for the rules of the *Acquis Communautaire* the sine qua non for their integration. For this reason, Europeanization may be defined as the strategic process of the national shaping of the shared rules of the EU member states, on the basis of shared representations and various alliances, as part of a dynamic that either supported or dampened the effects of globalization. In this interpretation one concept is central: national sovereignty. It is through the prism of national sovereignty that the strategies for adapting the constraints can be understood. But before we go further into this, let us make clear what the concept of Europeanization is not.

Europeanization is not the post-Communist transition, nor is it "post-Communism." We shall reserve the use of the term "transition" for the first moments of the exit from Communism in 1989–90, when the electoral and constitutional rules and the first measures on market stabilization were adopted. The aim of this study is not, then, to examine the paths out of Communism, of which the triple sequence of liberalization, democratization, and consolidation—together with the notion of pact—have done much to deepen our understanding in the wake of the work produced on the Latin American and Southern European transitions.[22] Nor is Europeanization "post-Communism." That term properly defines the 10-year process of the adjustment of economies and political scenes to the prerequisites for democracy and the market, a process that has had the central problematic of the transformation of property rights as its cornerstone.[23] This does not mean, of course, that the Union played no role in these different periods. On the contrary, it was substantially present from the beginning of the transformation of these states, either directly with Association Agreements and the finance granted—and also through the accompanying technical training—or more indirectly, through the influence exerted on various—constitutional and institutional—choices relating to public agencies, and so on. By asserting that the whole action of the Union cannot be reduced to this notion of Europeanization, our aim is to stress, by contrast, that we can only speak in terms of Europeanization when the Union showed itself to be the decisive actor; that is to say, when its pressure turned out to be irresistible, namely in late 1997 and early 1998 when it made adoption by the candidate countries of the entire *Acquis Communautaire* the absolute precondition for membership.

Ideas, Interests, and Institutions

Within this framework, it is worth lingering for a moment over one interpretive schema.[24] Rather than concentrating on the *formation* of the European rules, this is based on the examination of the national processes of their *integration*, the impact of which is facilitated or hampered by the very texture of the various national prisms, characterized, on the one hand, by shared representations and, on the other, by domestic institutions and, finally, by organized actors. According to this interpretation, the level of adoption, adaptation, or even rejection of the EU rules can be understood in two ways: in terms of the degree of openness or closure of institutions (an institutional "fit" or "misfit") or in terms of the capacity of certain groups to thwart or facilitate any process of adaptation. The facilitating or, conversely, inhibiting groups may take the situation forward or block it, depending on their power of veto. Thus, the more the national prisms attest to specific arrangements relating to long-term history or the power of interest groups, and the greater the particularity of the state in question, then the more pressure is exerted, leading to major conflicts between the two—supranational and domestic—poles. Conversely, the less resistance is offered by domestic prisms, the less pressure is felt and the more the rules are adapted without conflict.

Applied to the processes of change in Central Europe, this interpretive grid is productive for at least three reasons. First in understanding that the East European question is not a question of the formation of the rules of the Union, in which the candidate countries have never had a hand. It has strictly been a question for them of adjusting to EU pressure, not of participating in the formation of the collective space, even if Schimmelfennig is certainly right to analyze "political conditionality" as a pressure for relative adjustment: though it forced candidate countries to adopt adjusted behaviors, this was nevertheless accompanied, on the part of the EU, by the obligation to set a time limit for integration, indicating the amount of accessible benefits and seeking out the political partners capable of carrying the project through.[25] Moreover, the fact that the East European candidates did not participate in the formation of the common rules is a fundamental difference separating them from the countries of Western Europe—and even from those of Southern Europe, whose period of adjustment to EU rules followed their integration into the EU more than it preceded it.[26] Shall we, for all that, conclude that there was a "forced transference of norms" in the cases that concern us here?[27] We shall not, because it is the principle of sovereignty that explains the adjustment process, that process ultimately being particular to each state as a function of its own trajectory. Shall we also conclude that the candidate states had no feedback-effect on the rules? We shall not, if only because the membership criteria for any candidate have, since 2004, been supplemented by the obligation to hold a referendum in the member states, and the tools of intervention have been considerably enriched. The preaccession funds and control processes (action plans, screening, and monitoring) that have enabled the candidate states to be progressively socialized into EU rules are now part of the integration mechanism for every new member.

This is why this schema is also productive for understanding how domestic prisms, all of them characterized by the exigency to assert national sovereignty, have stood out against an extremely constraining pressure on the new states to open up their economies, both to benefit from all that has been shown to be lacking (capital, technologies, training, access to Western markets, etc.) and to meet the expectations of the European Union. Besides this, it is important to stress that the pressure to adapt has in certain cases been facilitated by the very absence of rules with regard to many policies that were entirely new for these states; and that, as a consequence, the European rules in some cases represented unhoped-for resources for some organized groups. Thus we shall conclude that, in both cases, EU pressure effected a redistribution of significant powers for several groups of actors. So far as these—facilitating or inhibiting—groups are concerned, we see in East European societies the influence of the former *nomenklatura*, of the political parties old and new, of the labor unions and also all the groups that, on one basis or another, found themselves favored by the previous regime; importantly, these groups will be covered in chapter one. To these may be added the "new" actors, those among the political parties and in the economic sphere, the new executives working with foreign partners, and single-issue groups such as those concerned with the environment, and so on.

The third reason for the interest in this analytical schema relates to the field of collective representations, which are too often assumed, where East European societies are concerned, to be factors of blockage or inertia, involving the so-called Soviet mentality. Now, in this dynamic process of Europeanization, in which Radaelli has reminded us of the importance of ideas, alongside the significant part played by interests and institutions,[28] the notion of "social learning" is an important output. It brings out, in fact, the notion of values shared by the different communities within networks backed up by mutual trust, growth of shared knowledge, and collective action. Such a notion enables us to reintroduce into the analysis two important advances made in analyses carried out in the West. The first relates to the so-called "constructivist" approach, which foregrounds the notion of "European identity"[29] and finds a common "core" of shared representations West and East. Among other things, this explains the extent of the demand on the elites of the EU15 to reunify, through the 2004 and 2007 expansions, a continent whose unity was accidentally broken at Yalta[30] and the sense of "moral reparation" involved in this. Here, to stress this common background is to stress, on the one hand, the identity common to both West and East, the reality of which had already been highlighted by the dissident movements before 1989[31] and, on the other, the choice of certain rules and the prohibition of others. In other words, the "common European identity" has force and, as Sedelmeier stresses, prohibits exit behaviors and favors certain groups (e.g., the policy advocacy groups). This does not mean, however, in the East European case, a continuum initiated by the Association Agreements, carried on by the Copenhagen Agreements in 1993, and reinforced by the reaffirmation of the *acquis communautaire*. In our view, the reaffirmation of the *acquis* as a sine qua non introduced a break into strategies, since its implementation, particularly with regard to Chapter Twenty-One (concerning regionalization and decentralization), called for the establishment of institutions that were both new and recomposed. It was these institutions that were crucial in completing the transformations accomplished before 2004 and the implementation of the structural funds after that date. This is why it is useful to draw on the advances of the second, so-called neoinstitutionalist approach, which, above and beyond transaction costs, stresses the notion of conflict to explain the consensuses achieved—consensuses to which the collective rules attest. What conflict are we speaking of here? The fundamental conflict that, in the East European case, is based on the former social constructs (institutions and behaviors) running up against the new operating constraints linked to the globalization of trade and membership of the EU. This is why the notion of path dependency has had substantial importance in the examination of East European transformations, because it has attempted to account simultaneously for the permanence of certain elements within the new human constructs, the radical novelty of the operating contexts and the reconfiguration of the actors' strategies at their base.

A Theoretical Paradigm, Path Dependency

Let us briefly recall the three basic elements that explain the decisive importance of this concept of path dependency and that we have mobilized for our purpose. First, continuity of processes, as a result of the series of constraints affecting choices. These constraints exclude alternative solutions ("lock-in effect") and enforce "compliance" with the path indicated. A second element is the continuation of trajectories taken by the actors. If actors follow the same path, they do so on account of acquired habits and, more broadly, of the advantages attaching to imitation or, conversely, the costs involved in breaking with habits. These logics of "self-reinforcement" thus ensure the success of the undertaking. The last element relates to the adoption by the greatest number of actors of those solutions that are already available. This is explained by logics of imitation, by group behavior, and by the perception of the advantages associated with repetition. For all these reasons, a suboptimal solution may win out over another, more rational alternative because it was the first to have been adopted and advantages ensue from choosing it and high costs from abandoning it. For this reason, innovation represents a cost that diminishes in relation to the duration of its rootedness or grows as a function of the absence of an environing milieu. Consequently, rule-bearing institutions promote both anticipatory capacities and common values and representations.[32] The latter both function as an incentive to repetition of the same behaviors and enable behavior to be adjusted. Rules ensure continuity of action, its correctness, and the satisfaction of the actors. They safeguard the permanence of communities and are, for that reason, legitimate. If we may assert that "history counts," this is because determinism bestows advantages by virtue of the fact that the structure of preferences is a historical construct. This is what gives grounds for rejecting a merely linear causality, which we might derive from a peremptory reading of North, as, for example, when he asserts that "path dependency" characterizes the influence of the past over the present.[33]

This approach was very largely in favor after 1990. At a point when everything was focused on breaks in continuity and the negation of past trajectories—providing scope for the policies that were violently thrust forward in the very early days of change—it stressed the importance of psychological continuities and the weight of memory and individual and collective experience.[34] Above all, it enabled the repetition of certain phenomena, the reemergence of a number of actors, and the revalorization of some dynamics belonging to the pre-1989 period to be explained, even though all operating structures were subject to radically new constraints and, hence, called for total redefinitions of action. Indeed, for this reason it was subject to a very great many critiques. Some stressed the nature of the choices made by researchers who foreground one historical phenomenon and turn it into the cause of others for the purposes of their own demonstration.[35] Others criticized the excessive determinism of certain causal series, as, for example, when the initial elections are built up into an explanatory matrix for all that followed.[36] Many works have criticized the fact that the very principle of causal imputation remains concealed. It has also been demonstrated that, within the industrial enterprise, the rupture occasioned by the introduction of a new technology could be combined with a high degree of continuity.[37] We shall endeavor in the following pages to show where continuities pertain and breaks occur. Now, these criticisms are admissible insofar as they do not downplay what is at stake in the analysis of the transformation of East European societies and economies. And what is at stake here? It relates to the capacity correctly to reconstruct the dynamics of the building of the various—most often disconnected—central and local equilibria on the basis of the combination of old elements and the new opportunities associated with the situation opened up in 1990.

A great many theoretical and empirical studies have endeavored to demonstrate the importance of this for the understanding of East European transformations in political science,[38] economics,[39] sociology,[40] geography,[41] or anthropology.[42] The objects of study have been very varied, ranging from social classes to interest groups, privatization policies to welfare-state reforms,[43] systems of government to systems of governance,[44] industrial companies to agricultural concerns, and regional dynamics to innovative local environments.[45] In each case, the approaches have highlighted three elements in the analysis. The first concerns the absence of a complete break in historical trajectories, the various authors preferring the notion of a partial decomposition of certain institutional elements and recompositions effected as a function of acquired habits and new rules. Thus, institutions are not born out of nothing, but are "recombined" with the aid of the trajectories pursued in the past that permit of adaptation to the new conditions. David Stark was the very first to stress that the way in which the pieces of the former regime broke apart would have "consequences for how political and economic institutions [could] be reconstructed. In short, the paths of extrication from state socialism shape possibilities of transformation."[46] The second element concerns the capacity of individuals and groups, who find in their own experiences and former trajectories the necessary resources to resist or to cushion the effects of the new rules of the game. Hence the disconnect between the logics specific to the centralized and the decentralized levels, between which there is no deterministic relation. The notions of network and informal relations have also largely won out, making relevant once more the founding analyses of economic sociology and the approach in terms of "embeddedness."[47] We shall show this to a considerable extent in part 2 of this book, focusing on recompositions of equilibria in enterprises, in agricultural concerns and, finally, in a number of associations. Hence, as the last element, the possibility of incorporating the notion of change or innovation into the very heart of causal series regarded as so many recomposed lines of development that are, ultimately, open to sudden bifurcations. For example, centralized contexts may permit the emergence of decentralizing dynamics, through which networked interest groups reveal new learning processes. New opportunities give rise to unexpected developments. Initially unforeseen actors may, like social movements, introduce themselves into a routinized game; new technologies may break a cycle of routines and impose different behaviors. The period between 1989 and 2004 in Central and Eastern Europe was neither a clean break, nor a time of pure continuity: it has the advantage of showing up the moments when history exerted its effects, when timescales were interrupted and when the various different heritages were recomposed, and under what factors and social and political relations of force these things occurred, leading to what learning process and what creative recomposition and, finally, to what legitimacy of the social, economic, and political orders.

CHAPTER ONE

The Legacies. Picture of a Political Economy of Soviet-Style Socialism

When we say "history counts," what do we mean by this expression? What counts? What remains from one period to the next? To understand the context in which change took place in 1989 and how it has been implemented in the states and societies of Central and Eastern Europe since that date, it is only right that we should specify what remains of the past. It is the aim of this chapter to identify the three fundamental mechanisms that ensured stability in Communist societies and left deep marks after 1989. These were: (1) the enterprise, because it was at the center of the whole system of values and production, the organization of territory and trade; (2) the welfare state, because the legitimacy enjoyed by the Communist states basically depended on massive redistribution, on the basis of a broad set of shared values and, hence, of very strong social consensuses; and (3) the political scenes, the surprising variety of which attested to the internal dynamics of the Communist Parties and hence to the reciprocal influences between Soviet-type societies and governments. Recalling these three mechanisms enables us to understand that, within a broad institutional uniformity—the same uniformity that entitles us to speak of a "Soviet-type system"—some countries were able to develop their own particular paths. Several groups of actors were in possession of very significant resources that they were able to exploit later, when the Communist institutions crumbled. This explains the importance of the notion of political, economic, and social capital that has been widely analyzed in the West and has acquired new significance in the study of East European realities.[1] This notion refers us, across these different periods, to a basic feature of institutions that is too often lost sight of the informality of institutional rules and consensuses, which means that, before 1989, institutions—even if they came under the overarching authority of the Communist Party—were appropriated to an enormous extent by the groups concerned, while the new institutions created from scratch after 1989 were not, by themselves, able to produce the expected collective action. By focusing successively on the examination of certain features of the economic order (the enterprise), the social order (the welfare states), and the political order (civil societies and parties), this chapter raises the question of the pertinence of resources, be it the various behaviors of adjustment to the shortage economy, work-based values and neighborhood solidarities, or resistance behavior within certain political organizations.

Industrial Organization, Territorial Concentration, and Autarky

What is significant in industrial organization of the Soviet type? First, there is the formidable concentration of material and human resources, which, despite the irrational management of the economy, gave rise to a high degree of internal cohesion. That so-called planned—or "centrally administered"—economy enabled a largely identical structure to be built up in every country. It was based on particular types of sector—the sectors of production and heavy industry—at the expense of consumption and light industry. It was, admittedly, the aim of this continual consolidation of heavy industry to provide these countries with an industrial infrastructure that had largely been lacking up to that point. It also suited the dominant ideology, which valued size, the better to ensure the consolidation of the "mass" working class and shore up within it the place of the skilled worker, the figurehead of socialism. This project of economic modernization involved the massive transfer of labor from the primary to the secondary sectors and, at the same time, of rural populations to the urban centers. The populations were subjected to a considerable degree of violence. This found expression in the various waves of nationalization of private industrial, artisanal, commercial, and agricultural property.[2] Industrial wage labor became the dominant form of work relations. This was also extended to agriculture, which, Poland excepted, was collectivized along the lines adopted in the USSR in the 1930s. Finally, labor was concentrated in more and more integrated units, which were themselves inserted into a set of strictly hierarchized industrial branches.

An organization of this kind was based on the interdependence of sectors and units of production. In the view of the Communist authorities, this was the only way to ensure the satisfaction of needs specified centrally and in advance, the transmission of orders and strict work discipline. The allocation of resources by the Central Planning Commission was carried out on a sector-by-sector basis, according to a hierarchy of large and small enterprises grouped within combines. Among the central activities of the sectoral directorate were research and development and training and skills centers. Foreign trade came under the authority, in each sector, of a Centre for External Commerce. The local enterprise had no great say in defining economic objectives. It merely had an executive function. It did not own its profits, nor could it set its prices itself. These were imposed administratively. Nonetheless, it played a substantial role in the locality. Industrial or agricultural units dominated the local markets for labor and goods. This industrial and spatial organization took place within an extended system of economic exchange characteristic of markets of the Soviet-type system, which assigned each country its place in the international division of labor.

The combination of the two elements—sectoral organization and the functioning of enterprises—contributed to shaping territories marked by a concentration of resources and a focus on monocultures. New industrial regions appeared alongside old ones, whose industrial potential was intensified. Towns, which were in many cases old market towns, were given a—most often monofunctional—industrial structure. Over the years, they acquired administrative functions, which were sometimes shared with the enterprise. Dynamics of territorial polarization, mainly due to the particular orientation of economies within the Soviet framework, reversed historical dynamics. These favored the Eastern regions, which were historically rural in the case of the Polish central plains and also Moravia, the Eastern parts of Slovakia and Hungary and Bulgaria. For their part the old Western regions were systematically put at a disadvantage on the grounds that they had previously had relations with the countries of the West. The Polish regions were discriminated against all the more for the fact that fears of the outbreak of a Third World War were stirred up by these border regions. For that reason, they found themselves overendowed with military hardware and garrisons, both Soviet and national. At the same time, the Western Polish regions, which were described as being "recovered" from the German "enemy," together with the northern and Western Czech regions, were subject to endless exploitation for symbolic prestige purposes and were a source of significant legitimation for the Communist authorities. It was on these lands that the very large majority of state farms were located, which the Communists expected to demonstrate their clear superiority over private operation. This nationalism tinged with triumphal voluntarism was, however, mingled with a fear of irredentism on the part of the populations, given the way the borders had been redrawn after 1945 and the presence in these areas of groups of nonallogenic individuals.

Moreover, all the regions bore the stamp of industrialization, including the traditionally agricultural areas. These filled up with farms that, over time, grew to gigantic proportions. Some of these specialized in livestock and others in arable farming, but they were subject to intense integration. In Bulgaria in the 1980s, they had up to 30,000 employees and stretched over tens of thousands of hectares. In this way, the enterprise became the engine driving local development. It fulfilled the expected functions in terms of employment, production, and, more rarely, training, but also all those functions previously assumed by independent, private units. The same went for administrative or judicial functions—a number of large units equipped themselves with a regional prison—and also the organization of festivities within and outside the enterprise and the distribution of various products that would formerly have been done by private stores or of alternative products that effectively served as currency in the vast local circuit of which the enterprise was the center.

Finally, the violence underlying the dynamic of social and economic transformation was able to exert itself only because one particular actor, the Communist Party, had concentrated all power in its own hands. It had subordinated all centers of power to itself. It had at its disposal a unit—or even a department—of secret police working in every enterprise, submitting everyone to its rule. Several enterprises had armed groups or military brigades, ready to intervene in case of disorder. They all maintained the myth that the enterprise was under siege and that the gains of socialism had to be defended at rifle point. When the enterprise held celebrations, they marched at the head of the parade. At the top, the secret police, the armed wing of the party, had extended its power into every organization, maintaining a constant climate of fear. In this way, central and local rule was achieved through the absolute domination of all organizations by the Communist Party. The political order was based in part on the integration into the decision-making process of the representatives of the combines in the main industrial sectors and the representatives of the trade unions. The highest official of the trade unions was an ex officio member of the supreme political body, the Politburo, while very often the directors of the main combines were members of the Central Committee. In all the countries without exception, the centers of negotiation and decision making were dominated by the *troika* of party, combined management, and trade unions. This led to a total subordination of all the levels of the various political, judicial, administrative, economic, and social structures to the party. The principle of "democratic centralism" gave formal expression to this subjection, which was illustrated in each sector by the various so-called *nomenklatura* lists.[3] The principles of differentiation and autonomy of the fields of public and private action disappeared, and any notion of local initiative was condemned.

The Real Functioning of Enterprises and Economic Crises

Long before 1989, a great number of observers condemned the irrational character of Soviet-style economies, despite their very high level of internal coherence.[4] We shall mention three components of that economic irrationality here: planning, the parallel economy, and dependence on the West.

The Irrationality of Centralized Planning

It was the basic aim of centralized planning that the disorder of the market would be replaced by the specification, from the commanding heights of the Communist organization, of all material needs and the means of satisfying them. This primacy of the plan gave rise, on the one hand, to the particular forms of ownership (collective or so-called public property) and, on the other, to the (vertical) modes of organization. In order to validate the central prescriptions, it was up to all the local actors to establish their own plans, in such a way that, when aggregated together, these would correspond to the intended overall plan, the aim being to create a situation in which all these elements contributed to setting centralized, concentrated organizations in place. Only such organizations were capable of facilitating the transmission of information and the requisite obedience for their practical implementation. This claim that planning and the circulation of data operated freely has been repeatedly criticized in a large number of studies. In reality, the processes of production were dominated by arythmia and the breakdowns led to substitution behaviors. These rendered inoperative all efforts to ground the organization of labor scientifically.[5] The mismatch that was observed between the prescribed state of affairs and the reality, which gave rise to the operational crises of that economy, was always ascribed by Communist officials to human malevolence alone. On every occasion, it was interpreted in terms of class hostility and the enduring presence of the former class enemy. Most often, the authorities concluded that there was a need to intensify discipline, which had been relaxed for a moment, and also to reinforce the mechanisms that had been responsible for the gap between prescription and reality in the first place. All the reforms carried out in the countries of Eastern Europe—and there were many of them—aimed to loosen the grip of central constraints at the enterprise level by giving unit managers greater room for maneuver. However, given the tight interdependence between the various sectors and enterprises, the effects of these reforms were to produce more breakdowns in interenterprise exchange. They led to the accumulation of bottlenecks, increased dissatisfaction, and intensification of the causes that had produced the original crisis. The irrationality of the economic system was thus reformulated by the politicians, as they aimed to correct the negative effects of centralization. Going to the source of what seemed to be the fundamental mistake—namely, this illusion of the total knowledge of the elements contributing to the definition of needs and the means of satisfying them—the British economist Alec Nove wrote that "Kiev mathematicians have established that, just to draw up a plan for the precise, completely integrated material and technical provisioning of the Republic of Ukraine for one year would take up the work of the entire population of the globe for 10 million years." There were many observers who had concluded from this that it was impossible to reform the centralized economic system, whatever the variants adopted by each country.

The Shortage Economy and Alternative Solutions

This aspiration completely to govern resources, both material and human, based on a total calculation of actions, produced a series of dysfunctions within organizations. Janos Kornai must be credited with having demonstrated the logic of this development[6] by stressing the systemic production of shortage (sellers' economy) and its reproduction by all the actors in the economic chain at all levels (substitution behavior). What the Hungarian economist defined as a "shortage economy" referred to this centralized economy dominated by suppliers (or, to put it another way, by sellers rather than customers), who knew no limits to their thirst for grandeur or their capacity to suck in resources. Credit was granted as a function of priorities laid down by the center, for the accomplishment of large-scale investment projects. Only such projects were able to fulfill the grandiose aims of the hierarchs in terms of industrial installations or armaments. Resources were allotted on the basis of the size and influence of interest groups. The latter were organized in combines supported by enormous political networks. Material well-being or mass consumption were not among the priority objectives and the sector of the consumption industries was, in consequence, largely neglected. In these conditions, there were no "hard" budgetary constraints, forcing financial discipline on actors, but only "soft budget constraints," which operated without any concern for losses or irrationalities of all kinds. This gave rise to Pharaonic projects, and the virtually unlimited expenditure on these could be based only on the rationing of demand. A chronic lack of resources ("shortages") ensued and hence an obligation for actors to forearm themselves, by accumulating human and material resources, against the inevitable interruptions that were going to occur. Hence the instances of excess employment, which some translate as "concealed unemployment" and continuous wastage, which the bloatedness of the repair sector was unable to bring under control. Hence, above all, the reproduction by everyone of the central constraint: namely, shortage. This resulted in many bottlenecks at the level of production, which impacted on consumers in the form of longer waiting lines or queues, and showed up in a phenomenon emblematic of this economy: waiting in line. This has been analyzed as the substitute for inflation for authorities that denied the existence of such a phenomenon within the framework of a socialist economy.

However, in both cases, the actors managed to find alternative solutions. Kornai has shown how, given the impossibility of obtaining the product one was waiting for, the producer or customer could do no other than direct his choices toward substitute products. Within enterprises, more or less effective, but always informal, makeshift solutions were implemented to find the missing input and, ultimately, fulfill the plan. An individual was tasked with finding the missing resources, both material and human. It was his/her function to check out the partners in the neighborhood of his enterprise, flush out the missing input, negotiate the barter with the partner and unearth the necessary labor. Within this circuit, the exchange of specialists was a form of currency, as were goods, so that, as payment for obtaining spare parts, for example, a partner would provide, for example, foodstuffs. Where consumers were concerned, a vast range of strategies was employed to find a replacement product and hence reduce waiting times and satisfy material needs in one way or another. The value of a good may well not correspond to its use-value, but to its value as currency in an alternative circuit.

Thus, far from promoting harmonious trade, the shortage system was based on discontinuity of exchange and the offsetting of product deficiencies. An entire economy functioned in place of the officially proclaimed one, inducing misappropriation, dissimulation, and dubious resourcefulness. The "second" or "parallel" economy has its origins in such behaviors. It covered enormous areas, which Stark and Nee have described as market economy substitutes within the plan.[7] The American economist Katsenelinboingen has described these parallel arrangements as a set of "colored markets." They reflected the vast spectrum of public tolerance, ranging from permitted, but hidden, activities to illegal, gangsterish ones, which at times fell foul of the law.[8] The degree of corruption was intense and affected more or less all trade. This term, "corruption," does not have the same range of reference as in market economies, where it refers to the abuse of public office for private ends. Nor does it cover the reality that will be examined in the next chapter, when we examine the forms of privatization after 1989. In a Soviet-type economy, where sellers dominate and relations of force are paramount, corruption appeared as a functional substitute available to individuals at different points in the chain of exchanges.[9] It facilitated economic exchange and ensured the satisfaction of the parties concerned. Where economists had isolated phenomena of transaction obscurity or informal relations, sociologists stressed resourcefulness, networks, social capital, and the autonomous social relations specific to a "shortage economy."

In this way, different levels of reality existed side by side, consisting of the official economy, the secondary economy and (for the armaments sector) the privileged economy.[10] Each of these involved particular forms of exchange, along with specific forms of currency and distinct social relations. Far from leading to homogeneous living and working conditions, Communism had led to the superimposition of spheres of action, each largely disconnected from the other. More or less appropriate behaviors were constructed for each of the different strata. They involved particular sets of representations and allegiances. There were so many responses more or less well adapted to the dysfunctions induced by the center, not the least of which was that "uncivic economy" reflected in cynicism and slovenliness at work.[11] In the 1980s, several Polish sociologists interpreted the splitting of public and private behavior in terms of dimorphism. The Romanian political scientist Daniel Barbu spoke of Communist double-talk as a form of "moral diglossia."[12] A vast literature has underscored the duplicitous attitude adopted toward the various public interlocutors, the crisis of values, and the loss of trust in institutions. The final crisis has been analyzed as a moment in which there was both a delegitimation of rules, perceived as unbearable, and a generalized defection of individuals.

Dependency on the West

No thoroughgoing reform was able to set this type of economy right. Given the interdependence between different areas and actors, any reform led to an accentuation of the initial failings. Dependence internally on informal solutions had its counterpart in a dependence externally on Western partners. But this led to identical dead-ends. Over the decades, the West emerged as the key resource for maintaining the Communist positions, once the Communist elites had reached the conclusion that they had gone as far as they could by way of the extensive use of local resources. In the late 1960s, the Soviet-type economies were faced with the fact that extensive development had come to an end. It had been made possible, over the preceding two decades, by the great shifts from agriculture to industry and the imposition of industrial wage labor on almost all kinds of activity. Efforts to bring about the change of economic regime that it was felt had to come took different forms in the different countries of Eastern Europe. In East Germany, it gave rise to a reassertion of the founding principles of Leninism and Stalinism, based on voluntarism, mobilization, and socialist emulation. Yet, from the 1970s onward, the debt to West German financial backers swelled. Romania firmly rejected any form of financial dependency and sought national salvation in the affirmation of a so-called third way, based on the rejection of both the Soviet and American models. The outcome of this decision, in its final decade, was a progressive asphyxiation of society, as it was forced to find resources for its development within its own borders. In 1989, it had repaid more than half of the 9 billion dollars of debt contracted 10 years earlier. Hungary decided to launch its reform program in 1968. It was to lead, through many advances and retreats, to that characteristic situation of "neither planning nor the market," though it would nevertheless gain it kudos with the financial institutions 20 years later.

Finally, in the early 1970s, when Gierek succeeded Gomulka, Poland opted for an original solution based on calculation of a rational exchange with the Western nations. The idea was simple and seemed obvious.[13] With the credit granted by the international backers, the country could have "turnkey" factories. These would enable it to produce quality goods that could be sold in Western markets to cover the debt interest repayments. The idea seemed all the more brilliant for the fact that it satisfied various different aspirations: first, those of the Leninists, who had always dreamed of hanging the West with the rope Communism had bought from it; second, those of the Western financiers who were then experiencing considerable expansion, and finally, those of the population, who glimpsed the possibility of greater opportunities for consumption. However, this conception was based on the idea that no obstacle would get in the way of the virtuous circle of development that had, at last, been found. This was to reckon without the oil crisis that the West was going to face from 1973 onward, and the Soviet sphere a little later. Credit became dearer. The quality of the Polish products did not come up to the mark. The combination of these two factors led to selling at a loss on Western markets and to products being left unsold in Polish enterprises. The crisis now developed, as Poland's debt increased and the incipient economic take-off was halted. Restrictions were imposed and discontent grew. The authorities' only response was to increase norms and tighten labor discipline. A price rise was decreed. This led to popular uprisings in a number of cities in 1976. Subsequently, with certain specific circumstances aiding,[14] revolt broke out four years later in the Baltic and throughout the entire country. Several economic historians date from the end of the 1960s the point at which the dependency formed that was, 10 years later, to plunge Poland—and, ultimately, the whole Soviet system—into an irreversible crisis when credit was frozen, generating an enormous sense of privation and a feeling that the rules of the system lacked legitimacy.[15]

Soviet–Style Welfare States

Between 1945 and 1989, states in both West and East based their legitimacy on the principle of the widest possible redistribution. This represented the condition for social integration and for the legitimacy of political parties, all of which advocated it. During the years of postwar boom in the Western countries, social welfare rights were provided not just on an occupational basis, but on the much broader grounds of citizenship. During this period, social expenditure increased considerably, around 8% per year between 1960 and 1975. This very generous system was characterized by a high degree of coherence between the different elements of contribution and payment, based on intergenerational solidarity between individuals. As Polanyi has shown, it involved an enormous degree of protection from the vagaries of the market and required an extended partnership. For his part, Esping Anderson has stressed the high degree of institutional coherence underlying this model, which was based on the strengthening of three basic communities: the political community in the form of the nation, the economic community in the form of the enterprise, and the social community in the form of the family.[16] It is this very broadly consensual model that turned out to be fragile, when, after 1975, it was undermined by three shocks: lifetime employment came into question; the family saw parental roles break up under the major impact of female emancipation; and the expectations of a continuously redistributive state eventually left it struggling to meet growing financial costs.[17]

In the Eastern bloc, the starting situation was different, even though the subsequent dynamic was broadly comparable. The consequences of the war and the establishment of Communism combined to promote reconstruction efforts in countries ravaged by the global conflict. The ideological project of the welfare state, carried forward by the new authorities, rested on the demand for egalitarian justice—according to the principle of recompensing each "according to his needs"—and on the desire to eradicate the deficits of the prewar years. There were names for these: unemployment, hunger, and homelessness. Within this context, employment was to be guaranteed for life. Housing became the major target of redistribution policies, to which was added the policy of subsidized prices for basic products. These three programs constituted the main thrust of social policies during the first 20 years of socialism. From the 1970s onward, a number of obvious lags emerged by comparison with Western policies. These were in the area of pensions, on the one hand, and family policies, on the other. The policy pursued, from this moment on, was deliberately one of a "union of the economic and the social," to quote the East German slogan. This translated itself into a degree of catch-up in several areas of social policy, though the Eastern economies began to fall behind those of the West at just this point— namely, the end of the 1960s.

Basing ourselves on the comparison between Hungary and the Western countries over the 20 years between 1960 and 1980, we can see that the two moved apart in terms of health expenditure, whereas Hungary caught up very significantly in the field of pensions and family policy. The treatment of pensioners was one of the prime targets of the Communist regime, in order to establish its authority and underscore the difference from the prewar years.[18]

As for family policies, they gradually came to occupy a central place in social provision, doing so for two reasons: first, to promote a probirth policy, given the low levels of fertility in most of the countries, and second, to justify the superiority of Soviet-style Europe over Western Europe in all matters relating to female employment. Day-care centers, parental leave, and family services were the pride of the Eastern bloc countries, which exhibited very generous family policies. Among the social advantages granted to families, there were, in all the countries,

Table 1.1   Social Expenditure in Hungary and the West, 1960–1990

	Social Expenditure (OECD) (% of Gross National Product)	
	Hungary	West
1960	11.30	15.62
1970	13.90	21.44
1980	19.60	29.99
1990	27.80	30.23

Source: This table is based on data found in Tomka, Béla, "Wohlfahrtsstaatliche Entwicklung in Ostmitteleuropa and das europäische Sozialmodell, 1945–1990," in Hartmut Kaelbe and Günther Schmidt (eds.), Das europäische Modell. Aud dem Weg zum transnationalen. WZB Jahrbuch, 2004, p. 133.

Table 1.2   Social Security Expenditure (% of GNP) in 1960 and 1980 (Hungary/Western countries)

	Social Security Expenditure in 1960				Social Security Expenditure in 1980			
	Health	Pensions	Family	Other	Health	Pensions	Family	Other
Hungary	33.1	38.7	12.20	16.00	17.50	55.10	13.30	14.10
West	15.39	49.98	17.28	13.02	30.32	45.99	8.04	9.19

Source: This table is based on data found in Tomka, "Wohlfahrtsstaatliche Entwicklung in Ostmitteleuropa and das europäische Sozialmodell, 1945–1990," p. 133.

a range of benefits granted for the first child, debt relief in respect of the next ones, and preferential treatment in housing provision. We may also add to this an extension of leave before and after the births. In the GDR, for example, women were entitled to six weeks' leave before—and 20 weeks' leave after—giving birth. After the 26 weeks' leave, mothers could take unpaid leave of 12 months, extendable to 18 months in the case of a third child. Furthermore, grandparents were also entitled to the same provision, which meant that unpaid leave could be extended to 32 or even 58 weeks.[19] In Hungary a similar program was still more or less in place in 1990. The same was true of Czechoslovakia. For this reason in particular, female employment was very high everywhere, particularly in the GDR and Bulgaria. Behind it was a desire for gender equality, which was reinforced by policies favoring abortion—in all countries except Romania. These liberal policies were, incidentally, at odds with the pro-birth policies, but they were in keeping with the ideological claims of Communism's superiority over capitalism, which was denounced as ine-galitarian. Here, politics won out once again, but at a very high cost to the community.

The Communist social state rested on three pillars that are somewhat reminiscent of Western communities, though differently oriented. The first of these was the national community, which won out over the pre-ceding regime, denounced as a regime of profiteers. The legitimacy of the Communist state was based on the elimination of "exploiters," the redistribution of the fruits of their labor to the workers and the singling-out of competent, deserving individuals, having regard to their level of social commitment. The second was the enterprise community, the central component in social, local, and territorial integration. The third was the family community to which the state delegated social welfare functions. The system was, then, very coherent, even if there were many gaps in the social safety net. There was an insistence on employment for all, at the cost of generalized wastage and very slack work discipline; on healthcare for all, even though the medical attention was sometimes very mediocre in quality; on guaranteed pensions, though these were a long way short of providing a sufficient income for old people who, in many cases, were forced to pursue an economic activity. Housing suffered from the poor quality of building materials and the tiny size of dwellings.

Gender equality was largely formal and there were significant inequalities, though these were not so great as in the West.

For this reason, the differences from the Western system lay primarily in the quality of health or pension benefits. These deteriorated markedly in the 1980s, by contrast with most Western countries. Moreover, the absence of democratic control of the system of redistribution represented a further difference between the two Europes. By contrast with the pluralism of management institutions in the West, the Eastern bloc was massively statist. Given the nature of Soviet-type trade unions, the delegation of some areas of the management of social affairs to the unions did nothing to affect this. This was the major failing of the system: there was no notion of comanagement whatever. Social negotiation was absent and contracts nonexistent. The paramountcy of politics in all circumstances left citizens bereft of all responsibility. The Soviet-style welfare state had not promoted active citizenship. A deep disconnect sundered the citizen from the welfare-state regime. The former was kept in a state of radical passivity, while welfare was consigned largely to the realm of assistance in a state that was always defined, rather, in paternalistic terms. Admittedly, waged activity was the sine qua non for the possession of social rights. Yet this did not mean there was a link between occupational status and benefit levels: there was no connection between contributions and payments. By contrast, if one did not work, one enjoyed no social entitlements. There was, in this way, a sphere of obligations, represented by the sphere of work, uncoupled from social entitlements the state had reserved for itself.

However, despite the failings we have just pointed out, one thing is certain: Soviet-style states were able to develop social policies of great scope, paid for out of the public purse. All of these provided the state with one of the most important foundations of its legitimacy. The other foundation was, most certainly, that of culture, of which civil societies were the vector.

Civil Societies

Two radically opposed schools of interpretation have attempted to define the notion of civil society in the Communist states. The first has attempted to present it as lying at the very root of societal consensuses, as these developed in a sphere removed from political opposition movements, and not necessarily in relation to the Communist political order. The second has seen "overt" crises as proof of the existence of societies massively opposed to the political order. These two schools of interpretation are to a great degree mutually exclusive, since the former stresses the history of everyday life, while the latter highlights long-run history. It will be the aim of the penultimate chapter of this book to show that the definition of societies before 1989 has largely determined the conceptions of civil societies after 1989.

Nonpolitical Societies

It is certainly the case that civil society did not exist in the sense in which Liberalism understands it in the wake of Locke, Montesquieu, or Tocqueville. The Communist Party exerted its monopoly of control not only over the state but over society. This constitutional principle governed the operation of every organization and found concrete expression in the appointment of virtually all officials by the political system. The hierarchies of nonpolitical organizations came under the aegis of the party at every relevant level without exception. Society was organized on corporatist lines, and collective life was strictly regimented. But we cannot conclude from this intensively controlled organization that individuals played no part in adapting their living environments. The extreme politicization of public life never eliminated the influence of private relations; moreover, public organizations never ceased to be subject to individual appropriation. This was the case not only with directly political organizations, such as youth, trade union, or neighborhood associations, but with all others, whether in the field of social action—with the Red Cross and Caritas—occupational bodies—such as the organizations of engineers and technicians across several industrial branches (including the car enthusiasts' clubs)—in the field of sport and leisure—with the prominence given to associations celebrating the folk heritage, not forgetting the animal protection societies and, more rarely, environmental organizations. All of these represented an extremely hardy social weft, in which party control was, admittedly, influential, but in which a rich fabric of social exchange was also to be seen, along with a distancing from politics and the enjoyment of private activities. In some countries, the churches represented a site of intense sociability within this landscape, provided that we remember the close surveillance they were under both from the party and the secret police, and the exceptional status the Polish church enjoyed after 1956.[20]

A number of intense sites of sociability left glowing memories behind them after they were eliminated in 1989. These included pensioners' clubs, women's groups in some factories, or rural clubs in the countryside. In Bulgaria or Poland, they had taken over the legacy of the prewar community groups. In many circumstances, under Communist domination, they enabled local conflicts to be settled. They also made it possible to produce and supply certain goods, by keeping industrial or village traditions in being. The sadness at their loss after 1989 is, for Chris Hann, proof of the strength of the bonds created and of the liveliness of civil society.[21] Finally, a special place must be reserved for allotment gardens, the "little gardens" for private use that allowed domestic agricultural production to take place. They had come to play a substantial role in social life everywhere. Often obtained through the trade union, they met several demands at once: the political requirement for social control overseen by elected officials; ideological demands, thanks to the valorization of leisure through work; and economic needs, by offering opportunities to raise a few animals, the production of which would turn out to be crucial in the last decade of the Communist regime. The "little gardens" represented an essential element of social life thanks to the safety-valve role fulfilled by the ownership status acquired by those who had them—namely the great majority of the citizens of Central and Eastern Europe. They also helped to develop networks of neighborliness. Social competition took place not on the basis of artificial campaigns, such as those organized by the trade unions in the factories, but of the growing of quality produce, the careful maintenance of the plots and the attention devoted to embellishing the huts, even if they were only little lean-tos. Time and again, the produce from these small gardens made up for shortages in the public food supply system, and individuals showed a distinct preference for such produce, particularly the fruit and vegetables, which were unpolluted.

We also must mention a number of aspects of workers' culture, which was so distinctive under Communism on account of the power given to the workers, the effects of which were so influential in the environment around the enterprise. The German sociologist Zapf has aptly characterized the GDR as a *Facharbeitergesellschaft* or "society of the skilled worker,"[22] and the Romanian sociologist Barbu has referred to work as the social contract of Communist society. That culture was built upon technical training and careers, occupational paths aiding social advancement and a system of occupational relations closely linked to political power. Admittedly, the constrained character of the trade unions was plain for all to see, with workers being forced to join them as soon as they were recruited. We must also add that the workers set great store by these social organizations on account of the resources at their disposal, foremost among these being access to health care and collective vacations. The latter were prized all the more for the fact that private alternatives did not exist. The workers had a very strong sense of their own appropriation of their contexts of action, as several studies were to show after 1990.[23] This related to the way technical work was valued by the Communist regime, but also to the impact of the enterprise on the local environment and the fact that entire generations of the same families had worked there. All these elements attest to a high degree of autonomous self-regulation by the workers or, in other words, to their negotiating power in terms of employment, time management, machines, and even products, albeit exercised highly informally. They were the pendants to the "second economy" within the enterprise. The workers thus had a great capacity to manage the crises that broke out over supply deficiencies, and also over the raising of norms or increases in the pace of work in certain periods. These conflicts often ended with the management backing down and paying up. This workers' culture was all the more powerful for the fact that it was constantly being talked up in public. It was based on the prestige of the major infrastructure projects that the regime idealized, and

backed up by the glorification of the local enterprise as the body providing all social bonds (catering, healthcare, housing, vacations, training,
festivities, distinctions, etc.). Much was made of the employment of entire
families in the same company, their technical specialization, and their
social mobility. The sense of "communitarization" of the enterprise was
thereby reinforced, in direct proportion to the paternalism of the leaders,
who found in it the source of their legitimacy. The equilibria of the villages rested on the same mechanisms. For individuals who had suffered
from extreme privation and deep inequalities before the war, communism
had satisfied the desire for equality of conditions and reinforced the powers of negotiation on the basis of exchange between the cooperative and
the little plot of land.[24]

The informal compromises that were typically struck in the working environment have been the subject of many analyses by sociologists
(Polish and Hungarian ones in particular). However, what shows up more
than in the West is the notion of a confusion over rules, for a whole
series of reasons that relate fundamentally to the very nature of the party-
economy. The running of that economy involved the workers constantly
in anticipating breakdowns or dealing with missing components. This
enables us to understand the consensuses built up around the extensive
flouting of the rules and to see power not as being assigned to a single
camp, that of the bosses, but as a relation of exchange between interde-
pendent actors. The Polish sociologist Andrzej Rychard has attempted to
explain the coherence of socialist legitimacy in Poland by presenting societal equilibrium as resting on a series of agreements granted in exchange
for advantages accorded to the citizenry.[25] First, in the sphere of values,
an enormous consensus prevailed around recognition of the value of full
employment or egalitarianism. Then, in the public sphere, passive compliance and outward shows of accord were reproduced in ample measure in
the ritualized events held in honor of the regime. In the material sphere,
the assent to Communist power depended on satisfaction being derived
in material terms. In these conditions, the dictatorial nature of political rule could be borne, provided that there was satisfaction in the symbolic and material spheres. In Hungary, some have spoken, for example, of
"Goulash socialism" to indicate the consumerist nature of the "contract"
uniting the authorities to their societies. But if material supplies began to
fail, then it was the delicate political balance (not fundamental values) that
was unfailingly brought into question. As a result, crises prompted radical challenges to the regime's political equilibria. At that point, a culture
different from the every day would emerge, with other values and other
references. Here, politics was the prevailing factor.

Political Cultures

The element of the tradition of political culture refers to the presence
or otherwise of popular mobilizations in recent history. This point is

essential because the presence of a social movement provides the *longue-durée* argument, rooted in the tradition of a society battling for recognition of its identity. This tradition refers back to the desire, expressed in the nineteenth century, to exist politically within the borders of a sovereign state, a desire denied by the existence of empires.[26] At that date, all the countries of Central and Eastern Europe had ceased to exist as sovereign states, some of them not having existed for several centuries. Others never had existed. The nation did admittedly exist, expressive of an ethnic group endowed with its own language and, on occasion, with a religion. It was, however, lacking in any particular state configuration by dint of the membership of the former countries of the German, Austro-Hungarian, or Ottoman Empires. The question of dependency on a foreign state—and hence the opposition between society and state—reemerged from 1945 onward. This is why the nationwide risings that took place between 1945 and 1989 all made demands for national sovereignty and for all that went with it in symbolic and cultural terms. To claim a place in this history of peoples fighting for their autonomy was to call into question the status quo established at Yalta, which had fixed the relations of political dependency after 1945. Peculiar to the countries that saw popular movements against the Communist parties, as opposed to those that did not, were three factors: reformers within the Communist parties, the role of the intellectuals for all the countries cited, including the GDR, and the place of the working classes, as in Poland. In all these cases, historical references to the nineteenth-century nation played a part, with the Hungarian uprisings of 1848, the Polish revolts of 1830 and 1863, and the birth of Czechoslovakia. Such popular risings were not experienced in every country. Far from it. The Baltic countries, incorporated into the USSR, were not able to express any kinds of demand, so much did their membership of the Soviet Union imply their strict submission to the domination of the Moscow authorities. The denial of any national past and the refusal to recognize the slightest demand for autonomy were based on the large-scale elimination of the prewar elites and the massive arrival of Russian, Belorusian, or Ukrainian populations, to whom all the responsible positions were allotted. From this point of view, the Baltic countries and the Balkans share a common destiny that sees them united over the *longue durée* by a history of territorial fragmentation. This produced such population mixes and divisions between majorities and minorities that, within the context of an extremely violent Soviet occupation, the collective capacities for the affirmation of national unity had apparently been eliminated. Bulgaria is, no doubt, an exception in this regard, on account of the absence of Soviet occupation, and of the greater closeness between the two states, due, among other things, to the part played by the Russians in the rebirth of Bulgaria.

The Balkan Case

In the Balkans (or, more exactly, in Romania and Bulgaria), there were no risings of a national coloration during the 50 years of Communist domination. How is this to be explained? Doubtless by the very violent repression meted out to the representatives of the bourgeoisie, a class that had, moreover, made its appearance rather late. In fact, it barely existed before the last quarter of the nineteenth century, particularly in Bulgaria. The Bulgars, dominated for five centuries by the Ottomans, had been confined to an almost exclusively rural system. Admittedly, rural traditions and religion had been respected within the Millet system, but without being taken in hand by an autochthonous aristocracy.[27] The land-owning nobility were Ottoman, and when the Turkish armies were defeated by the Russians, who liberated Bulgaria in 1877, they left behind a country with hardly any institutions or powerful urban social groups. The country was predominantly rural. There was mass illiteracy. The bourgeoisie had only just begun to develop during the century, mainly in the banking and industrial sectors. It had financed the churches and schools from which the intelligentsia that was to take power in 1878 emerged, though the Central Powers were to impose a foreign king on that stratum as supreme political authority. Here, as in Romania, and more generally elsewhere in Central Europe, the models were directly taken from the West. Democratic institutions were often tacked on to societies dominated by rural structures. Among several groups, demands for purity and appeals to past greatness prevailed. During the interwar period, Romania (but not Bulgaria) was ravaged by the national question. The relationship with minorities was the breeding ground for the Romanian nationalist extremism that was to culminate in the alliance with Hitler.

The situation was highly differentiated in the Balkans at the end of the Second World War; though Yugoslavia had resisted sternly, certain countries had made substantial compromises with Nazism. For its part, Bulgaria had pursued an ambiguous policy. Russophile as a country, but allied with the Germans, it resisted handing over its Jewish population to the Nazis until 1943. There was economic devastation throughout the region. And the Soviet occupation proved backbreaking, except in Yugoslavia, Albania, and Bulgaria. Countries had to pay up, even though they were ruined. The only political culture that prevailed at that point depended on loyalty to the Communist Party, whose aim was to restore pride on different foundations. In Bulgaria, this meant the collectivization of land and rapid industrialization. In other words, it meant the Sovietization of a country that its leader Todor Zhivkov later dreamed of merging into the USSR as another Soviet republic. Gerald Creed argues that there were similarities between the prewar cooperative spirit and collectivization under the Communist authorities; he uses this argument to point up the extent of consensus within the country and thus account for the absence of revolt against the Communist Party.[28] By contrast with this new-style nationalism, Romania chose a path of nationalism anchored in a revamped tradition; this was based, of course, on the typically Soviet type of development, but a development articulated politically to demands for nonalignment. During the 1960s, Ceaucescu decided to take up the torch relinquished by Tito. He attempted to find a midpoint between the USSR, whose hegemonic intentions he denounced (Romania went so far as to condemn the invasion of Czechoslovakia in 1968), and the United States, which was guilty of capitalist exploitation. This nationalist rhetoric would turn into a phobia of other countries, an overestimation of—both material and symbolic—self-sufficiency, and the crushing of any alternative thinking, a move made possible only by police surveillance of a kind unrivalled elsewhere in the Eastern bloc and by a dictatorship exerted by a paranoid family.

Popular Mobilizations

The countries that experienced various uprisings during the Communist period were quite different. The importance of these risings can be gauged by the emergence of political community organizations and the evolution of the various Communist parties. The frequency of these uprisings and their intensity varied from one country to another. With the exception of the days of "Solidarity" in Poland, which ran from August 1980 to December 1981, the risings were spread over a short period—two weeks in Hungary in 1956, four months in Czechoslovakia in 1968—or even a very short period in the case of the GDR in June 1953. Despite their brevity, they were decisive on three counts. First, because they showed up to the majority of people—and particularly to the West—the fundamentally illegitimate character of the rules and the massive rejection of Communist domination by the popular majorities that had risen against the parties. Because they marked the point at which the veil of lies erected by the authorities was torn down, the crises gave an insight into the societal equilibria and totalitarian nature of the Communist regimes.[29] The campaigns of repression that followed in each case brought definitive proof of this. The aim pursued by all those in charge of such campaigns was to show, through bloodshed, social and occupational demotion and banishment, that it was not possible to move beyond the Communist regime. In this way, the Communist authorities sought to convince the citizens that there was no other conceivable political horizon than that imposed by Moscow's domination.[30]

They were decisive, moreover, because they had major long-term effects on the triggering and shape of the 1989 uprisings. For this reason, they reveal themselves to be vectors of a strong national identity, rooted in the society, in its struggle against the occupying power. The Hungarian revolution of late October/early November 1956 was a movement of substantial scope, both in its international political significance and the repression to which it led domestically. During the

32 years of Kadar's dominance, it was an absolutely taboo subject in Hungarian society. Yet this did not prevent public memory of the event in 1988 from being one of the major triggers of the demonstrations that occurred at that point, which led directly to the final crisis.[31] The short period of the Prague Spring in 1968 and its aftermath in 1969 were significant both for the scope of the demands for national autonomy that emerged and for the way the exhaustion of the internal reform model was demonstrated. The notion of "socialism with a human face" lost credibility once and for all. The "Prague Spring" gave way to a regime dominated by dull, grey old men with no sense of vigor. Society was crushed by the extent of the repression. But that repression prevented neither the emergence of Charter 77, nor the rebirth, 20 years later in 1989, of the nation, under the aegis of the dissident movement, even though we must point out that the spark was ignited, in that country, by demonstrations on the part of students too young to have known the 1968 movement.[32]

These popular movements were decisive in the development of the Communist parties themselves. The great majority of them drew the conclusion that the reinforcement of Leninist principles was the only route to follow. And their Soviet protectors certainly intended to persuade them of this in every way possible. The dynamics of "normalization" all involved the reinforcement of the "hard-line" currents within the parties and the expulsion of "reformers." In Hungary, this led to the execution of the reform Communist Imre Nagy and his ministerial associates in 1958. The second effect was, then, to expunge these reforming forces from the parties and to set those parties in a mould of strict orthodoxy. Projects for reform were left to wither on the vine, even if this meant that their advocates were pushed into silent—or, exceptionally, open—opposition. The third effect was to accentuate the splits between Communist parties, the dividing line now running either between them and groups outside the party (which was the case in Czechoslovakia) or within the party itself in the case of those parties that had experienced no frontal opposition to their own societies. It was these "reforming" wings that would be promoted by the Gorbachevian dynamic in 1980s Romania and Bulgaria, and then propelled into power in 1989. Hungary is an exception to this pattern on account of the evolution of Kadarism, which we shall examine below. So too is Poland, as a result of Solidarnosc, of course, but also because of the reform introduced by Jaruzelski and his team in the 1980s.

Solidarnosc, the Exception

In many respects, the "Solidarnosc" movement seemed to represent an exceptional moment in the history of Central Europe.[33] It was exceptional, first, in the magnitude of its dynamic, as it managed to unite 10 million members behind a charismatic leader, Lech Walesa. Developing within a highly structured organization that was decentralized from the outset, the better to counter Communist centralism, it had a program that proposed to see the state recast entirely by the society. It was also exceptional insofar as it constituted the latest link in a long chain of uprisings that Poland had seen since 1945 that, on each occasion, further ate away at the basis of the regime. The workers' self-management councils, promoted after the 1956 rising, were destroyed two years later. Admittedly, part of the working class was overtaken by apathy, but they nevertheless constituted the basis for the reform project that was to be reforged a quarter of a century later.[34] The anti-Semitic campaign launched against Warsaw University in 1968 would be an eye-opener for many intellectuals, several of whom had deserted the party in the previous years. The crackdown on the workers in the Baltic and in Lodz in the winter of 1970 and in January 1971 would, for its part, contribute to driving a massive, enduring wedge between the working class and the party. It marked that class's break with the party. Five years later in 1976, the crackdown on the workers in the cities of Radom, Plock, and Ursus was to be the final straw that prompted several intellectuals to speak out publicly and act concretely to assist the victims of the repression and their families.[35] This organization was to come to full maturity four years later when the first free trade union in the Communist world emerged on the Baltic coast, with a number of intellectuals as advisers. This coming-together of all classes in a body rooted within industry was exceptional. It meant that Solidarnosc was simultaneously a trade union and a social movement.[36] For some observers, its unrivalled originality in Communist Europe related to the active cooperation between the working class and intellectuals, who were the main actors in socialist industrialization.[37] For that reason, these sociologists do not hesitate to speak of the emergence of a class consciousness, based on the recognition of the barriers between dominant and dominated.[38] Solidarnosc was also exceptional in the linkage it was able to make between secular and religious forces, under the authority of the Catholic church, seen as representative of the people in the darkest hours of the nation's history. It was exceptional because it represented the archetype of civil society in its traditional and modern versions: the former in taking over the ideals of the self-management movement, rooted as it was in Proudhonian labor solidarism, and the latter thanks to the frontal opposition to totalitarianisms, anchored in resistance to the occupying Nazi forces and to domination by Moscow. The political culture of dissidence exemplified by Solidarnosc was embodied in the program of the Self-Managed Republic, as conceived by the members at the first congress in September 1981. That program advocated founding the state on the twin pillars of civil society and self-management in the enterprise. In this way, Solidarnosc was proposing to fulfill the dream of uniting the producers and their product in nonalienated labor, leading to a society based on public enterprise. It is this conception that was shattered in 1989 under the twin blows of economic liberalization and the differentiation of interests.[39]

Forms of Political Domination

After examining the economic structure and the welfare states, it remains for us to analyze the political sphere. Here diversity won out by a long way over uniformity because of the long-term legacies, the developments that emerged between 1945 and 1990, and the ethnic composition of the various countries. Totalitarianism was the lot of all the countries in the 1950s, reflecting the generalized adoption of the Stalinist model after 1953. This evolved toward less rigid forms in certain countries, but without it being possible, ultimately, to give a clear account of the nature of Soviet-type political domination. The classifications that have emerged are of probative value mainly for the understanding of certain phenomena specific to the later, post-1989, period.

Classification

Throughout the existence of the Communist regimes, one element remained unchanged: the monopoly of power held by the Communist Party, together with its absolute primacy in the state and society. This principle was inscribed in all the national constitutions. From this standpoint, there was no evolution whatever over the 40 years of Communist Party domination. Yet this is not all that is to be said on the development of the various national scenes. In a landmark work, Zbigniew Brzezinski and Karl Friedrich defined totalitarianism by the presence of a party state and, more broadly, by the monopoly of the means of information, the planning commission, a secret police, and violence employed as a means of governance. If some authors subsequently take the view that the nature of the regime changes, they do so on the basis of the accumulation of several factors:[40] Stalin's death in 1953 and the increased importance accorded to the body of higher party officials (the Politburo); the abolition of the Gulag and its transformation into a less violent system of repression; the pursuit of a different social equilibrium, still based admittedly on the unchanged principle of party domination, and still imposed by force, but depending also on the wider integration of a number of segments of the population into collective life, and hence more consensual. Moreover, some countries had powerful opposition movements, while others did not. These developments prompt Juan Linz and Alfred Stepan to make distinctions, in an important work, within the category of posttotalitarianism, subdividing it into three subcategories. The first of these refers to the regime known as "Early Posttotalitarianism." This characterizes the situation in Czechoslovakia between 1977 and 1989, when Gustáv Husák's regime falls back on a strategy of repression and the freezing of former gains and leaves only the party-state standing. The second is "Frozen Posttotalitarianism." This enables us to distinguish the countries where the unchanged domination of the party endures side by side with a civil society. An example would be the GDR. The concept of "Mature Posttotalitarianism" defines those countries where everything has evolved except domination by the party, to the point, indeed, where certain elements of the market economy have been incorporated, as in Hungary. With the latter case, "growing pluralism" and the emergence of a parallel culture overturn the notion of totalitarianism, as is highlighted by the Polish case.[41]

In another major work published in 1999, Kitschelt deepens this approach. He analyzes the profiles of the parties and the choices of public policies and political programs on the basis of the different legacies left by a number of historical periods.[42] The question is: what are the elements that are to be regarded as pertinent in accounting, on the one hand, for the modernization of the Communist regimes under the effect of increased bureaucratization and, on the other, for the post-1989 trajectories. Kitschelt isolates five elements: the importance of the prewar period and whether it gave rise to parliamentary democracy; the existence of a Communist Party and a substantial working class and peasantry; the dynamic of the conquest of power by the Communist parties after 1945, through elections and coups, as with the Prague coup in 1948; bureaucracy, based both on clans and on relatively formal elements; pluralistic tolerance in the economic and political fields; and the conflicts and crises experienced by these societies. From these different factors, Kitschelt establishes the impact of the cognitive and institutional legacies that enables him to answer the question why one particular option imposes itself rather than another. In this way, several types of regime may be distinguished. The first type is that of sultanism. Borrowed directly from the work of Max Weber, this category has often been used to examine the forms of Communist domination.[43] It highlights the importance of patrimonialism, the charismatic figure of the leader, the fusion of the public and private spheres, and the existence of the clan and the unwarranted interference of the leader in the law. In an effort to go more deeply into the features of this patrimonial regime, Kitschelt stresses the existence of a clique or clan, corrupt administrative standards, weak urban networks and undeveloped working classes, strong rural features attesting to vast agrarian societies, and the presence of submissive religious leaders. The countries that come under this category here are Bulgaria, Romania, and, more widely, the countries of Central Asia and the Caucasus. Communism imposed itself there by implementing two strategies. The first consisted in basing itself initially on the peasants by means of land redistribution (on a very small scale in Bulgaria), the better to push them aside subsequently with generalized collectivization. The second developed on the basis of a large-scale industrialization policy, conceived as a strategy of import substitution. Hence an extremely violent process of the construction of Communist society, which led to a radical upheaval among classes and the construction of distinctive societies. What were the reasons for the success of these strategies? Kitschelt's answer is the absence of urban tradition and preexisting networks within the working class or the bourgeoisie. This, he contends, is why there are features of clientelism, and why co-optation is a principle of recruitment; it explains also the enormous social mobility of the peasants toward the towns and industry, the subordination and submission of the intellectuals and the weakness of the working class.

The second type of Communist regime is identified by Kitschelt as the "national-adaptive." It is illustrated by the relative separation of political regulation and state administration, on the one hand, and by the recognition of civil rights. This type of regime is based on the pragmatic combination of the maintenance of the public monopoly (in terms of information, ideology, and, above all, the preeminence of the party) and a relative tolerance, in the economic field, of interest groups and informal networks that are not necessarily linked to the Communist Party. Hungary is the archetype of this compromise; so much was it defined by the slogan of "Neither plan nor market" that it earned the regime the tag of "new type." In this particular case, the Communist party yielded over the vision of modernization as cultural project and also over ideology, and hence over official truth. This is why Poland, in its last phase of the 1980s, also falls within this category. The third type identified by Kitschelt is that of "authoritarian bureaucracy." He presents this as the most direct heir to totalitarianism in its Stalinist version, when extreme faith in Soviet organizational demands dominates as a principle of action. It involves rigorous party discipline and the party's total ascendancy over all organizations, repression of the slightest opposition and the spreading of fear in society. Countries like Czechoslovakia and the GDR fall into this category. Before the war, they were pluralist democracies with Communist parties rooted firmly in the working classes, which were themselves highly developed.

Ultimately, Kitschelt's analysis boils down to constellations of factors linked to socioeconomic backwardness in the first case, cultural and societal advances in the second, and bureaucracy in the last. It is, more or less, these elements we have to look for when examining the post-1989 transformations so far as "legacies" are concerned. Rather than strict causality, in which an earlier phenomenon could be said to produce a precise, circumscribed effect in a later period, it is better to focus on the aspect of "affinity" in the imputation of causes: not a strict concordance, then, but proximities. These "affinities" enable us to stress the characteristics of "confused mixity" that pertain in the Communist period, and the dynamics of differentiation after 1989.

Random Definitions, Confused Realities

For this reason, taken literally, Kitschelt's classification is open to several objections and deserves to be seriously scaled down. The GDR, which Kitschelt ascribes to his third type, implements a mode of exit from Communism in 1989 that in fact makes it closer to the second type, a societal opposition united around the "Round Table" with reform Communists. Moreover, it is hard to see how the East German case and that of Czechoslovakia can feature in the same category on the mere pretext that they can both be said to be highly industrialized, centralized countries in the years before 1939. In the 1970s and 1980s, there was no equivalent of Charter 77 in the GDR and the small number of East German social groups allied with certain evangelical movements cannot be equated with the movement led by Havel, even though that also represented a very small minority. Nor do the social mobilizations in 1989 conform to an identical pattern. The pathways of national transition differ widely. They led in some places to subsequent local mobilizations that were radically different in the two cases.[44] Moreover, the attribute of clientelism, which Kitschelt seems to ascribe, before 1989, only to the Balkan states, may in reality be extended to all the countries. Communist domination was based, centrally and locally, on relations of patronage and loyalism. From this standpoint, the East German enterprise was no less clientelist than its Polish counterpart. The trait of patrimonialism was shared, ultimately, by all cases of the Soviet type, because the Soviet-type economic structure applied in all the countries. Potential "cultural" or "national" features could be identified at the micro level, but they were not such as to modify the systemic constraints that applied across the board. On this count, it is not at all easy to distinguish Romania and Bulgaria from the other countries of East Central Europe. Though it is not difficult to show the long-standing inclusion of these two countries in the Ottoman Empire, can we nonetheless deduce that they are more bound to tradition, to patriarchal authority, to confusion between household and enterprise, and, by extension, to the clan, than are the other countries? We should have to explain why a Round Table was held in Bulgaria in 1990, which, if we followed Kitschelt, would actually rank this country among the second type. In other words, even if the categories were fully acceptable, they did not produce the expected effects.

The difficulty of precisely defining and correctly assessing the variations that may have arisen within this type of political regime reflects the confusion Max Weber attempted to deal with by employing the concept of "patrimonial bureaucracy." In coining this concept, Weber brought together two terms—bureaucracy and patrimonialism—that are, in ideal-typical terms, mutually exclusive. Their combination enables us to understand how the Communist states were able to be the site of bureaucracy—and hence the domination of rules—and simultaneously to reflect an order whose mechanism owes much to tradition, to the figure of the leader and generalized submission to that figure. In short, we are speaking of an order that, far from displaying the legal rationality specific to the bureaucracy of developed states, intermingled the procedural and the authoritarian types. This system could not, in fact, be defined by the sheer domination either of rational rules or of tradition. On the contrary, it could not be analyzed without drawing on both these categories. The dynamics of "dedifferentiation," highlighted by a large number of—particularly German—sociologists as a consequence of the domination of the party in all areas of collective action, had led to a confusion of the different—political, economic, and social—orders, not to mention the public and the private. Corruption, the grey economy, and informal relations were a consequence of this. For these reasons, the notion of "bureaucracy" applied to the GDR was perhaps the index of a greater concern with rules than elsewhere, but assuredly not of the absence of relations of patronage and clientelism. We may even hypothesize that this concern with respect for Leninist orthodoxy, which was so particular to the GDR, had led, as a result of the features of the Soviet-type system, to an even more pronounced mixing of genres than in the other countries and, consequently, to a greater confusion between the different orders of action.

Furthermore, the concept of "authoritarian bureaucracy" is equally questionable. It does not exactly seem to correspond to the authoritarianism that has been ascribed to several Soviet-type regimes, such as the Hungarian in the 1970s and the Polish in the following decade. The term "authoritarianism" seems appropriate to designate a regime in which a less arbitrary rule dominates than in the foregoing cases and that is more predictable. The dominant features of authoritarianism are, thus, growing pluralism, leadership, and a less tangible role than before for ideology. Drawing on the writings of Samuel Huntington and Barrington Moore, Peter Sugar has defined authoritarianism as a deviation of democracy specific to regimes that, though they have properly formulated constitutions, render criticism of their nonconstitutional behavior difficult or impossible.[45] These regimes may then tend either toward democracy or toward forms of heightened tension. These are regimes in which the separation of civil society and the state has not taken place. Hence the domination of a class or a group, which is, in many cases, the bureaucracy. In this sense, a regime that falls into this category may be defined as a premodern state, since neither pluralism nor class consciousness predominates.

For these various reasons, attempting to classify the political regimes of the East European states before 1945 enables us, above all, to grasp the weight of certain traditions and then to understand certain elements specific to the later period. Crude as they may seem, because of the confusion inherent in Communist-type domination, these classifications enable us to account for three elements: the first concerns certain pre–Second World War trajectories; the second refers to the relations of force that resulted in part from these after 1945; the last relates to civil societies under Communism. The consequences that may be drawn from certain features brought out in this way enable us to reply, in part, to the question of the impact of legacies and of the theoretical issues that will dominate the post-1989 period.

Conclusion. What Legacies?

Economic Cohesion and Social Consensuses

The very high degree of economic, sectoral, and territorial concentration specific to the Communist states enables us to see the substantial capacity for self-defense this afforded the central and local actors at the point when change came in 1990. It was in order to reduce the power some local political officials had derived from this concentration that the central actors launched a number of campaigns against them. But these actions, whether political or economic in nature, merely ended up reinforcing the power of these "feudal fiefdoms" and obliged the centers to form alliances with them. This was the case with the party administration and with the civil service in general and, of course, concomitantly, with the managers of industrial and agricultural enterprises and the officials in charge of distribution circuits. Though it was formally subordinate to the party, Soviet-type bureaucracy was, first and foremost, structured by interest groups firmly rooted in the various sectors and territories. This means these groups had enormous impact and great influence over local milieus, which were very complex because of their high degree of integration. Such phenomena contributed after 1990 to these groups being able to manipulate the laws to a large extent. Moreover, they were able to thwart a number of initiatives for change, among them the entry of foreign investors. They were able to readjust a number of political, economic, and social equilibria to the advantage of various coalitions formed either among themselves or with foreign partners. We shall see this in the next chapter.

More broadly, we have noted the strength of social consensus in these societies as a result of the scale of welfare state provisions. Such a level of consensus enables us to understand both the resistance displayed toward any reform project and the risk to the authorities of embarking on such a policy. Several elements peculiar to the functioning of the social welfare regimes turned negative after 1989, including the absence of any connection between social contributions and benefits, the understanding of the respective roles expected of the state and the citizen, the defective bureaucracy and the generalized egalitarianism. This principle of egalitarianism found itself, in reality, undermined by the existence of special arrangements, which took into account services rendered under various headings: military, political, bureaucratic cultural, artistic, or sporting activities. As a result, a substantial number of individuals were concerned. All the Communist states had accorded considerable scope to interest groups in which there were, alongside the representatives of the *nomenklatura* and military men, peasants, miners, and, more generally, employees in the heavy industry sector, and a number of intellectuals, artists, and athletes. All these groups enjoyed significant facilities so far as sanatoria and clinics were concerned, and also holiday hotels, spa facilities, retirement homes, and so on. For all that it had produced some profound inequalities, this clientelist regime had managed to satisfy a great number of individuals. These observations suggest we have to take the view that, even though they were massively rejected in 1989, the Communist regimes enjoyed significant support within their societies. More deeply, the values of full employment and egalitarianism were widely shared. These values had forged what, by common consent, we term "societies of the Soviet type."

Break or Continuity?

In this context, the debate on institutional change after 1989 has been polarized around the categories of break or continuity. Those who argue for a break with the Communist legacy have contended that the very nature of Soviet-type societies made any adjustment impossible and that the nature of the market called for new contexts of action.[46] As a consequence, the new rules had to be based on the prior elimination of any trace of the past. Only the radical destruction of the old structures could guarantee redevelopment. In a striking résumé of the situation, Janos Kornai has systematized the task to be accomplished by identifying, term by term, the respective ideal-types of the socialist and capitalist systems. The conclusion clearly forced upon him is that there is no possible accommodation with the Communist legacy and that a radical break is required to move from the one system to the other. A strong impression has to be made on people by suddenly and rapidly implementing rafts of measures that break with the past.

Table 1.3 Model of the Socialist and Capitalist Systems

Model of the Socialist System				
1⇒	2⇒	3⇒	4⇒	5⇒
Undivided power of the Marxist-Leninist Party	Dominant position of state and quasi- state ownership	Preponderance of bureaucratic coordination	Soft budget constraint; weak responsiveness to prices; plan bargaining; quantity drive	Chronic shortage economy; sellers' market; labor shortage; unemployment on the job
≠	≠	≠	≠	≠

Model of the Capitalist System				
1	2	3	4	5
Political power friendly to private property and the market	Dominant position of private property	Preponderance of market coordination	Hard budget constraint, strong responsiveness to prices	No chronic shortage; buyers' market; *chronic* unemployment; Fluctuations in the business cycle

Source: This figure is based on Kornai, Janos, "What the Change of the System from Socialism to Capitalism Does and Does Not Mean," *Journal of Economic Perspectives,* Winter 2000, 14 (1), p. 29.

In the second part of this book, we shall look at the consequences of such a profession of faith in respect of the reforms of public policy and the style of public management that were then implemented (see chapters two, three, and four). Their effects often gave rise to unexpected situations, given, precisely, the capacity for resistance mentioned above. As for the continuity theorists, they have instanced the widespread lack of understanding of these complex ensembles to stress the need to take account of the particularity of the elements of the socialist legacy. They have done so not to rescue dictatorship, but to make clear that system change is rooted in the continuity of certain institutional and behavioral dynamics. The latter are able to explain that the creation of rules takes place in existing milieus. It mobilizes lived experiences. It calls on the individuals in place. It selects elements from the past. It preserves the reference to the "long-term" through its treatment of the recomposition of legacies and their hybridization with the new constraints. Part 2 of this book will be concerned to show this by analyzing the local processes of industrial and agricultural, trade union, and civic recomposition. Far from presenting themselves as a "tabula rasa," the societies of Central and Eastern Europe took account of the accumulation of elements that we attempt to bring together in the table 1.4.

Working from the preceding data, we may isolate a number of long-term factors, which are elements that can properly enter into the analysis of economic, social, and political change after 1989. The first of these relates to the economic and social structures that, like Bulgarian, Polish, and Romanian agriculture, remain virtually unchanged throughout the twentieth century. We are speaking of features that will be analyzed in chapter six, such as the very small size of farms, agricultural excess employment, the absence of specialization and technological backwardness. The second factor relates more to collective behavior, be it uprisings of civil societies against the Communist regime—though we saw the very limited character of these in the introduction to this work (they were limited largely to Poland, and to a lesser extent, to the Czech Republic/Slovakia and Hungary)—or the absence of any uprising on a national scale, as in Romania and Bulgaria. These two types of behavior are important for understanding the capacity for resistance of interests group, whether oriented toward contesting change or greater inertia. The fact that Hungary managed—uniquely in the Eastern bloc—to establish links with foreign managers during the long phase of reforms initiated in 1968 turns out to be equally useful for understanding the gradual later opening-up to foreign investment. By contrast, the very high concentration of economic units—common, admittedly, to all the former Soviet-type countries, but more marked perhaps in the East German and Czech cases on account of their earlier industrial history—is able to explain the higher resistance to any modification of equilibria—economic in the case of foreign investors, or political in the case of decentralized redistributions. This is what the next three chapters will show.

No doubt we should add to these factors the two decisive elements that have been present for almost 50 years: on the one hand, urbanization, which has seen significant upheavals, particularly in respect of the capital cities, though many fewer in the fabric of intermediate towns; on the other, education, with the almost total eradication of illiteracy and the massive spread of technical—and, to a lesser extent, university—education. However this may be, the factor of the massive presence of the primary sector in Poland, to which we may add a powerful and established civil society and a long period of abortive economic reforms, provides a framework in which to understand the violence with which change was introduced into the country after 1989 and also the potency of the reactions to any radical form of change. Hence the violence of the conflict and the uneven character of change. By contrast, the power of the rural sector, the absence of a national-scale civil society, and the lack of openness to foreign partnerships in Romania and Bulgaria help to explain the difficulty of introducing change there and the extent of the manipulation by the reformed Communist elites. Violent, uneven, and generally involving enormous conflict, change in post-Communist Europe was, in part, to reinforce a number of these features by lending them renewed vigor as so many maladaptations, while making the actors into so many "veto players," and was, in part, to lead to the rearrangement of these same factors. Confronted with the new rules of the game, the sectoral configurations of which we shall examine in the following chapters, the legacies of the historic "long run" have provided the opportunity for permanent adaptation as the interests of the various groups involved have dictated.

Table 1.4 Synoptic Table of the Countries of Eastern Europe, Prewar, Postwar, Post-1990 (Excluding the Baltic Countries)

	GDR	Czechoslovakia	Poland	Hungary	Romania	Bulgaria
1919–1939						
Ethnic Composition		51% Czech 23% German 16% Slovak 5% Hungarian	65% Polish 16% Ukrainian 10% Jewish 6% Byelorussian 2% German	87% Hungarian 6% German 5% Jewish	75%, Romanian 6% Jewish 4% German	87% Bulgarian 10% Turkish 1% Jewish
Per capita industrial GNP 1938[a]		60%	23%	34%	11%	19%
Direct foreign investment[b]		30%	40%	24%	59%	18%
Agriculture in 1930[c]		35%	68%	55%	70%	72%
Fewer than 2 hectares		26.3%	30.3%	71.5%	52.1%	27.0%
2–5 hectares		43.8%	33.4%	21.5%	22.9%	36.1%
5–10 hectares		29.0	36.0%	15.1%	24.2%	36.8%
More than 100		0.9%	0.3%	0.9%	0.8%	0.1%
1945–1989						
1945	Destroyed	Victorious	Victorious	Defeated	Defeated	Defeated
Insurrections	1953	1968	1956; 1968; 1970; 1976; 1980; 1981	1956	—	—

Economic regime	Centralized. Reformed in 1960, 1970	Centralized Failed reform in 1968	Reformed in 1970, failed reform in 1981, and the 1980s	Reformed in 1968 "Neither plan nor market"	Centralized	Centralized Reform in 1960, 1970, 1980
Agriculture 1990	12%	8%	22%	18%	25%	25%
Public sector contribution to GNP (NMP)[d]	99%	91%	83%	93%	98%	99.3%
1989/1990	Round Table	Low	Round Table	Gradual (88)	High	High
Successor to the Communist parties[e]	PDS	CP	Reformed SDL (Democratic Left Alliance)	Reformed MSZP	Reformed	Reformed
Debt (billions of $)		4.6	35.3	15.8	4	8
Inflation		Average	Very high	High	Very high	Very high
Minorities 1990 (the 2 largest)	1% (Sorbian)	3% Hungarian, Roma	0.8% Ukrainian 0.8% Byelorussian 0.1% German	5.6 % Roma	4.5% Roma 6.6% Hungarian	3.7 % Roma 9.5% Turkish

[a] Balcerowicz, Leszek, *Socialism, Capitalism, Transformation*. Budapest: Central European University Press, 1995.

[b] Bairoch, cited in Janos, Andrew, *East Central Europe in the Modern World: The Politics of the Borderland from the Pre- to the Post-Communist System*. San Francisco: Stanford University Press, 2000, p. 135. Base 100 is that of Great Britain.

[c] Mihaly, "Industry and Foreign Capital," in M.C. Kasers and E.A. Radice (eds.), *Economic History of Eastern Europe, 1919–1975*, Oxford: Clarendon Press, 1985, p. 114.

[d] Cf. Berendt, I., "Agriculture," in Kasers, M.C. and E.A. Radice, *The Economic History of Eastern Europe, 1919–1975*, 2 vols. Oxford: Clarendon Press, 1984, p. 154; Wädekin, Klaus Eugen, "The Place of Agriculture in the European Communist Economies: A Statistical Essay," *Soviet Studies*, 29, August 1977.

[e] Net material product. Wild, Gérard, "Economie de la Transition: le dossier," in Colas, D. (ed.), *L'Europe post-communiste*. Paris: PUF, 2002, p. 341.

PART 1

The Formation of the Central States

The Reforms of Ownership, Social Welfare, and Administration

In 1989, what was the state in Central and Eastern Europe? It was, first, a structure in total disintegration, on account of the loss of complete control by the Communist Party that previously structured it. The expression "party-state," applied in the earlier period, was employed to signify, among other things, the disappearance of the state as controlling authority above, and distinct from, all other institutions, as a result both of its subversion by the ruling Communist Party and of each national Communist Party's subservience to the Communist Party of the USSR. After 1990, the general retreat of the Communist Parties in response to the wave of East European revolutions and the adoption, at that same time, of pluralism and open trade led to disorder and a substantial level of competition between the various organized groups. In the institutional void that opened up at that point, some groups that had enjoyed considerable favor under the previous regime were sometimes better placed to carry out change than those that emerged without experience or genuine resources. Though this initial situation enables us to account for the way public assets were taken over in the early moments of transition, it does not explain the full range of issues associated with this change, which was neither a matter of the mere reproduction of preexisting equilibria, nor of the imposition of entirely new institutions.

In part 1, we shall attempt to show that, far from being subjected to straightforward privatization by interest groups, based most often on the principal coalitions among the pre-1989 *nomenklatura*, the post-Communist states were constructed in a number of stages: they were built, first, on the appropriation of public resources by interest groups—most often the political parties in collusion with economic groupings—and second, on the construction, either at the same time or later, of public agencies based in part on the preexisting bureaucracy. These transformations reshaped the field of alliances internally, between certain social groups, and externally, with a number of foreign partners. The reform of ownership was a key moment in state-building, because it made possible the other stages represented by the reforms of the welfare state (chapter three) and regional reforms (chapter four). In Eastern Europe, states subject to the rule of law provided the starting point for processes of reconstruction of the national edifices. It had its roots in the various procedures for the transformation of public property, and in the elaboration, by degrees, of trade rules, guaranteed both by the alliances formed with foreign partners, by the social consensuses that ensured their stability, and by the European Union, membership of which represented the target of all the governments concerned.

CHAPTER TWO

Privatization and the Formation of East European States

The analysis of privatization policies in Central and Eastern Europe brings out the shift from the predatory capitalism of the earliest transitional stages to a capitalism regulated on a more legal basis. This process was indicative of the increasing rationalization of economic, political, and administrative arenas that ensued from the formation of alliances between various domestic and foreign actors. The opening of borders in 1989 and globalization played a key role in the dynamics of the transformation of public ownership, and even though the European Union had less of a part in this, the EU was nonetheless an important actor in introducing the rule of law and ensuring that investor guarantees prevailed. This transition neither indicates an internal necessity, leading irreversibly from the one form of capitalism to the other, nor does it show identical forms being adopted that would enable us to speak of an "East European" type of capitalism. This chapter analyzes the three stages of this process of East European state formation, stressing, first, the intense dynamic of initial capture by interest groups, second, the process of rule formation thanks to the consolidation of the public agencies, and, third and last, the redistributive capacity of the new states.

Representations of System Change

Techniques of Change

The recipes of free-market liberalism that had been all the rage in the decade preceding 1989 under the auspices of "Reaganism" and "Thatcherism" were widely brought into play to restructure the Soviet-type economies. Reformulated by the IMF and the World Bank into the so-called Washington Consensus plan, these recipes had the enormous advantage of providing a simple, systematic response to an extremely complex situation. Among other things, they advocated three types of coordinated intervention:[1] a currency stabilization plan at the macro-economic level, a privatization policy at the institutional level, and freedom for the individual actors at the enterprise level. This economic policy mechanism, promoted by prestigious experts of the monetarist Chicago School and bathed in the glow of successes achieved in Latin America and the UK, was underpinned by a representation of economic actors that was likely to meet the expectations of the populations of the former Soviet bloc. It assumed the freedom of the individual actor, liberated from all collective constraints and driven only by his own rationality, provided that the obstacles to the free exercise of that rationality were removed. In the event, these obstacles were the state and the intermediate organizations, that is to say, the trade unions and, more generally, community-based bodies. This is what the Czech prime minister Václav Klaus had formulated explicitly when he asked, "whether we want a standard system of relations between the citizen (and community) and state, supplemented with voluntary organizations, or whether we will create a new form of collectivism, called civil society or communitarianism, where a network of 'humanizing,' 'altruising,' morals-enhancing, more or less compulsory (and therefore by no means exclusively voluntary!) institutions, called regional self-government, professional self-government, public institutions, non-profit making organisations...councils, committees and commissions...are inserted between the citizen and the state."[2] In this perspective, which has been largely dominant, the founding view of the new economic order was based on the elimination of social mediations and public authorities, leaving in place only rational actors, who were alone empowered to reorder relationships and networks of exchange in accordance with their free will.

By virtue of this logic, privatization seemed to be a procedure of a purely technical order. It was to obey a set of recognized, effective prescriptions (those of free-market liberalism), to enable the former authorities (the Communists) to be eliminated and lead to the creation of law-governed states (understood as states guaranteeing property rights). From this "good" economic structure the political order would necessarily ensue. In this systematic progression, democracy was not an indispensable mechanism, since the success of politicoeconomic transformation was guaranteed by the mere fact of having the "right" macro-economic tools to hand. Nor did these tools have to be subjected to public discussion. Their performance had been observed in earlier cases and was a basis for unconditional acceptance. This is why most of these procedures for transforming ownership rights were entrusted to units that were most often answerable to the Ministry of Finance, but not subject to national parliamentary oversight. Since, moreover, time was of the essence, given the seriousness of the problems and the increasing scale of social expectations, the advocates of short, sharp solutions largely won the day. They assumed that the combination of speedy decision making, the secret dimension to the deliberations, and the burden of the new constraints would instantly produce a new situation. This was the promise of the "sunny uplands" (*blühende Landschaften*) made by Chancellor Kohl, seeking reelection as leader of the German government in 1990.

This set of ideas and change-management tools was embodied in the so-called shock therapy policy implemented in Poland. In that country the "shock" was, in fact, merely partial, since the process very soon ran up against unforeseen obstacles connected with the state of the social forces in play. Once the currency stabilization plan was implemented, questions arose concerning modes of privatization and the necessary local support. Elsewhere, in the other countries of the former Soviet bloc, these prescriptions were also followed to a greater or lesser degree, though with a certain time-lag. Why this time-lag and why this incomplete realization of a plan presented as the embodiment of efficiency and clarity? The answer is largely because the various—political, economic, and social—interest groups broadly maintained continuity with the past rather than making the much-heralded violent break with it. These groups, lying at the intersection of the pre- and post-1989 worlds, and at the hinge of politics and the economy, attested, by their attitudes, to the intimate confusion between the two fields that prevailed before 1989. At the same time, they were the promoters of the new legality. What we have to account for here, then, is this transition from the confusion of these two fields—a situation conducive to the takeover and "privatization" of public goods by particular groups—to the establishment of legal rule. More generally, inquiry into privatization policies leads to inquiry into the formation of the new post-Communist states and their relations with the European order of which they are a part.

Violence and Legal Rule

Above and beyond the multiplicity of forms that have eventuated historically, one type of capitalism seems to have emerged from this transformation process. This corresponds to the "subtype" of *political capitalism* that Max Weber ascribes to transitions characterized by war or revolution—periods in which profits are extorted, through predatory activities, by the political leaders dominating the country. This type of intervention, of which the mafia is the most extreme form, constitutes, in Weber's view, one of the pillars of market orders. The latter are based, in effect, on relations of violence, whose origins are necessarily kept silent—or even forgotten[3]—but their process of development often leads to the production of legal rule. They thus develop a view of the market as a site from which traditional state monopolies are excluded, to be replaced by other monopolies, dependent in this case on formal purposive rationality. It is this process of legalization based initially on violence that leads to continuity of ownership, safeguards trade, and redefines social status. If the earliest dynamics of change in Central and Eastern Europe took place within a context of "weak" states, their lasting continuation required the consolidation of bureaucracies based on competence, a consolidation that gave rise to a conflict between the various specialized administrations battling against the political authority. Extortion and legislation are the two stages that characterized the transformations of property rights after 1990, soon to be complemented by the redistributive policy that accompanied the emergence of the new economic actors.

The Strengthening of Interest Groups

The question of the funding of political parties was a basic element in the dynamics of privatization, at a point when the abolition of the one-party states was opening up generalized political competition. First, in 1990, all the countries without exception were short of liquidity, and that situation was aggravated for some of them, such as Poland and Hungary, by considerable indebtedness (see table 1.4). Second, the emerging parties, with the exception of the inheritor-parties to the Communists, had hardly any resources, except the enthusiasm of their activists and the willingness of their officials to occupy leadership posts. In this connection, positions acquired before 1990 were a determining factor.[4] Privatization emerged from the outset as the best way not just to obtain funds but also to construct the clientelist networks that these emergent parties cruelly lacked. They had to build up electoral bases by forming alliances with certain representatives of the leading economic groups. A number of strategies were implemented to this end.

Resource Conversions and Transactions

The theory of the conversion of resources by the former economic officials allied to the Communist political elites has met wide success, on the grounds that it accounts for the initial dynamics of transformation.[5] It reinvigorated the Paretian theory of the conversion and reproduction of elites by showing that, in periods of uncertainty, individuals endowed with resources under the former regime are more able to influence decisions and gain positions of responsibility than the others, if there are no external controls to prevent this.

The Conversion of Elites. Political,
Intellectual, and Family Capital

Long before the actual end of Communism in 1989–1990, the Communist elites had managed to convert their political and economic resources by taking advantage of the uncertainty created by Gorbachev's policy line within the Soviet bloc. The phenomenon affected every Eastern bloc country, from the most "open," such as Poland and Hungary, to the most "closed," such as Bulgaria and the GDR. During the brief period preceding the collapse of the regimes, the last Communist parliaments adopted laws permitting the creation of private companies and the establishment of joint ventures. Private companies or even banks were thus created entirely legally. They were able to siphon off incoming finance, particularly the funds that came in later from the European Union.[6] These resources enabled the new officials of the reformed Communist parties to maintain their local networks almost intact. Similar decisions were taken in Bulgaria from early 1988 onward, introducing the possibility of the leasing of several state enterprises. In January 1989, decree 89 cleared the way for the beginnings of privatization. By September of the same year, there were already 5,520 private firms.[7] Decrees 74 and 129 of 1990 completed the arrangement, permitting the leasing or even sale of goods that were to be replaced and were no longer required. This gave rise to a large-scale privatization of military equipment. Decree 111, dated November 14, 1990, authorized the transformation, lease-sale or transfer of a number of state concerns largely in the metallurgical, oil, or food sectors, formerly managed by the external trade agencies. It was this dynamic that gave rise to the emergence of several economic groups, including the Multigroup conglomerate.[8]

This conversion theory echoed a suspicion very widespread in public opinion that the post-Communist transformation had led to the enrichment of former officials, of both government and opposition. There were doubtless preliminary understandings leading to the negotiations that ushered in regime change. This enormous movement of private appropriation by the former economic managers, but above all by the political officials who underwrote this conversion, was referred to as "red privatization." But if there were corrupt practices on the part of the former officials, this is because the new political authorities had created legal and organizational conditions that made such a dynamic possible. The phenomenon of hybridization of politics and economics operated to the advantage of the parties. This thesis underlies the approach of David Stark who showed, as early as 1992, how the processes of interdependence between economic and political interests had operated through the institutional set-ups constructed after 1990.[9] He particularly stressed the dynamics of resource conversion by the managers, in collusion with the central bureaucracies, noting, in conclusion, that the *nomenklatura* lists had been the matrices of change, at least in the initial period. There has been a great deal of research on occupational status profiles, particularly on the elites, and less on the other social categories.[10]

Two arguments have long been prevalent in explaining the origin of the elites. The so-called resource-conversion theory posed the question of the circulation or reproduction of elites. The family tradition thesis highlighted the importance of inheritance and also of social skills. Both theories showed up a broad continuity between the two periods, pre- and post-1989. The circulation-of-elites theory has only really been applied to a single case, that of the former GDR, where, in the few months after unification in October 1990, all the central officials of the economic bodies were dismissed and only local political officials were able, in some places, to hold on to their posts. As for the reproduction thesis, it was deployed to indicate that the elites changed jobs without losing their status as leaders, the question here being which elites were concerned and what was the level of circulation between the political and the economic sphere, and, above all, to what post-1990 period the thesis referred. Szelenyi and Szelenyi were able to show that the key factor was the origin of the *nomenklatura*, depending on whether that term referred to the elite underpinning the Communist regimes or the elite that was formed in the 1960s and 1970s on a more technical basis, but did not reach the heights of power. The latter were the more successful in their conversion, passing easily from their political positions to an economic function. What is true of Hungary would also seem to be true, with a little variation, of the other countries of Central Eastern Europe. For some observers, the thesis also remains relevant to the Balkan countries where the former elites of the intelligentsia enjoyed major advantages for converting their resources and remaining in their posts.[11] However, "political capital" is said to have had more of an effect here than elsewhere, this is confirmed in the doctoral thesis of Nadège Ragaru, who also stresses the greater influence of "political capital" in Bulgaria, the importance of networks, particularly those linked to security, and the variety of individual trajectories of members of the "intelligentsia," who were faced with multiple dynamics of ascent and decline.[12]

Two Strategies of Collusion

In the view of several observers, such collusion was possible because of the scarcity of domestic capital and the political elites' desire to remain in power. Once the potential resources that an enterprise represents for the (domestic or foreign) buyer have been assessed, two strategies can be identified. When an enterprise has a captive market and, potentially, substantial financial resources, it merely has to be assured of finance to guarantee that it remains in the hands of domestic leaders. The political field then favors the domestic sector through privatization, setting aside foreign bids, even if they are higher. On the other hand, when an enterprise has a market, but no capital, the restructuring of that enterprise entails financial investments that are beyond the reach of the local actors. This was the case in the automobile sector, which, as could be sensed with little fear of error in 1990, was going to enjoy a substantial expansion, or the building materials sector, given road infrastructure needs and the availability of European aid. In that case, the call for foreign investors was organized by central actors colluding with the directors of the enterprise, in order not only to establish an optimal price, but also to guarantee themselves incomes. Some negotiations thus involved the maintenance of the former managers in their posts.

The case of Poland provides a particularly good illustration of the process whereby interest groups have their positions consolidated by party authorities. On this point, there are two theses partially at odds with one another. The first takes it as read that it was the political parties that, despite changes of government, defined the sectors and enterprises deserving of support. From this perspective, it was the party organizations that constituted the economic elites after 1989.[13] Noting the frequency of the above-mentioned changes of government (they occurred in 1993, 1997, 2001, and 2005), it has been argued, in a second approach, that, in a political context characterized by a high volatility of choice between parties, it is entrepreneurs who have significant leeway to vary their choices. Thus, both Wasilewski and McMenamin conclude that the entrepreneurs are "not politicized on party lines."[14] In their view, business people take account of the volatility of the political sphere and the variation of electoral results to "shop around": far from serving a single party, they finance several. Since each election sees the preceding government team dismissed, entrepreneurs can diversify their "offer" all the better. Their influence is stronger for the fact that the parties often mutually accuse each other of being financed by an entrepreneur and hence of being corrupt. According to this logic (the accusation of corruption), those who were closely associated with a party would become members of the boards of the state enterprises. Schoenman and McMenamin take the view that such a logic applies to all the former Eastern bloc countries.

Corruption, a Generalized Phenomenon

The extreme form of this confusion of the political and economic spheres was doubtless embodied in the interest groups associated with a number of security firms. Nadège Ragaru has, in various of her writings, stressed the importance of the private security agencies in Bulgaria, which were made up of three groups of people: former members of the secret services, former sportsmen and members of the *nomenklatura*.[15] Their aim was to transform certain state monopolies into milch-cows for their own personal benefit and they were largely aided in this by an uncertain political situation since, between 1989 and 1997, there were no fewer than 11 successive governments. Yet the entire Bulgarian privatization process cannot be reduced to this dynamic, which is in fact best illustrated by the exemplary case of one of the largest economic conglomerates of the period, Multigroup. Multigroup is of interest to us here mainly on account of the diversity of its acquisitions, which range from a great number of state monopolies, particularly in the food sector, to the control of gas supplies, which involved close cooperation with the main Russian partner, Gazprom. If these studies are exemplary, this is because they exposed the misappropriation, on a very grand scale, of public resources by actors situated at the interface of the economic and

political spheres, exploiting these two spheres alternatively or simultaneously, by creating and destroying front companies, against a background
of criminality, but also, at times, of legality. The law did, on occasion, provide advantages when the losses brought about by uncontrolled
criminality were regarded as too deleterious. Reinforcement of the legal
apparatuses and, more generally, the control of the administrations by
gangster cliques has been one of the strategies pursued, alongside the
ransacking of the public resources. In 1997, the decision to bring the
financial and banking sector under the authority of a currency board had
the effect of stabilizing the exchange rate and the value of the national
currency by preventing the manipulation to which it had been subject
to from different groups.[16]

However, when it comes to the intermingling of politics and business, Bulgaria is not an exceptional case. Widespread and unremitting
corruption seems to have gone hand in hand, from the beginning, with
the transformation of the economic system and the consolidation process of political parties. In the former GDR, 62,000 cases of economic
crime—21,000 for the city of Berlin alone—were brought against almost
10,000 individuals. To the manipulations of interest rates in connection
with monetary unification properly so-called in July 1990 and the embezzlement of considerable sums by the former Deputy Minister for External
Trade, Alexander Schalck Golodkowski,[17] can be added the falsification
of accounts, the manipulation of company funds, the misappropriation
of national and EU subsidies and money-laundering. The total amounts
concerned have been estimated at 26 billion DM. The Treuhandanstalt
deserves special attention here. The privatization authority was note-
worthy for the lack of internal or external oversight, false accounting,
the selling-off of companies without proper evaluation, wild speculation
on land prices, particularly in Berlin, and dubious tendering practices.
The Treuhandanstalt was not required to make profits, but to sell off the
industrial heritage of the GDR as quickly as possible. Instead of taking
account of the true value of enterprises at the moment when the property
was transferred, its officials often falsified the situation to be able to sell
the greatest possible number of companies, even if it meant selling them
at the nominal price of one deutschmark.[18] In other words, corruption
was not the sole prerogative of illegal organizations. It seems, in fact, to
have pervaded all organizations whose modes of intervention were characterized by secrecy, lack of external or democratic controls, and the use
of violence, legal or otherwise.

In the Czech Republic, the scandals led directly to the fall of Prime
Minister Václav Klaus in 1996. Unclarity surrounding transaction
rules made a great deal of insider-trading possible, enabling companies to be sold off at low prices or at different prices to different buyers.
Accusations of misappropriation of funds were leveled at civil servants,
senior privatization officials and ODS (Civic Democratic Party) leaders, who were said to have benefited from favorable sell-off prices in

exchange for bribes. Collusion between enterprise managers and public bank officials was alleged.[19] Ultimately, the Czech case gave the lie to two fashionable theories: the theory that good practice demanded a swift sell-off of companies and the theory that only political stability produced positive outcomes. This enabled Mitchell Orenstein to suggest, on the basis of the Polish case, that slowness is sometimes more efficient, and that changes of government personnel often give evidence of greater oversight on the part of society. In this, he is attesting to the reality of democracy, which is alone capable of reducing corruption. However, against this argument, Alexander Surdej has pointed out that a slow approach in Bulgaria had created the conditions for a massive decapitalization of enterprises and, generally, such dynamics had advantaged the former holders of power.[20]

We may add that Poland, which, unlike the Czech Republic, passed through many changes of government, was not exempt from corruption—indeed, far from it. An enormous number of Polish politicians have been mixed up in "scandals," from the Gudzowaty affair—named for the Polish citizen who was able to build up an industrial empire thanks to his contacts within the state, and particularly with President Kwasnieski to ease the connection with Gazprom—to the Rywyn affair, which bears the name of the individual who sought to corrupt journalists in the attempt to have a law passed to his own advantage. It should be said that corruption was not by any means confined to former Communists. Under the "right-wing" governments led by Buzek between 1997 and 2001, 22 ministers or their equivalent were dismissed from their posts, most of them for corruption. In 2001, the dealings around the sell-off of the telecommunications operator led to the resignation of the entire ministry. There were more scandals under the next government, led this time by the former Communists of the SLD (Democratic Left Alliance). The last period of the Miller government was undermined by "scandals," the Rywyn affair involving several members of the parliamentary majority, including the prime minister. The uninterrupted succession of such cases of economico-political misappropriation of funds over 15 years definitely explains the rise to power of the Law and Justice Party (PiS) in 2005.

In Romania, the whole of the political class was mixed up in the Rosa Montana goldmine scandal. After being closed down for destroying the fauna and flora of the Tisza Basin, when it had leaked cyanide into the river, the mine was very quickly reopened under the auspices of a Romanian/Canadian company. As a result, Budapest threatened Romania with the use of its veto to prevent it from joining the European Union in 2007 as planned. In Hungary, Viktor Orban, the prime minister from 1996 to 2001, was criticized for acquiring a vineyard in the Tokay, listed among the first ranks of Hungarian wines, for a nominal sum. He also enabled several members of his family to make illegal fortunes, including his own father, who acquired a state-owned mine without any public tendering process taking place. Prime Minister Madgyessy had to stand down after accusations made against him by his liberal rival (the SZDZ) that he had done nothing to control increasing corruption in political circles, and that he had even been involved in it. His immediately designated successor, Ferenc Gyurcsány, was incapable, for his part, of explaining the shadowy background to the acquisition of his immense fortune in the early 1990s. In Bulgaria, Stefan Sofianski, the mayor of Sofia, was accused of selling a company at a price 10,000 times lower than its actual value. After being found guilty and removed from his post, he was amnestied two months later and restored to his former position.

Initially, privatization policies strengthened the position of interest groups everywhere. Prominent within those interest groups were the political parties that, as a result, became, as the sociologist Attila Agh argues, "super actors."[21] Now, these groups, which were consolidated by the dismembering of the state, are the very ones that were capable of strengthening the state in its function of overseeing the legality of the procedures and rules they themselves formulated. Why, then, at a particular point did legal rule win out over the traditional—or even the "gangster"—order? What new political structure came into play at that moment to modify representations and induce the actors to modify their strategies?

State Autonomy and Public Agencies

The Sources of Legality

The first answer to this question relates directly to the nature of the former Communist states. As we showed in the previous chapter, several observers have attempted to differentiate between these states on the basis of the level of bureaucratization they had reached before 1990.[22] Under the Communist regime, the pursuit of legitimacy by the ruling parties had led, from the death of Stalin in 1953 onward, to a greater level of respect for legality. His successors attempted to legitimate the central power by creating a new form of respect for "socialist legality" by reducing arbitrariness in the legal system, abolishing the Gulags and strengthening the legal apparatuses by training up more highly competent personnel.[23] The Berlin political scientist Glaessner was able to show that the desire evinced by all the hierarchy of the GDR, from Ulbricht's time to Honnecker's, to see East Germany move to the forefront of Soviet-type modernization led to a constant reinforcement of "socialist legality" and, with it, of legal tribunals, the bureaucracy and the training of state functionaries. The GDR, analyzed by some as heir to the Prussian bureaucracy, had taken legal formalism to the point of caricature by combining it with the Bolshevik principles of mass mobilization and socialist emulation. The second answer, largely analyzed in terms of rational choice theory, relates to the demands of enlightened self-interest after 1990.

Certain former political or economic officials recognized they had more to gain by respecting the law, which they had themselves established, than by continuing to follow the previous rule, which had not guaranteed their security. Hence the "red privatization" of the early years, mentioned above. Moreover, it became necessary to combine particular party interest with the interests of the foreign investor, who would not come in unless he could be sure of recovering his investment and could repatriate his funds at will. The classification of countries at financial risk by the international organizations responsible for monitoring legality played a major part in the bureaucratic adjustment and the concomitant arrival of direct foreign investment. The Balkan countries were at the top of this list for a long time and when Hungary was added to this group in 1994, the Budapest government was forced into adjusting its public expenditure and reforming its welfare system.

A third and last answer concerns public pressure for the maintenance of collective security or, to put it another way, it concerns the demand for justice that showed itself in some countries from autumn 1989 onward. In this connection, democracy undoubtedly had decisive social effects that in part made possible the oversight of political practices. In the Bulgarian case, there was pressure of this kind coming up from the streets as early as 1990, though it was not until the winter of 1996–1997 that popular demonstrations triggered a dynamic capable of reinforcing the rule of law.

Public Agencies and Rational Behavior

In this way, in order to be able to benefit from the fruits of privatization, the central actors had, at one point or another, to exploit the existence of state guarantees. To this end, they created public agencies of delegation, regulation, or management. These agencies enabled a general interest to be formulated, distinct from that of the interest groups, by drawing on bodies of newly trained specialists, which were a key factor in the growth of the middle classes. However, the construction of the rational legal order, however imperfect it was, took place against a background of violence and conflict. In this process of the replacement of a more or less criminal order—independently of any evolutionist dynamic—the European Union played an important role, first by contractualizing bilateral relations and, second, by assisting the candidate states financially and making their membership dependent on respect for norms of public management. However, before the *Acquis Communautaire* became incumbent on all the candidate states, it was national forces that played the main role in the transformation. Integration into the EU was preceded by internal transformations of the candidate countries, which means that Europeanization cannot be reduced to that integration alone.

In some countries, the public agencies overseeing the transformation of property rights appeared as early as 1990, in the form of privatization (or ownership) institutions. Though initially part of a Privatization

Ministry, these agencies later became more autonomous, while remaining most often under the authority of the Finance Ministry. They were initially made up of a few departments, created rather chaotically, given their lack of experience of the field and, above all, the general lack of data on the industrial portfolios it fell to them to manage. They thus had to gather together the various data that were in the hands of the great number of sectoral ministries operating before 1989, which were not unified in a single Industry Ministry. Given the situation in 1989, these ministries tended to become autonomous, seeking to cash in their data, particularly with private investors who had no information whatever about the enterprises they were proposing to acquire. Moreover, the various privatization agencies were tasked with specifying and implementing transformation procedures, whether these took the form of commercialization (that is to say, being entered in the trade register), liquidation or sell-off, the latter being either whole or partial. Other procedures also appeared, by which groups, rather than single enterprises, were sold off, through the establishment of Investment Funds that were themselves managed by public bodies. All of these led to a consolidation of bureaucracy, to the specialization of civil servants and the construction of a fund of technical knowledge. Thus, from 1992 onward, in parallel with the law on the transformation of enterprises, the Slovene authorities put in place a Development Fund in the form of a public agency tasked with the restructuring of companies, and the management of—and financial assistance to—those companies. In 1993, this fund was backed up by the creation of development agencies for SMEs (Small and Medium sized Enterprises).[24] Wherever they appeared, these privatization and development agencies provided evidence of the reality of the notion of the general interest, both by way of trade rules and by strengthening administrative and management apparatuses.

The bureaucratization of procedures gave rise to an expanded body of law, enhanced the importance of lawyers, and, more generally, swelled the ranks of state functionaries. Moreover, it created a requirement for the development of internal procedures of oversight and for staff training. In the Czech Republic, under the Klaus governments, numbers in the central bureaucracy rose by 77%. In Poland in 2004, the department in charge of the structural funds, at the level of programming and monitoring, grew by 150%, to which we may add a growth in regional administrative personnel of 80%. Bureaucratization and centralization went together, particularly as the development of a national public agency was everywhere accompanied by the creation of subsidiary bodies in the regions, most often within the regional civil service. In parallel with these developments, agencies charged with managing agricultural property also appeared and, later—under the influence first of the World Bank, then of the EU—employment agencies. One of their tasks was to retrain the staff laid off from the public companies and, at times, to relocate them in other public enterprises. Under EU influence also, development agencies were created from 1995 onward. These operated initially in harmony with the first support programs aimed at SMEs, but later they worked with wider regional development programs. When regional transformation policies took shape in the late 1990s, these development agencies were often attached to the decentralized authorities.[25] They were responsible for the management of funding, for interfacing with the central and local authorities, and for supporting projects. In this respect, they made a massive contribution to spreading a kind of behavior oriented toward respect for rules and procedures. They led to the recruitment of qualified individuals on the basis of high skill levels (though appropriate salaries were not forthcoming). That it was possible for them to be dominated in certain circumstances by interest groups and, particularly, by members of the party in power, is an acknowledged fact. Indeed, the politicization of the civil services found expression, when political power changed hands, in the EU-trained staff systematically losing their jobs. This was one of the criticisms commonly leveled against the agencies in charge of the rural preaccession funds (SAPARD). After 2004, the new civil services were notable for scandals relating to the misappropriation of state funds. It was, nonetheless, through these development agencies that the commission was able to exert control over procedural legality and make the allocation of funds dependent on respect for procedure. The countries that adopted the rule of law—meaning the independence of the judiciary—without delay were the first ones selected by the commission in Brussels for EU membership. The others saw their candidacy postponed, if not indeed rejected.

The Redistributive State

The third modality of post-Communist transformation of property and state-building, after seizure by political elites and transformation by agencies, is the one that refers to the capacity of public players, through fiscal and monitoring policies, to distribute economic actors over defined spaces. In so doing, the state redistributed social roles and played its part in the polarization of spaces. This it did with public enterprises and direct foreign investors.

Fiscal Policy

Fiscal policy is one of the most important tools enabling the central state to exert control over the economic, social, and administrative structure. Setting the tax base is a prerogative of the central state that ensures it of supremacy over its own administrative hierarchy, domination of the regional governments, which are forced to negotiate over their resources, and authority over the beneficiary groups it seeks to identify. The "fiscal linkage" is a classic form of linkage by which states achieve their domination.[26] Now, as chapter four will show, regionalization policies did not necessarily lead to a devolution of financial resources to the regions. Though local communities have seen their prerogatives expand over the past two decades, conflicts over budget allocations have been constant sources of strife between the centers and their regional peripheries.[27] The center has remained the central power. It is the center alone that has decided the tax base in its various forms, often without accounting for its actions. The citizens have remained in ignorance of the public expenditure they have had to bear, and the politicians have not had to explain themselves in ways that would potentially have been costly in electoral terms. Moreover, the availability of international sources of funding has enabled the state not to depend on more expensive domestic sources of private finance. These sources have enabled it to implement autonomous redistributive policies.[28] And, to be efficiently implemented, this policy presupposes the existence of stable legal rules and an efficient bureaucracy.

In this regard, in post-Communist Eastern Europe, foreign companies have not been treated on the same footing as domestic enterprises. The former have been subject to tax levels set by each state and relatively well-known to everyone. By contrast, domestic companies have been more able to negotiate their liability under cover of the obscurity of the rules. On the basis of an examination of the 500 leading Polish companies, Roger Schoenman has shown that company taxation rates were very high for direct foreign investors, but low for domestic companies.[29] More exactly, companies with largely private capital (direct foreign investors or domestic) were called upon more than public-private joint ventures to settle their tax bills. Among these, foreign companies were taxed the highest. Moreover, the leading companies in the list paid relatively more tax than those lower down. Amounts of unpaid tax are much higher in the case of state enterprises than in private companies. In Romania this overdue tax represents 14% of the capital of private companies, but it is as high as 53% in the case of public enterprises.[30] We may conclude, then, that those in possession of state capital were more able to bargain over their liabilities to the public authorities than the others, who were more highly taxed. Of the 500 largest Polish firms, which represented 40% of the GDP in 2000, a third were in the hands of private capital, a third in state hands and a third in foreign ownership.

Redistribution and Territorial Development

However, foreign investors have not simply been discriminated against. Far from it. Investment support policies have largely favored them. "Special economic zones" have burgeoned in all the countries. Based on the principle of exemption from certain taxes—mainly land taxes, but also taxes on profits in some cases, such exemptions sometimes lasting for 10 years—these instruments were intended both to make up the missing links in terms of technology and to recreate local employment and, consequently, the skills base. These zones have been negotiated with the regional and local partners, but on account of the tax advantages they have offered, they have first and foremost required the support of the central state. Having initially been created to promote employment in the areas in deep crisis, they were subsequently located mainly in the regions of economic dynamism, being less commonly found in areas of industrial decline. In other words, the central economic development support policies have reinforced the wider dynamics of redeployment that have seen investment massively localized in what are already, in most cases, growth regions and sectors. By contrast, the development of—chiefly rural—crisis-ridden environments was largely the responsibility of local actors, before the programs supported by the structural funds attempted to overcome their backwardness. The policy of the creation of special zones has generally been underpinned by the idea that development should be concentrated sectorally in already developed geographical areas. This conception also underlies in part the approach in terms of "clusters," widely developed in the West and subsequently taken over in Eastern Europe.[31] After 1990 these "clusters," which are found in all the countries, designate either new geographical areas revitalized through new technologies (like the automotive cluster in the area that links the cities of Budapest, Bratislava, Prague, and Katowice), old areas experiencing growth as a result of new demand, or specific rural, agricultural activities reorganized by a multinational, such as Danone with its berry-fruit production in South Eastern Poland.[32]

The new territorial dynamics largely tie in with the long-term opposition between the occidental regions of the countries concerned—regions adjoining the Western countries whose development they have shared in other periods of history—and the eastern regions, marked by a collapse of collective agricultural structures. In reality, the latter regions have never in their history known articulated development. In this regard, the Communist period—when, in an attempt to achieve a coherent working of land unfavored by nature, the great collective farms were established—represented an exception. A factor that made matters even worse in the post-1989 period was that these areas undergoing a massive agricultural slump adjoined territories that were even more in crisis than they were: Russia to the north of Poland (the Kaliningrad oblast), Belarus and Ukraine on the eastern border of Poland, Slovakia and Hungary, and, in the case of Romania, Moldavia.[33] All these adjoining countries remain centralized, which hampers cooperation with the East European regions even more, given that they now have decentralized political authorities.[34] We shall see this more clearly in chapter four on decentralization policy, and in chapter nine, which deals with the Euroregions.

This very high concentration of direct foreign investment in the capital regions in the first post-Communist decade diminished greatly after 2004, particularly as a result of the structural funds, which have attempted to reduce territorial inequalities.[35]

Table 2.1 Regional Concentration of Direct Foreign Investors in the 1990s

Bulgaria	More than 51% in Sofia (41%) and the Sofia region (11%), 19% in Varna
Czech Republic	47% in Prague and the Prague region
Estonia	81% around Tallinn and in the Harjuma region; 10% in the Tartu region
Hungary (1998)	60% in Budapest (49% + 11% in the Pest region), 12.5% in Györ-Moson-Sopron county; and 5.9% in Borsöd-Abauj-Zemplen county
Latvia	52% Riga, 7% Daugavpil
Lithuania	83% concentrated in the 3 main cities: Vilnius (60%), Kalipeda (12%) Kaunas (11%)
Poland	Widely spread, with Warsaw 10%; Mazovia 10%; Poznan 9% and Upper Silesia: 9%
Rumania	48% in Bucharest, 6% in Timis, 4% in Prahova
Slovakia	Circa 50% in Bratislava and region; Tarnava 9%; Kosice 8%; Trencin 7%
Slovenia	Mostly around Ljubljana

Source: This table is based on Daniel Vaughan-Whitehead, *EU Enlargement versus Social Europe? The Uncertain future of the European Social Model*. Cheltenham, Edward Elgar, 2003, p. 393.

Conclusion

Since the fall of the Communist regimes, state-building has not proceeded at the same pace or in the same ways in all the countries of former Soviet Europe. Some countries have progressively passed through the various stages, while others have fallen behind or barely begun at all. The massive initial politicization of the processes (in which the parties in contention won out if they had previously accumulated resources) was followed by a period in which foreign investors—most often, multinationals—weighed in heavily. During this stage, when the rule of law became firmly established, the democratic demand was the decisive factor, seconded by—widely differing—national bureaucratic traditions.[36] Even though the initial privatization model made no call on it, democracy functioned in the end to safeguard the later development, particularly as the European Union quickly became the magnet for countries that would be selected on the basis of their "good" governance. And it was democracy that, at the electoral level, penalized those who had taken advantage of their positions to appropriate public property, whether in Poland, the Czech Republic, Hungary, or, subsequently, Bulgaria, and Romania. Later on, it was democracy that, at the economic level, guaranteed the sustainability of investment.

In this sequential transition dynamic, there is a clear movement toward the bureaucratization and rationalization of procedures. This has translated, among other things, into a complexification of social structures, a specialization of functions and an autonomization of fields of action. However, this dynamic of change has in no way expressed a division between corrupt interest groups, on the one hand, and "transparent," "honest" direct foreign investors on the other. We shall endeavor in chapter six to show that the greater rationalization of transformation processes as a result of foreign investment have actually taken place against a back-ground of misappropriation and the flouting of initial commitments. The salaried employees were left out of the decision-making process on many occasions and insider-trading was rife. But, unlike the initial players, the foreign actors, including those from the European Union, brought about an expansion of fields of intervention, both private and public. They made the development of new tax policies possible, leading to the consolidation of domestic companies and larger-scale redistribution policies. These various dynamics enabled specific national paths of development to be mapped out within a radically different set of constraints. These paths were, admittedly, carved out as a function of past trajectories, but also of the opportunities afforded by the post-Communist period.

CHAPTER THREE

The Reforms of the Welfare States

Given the pressure exerted by the measures adopted under the "Washington Consensus," one might have expected the introduction in the 1990s of a massive reform of the welfare states, along the lines of Chilean-type liberalization, as implemented in the 1970s and 1980s. Here again, however, as with the reforms of property rights, the national centers asserted their sovereignty. Globalized models, together with European prescriptions, were widely adapted to fit in with national trajectories. A number of interest groups came together to thwart the wholesale adoption of programs developed at other times and in other cultural spaces. And because the European Union is not very demanding in this regard, on account of its desire not to see its own high level of protection dented, it allowed the international monetary institutions free rein to exert pressure, without the final architectures arrived at actually giving the impression of a totally liberalized Central and Eastern Europe. Far from it, indeed. A variety of eventual patterns predominated. This is what we intend to demonstrate in this chapter, after analyzing the prevailing political contexts at the point when the decision to reform social systems was made. In many places continuities combined with sizeable innovations, though they never produced a typical Eastern European model of a kind that might be added to the various existing typologies.[1]

The Political Contexts

The crisis in the finances of the new East European states had its source in an accumulation of the same phenomena that affect Western economies: an increase in unemployment and a mismatch between contributors and beneficiaries; longer life expectancy and a mismatch between the active and the inactive; depleted public funds and increased expenditure. In the same way as in the West, but even more dramatically given the scarcity of resources, needs grew in Eastern Europe and revenues declined. Demographic projections for 2015 all show a diminution in the populations of Central Europe—not so great in Poland, but very distinct in

Table 3.1 Total of East European Populations and Projections for 2015 (in Million)

	1980	1990	2001	2015 (projections)
Bulgaria	8.846	8.767	8.191	6.8
Czech Republic	10.316	10.362	10.267	10.0
Estonia	1.472	1.572	1.367	1.2
Hungary	10.709	10.324	10.005	9.3
Latvia	2.509	2.613	2.366	2.2
Lithuania	3.404	3.708	3.693	3.5
Poland	35.413	38.038	38.644	38.0
Romania	22.133	23.211	22.431	21.4
Slovakia	4.963	5.288	5.403	5.4
Slovenia	1.893	1.996	1.990	1.9

Source: This table is based on data found in United Nations Economic Commission for Europe, *Economic Survey of Europe*, Geneva, 2003.

Bulgaria and Hungary. They show up a continuous decline over 30 years. By revealing the depth of the crisis of the public finances, similar data raise the question of the reform of the welfare states.

The Initial Absence of a Program

Unlike policies for transforming property rights, social policies seem to have been the subject dealt with least in the first years of transformation. This was the case because in 1989, by contrast with what occurred in the economic field, no program was ready. Other priorities were on the agenda—property rights in particular. And, first and foremost, the desire for social peace was dominant in this highly turbulent period. At this stage, unemployment was regarded as a temporary evil and many actors believed that the expected resumption of growth would soon eliminate it. There was, then, continuity with the highly spendthrift Communist regime. When it became clear that the crisis was going to be a long-term affair, far from disappearing, this mental mechanism was reinforced by the simple fact that no alternative policy was available and, given the growing uncertainty, it was better to leave the existing arrangements in place. The use of early retirement became generalized at the central level to offset the successive shocks of recession, while simultaneously in the enterprises, previous social benefit levels were maintained in the areas of social services, childcare, health care, vacations, and employment. The Soviet-style welfare state, based on the promotion of labor, extensive paternalism, and clientelism, remained unchanged in the initial years, whereas financial constraints had tightened fiercely. From a strict economic point of view, the situation may be said to have required vigorous action, which Kornai had no hesitation in demanding.[2]

As in the case of the transformation of property ownership, interest groups brought their influence to bear. The pressures to modify the pre-1989 universal system ran up against the majority's determination to keep it in being, despite the high levels of public expenditure it occasioned. In the three branches of health, pensions, and employment insurance, costs were too high, whereas receipts seemed too low. This just shows how enduringly attached the majority of the population were to generous welfare states and what tensions this generated, given the financial constraints.[3] The second phase began after 1995 when it became impossible to ignore the reality of the financial crisis and the high levels of unemployment. The European Union grew insistent that something must be done, without however presenting any concrete solutions.[4] It was, in fact, the World Bank that led the way, both in terms of macro-economic analyses and financial regulation policies. This was the period when the Left, back in power in Poland, Lithuania, and Hungary, were to adopt rafts of measures from which their free-market successors would subsequently row back somewhat, in the face of growing discontent. In certain countries, then, we saw a kind of "role reversal" in which "Left-wing" governments implemented reform policies that "Right-wing" governments had been unable to apply. Elsewhere, where financial constraints were less onerous, particularly in the Czech Republic and Slovenia, the new architectures were more consensual, but just as costly. Poland saw both the largest fall in GNP and the largest growth in social budgets—from 17% in 1989 to 32% in 1995.[5] In the Czech Republic, the figure rose from 25% to 30%. The only exception to this was Romania, where there was an upturn in growth from 1996 onward, after a long period of sluggishness.

Public Expenditure

Social expenditure was considerably lower as a proportion of GNP than in the West, catch-up not being achieved before 1990, as we saw in chapter one. After that date, we may, however, note substantial growth. This was a mark of the resolve not to completely dismantle the old redistributive edifice and even, in certain countries, to make it more robust. This was, indeed, the case in all countries except Hungary and Slovakia, Poland, for its part, barely having reduced its social expenditure as a percentage of GNP. In absolute figures, some countries, such as Poland and Hungary, came close to the European average of the 15-member EU. In relation to Standard Purchasing Power (SPP), the difference between the two parts of Europe increased. Taking the EU15 figure as base 100, Poland achieved a score not much above 30. By comparison, Luxembourg was the leading nation with 165, while Denmark scored 122, Austria 117, Germany 114, France 113, Italy 97, Greece 62, Spain 60, Ireland 60, and Portugal 57.

Moreover, the amounts devoted to the three policy areas of employment, health, and pensions shifted significantly to the advantage of pensions and to the detriment of employment. While the employment crisis was unprecedented for most of the countries, bureaucratic measures for handling unemployment won out. Throughout the decade, criteria for the granting of assistance were constantly tightened, as various legislative changes were introduced. In Bulgaria no fewer than 8 laws were adopted while in Poland there were 11. The outcome was a substantial reduction both in the amount of benefits and the number of beneficiaries. Passive measures greatly exceeded active ones, reducing the sums granted for assistance with training or enterprise-creation, while child-benefit payments were cut significantly and were, indeed, among the largest reductions made.

Coverage rates (which indicate the number of unemployed eligible for public assistance) were generally below 50% of the registered unemployed figure, except in Hungary and Estonia. The replacement ratio, which indicates the amount of benefit as a percentage of the average wage, was set very low, in order to encourage the unemployed to look for work. For this reason, some observers have described this as a "workfare" system.

Where health policies are concerned, expenditure stood on average at 4.5% of GNP, when the figure for the old member states was at the time 8.6%. All the countries favored a substantial decentralization and privatization of insurance schemes and of health services. As a result, these

Table 3.2   Public Social Expenditure as a % of GNP

	1996	1998	2000
Bulgaria	12.1	14.9	17.9
Czech Republic	17.4	18.1	19.5
Estonia	15.9	14.74	15.2
Hungary	24.8	24.2	23.2
Latvia	17.5	17.6	17.8
Lithuania	14.2	15.8	15.8
Poland	31.0	29.5	29.9
Romania	10.6	13.8	13.9
Slovakia	23.28	21.88	21.7
Slovenia	25.5	26.1	—
EU 15			27.6

Source: This table is based on data found in United Nations Economic Commission for Europe, *Economic Survey of Europe*, Geneva, 2003.

Table 3.3   Unemployment Benefit Relative to the Minimum Wage in 2002

	Unemployment Benefit as a Percentage of Minimum Wage	Minimum Wage as a Percentage of Average Wage
Bulgaria	40.9	39.8
Czech Republic	57.4	34.8
Estonia	21.6	31.5
Hungary	60.2	42.7
Poland	62.7	34.3
Slovakia	69.2	36.9
Slovenia	92.9	41.4

Source: This table is based on data found in United Nations Economic Commission for Europe, *Economic Survey of Europe*, Geneva, 2003, p. 198.

Table 3.4   Coverage Rates and Replacement Ratios, 1998

	Coverage Rates (number of unemployed receiving insurance payments)	Unemployment Replacement Ratios (insurance/wage)
Bulgaria	24.8	29.0
Czech Republic	48.8	24
Estonia	59.3	7.5
Hungary	73.9	27.5
Poland	23.1	36
Slovakia	27.0	32.8
Slovenia	32.6	43.9

Source: This table is based on data found in United Nations Economic Commission for Europe, *Economic Survey of Europe*, Geneva, 2003, p. 88.

measures created vast regional imbalances, together with thoroughgoing restructurings of hospital facilities, which had to cope with substantial cuts—particularly reductions in the number of beds. Quite naturally, a correspondingly great emphasis was placed, as a result, on the family structure and on individualized insurance. In most cases, the social insurance system was entrusted to a national administrative body, independent of the state, and responsible for collecting and distributing monies. The differences between the new members relate largely to the fact that some countries, such as Latvia, Poland, Romania, and Bulgaria, have adopted the principle of a plurality of resources, based on taxation and voluntary insurance, while others have relied entirely on taxation.

The Actors

Interest Groups and "Epistemic Communities"

There were a very great many interest groups opposed to any reform of the pension systems. Let us take the Polish example. In that case, the farmers were involved, and they had little interest in seeing any change to the existing regime, since there were two active contributors to the scheme for every two pensioners. The deficit was covered by general social insurance or, in other words, by the other wage earners, which gave the agricultural beneficiaries no incentive to change the scheme and that, even worse, thwarted the anticipated modernization of the primary sector.[6] Alongside peasant farmers, who represent more than 20% of the social structure in Poland (but up to 30% in Bulgarian and 40% in Romania), we may also note the sizeable influence of employees in heavy industry, a sector in which enterprises were highly concentrated regionally, as we pointed out in chapter one. Hence the massive presence of groups linked, in one way or another, to the members of the old *nomenklatura*, and, even more, of employees eager to see the retention of the former scheme of social benefits paid by the public enterprises. The reform of the social benefits paid to miners proved very difficult to accept for those concerned, even when there was no longer any justification after 1990 for the payment of sums in lieu of milk or coal allocations, which had originally been granted in the 1950s. To these occupational groups were added the political parties, whose various clienteles all had an interest in keeping the existing system in being. Who were these people? Or, more to the point, which political groupings were the exceptions, given the pressure exerted by these regionally very powerful groups? The answer is, mainly, the free-market liberals, who made substantial cuts everywhere in social budgets at the beginning of the 1990s, without, however, reforming the system effectively. In this way, as in the case of the Polish finance minister, Balcerowicz, they induced the various interest groups to coalesce against them. As for the social-democratic parties—the ex-Communists—to whom it often fell to implement the reforms later, they adopted them very much against their will. The foreseeable effect of the *laissez-faire* of the early years was a product of the pressure exerted simultaneously by the growth of expenditure, the collapse of GNPs, and the spiraling rise in the number of benefit recipients and early retirements. Enterprises invited to rationalize often then negotiated on the basis of the grey economy, involving clandestine working and nondeclaration of incomes. Everyone "came to an accommodation" and clientelism acquired renewed vigor.

Epistemic Communities

Over and against these groups, which reflect the national structure of different interests, stood another coalition of actors, whom a number of specialists have dubbed an "epistemic community." This term enables us to highlight the influence of ideas within broadly transnational communities.[7] Basing themselves on the approach of Pierson, who argues that the diffusion of innovation presupposes an epistemic community and a structure of innovation, Orenstein has examined the vast movements that attest to the importance of international organizations diffusing "models." The "epistemic community," for which great international organizations like the World Bank and the IMF were the vectors, intervened on the basis of well-established reform programs, based on the work of recognized experts, whose successes (though not, to any great degree, their failures) were widely trumpeted.[8] The starting point for their intervention was agreement that the existing systems were bankrupt for reasons of corruption and mistakes in the management of funds. Firm in this conviction, they proposed that there should, in all circumstances, be reform of the Finance Ministry and that this should relate to the payment mechanism. The *idée-force* was the depoliticization of the process, which in the end only a free-market, authoritarian regime, such as that of General Pinochet in Chile, could guarantee. The conduct of such a policy was backed by the authority of the "Chicago Boys." This theoretical posture marked the triumph of an "epistemic community," which, thanks to globalization, permitted the widespread diffusion of reforms of a neoliberal cast, reforms directly imposed against Keynesian-style policies. As part of broad currents of international exchange, these communities had available to them a vast panoply of recipes that were diffused to their local allies.

Who were their intermediaries in Eastern Europe? Initially, the central actors with, first, the groups of experts working in the agencies, ministries, and national research institutes. Kataryna Müller argues that the crisis often came to a head when the civil servants in the Budget Ministry clashed with their colleagues in the Labor or Social Affairs Ministries. In the Polish case, an intermediary with great support from the World Bank played "Honest Broker" between the different parties and enabled deals to be worked out. This is the reason why plans barely came to the attention of the public at all and why there was even less collective discussion of them. The complexity of the procedures provided an argument for evading any discussion of the possible negative effects of the decisions made. As during the privatization reforms, secrecy around the measures adopted proved to be a key to success and dissimulation served as a basic principle of public management. Everywhere, the new laws were presented hastily ahead of the elections. The citizens were not able to exercise any oversight. The trade unions were kept out of the decisions, if not indeed ousted from them. The investment funds were given a systematically privileged status (with a few exceptions, notably that of the Czech Republic), though there was no justification for such decisions and no one could guarantee their certain success.

And yet in spite of these features, which are clearly far removed from democratic principles, these reforms were widely accepted. This is what we have to explain. The fact that they did not lead, in reality, to the pure application of the Anglo-Saxon model, based on pension funds and the privatization of welfare systems, is one explanation. Far from fading away before the preeminence of the funds, the state everywhere reaffirmed its position. The second element relates to the fact that these reforms were adapted to national traditions and, moreover, that they targeted certain disadvantaged populations. In combination, above and beyond the dissimulation that prevailed when they were adopted, these explanations enable us to account for the building of social consensuses. These were based on conflicts between interest groups, representative of the equilibria of the foregoing period, and the transnational communities associated with certain representatives of the national bureaucracies.

The Implementation of the Reforms

Without budget crises, no need for reform is actually felt. Even though everyone is aware of the need for reform, routine, and interest groups, as we have just seen, prevent any change. In Kataryna Müller's view, reform is possible when the crisis of the pensions system (and more generally of welfare systems) is taken seriously and when a broad range of factors are combined that have to do with dynamic political leadership (particularly in the person of the finance minister), the importance granted to the international financial institutions (IMF/World Bank), the elaboration of an intelligent reform design, and the capacity to act and thwart the opponents of reform.[9] For Orenstein and Haas, reform is possible when free-market or social-democratic ideas dominate, expressed by experts who are capable of negotiating and who enjoy both the support of the international institutions and a broad degree of social acceptance. All these elements played a part in the adoption of the various reforms in Central and Eastern Europe. It wasn't the least of the paradoxes that it was often the ex-Communists (allied with some liberals), restored to power, who implemented the free-market liberal policies that were initially expected from the parties of the Right or Center. In each case, social consensuses based on strong group interests played a part in reformulating the liberal orientations of the reforms, as it happened with the Polish and Hungarian policies.

Polish Reform

The crisis in the public finances brought an understanding of the need for reform in Poland. Between 1989 and 1992, the number of pensioners rose from 17.9% to 23.1%, while the level of pensions went up in the same period from 66 to 387 zlotys. The proportion of GNP devoted to social expenditure rose from 50% in 1989 to 54% in 1994. In 1989 14.5 million Poles paid into the social security scheme, but in 1995 the figure stood at 12.6 million. There were two workers for two pensioners at the KRUS, the agricultural insurance fund.[10] The neoliberal transition of the early years was characterized by an indexing of unemployment benefit to wages, assistance granted to local authorities, and the adoption of active employment measures of limited scope. A very high number of people took early retirement pensions, but as the sums paid out were relatively low and not targeted (they were equal for everyone), many low-income individuals were compelled to carry on working. In this, there was little change from the one period to the other. Though the principle of social assistance was adopted, obtaining such assistance nonetheless signified the end of "welfare payments," particularly the provisions relating to housing; hence the weak incentive character of the measures. Moreover, substantial sums were allocated to pensions and, hence, far less for employment or for "welfare." This latter was not paid on a means-tested basis, as in the Czech Republic, or related to a universal citizenship, as in Hungary. It functioned as an exit door and was not targeted at the poor. Paid without distinction between persons, the sums were low. Unemployment benefits were not correctly targeted. Ultimately, in the view of several observers, the introduction of a liberal system turned out to be very expensive, because it was poorly directed and not properly targeted.

In 1993 the Left returned to power under the leadership of the former Communists, now converted to Social Democracy, in alliance with the peasants. Its policy was to relaunch growth, reduce the public element in the deficit by means of restructurings, and increase social expenditure. A guarantee fund was created for the workers (to cover enterprise insolvencies). Kolodko, the minister who introduced this reform, wanted to create similar funds for all private and public enterprises. A program for employment activization (for young people) and against unemployment took shape, while, after 1995, tripartite negotiations were restarted in order to win the social actors over to reform. However, the latter initiative held little interest, given the sidelining of the trade unions, the weak desire of the employers to participate, and the absence of delegation on the part of the state, which retained control of the overall situation. In very many cases, the tripartite forums seemed more of an alibi than a recognized partner. The weakness of Polish reform had to do mainly with the disorderly relations between the center and the regions, the incomplete privatization of the health funds and the large extent of informal payments. And yet, despite all this, the reform was a success.

The SLD, the reformed former Communist Party, got its pensions bill through before the elections of 1997. This reform of pension funds enjoyed broad popular support, a product of the neoliberal/social-democratic combination. The first "pillar" of the scheme offered a guarantee in the form of a minimum retirement pension for a given period, at the same time as it provided incentives to work longer. Men were allowed to retire after the age of 65 and 25 years of work, women after the age of 60 and 20 years of work. The second "pillar" involved contributions to private funds chosen by the employee. For employees aged under 30, contribution to the fund was obligatory and for those between 30 and 50, it was a matter of individual choice. As for charges, these were fixed at 12–22% of gross wages processed by the state insurance funds and 7.3% by private funds, to which was added the charge of 17.48% for the sickness funds. In the short term, we are speaking of a system that was highly onerous for the state that, while meeting its commitments inherited from the former regime, had, at the same time, to commit itself to allocating part of its income tax revenues to the private funds. In the long term, the creation of the private funds was seen as the way to lighten the burden on the state and to promote growth, on the basis of a commonly held belief that capital-market growth and the growth of investment were linked in a virtuous circle. For its part, the growth of investment was supposed to generate higher wages, hence higher tax revenues, and, ultimately, the share payable to the private funds. This conception is justified so long as the investments made by the pension funds are well-managed and there is no break in this particular virtuous circle. It was no doubt the perception that there might be such a break and hence the desire not to undermine the social consensus that led the Polish authorities not to liberalize the system more. The "Left" was thus given credit for not dismantling the social safety net, while at the same time achieving compromises between the different positions by maintaining intergenerational solidarity.

The Hungarian Case

From 1989 onward, Hungary also ran a substantial debt and serious public deficits. However, the trade unions blocked all reform and even managed to raise what were already high benefit levels (cf. chapter one). Pregnant women were granted six months' maternity leave, paid at 100%. Up to the second child, they received 60–75% of their wage, together with an allowance that had previously been reserved for the third child. Added to this was an allowance for the poorest households, social assistance for the long-term unemployed, and other benefits delivered by the local authorities. For these various reasons, the social state remained extremely generous, a state of affairs violently denounced by Kornai.[11] In 1994, the reformed Communist Party came to power, inheriting this very burdensome social system; 7% of GNP was taken up in social expenditure at that point, when GNP was, in fact, falling. The Left, in a majority with 37% of votes and 54% of seats, decided nonetheless to govern in coalition with the Alliance of Free Democrats (SzDSz), which had not participated in previous government coalitions. This alliance enabled it to get through the reform, which it hatched with the World Bank. A tripartite body, the Council for National Reconciliation, was formed in 1994. In February 1995, the government imposed an extremely harsh reform regime (known as "Hungarian shock therapy") and the Left turned out to be much more economically liberal than the Right. Why was this? For a whole series of reasons, relating initially to the major financial crisis, which put the country at risk of a Mexico-style crisis. At this point, international financiers ranked Hungary uppermost among the at-risk countries. In the end, the failure of the social pact marked the end of a "gentle" exit from the Communist-type system or, to put it another way, a "graduated" exit, as the Hungarian path had been styled.

After wide-ranging negotiations between the tripartite body, the six employee trade unions and the nine employers' organizations, Lajos Bokros, the finance minister, proposed a reform plan that included devaluing the forint by 9%, an 8% tax on imported goods, cuts in the social budgets, which fell from 29.5% of GNP to 24.3% in 1996, and an end to the indexation of benefits to inflation, which had reached an annual rate of 20%. Civil service wages were cut by 5%; a severe 3% reduction of the deficit led to massive cuts in support for families and children, and the retirement age was raised to 62 for men (it had previously been set at 60). If these measures had been adopted, two-thirds of Hungarians would have been affected, and this led to massive demonstrations on the part of students and workers.

The harshest criticism of this plan related to the introduction of means-tested benefits, which are in reality doubly disadvantageous, since they increase poverty. The administrative costs of oversight increase, without there being the slightest assurance that monies will be redirected toward those who need them most. The cuts in family expenditure were felt the most bitterly. A year later, in February 1996, Minister Bokros had to stand down. Before leaving his post, he launched his radical pension funds plan, inspired by an American adviser Adam Gere, a fervent proponent of the Chilean method, which prescribed that all or almost all insurance contributions had to be directed toward pension funds, with a minimum of guaranteed pension rights. But after much conflict and discussion, the plan was challenged and a compromise was found on the basis of a balanced system of public and private provision. Over time, the private-sector share fell to 30%. Peter Medgyessy, who succeeded Bokros, managed to achieve a consensus between the finance minister and the minister of health (by threatening his own resignation). In July 1997, after six weeks of debate, the new plan was adopted by the parliament. This provided for a first "pillar" covering three-quarters of the monies and a second covering one quarter. In the face of the wave of strikes led by the taxi drivers, the authorities committed themselves to maintaining a high level of redistribution. Expenditure on pensions and social benefits rose as a result. The fixed portion of pensions increased. In 1998, the Right, returning to power, challenged the Left's free-market reforms. It reestablished the principle of solidarity, decreased the element of private provision in pensions, and increased the element provided by the state, and rehabilitated the principle of citizenship in the granting of benefits. In the view of Tomka, there was no liberal reform of the welfare state in Hungary, any more than in the other former Communist-type countries. The sickness insurance systems had retained their universal character. The idea of social assistance as a residual provision, which in the view of Esping Andersen is what characterizes liberal regimes (USA and Canada), was given short shrift in Hungary.[12]

The Variety of Models and National Situations

Social Consensuses

Using the Chilean example as their guide, several observers have taken the view that only an authoritarian regime could combat organized interests. In contrast to that conviction, which was widely shared in 1990, the extension of the principles of the reform of social systems in Eastern Europe would tend to prove that reform can be carried out democratically, or less violently than the hyperliberal prescriptions suggest. The problem is to characterize the consensuses arrived at the expense of the citizens—given the skew, highlighted above, in terms of asymmetry of information—and the secret character of the procedures employed. The populations were, in fact, kept in ignorance of the risks being run with pension funds, and measures were adopted in secret, just before elections, in such a way that no one paid attention to them. The introduction of such reforms in the middle of electoral campaigns and the low impact of these reforms on the votes cast make the case for an asymmetry of information and for the inequality of citizens in the face of government, particularly as several observers noted a glaring absence of policy coordination. Policies on childhood and housing, to which the former regime devoted the better part of its energies, suffered especially. Moreover, decentralization to the local levels created major inequalities, particularly in Poland. Welfare policy, delegated largely to the local authorities, suffered from glaring funding shortages.

In spite of all these points, however, it seems that success in this area was based on a massive "social acceptance" of reform. To explain this, we no doubt have to recall that the reforms went hand in hand with social packages aimed at those categories of people most affected by the changes. We have, then, to accept that the processes were, in one way or another, legitimated. Though the citizens did not participate in the drafting of the reforms, they did at least seem to have benefited from them once they were implemented. As Zusza Ferge and G. Juhasz argue, "The institutions of social protection—supported by the majority of citizens—could have been altered without major destruction."[13] This is confirmed by another Hungarian observer, for whom "the new democratic governments reacted by introducing new welfare state programs and new institutions that would be better suited to market conditions, but the reforms were cautious."[14] One of the most important innovations here will have been gaining acceptance everywhere for the adoption of a national insurance scheme funded by contributions. This was the case in Hungary in 1991, in the Czech Republic in 1992, and in Slovakia in 1993. Not until 2000 was it adopted in Bulgaria, Romania, and Poland. And yet observers stress the problematical installation of this National Insurance Scheme, given the increased levels of unemployment and, hence, the lower number of contributors, and the reluctance to accept it on the part of employers and employees.

The variety of national situations revealed the strength of the domestic consensuses inscribed in particular historical paths. Each country combined traditional elements with their own evaluations of their situation and ended up not unilaterally adopting a "hard-line" liberalism that would have presented pension funds as a panacea. Lithuania was the only country (with Kazakhstan) to have adopted something almost identical to the Chilean "three pillars" model, doing so the better to differentiate itself from Russia and with the aim of gaining entry to the European Union. The Czech Republic and Slovenia retained their systems in their totality, rejecting the second "pillar" and reforming the first. These two countries did not have heavy debts in 1989. In both countries, there seems to be a high correlation between this low level of indebtedness and a tripartism that was more active than elsewhere, a high degree of consensus over privatization, and a real political will for cohesion with a neocorporatist system. Unlike the Czech Republic, Slovakia adopted the principle of the second pillar; 60% of Slovaks are said to favor this system and, in the summer of 2005, 8 funded insurance schemes shared 945,000 private contracts between them. It was expected that Hungary would implement a very liberal system, yet this did not eventuate. The citizens showed their attachment to a European model based in large part on solidarity. In the end, the first and second pillars were balanced in a two-thirds: one-third relationship. Poland, which is often presented as dominated by free-market ideology, demonstrated a pattern of specific national alliances between the state, occupational interest groups, and the great majority of the population. In that country, as in Hungary, there was the same relationship between the first and second pillars: 62.4% for the first, 37.4% for the second. Capitalization is obligatory for a certain age range. All in all, most of the countries fought to maintain a system that is, at least in part, universal.

Borrowings and National Pathways

In this vast laboratory of welfare-state reform, several "models" were at work, producing a variety of combinations. Many observers felt justified in criticizing the weak impact of the European Union, its formalism and the frequent lack of content of its recommendations. In the employment field, the Commission did, admittedly, make its influence felt, with the Lisbon Strategy, which foregrounded the objectives of employability, entrepreneurship, adaptability, and equality of opportunity. Regarding employment, each of the EU candidate countries was invited to draw up a Joint Assessment Paper with the commission, in which the main national objectives were laid down. Moreover, exchanges of experience and shared assessment were extended thanks to the implementation of the "Open Coordination Method" (OCM). However, the results were mixed.[15] On the other hand, the distinction between active measures (training and assistance with employment creation) and passive measures (unemployment benefit) was applied everywhere, leading to the establishment of labor offices and the training of staff specialized in providing assistance to jobseekers. Bureaucratization went hand in hand with the specialization of civil servants' skills. The European Union also intervened in the pattern of pensions provision, but it was the World Bank and the IMF that most made their influence felt in this connection, linking the principle of the introduction of reform to the granting of loans. The social insurance schemes, which were largely supported by the World Bank in all matters relating to child support and targeted assistance, were in reality very close to the aims of the EU.[16]

What part does the influence of history play in all this? The countries' pasts as part of the central empires seems to have been crucial. In the Western part of Poland, under German domination, an unemployment insurance scheme had been introduced in 1924. From 1929 onward, pensions were paid out of employees' contributions. In the Czech Republic, the importance of Mazaryk's social thinking found expression in non-contributory social provision, the role of the state, and the importance of Czech solidarism. Unemployment insurance was introduced there in 1921. Tomka speaks of the complete adoption of the Bismarkian system. However, to explain certain features, such as the importance accorded to pensions policies in Poland, some observers, such as Kapstein and Milanovic, refer rather to the domestic balance of forces, a factor to be seen in parallel with the slowness of privatization. In their view, the interest groups won out by a long way in both areas. The Czech Republic acted differently, according greater importance to employment policies. For Orenstein and Haas, this can be explained by the predominance of-neoliberal or social-democratic—economic ideas in strategic decision making.

These are so many elements that enable us to highlight several features of the "path dependency" approach, first isolating the nature of social consensuses. Taken together with a long-term perspective, these make a case for a strong representation of social cohesion that orientates the preferences and interests of the various groups. Next comes innovation, which refers to an external "model," but a model relayed internally by intermediate actors whose social struggles enable that model to be reformulated as a function of the various trajectories and interests. Finally, the broad dynamic of recomposition at work in the reform of welfare systems enables us to distinguish both a ruptural process—made possible by the initial financial crisis that marked the point of exhaustion of the previous operating structure—and a process of continuity, by way of the "recombination" of references and the adaptation of the different interests.

Conclusion

It took a decade to implement the welfare reforms necessitated by the financial crisis that hit almost all the countries. Given the economic and social issues associated with this reform, the speed of adaptation of the former Soviet-type countries is worthy of emphasis. The previously missing link between wages and payouts to each insured person was established, as was a division of contributions between employers and employees. As we reminded the reader in chapter one, this was a crucial requirement in the transformation of the Communist systems. In most cases, the capitalization system came into being, without however imperiling the classic regimes of contributions based on wages. Above all, these reforms were implemented on the basis of expanded social consensuses, despite adoption procedures that were often obscure, if not indeed undemocratic. Though there are still many obstacles where relations between the central and local levels (politically, with respect to everything relating to employment policies) or the regard for certain European Union objectives—particularly gender equality—are concerned, they are not such as to endanger the adjustment dynamics of the countries of Central and Eastern Europe. We shall, however, come back in chapter eight to the deficit of social regulation when we examine industrial relations.

Moreover, none of the various national set-ups arrived at seems to be the product of conforming to an existing model; though neither does this signify the emergence of a particular "Eastern European model." None of the three models advanced by Esping Anderson seems to have imposed itself on a country: in reality, all the countries have borrowed elements from each, and the resulting product does not constitute any typically "East European" model. The importance of the rural phenomenon, the influence of the family, and the primacy granted to pensions mean that some countries, such as Bulgaria and Poland, have been compared to the Southern European model,[17] but this is not systematic. Tomka comes to the conclusion that the various outcomes are "faceless" configurations.[18] Ultimately, the innovative aspect lay in the combination of elements belonging to the two—Bismarkian and Beveridgian—models, insofar as national choices have included universal assistance, contributions made by the insured, and the balance being made up in the form of personal insurance. More generally, there was a shift from a system based on the enterprise to a more decentralized system with regional insurance funds, individualized contributions, and a high level of outsourcing of services.

The influence of national trajectories has been determinant in the adaptation of the constraints exerted either by international organizations—as in the case of pensions or health policies—or by the European Union in relation to employment. More generally, European prescriptions functioned as a damper on the very free-market liberal measures advocated by the international organizations. In the end, however, many critics denounced the lack of content of these prescriptions and their too frequently formal character. The same type of criticism was heard over the policy of administrative reform, which is the subject of the next chapter.

CHAPTER FOUR

Regionalization Reforms and the Redistribution of Powers between Central and Regional Actors

A third crucial public policy, after those of privatization and welfare systems, is that relating to the reform of the state and to regionalization and decentralization. This chapter will attempt to cover this subject, first stressing local policies and, second, regional policies, between which there was a time-lag. The examination of these policies will enable us to highlight the crucial topic of administrative modernization, particularly as affected by preparation for the management of structural funds. Unlike the policies of transformation of property rights or even of welfare systems, the European Union played a major role in the public administrative modernization policies. It has a "model" available for this purpose, which is based on a type of administrative division, a method of intervention (the "Community method"), development tools and an objective of getting closer to the citizens, and, hence, of promoting democracy. If the concept of Europeanization is pertinent, it is so in respect of this public policy. Given the particularity of the historical trajectories and national situations in which these processes of Europeanization have taken place, the results have differed widely between countries. In some cases, the imposition of the European Union "model" has turned out to be counterproductive. The union has often given evidence of its incapacity to adapt to novel situations, generating new resistances or strengthening the actors hostile to any decentralization. This has particularly been the case in situations where the priority for the candidate states was to promote not the model of local democracy, but a model of central authority over the different component elements, particularly minorities. This policy has thus been decisive for understanding the transformations of the post-Communist societies: not only because it rounded off the dynamic of the states' recomposition on the basis of a massive adaptation of EU rules to the post-98 legacies and issues, showing up the crucial influence of the EU, but also because by enabling a vast redistribution of powers to take place between the center and what it was previously customary to call the peripheries, it both promoted the emergence of new regional actors and, in certain circumstances, strengthened the central powers.

Historical Stakes and a Theoretical Approach

The administrative reform that dominated public decision making in the late 1990s and, in some countries, the early part of the next decade represented one of the key phases of the democratic consolidation initiated 10 years earlier. First because, with the project of decentralization, a crucial swath of the old system of Communist domination disappeared and, with it went also a style of public intervention composed of authoritarian command, strict obedience on the part of subordinates and, more generally, contempt for the citizen. By putting an end to several decades of Soviet-type centralization, the aim in 1990 was both to set up competent administrations and to promote citizen engagement. This was all about the "civic political culture" that came out of the social movements of the late 1980s and has had such a rough ride since, as a result of the privatizations and economic transformations. The goal was to revive individual public responsibility, in parallel with enterprises, which had been invited to revive individual private initiative. Now, from the outset, the question of decentralization, which was supposed to consolidate the post-Communist democratic state, ran up against the will of central political authorities that were resolved, if not to thwart any local initiative, then at least to control the dynamic of such initiatives, which they regarded as centrifugal. What happened in relation to administrative reform over the entire decade of the 1990s, and particularly at its end, thus fitted in fully with the logic analyzed in the foregoing chapters, where we have seen the central levels combining with external authorities to reinforce their domination, while being prepared to form alliances with certain local actors to achieve balances of forces specific to each particular case. Within this framework, the European Commission played a key role in setting the rules of the game. However, strictly national configurations were determinant in every case, whether the centers sought to assert their authority over their own hierarchies and whether regionalization took place in a multiethnic framework—thus creating tensions between the majority and the minority and leading to greater centralization of power—or emerged in more homogeneous countries.

These remarks have their place in a theoretical debate; recalling this debate enables us to review the spectrum of solutions that forced themselves upon the actors and the—radically opposing—ways out that were chosen.[1] Three conceptions of regionalization prevail where the redistribution of power is concerned, depending upon the position and significance of the actors involved. The first relates to minorities, whose legitimate demand for regionalization may possibly lead to demands for autonomy that endanger national unity. We can easily understand why, in these conditions, the debate on decentralization began badly in some countries, particularly the Baltic and Balkan states. The European Union's proposal on regionalization was at odds with the exigencies of sovereignty in all the various constitutions. The second conception refers to the dynamic of territorial regionalization that introduces a high degree of tension between the central and local levels, while claiming to establish a balance of powers. The risk here is that a confusion of—both statutary and financial—delegation will be arrived at, and hence at a dilution of the responsibilities of certain actors. Given the asymmetry of resources, recentralization is often the outcome. The third type of regionalization is the one exemplified and advocated by the European Union, which regards the mobilization of social and economic actors in regional networks as paramount. More than regionalization, it is the notion of the pertinent level of action that carries the day here, together with the concept of "subsidiarity." Within this framework, one method is to be followed: that of "multilevel governance." This claims to bring the partners of both the vertical and horizontal levels together in a more associative vision of democracy. But we shall see, here too, that in the end, for various historical—and political—reasons, this framework imposed itself on only a very small number of candidates. This pattern, that reflects the influence of German state structures in particular, turned out to be partially maladapted to the various East European configurations.

The End of Communist Centralization and the Difficulty of Decentralizing

What Is at Stake in the Abolition of the Centralized Model

Three things were at stake in putting an end to the centralized nature of the civil service in 1989: justice, efficiency, and democracy. First and foremost, there was the question of justice, so greatly had the center's absolute domination of the regions been felt by many citizens as a denial of their rights. Communist domination had meant the supremacy of the center over any regional imprint, such a thing being denounced, from 1945 onward, as a relic of the past. The central power of the capitals had been asserted against the regions and localities, and hence against any distinctive feature, linguistic or architectural. Minorities had been denied the use of their languages, most often on the basis of declarations of loyalty to the majority ethnic group, which was numerically superior, as in Polish Silesia or politically superior, as in the case of the Baltic republics. Many historic buildings had been destroyed, statues had been knocked down, and street names removed. Others had replaced those that had no historic resonance whatever. In the lands reclaimed from the German enemy, particularly in Poland or in the Sudeten area of the Czech Republic, discriminatory policies had meant that an individual from these peripheral parts was never appointed regional governor, and the representatives of the central districts received systematic support, by way of the collective farms, against the private peasants. A whole string of Soviet and national garrisons had been placed along the Western borders. Conurbations centered on industrial activities had been built near historic towns, such as Nowa Huta, built a few miles from Cracow or Eisenhüttenstadt built near Frankfurt an der Oder.[2]

The second matter at issue was efficiency. The supremacy of the Communist Party had been accompanied immediately, on the seizure of power in 1945–1948, by the imposition of the organizational principle of "democratic centralism." This applied to all organizations and hence to the civil service. This was taken directly from Lenin, who had himself taken it from his readings on the military system, and signified the predominance of the centers over the so-called levels of execution. This found expression, in each organization, in the superiority of the higher level over the lower, which in return owed it obedience, and the so-called election of each decision-making level. The center thus won out over the periphery, whatever its nature, and the local level was reduced to a mere link in the chain of a vertical hierarchy on which it was totally dependent. In the 1960s and 1970s, the intermediate levels between the region and the municipality had been eliminated. This happened to the *Kreise* in East Germany, as it had in the early 1950s to the *Länder*, which were replaced by a division of the country into 15 *Bezirke*; a similar thing happened in Poland, where the intermediate (county-type) levels, the powiats, had disappeared when the provinces (voivodships) were reorganized and expanded from 15 to 49 in 1975.[3] Corresponding to this territorial centralization was the integration of virtually all economic organizations into the central unit of production, the combine. This integration had led to the elimination of several functions previously performed by the civil service, which were now carried out by the local production units. Social development was taken over in this way, for example, as was local public order, with the combines often having their own internment facilities.

Transforming the old administrative hierarchy after 1990 meant freeing the territories for what had been stifling them: centralized political hierarchies and concentrated economic units. It meant putting an end to the confusion of functions and, as a result, redefining the objectives of each institution. We can, then, understand why the question of the transformation of property rights necessarily preceded that of the transformation of territories, and why, leaving aside the historic twists and turns, specific to each country, regional reforms represented the last stage in the great post-1989 transformation. Reforming the administration meant ending the threefold system of domination: political domination by the party, financial domination by the central allocation of funds, and economic domination by the combines. Thus, the restoration of the prestige of the territories in 1989 necessarily involved the reassertion of local power, which had been denied under the previous regime. To reestablish the old municipal and regional rights was to anchor democracy at the local level. This was recognized very early on by the Polish legislature when it conferred important powers on the municipalities in March 1990, particularly in terms of local development. Similarly, in Hungary, a very substantial decentralization movement emerged, quickly delegating decision making to the local level and depriving the regional authorities of many of their prerogatives. However, though this decision was part of a dynamic of total redefinition of the administrative structure of the state, it was nonetheless very soon blocked, because the notion of centrality of power eventually won out in all spheres. Everywhere, the rediscovery of state sovereignty brooked no infringement of the principle of national unity, whether in respect of minorities or competing political actors, national or international—beginning with the multiethnic countries that were facing substantial tensions. Moreover, as we showed in the previous chapter, the public finances were markedly failing.

The Constraints of Sovereignty

For the Baltic states that had been sacrificed to the Germans under the secret Germano-Soviet pact of 1939, then to the Soviets following the USSR's entry into the war in 1941, there could be no question of granting equal citizenship rights to the Russian minority, particularly as that minority was numerically very significant—representing more than 30% of the population in Estonia and Latvia—and largely concentrated in the main cities. That minority still held the levers of economic power and could still use them, if only to foment disorder. By asserting the constitutional principle of national unity and by making the obligation to speak the majority language one of the qualifications for citizenship, the aim was to deprive the former masters of their citizenship and, thereby, confiscate their economic power. In the Balkan countries, the situation was different. The minorities did not represent a significant economic power there, with the exception of the Magyar minority in Romania, concentrated in the Transylvanian region and supported by their mother country. As for the Bulgarian authorities, they were confronted with a substantial Turkish minority that was firmly resolved to see its political rights restored, given that everyone had recognized the irrationality and iniquity of the measures implemented in the latter years of Zhivkov's reign. Bulgaria's Turkish minority, representing almost 10% of the Bulgarian population, had in the years 1984–1985 been subjected to a policy of forced assimilation. From the end of 1988 onward, 300,000 individuals had been compelled to go into exile in Turkey. Their property had been hurriedly disposed of or abandoned, and the signs of their historical presence wiped out. Even Slovakia feared the demands of the Hungarian minority on its southeastern flank in the Košice region. For all these countries, identity claims and the demand for national sovereignty won out over any other particular considerations. This is attested by the constitutions of each of them, which passed into law in the 1990s. These affirmed the unitary, indivisible character of the state, on the one hand, and the rights of minorities, particularly in terms of education, culture, and language, on the other. The latter were specified as individual rights in Romania, Bulgaria, and Slovakia, whereas Poland, Lithuania, and the Czech Republic safeguarded them on a collective basis.[4]

Political Parties and Local Action

Does this mean that where homogeneous populations predominated, regionalization won the day? Not at all. In Poland and Hungary or in the Czech Republic, other considerations came into play, beginning with the political factor, though its effects were in each case differentiated. In Poland, as we have said, the law of spring 1990 on the municipalities went a long way toward devolving power to the localities,[5] even if many voices were very quickly raised to criticize the absence of a corresponding level of financial devolution. The fact that the state coffers were empty at this point would seem, in the eyes of certain observers, to be the real reason why the central Warsaw authorities blocked the process, though they alleged other motives linked, inter alia, to the international situation. In fact, the reluctance of the German Chancellor Helmut Kohl, on internal political grounds, to recognize the inviolable character of the Oder-Neisse border, together with the nearby collapse of the Yugoslav federation in 1991 as a result of the autonomist demands of certain republics, came at just the right moment to enable the Warsaw authorities to plead the danger of national break-up if regionalization was implemented. In this way, the dynamic was halted for many years, even though the debate went on, actively until 1995, and more attenuatedly thereafter. Even though it is the case that, as early as 1991, the chances of successful reform were greatly reduced, the failure of the various different proposals was nonetheless down to a powerful coalition of groups that had no interest in seeing change to the dispositions inherited from the Communist period. Around the elites of the cities of the voivoidships slated for certain disappearance, these—conservative—groups created a coalition involving representatives of the church and the surrounding rural populations. The fact that they had the attentive ear of the political parties, all of them centralized, made them the more able to thwart any redrawing of the administrative map. For these parties, particularly the newcomers to the political arena, who were cruelly short of regional intermediaries, they represented a precious source of support. From the outset, then, the structure of interest groups came into direct conflict with the decentralization project promoted by the European Union, even though that project had the support of many citizens, backed only by the liberal parties.

This lack of regional intermediaries for the centralized parties has also characterized the Czech Republic, though it has done so to a quite different pattern, which can fruitfully be compared to the former GDR, showing just how much the origins of the centralizing (in the Czech Republic) and decentralizing (in East Germany) dynamics have their roots in the period of transition.[6] In East Germany, the social movement first emerged in the cities of Leipzig, Dresden, and, to a lesser degree, Rostock, where the small oppositional groups of the 1980s had developed by articulating demands relating to the environment, to dialogue with the reform Marxists and to human rights. After their defeat in the legislative elections of March 1990, these groups put their local rootedness to good use in the reconstitution of the municipalities. As a consequence, the institutional change that was introduced centrally mainly under the aegis of the Treuhandanstalt, was introduced at the regional, and particularly at the local, level by the actors of the social movement. Being elected in large numbers in the assemblies, they took charge of public action.[7] The Czech situation was different, insofar as the political authorities there remained faithful to the rigid principles of a centralization of action, taking no regional partners on board, for fear that they may be overshadowed by them. Seen from this angle, the slightest attempt at regionalization could only be seen as a diminution of the central power and hence of national unity. By contrast, Czechoslovakia's centrist, free-market ODS party (Civic Democratic Party), which structured political life from 1990 onward, was characterized by a centralized political organization under the leadership of the uncontested and authoritarian Vaclav Klaus. The only advantage that party saw in decentralization was the possibility that, by increasing the number of regional partners, it could divide its opponents and thus reinforce the center. Klaus shamelessly argued that regionalization was synonymous with the growth of bureaucracy. He was, however, entirely aware that between 1991 and 1997 the central bureaucracy increased by 77%—further proof, if any were needed, of the gap separating Klaus's rhetoric from his political practice.[8] For these reasons, the successor to the strictly Marxist Czech Communist Party, the KCSM, was the only party to equip itself with representation in the regions. If it continued to operate at this level, this was largely because it was alone among the parties—or almost alone—in being financed by contributions from its activists, and hence was closely dependent on them for its program and action. From the comparison of the Czech and East German cases, one can see that the centralized implementation of institutional and political change could both be accompanied by decentralized public action and based on the absence of such action in the regions or locally. It was the legacies that made the difference here, that is to say, the elements that were inherited from the Communist period and also from the 1989 transition. As a result of these legacies, the particular modes of organization of the groups both in government and in opposition were brought to bear.

Only Hungary and Poland carried out significant reforms, though long before the end of Communism—indeed as early as 1987—there had been discussion in Hungary of the need for decentralization. A coalition of intellectuals and members of the opposition had emerged to discuss the subject. In 1988, the Left wing of the Communist party led by Imre Poszgay had gained the upper hand over the nominal party secretary Janos Kadar. Its program advocated decentralization and municipal autonomy. In its institutional form, this decentralization was based on three pillars, the first of which was the ability of the municipality to form itself into an autonomous unit, provided it had a school and a doctor. In that case, it was given the opportunity to undertake its own development, by agreement with an intermediate authority at the local or regional level, led by an authorized representative, whose task was to ensure the proper conduct of affairs. The second pillar was the *Komitate* or districts: this level, which had existed for many centuries, had been destroyed by the Stalinists in the 1950s and incorporated into the basic units, the *Oblasts* (the Soviet term for region); 19 of them were reestablished on October 3, 1990 as organs of local self-administration. A *Komitat* was governed by a council whose members were elected by the municipalities. The third pillar was the Republic's authorized representative, heading up one of the eight regions that were regarded as intermediate authorities of devolved state power. It fell to him to coordinate the action of the municipalities and the *Komitate*. Several studies have criticized both the excessive number of small municipalities, the inordinate tasks placed upon incompetent personnel, and the excess of formality in the operation of the *Komitate*.[9] Given that the position of the Republic's authorized representative was not strong enough, the need for further reform rapidly made itself felt.

The Weakness of Organized Action

The frequent failures met with by the first efforts at a transformation of the state architecture remind us of the weakness, on the one hand, of community organizations and, on the other, of the political parties. We shall have the opportunity to return in the last two chapters to this aspect, where community organizations and political parties are concerned. Let us simply stress here that history is an important factor in accounting for this weakness. Where regions were important historically, their borders have lasted up to the current period. The question of how the old administrative divisions are to be redistributed has fuelled debate since 1990. This is the case in East Germany, where reform of the *Kreise* represented one of the most important moments of the democratization of public life after more than 50 years of (Nazi and Communist) dictatorship.[10] It is true also of Poland, where the old boundaries or, in some cases, the supersession of those boundaries as part of new proposals have often fuelled public debate, and equally true of Hungary, though in that case only with regard to municipal boundaries.[11] By contrast, we find no debate in the other countries where, historically, the notion of region is nonexistent.[12]

Furthermore, the revival of the debate after 1997–1998 occurred in the three countries where the question of local civil society arose.[13] That debate was not seen elsewhere, since the weakness of civil society does not, in some circumstances, exclude a high level of mobilization of local groups that are able to articulate interests linked to tradition. We shall see this more clearly in chapter eight.

As for the weakness of political actors, this can be seen in the absence of political intermediaries referred to above. To define the political parties in this post-1989 period, the Berlin political scientist Gert Joachim Glaessner has spoken of "organizations in search of their social base."[14] This is a strong point, reflecting as it does the wider upheaval that seems to have characterized the whole period, which is distinguished by the establishment of institutions, but institutions from which the actors seemed to be absent. Gernot Grabher also expressed this powerfully when he spoke, in the economic sphere, of the emergence of a capitalism without capitalists.[15] This was repeated in the dynamic of decentralization and then with the action of the NGOs and community-based organizations. The development of collective action was everywhere accompanied by an absence of activism. It was entirely as though the institutions had first been defined by a number of groups, containing not very many people, and then attempted to target the actors corresponding to, or adapted to, the missions with which those institutions had been entrusted. In this context, to define the parties as organizations in search of a social base amounts to asserting that they can only be organizations in which strictly partisan interests, limited to small groups, predominate—to the exclusion of any other. This is the conclusion arrived at by German sociologist Helmut Wiesenthal, when he asserts that "the governing parties struggling for a monopoly of decision-making regard private-interest organizations as particularly dysfunctional [systemwidrig]... To the attempt by social organizations to function autonomously, they react with ignorance and apathy. The political systems of Eastern Europe thus seem self-referential, which means that they are uncoupled from social aspirations and the definition of problems. Given that one cannot imagine a civil society that aspires to autonomous existence functioning without the extra-parliamentary means for its own organization or coordination, then we must in the end accept that it is the parties that constitute a series of obstacles."[16] Later, even when the regionalization laws were passed, the parties would find themselves criticized for jamming the system, as in the case of the parties in Slovakia, where, in the words of one observer, "the politicians are still following their individual interests with the aim of transferring centralism to the large districts and preserving their own party influence over as many territories as possible." Absent or under-mobilized community organizations, parties cut off from their grassroots (not to mention their programs)—these were all so many gaps that would be reflected in later policies when the European Union made regionalization a sine qua non of integration in 1998.

The Vitality and Limits of Municipal Action

In the late 1990s, only a single raft of state and administrative reform had, then, been implemented. It was, however, a very important one, since it concerned the municipalities.[17] In most cases, the reforms brought about a significant fragmentation, which left the Czech Republic, for example, with a form of local government as highly dispersed as the French, since it had 6,230 separate municipalities, one of the highest figures in Europe. Hungary had half as many with 3,131 and Poland had 2,483.[18] Intermunicipal cooperation was relatively undeveloped. There were, in fact, no very binding ties between municipalities in Romania, Slovakia, and Poland, though intermunicipal syndicates were permitted in the Czech Republic. They were also allowed in Hungary, where municipalities with fewer than 1,000 inhabitants—80% of the total number—were required to create intermunicipal associations. In Latvia, the new law of 1998 established 10 "areas" (groupings of local communities) in place of the 7 cities and 23 rural municipalities. In Estonia, the reform of 2002 attempted to bring towns and rural municipalities together into larger groupings, but the outcome was negligible (49 towns became 46 and the number of rural municipalities rose from 209 to 295). Where the status of municipalities is concerned, everywhere except Bulgaria the status of rural districts is different from the urban. This is a direct consequence of the membership of the old empires, when, for example, Hungarian and Czech towns and cities possessed local autonomy and could incorporate the surrounding rural districts. On the other hand, because they enjoy a special status, the capitals achieving high rates of development can enable the less developed surrounding areas to benefit from this. Where local executives are concerned, almost all are elected for a four-year period. There is, however, great diversity among them, depending on whether the mayors are elected directly by the citizens, as in Hungary, or by the local councils, as in the Czech Republic or Poland. The municipalities have significant prerogatives in terms of urban transport, the environment, waste management, and water, some of which are shared with the state's devolved authorities, as are matters generally relating to health, economic development, environmental protection, and tourism. The state, for its part, retains control over security, public order, infrastructures, and employment in the public sector, even though, in the latter field, the Polish, Latvian, and Czech regional authorities play a key role in the payment of teachers' salaries. This is, in fact, the largest budget head in the structure of local budgets, followed by housing and municipal expenditure, whereas management services come in last place.[19]

The picture is also a very varied one in terms of financing, even though fiscal autonomy remains generally very limited right throughout the period. In a general way, centralization has been exercized at the expense of the various local levels of government, which have been forbidden to raise taxes on their own account. There were, in fact, many obstacles in their way. Where property taxes or local income taxes were concerned, criteria for assessing property values were lacking, land registers defective, and the institutions for the collection of such taxes nonexistent. Equally absent was any experience on the part of local officials. Hence, the centers retained their power, often with the consent of the local authorities, which were thereby relieved of one additional burden at a point when they were overwhelmed with new tasks. If they had been granted partial autonomy in the collection of taxes, local leaders would have had to clearly specify the assessment criteria, which would surely have had an effect on their electability. For these reasons, the field of local taxation remained wholly cloaked in obscurity. This exempted the public authorities from having to provide accounts and deprived the citizens of any knowledge of the cost of public goods.[20] This attitude was reinforced by the behavior of the European Union, which did not, in the event, call for any fiscal decentralization. For these various reasons, the volume of transfers remained massive and the proportion of preallocated budgets predominant. In Poland, the Czech Republic and Hungary in 2007, the largest part of local revenues came from transfer payments from central government. Like Lithuania and Latvia, these countries have no leeway for setting property taxes. Slovakia is the single case of relatively broad municipal autonomy, as is attested by the lack of interest shown by the central authorities in local taxation. The governments led by Vladimir Meciar had their eyes fixed on the privatization of industrial property, not on local government. In Romania and Lithuania, tax revenues account for around 80% of local government income. The tax revenues shared are mainly those deriving from income tax. As for state subsidies and aid, these are most often monies targeted at "delegated commissions." There is no doubt that the prospect of EU membership has influenced the extent of local authority expenditure as a proportion of GNP and as a proportion of public expenditure; these figures are falling in most of the countries, Poland being the exception.

The Case of East German Reform

The law of 17 May 1990 on municipal reform in East Germany bore the imprint of two legacies.[21] The first was German law, which now had to be incorporated into legislation (even though German unification would only assume legal form five months later on 3 October). On this basis, some tasks were taken over by the higher regional and federal levels (such as the economy, the environment, or agriculture, in the former case, and labor and finance in the latter), whilst others, which were previously carried out by the industrial combines (*Kombinate*) fell to it, such as social affairs and culture. The political scientist Gerhard Lehmbruch has used the expression "institutional transfer" to highlight the total takeover not just of municipal tasks, but of organization by office (*Amt*) and department

(*Dezernat*), with each level taking over the principles relating to personnel, finance, and law.[22] The contribution of Western specialists was significant in the technical posts relating to finance and the economy and in the *Hauptdezernat*, 20% of whose staff, on average, were West German citizens.[23] The second legacy was specific to the 1989 "turn" (*die Wende*). That legacy, left by the social movement, made direct participation of the citizens in the election of their mayors obligatory. The aim was to promote the self-expression of the citizenry in the wake of the Round Tables that had sprung up more or less everywhere. And it was at this local level, that the activists of the *Wende*, brought together in "municipal parliaments," expressed themselves best and, in fact, got rid of the former Communist officials.[24] In the first local elections of 6 May 1990 three quarters of the mayors were removed from office, together with three quarters of the members of the municipal councils, half of the offices and half of the *Dezernate*.

However, it was this very dynamic of "institutional transfer" that some observers saw as the cause of the successes and others as the source of the obstacles encountered at the local level after 1990. The first group contended that the new framework had enabled not only certain East German legacies to be taken over—of local provision and participation, as at the time of the *Wende*—but also innovations in municipal management. This was the case, for example, with local employment policies, which promoted the establishment of employment units (*Arbeitsgesellschaften*) that brought together the most important local actors under the aegis of the mayors.[25] But, though alternative solutions were proposed, the effects of the importation of rules could not mask the "colonial" aspect of the transfer, which found expression in certain quarters in the acute lack of a sense of participatory democracy, often generating feelings of apathy. This exogenous character of the rules was highlighted all the more for the fact that, at the very moment when the administrative system was transferred (chiefly, the municipal system, but also that of the *Länder*), it ran into considerable operating problems in the West.[26] The alignment of the East German municipalities with the West German organization led, initially, to a swelling of civil service ranks as a result of the transfer of personnel (who had previously been located in the combines and were assigned to tasks that were now to be devolved to the municipalities). Drastic reductions were very soon imposed so that the figure for "civil service employees per inhabitant" could be met. Thus, in four years, local government staff fell from 662,000 in 1991 to 438,000 in 1995, while the number of statutory civil servants was 2% in the East, as against 21% in the West. Furthermore, the divergence of trajectories between West and East increased because, during the 1990s, the West German civil service, faced with major financial problems, had implemented a modernization of its different components, based on the "new public management" method, which was borrowed from the American model and founded on the notions of flexibility, groups, and project management. These notions brought about a reduction in hierarchical levels, a greater emphasis on exchange, the decentralization of resource management, job redefinition, and the reorganization of administrative units. These cultural and organizational developments were necessarily at odds, after 1990, with the needs of the East German partners, who were grappling with radically different problems. Paramount for them were the issues of deindustrialization and its corollary, mass unemployment. The modernization of the civil services that, in the West was carried out in the name of a more or less shared flexibility, was imposed in the East in the form of staff restructurings that obeyed exogenous rules and were not a response to the problems of the day. In these conditions, it seems that the innovations that emerged at one point and thus reflected preservation of the spirit of the *Wende* corresponded only to a very brief moment, that of the very first years. From 1994 onward, the routinization of procedures—in other words, the operation of West German rules—won out, together with the associated problems.

Decentralization and Regionalization

Though the European Union turned out to be the central actor in reviving the debate on regionalization and, particularly, in the adoption of regionalization laws after 1997, this was not a forced transference. On the contrary, domestic actors—chiefly, the political parties—very much made their influence felt in determining the final configuration, and whether regionalization led to decentralization or the take-up of the EU's imperatives led only to adjustments that remained, in the end, rather formal. Whatever the configuration adopted, one thing is sure: the reform was in no way to threaten the state's sovereignty over its territory. It had to fit in with the framework of a unitary national state. Article 11 of the Polish regionalization law stipulates that, by their development policy, the regions are "maintaining the Polish national character." The Bulgarian constitution of 1991 proclaims, as early as its second article, that "the Republic of Bulgaria is a locally-managed unitary state. Autonomous territorial formations are not allowed." Romania followed suit in article 2 of the new constitution of 2003.

Regionalization and Democratic Debates

In the three countries of central Europe, the Czech Republic, Hungary, and Poland, the principle of regional reform enabled the parties to position themselves, particularly in relation to pre-1989 historical traditions and to the initial decisions adopted in 1990.[27] Given the lack of real content of the EU "model," national configurations won out after much conflict.

This was the case, first of all, in Hungary. Decentralization was seen there as a way of moving beyond Communism, which was equated with centralization. The references to history were, however, made as a function of partisan interests. For conservatives, the restoration of the regional division into counties was a reference to the founder of the Hungarian state, Stephen I, who triumphed over local particularisms and preserved the unity of the homeland. On these grounds, the conservative party, FIDESZ, gave its preference to regionalization on the basis of the appointment of delegates (akin to French *préfets*). By contrast, their liberal opponents in the SzDSZ Alliance of Free Democrats—Hungarian Liberal Party), committed to a social vision in which civil society was paramount, argued not for "counties," but for local power. Thus the liberals contested the conservatives' vision, which they denounced as reactionary because it went back a thousand years and was based on the negation of civil society, whereas the conservatives of the FIDESZ (Fidesz-Hungarian Civic Union) criticized the liberals of the SzDSZ for taking advantage of the absence of civil society to get their law through. Amid these opposing conservative and liberal voices, it was easy for the former Communists to criticize the excesses of the 1990–1994 period, characterized by excessive decentralization. Though they did not call for the restoration of pre-1988 centralization, they argued for a reform that would incorporate the prerequisites of the European Union. All the parties accommodated the adaptive pressure of the EU, then, each one ultimately taking the view that the Hungarian vision should win out.[28] In the end, the counties are rather formal constructs, more statistical than anything else, designed to meet the expectations of both the European Union and the many advocates of sovereignty, who felt threatened by too much delegation to the local level.

As with the reforms of the welfare systems, the programs that were adopted had their origins in the various changes of government. The passing of the law on regionalization in the Czech Republic was, in fact, the result of the defeat of the Center-Right coalition in 1996. This enabled a vote on the constitution to be tabled one year later, even though long years were needed before the final territorial division was adopted. In fact, this only assumed definitive form in 2004. In Slovakia it was the Left that was hostile to the decentralization project, whereas the Hungarian-speaking minority wanted to have its own regional government, a plan rejected by all the other parties. The constitution and the division into eight regions were adopted in 2001, which still raises a number of questions relating mainly to their small size. As for Poland, though it was the first country to adopt the law in July 1998 and to implement it on 1 January 1999, it was only when the next legislature was elected with a Left-wing majority in 2001 that there was a genuine response to the imperatives of administrative modernization.

What really stirred people into action were the particularities of the territorial borders of regions and districts. Some groups—particularly the mayors concerned—wanted these borders to correspond to historic regional boundaries, as in Polish Silesia or in Bohemia-Moravia.

Others wished to argue for regional particularity on the basis of historical precedent. This was the case, for example, with the German minority in the Opole voivodship. Other regional elites demanded that they
retain a regional prerogative on one basis or another. This occurred in
two Polish regions. They preferred to divide the capitals of the voivodship and of the region between two previous regional capitals (Bydgoszcz
and Toruń; Gorzów Wielkkopolski and Zielona Góra) rather than submit
to a single authority. More generally in Eastern Europe, it was historical
identities that counted. Where they existed previously, the debates were
lengthy and fierce. Where they did not exist, the decisions were taken
without debate. There was, thus, a significant split between final designs,
depending on whether they fitted into local trajectories—and, for these
areas and regions, learning was important—or whether adaptation pressure operated in national contexts characterized by an absence of references, in which case formalism won out as, we may fear, did a distancing
of the citizens from the process. Where local actors were able to assert
their interests, outcomes may not have been totally in accordance with the
prescriptions of the European Union, but they turned out, on the other
hand, to be more democratic. By contrast, where the actors were absent,
formalism predominated. This provides additional evidence that the pressure of EU rules had differential effects depending on the initial national
situation, on the power of veto of the central authorities and on the presence or otherwise of "facilitating" groups.

Administrative Modernization

With the obligation to implement administrative reform as part of
Chapter 21 of the *Acquis Communautaire*, and with the civil services being
readied to manage the structural funds, the European Union played a

Table 4.1 Territorial Structure in 2004

	Municipalities	Number of Inhabitants per Municipality	Provinces	Regions
Bulgaria	263	28,000	28	6
Estonia	247	4,200	—	—
Hungary	3,154	2,700	19	7
Latvia	540	3,000	26	5
Lithuania	61	58,800	10	—
Poland	2,489	15,000	373	16
Czech Republic	6,237	1,500	—	14
Romania	2,862	7,000	42	—
Slovakia	2,871	1,700	—	8
Slovenia	192	8,800	—	—

Source: This table is based on data taken in Dexia, *Sub-national governments in the European Union: Responsibilities, Organisation and Finances*. Paris: Dexia Editions, 2008.

central role in the post-1989 modernization of the state. And yet, by confining themselves simply to specifying procedures, without ever intervening at the level of the content of the policies advocated, the Brussels Commission may be said, in an initial period, to have deliberately favored the central authorities. The latter were unexpectedly reinforced by the decision in 2002–2003 to deprive the regions of the right to set out regional programs, within the framework of programming, even though regionalization, as we have seen, was the subject of a particularly important debate in the preceding years. For these two reasons, European regulation can be said to have been of substantial assistance to the national actors. The rest was left to learning "on the job" and to random outcomes. Even if we have to record a very distinct strengthening of the regions in the new programming exercise—that of 2007–2013—they have obtained at most 25% of the total funds, leaving the larger part of the prerogatives to the centers.

Administrative Programming—A Necessary Exercise

At the time of regionalization and preparation for fund management, the European Union effected a "revolution" within civil services broadly comparable to the revolution foreign investors brought about within enterprises. The need for all public services—both central and regional—to specialize, in order to perform the new development tasks, can be equated with the implementation of technical rationality that is exemplified in industry by the notion of "process." The administrative approach required by the EU is not greatly different, in fact, from the process of industrial decision making. The elements of anticipation, planning, and programming came to the fore, together with teamwork, and information-distribution and networking.[29] Let us briefly enumerate the four stages any public service in charge of strategic programming must imperatively follow, in order to understand how, by its intermediation, the process of rationalization equates with that of bureaucratization.

The first stage is that of a definition of aims to be pursued, by setting out the diagnosis of the situation as one sees it. It calls for a prioritization of the problems identified, together with an examination of the strengths and weaknesses of the field and of the actors involved. The second phase is that of the identification of a strategy. This divides into priorities for intervention, which themselves break down into a number of measures in which each element of the priorities is specified in detail. The third stage is that of budgets. These are broken down into the annual sums required for the execution of the priorities and measures, and established on the basis of cofinancing, which indicates the various public and private partnerships involved in the program. The last stage relates to the various internal and external controls. The internal controls are carried out by the various responsible national bodies and by independent committees, while the external controls are carried out by the commission's services. This method was based, then, on the founding demand of rationality, which states that, for any prescribed end to be achieved, adequate means must be deployed correctly. Despite its banality—for the foregoing does nothing but formalize the elementary principles of technical rationality—this represented a radically new departure for individuals—the civil servants—who had never been accustomed to taking decisions for themselves, but had simply been used to obeying higher orders. The extreme politicization of the public services before 1989 (and, to a large extent, until the post-1998 reforms), the violent turnabouts in political decision making and the inflation of rules had led to a generalized elimination of individual responsibility. For this reason, as we stressed in chapter one, rational-type bureaucratization ran radically contrary to the practices of Soviet-type bureaucracy. It represented a key moment in the learning of rational rules, which implied a steep learning curve for all the civil servants who were faced with the need to adopt an approach that forced them to make decisions—if only at the initial level of assessing a situation—and take responsibility for their consequences, with regard both to priorities for intervention and funding implications. In so doing, it made both politicians and civil servants answerable to the citizens for their use of public funds.

In this process of intervention, the notion of partnership was central. In its turn, that notion covered two dimensions that make up what is normally termed "the Community Method." The first of these relates to the vertical axis of cooperation inherent in governance, which brings into play all the various actors from EU to municipality level. The second—complementary—dimension requires that public action be backed up by private partners or even partners from the community sector. This is what is normally termed horizontal governance. Concretely, in respect to programming carried out for the purposes of structural funds, this involved authorizing regional authorities to formulate their own strategic development and regional plans in which the cofinanced projects had to figure. In the event, the principle of subsidiarity—and hence the specification of the region as the originator of regional strategy—was restated on several occasions.[30] By this, the commission clearly intended to indicate its support for regional actors, the better to circumvent the central bastions, which were often denounced as the haunts of the former *nomenklatura*. In this period when the legacies of Communist centralization were being swept way, this was a major issue, since the objective was no less than to satisfy the combined need for justice, efficiency, and political culture. The three principles were closely linked, insofar as the development plans (efficiency) were the work of elected executives (democracy) that enabled cooperation to take place between the various actors (political culture).

An Ambiguous Choice

Now, this is where the paradox of East European administrative modernization lies, in the final moment preceding integration in 2004.

The intervention from Brussels in fact ran partially counter to the initial principles underlying its conduct. Purely on its own initiative, the commission decided to recentralize the whole programming procedure. Rather than allow the regions to determine their development plans themselves, the commission invited the centers to seize back the initiative and determine regional policy. By so doing, it played a large part in reinforcing the power of the centers, thus forming part of a dynamic that can ultimately be said, as we saw in the foregoing chapters, to have characterized the whole style of public management of the reforms. Why did it act in this way? Because, from 2000 onward, it took the view that the regions were not capable of formulating their development plans themselves.[31] This peremptory assertion, never supported by rational argument, led the commission's services—mainly those of DG Regio—to delegate the elaboration of the whole of the regional program two years later—first in Poland, then later in the Czech Republic—to the central Ministry of the Economy.[32] Two conflicting arguments have been advanced to explain this surprising turnabout. For researchers at the University of Sussex, the conflict between DG Enlargement and DG Regio explains it.[33] It was a question of promoting either centralized or decentralized management. The former option won out, thereby proving that the commission is not a unified actor. It is said to have hesitated for a long time, stressing the two aspects of democracy and efficiency or, in other words, first giving leeway to DG Regio, then to DG Enlargement. The latter carried the day as the deadline for accession approached and the question became increasingly urgent. According to other observers, the primary factor was fear of the corruption prevailing in the regional administrative bureaucracies. Given their lack of sufficient experience, it was thought preferable, according to this interpretation, to pursue dialogue with the central public services. The fear of a recurrence of the criticisms that beset the Santer Commission over its lack of financial control over public funds is said to have taken precedence over all other considerations.

In acting as it did, the commission was thumbing its nose at the advances made over four years by the regions, which had adjusted to its demands for modernization without complaint. It felt it could take it upon itself to disregard the principle of subsidiarity. This is why what dominated was not so much support for policy content as a bureaucratic observance of regulations. This found expression, with twinning policies, in an excessive formalism and calls for the incessant submission of reports. This attachment to written procedures meant paying less attention to the cross-fertilization of the various interventions from experts and advisers.[34] In acting in this way, the commission overlooked the fact that regionalization could, as a consequence, be entirely manipulated by central political players, as in the case of the party of the Hungarian prime minister, Viktor Orbán. Orbán was accused of profiting from his position to safeguard his personal assets and favor his family to a considerable extent.[35]

By acting as it did, the commission not only did not break with a centralizing dynamic that ran through the entire post-1989 transformation, but contributed, above all, to ratifying a type of behavior that its entire tradition actually rejects. Before 2000, many writers were alarmed by the prospect that European construction, which had, from its inception, been a "bottom-up" process, should run up against a dynamic of institutional construction that had, since 1989 in Eastern Europe, gone in the opposite direction. Yet it was by its own action—to soothe an anxiety fuelled solely by its lack of knowledge of local situations—that recentralization took place. For this reason, it incurred legitimate criticism from those in the regions, who found evidence in the contempt with which they had been treated of collusion between the central and the Brussels authorities against any kind of local democratization. Quite clearly, the civil servants in Brussels were, in the event, bound to enjoy a favorable reception in the central ministries, for whom regionalization had often been seen as a defeat or, at the very least, a loss of power. The effects of such a decision were felt all the more painfully, at least in Poland, for the fact that the Ministry of the Economy was, in the event, somewhat behind in meeting its initial commitments. Worse, it approved a number of decisions that were rather objectionable so far as regional aspirations were concerned. Ignorance of local realities and unfamiliarity with local actors combined to make programming a solitary exercise, carried out without any oversight on the part of those to whom it was to apply. The sessions at which the results of programming were presented to the actors in the local communities turned almost exclusively into great orchestrated set-pieces, to which the social actors were not invited. On the other hand, the job of informing the municipalities, the prime beneficiaries of the funds, fell to regional civil servants, who were not at all familiar with the programming guidelines whose principles they were in fact supposed to defend.[36]

The Critique of Formalism

These criticisms came together with criticisms of the often largely formal character of EU intervention, on the grounds that it could be said to be more concerned with the form than the content of the policies implemented. The respect for conditionality (the external constraint) could be said to prevail over the examination of policy content. What was seen in respect of social policies in the preceding chapter is largely confirmed in the reforms associated with European funds. The core of the criticism related to the fact that the European experts adopted normative behaviors when the local actors really needed precise, concrete advice in organizational matters.[37] The contention was that no directive on the way of concretely constructing administrative bodies was given. Neither the regulations nor the guidelines were of any use in this regard. As article 8 of the European Council Regulation stipulates, "In application of the principle of subsidiarity, the implementation of assistance shall be the responsibility of the Member States, at the appropriate territorial level according to the arrangements specific to each Member State, and without prejudice to the powers vested in the Commission, notably for implementing the general budget of the European Communities".[38] From this, several researchers have concluded that there was a regrettable absence within the European Union of any indication about regionalization so far as administrations were concerned. Whereas the implementation of the structural funds must follow a very strict procedure of allocation and monitoring, no institutional model ultimately prevailed. At a point when the commission was emphasizing the virtues of the "Community Method," which was regarded by some as the "added value" that its policy provided, it proved incapable of furnishing the necessary framework for its implementation. Yet the creation in 1994 of "DG Enlargement" had given the impression that the technical assistance aid provided would match up to the lessons learned from the experiences of states with weak administrative structures, such as Portugal and Greece. The same went for the reform of the PHARE program in 1998 and the stress on supporting "institution building" through twinning projects. Moreover, given what had been learned from certain instances of embezzlement in some southern European countries, a clear policy should, according to these critics, have been formulated. Whatever the choice—efficiency or democracy—it would have been necessary in any event to provide the greatest assistance, and, particularly, to deliver the missing institutional key. A criticism of this kind connects with a wider critique with regard to the almost exclusively juridical aspect of European Union intervention that, in the view of some observers, could be explained by the predominance of lawyers in the commission's various departments.One is justified in thinking that the criticisms frequently addressed to the central and regional administrations after 2004 regarding the obscurity of procedures, the selection criteria for beneficiaries of the structural funds, and the absence of publicity around debates has its origin in this.[39]

However, let us draw three lessons from this very heated debate that went on during the last phases of preparation for integration. The first is that, thanks to the often very formal character of the EU's prescriptions, national actors were able to have their own points of view prevail, and hence, ultimately, assert their national sovereignty. The highly formal character of EU interventions conforms to the very nature of the union as a union of member states in leaving to those member states the last word when it comes to applying the common set of rules. What would have been said if the commission had added a single organizational model to what were already very restrictive rules? The second concerns the highly conflictual nature of the recomposition dynamic between the centers and the peripheries, and the redistribution of powers between the two. It reveals the substantial impact of the EU, not only at the level of the policies, but also of the polity of each country. This is a notable difference in what is meant by Europeanization between West and East.[40] Though the central administrations were in fact much better treated by the European partner than their regional counterparts, the latter were nonetheless responsible for a large part of their development in the new programming period 2007–2013. For all these reasons, the EU played an active part in the modernization of public administrations by, in the end, reinforcing the political architectures that promote the autonomy of the—economic or administrative—fields.

Conclusion

The reform of the centralized public architecture that was the preliminary to preparing for the design and management of European aid represented the last, immense task to be confronted in the institutional transformation of the Communist legacies. It revolutionized the modes of exchange between the center and the local periphery, and the basis of public decision making. Despite the very great number of difficulties, the new administrative configurations now exist. The regions—even if they were mere planning tools—were mapped out and operate. Administrations have been put in place and civil servants appointed. They manage funds, implement development programs, and negotiate with the center. Despite their formalism, which some find objectionable, we may suppose that, with time, these regional configurations will be capable of engendering processes of identification. A number of regions in the West, which were just as formally created, have already given proof of this. Several of them were constructed upon the antagonism of the cities that form part of them. They have nonetheless created a strong sense of belonging, on the basis of regional identities. Others have failed in this. In Central and Eastern Europe, administrative reform found its complement in the radical reform of the modes of behavior of the administrative staff. Admittedly, criticism has continued to be leveled against the maintenance of a practice that, with each new team elected, consists in dismissing those previously in post. This "spoils system" policy, as it is called, has proved very expensive, insofar as many of the functionaries trained by the EU have been trained to no purpose. Nonetheless, given the benefits of following common prescriptions and the costs of not doing so, it is probable, over time, that an adjustment will emerge toward greater respect for procedures and for the efforts made by the commission.

For these reasons, this reform has brought to a close the dynamic of institutional adjustment, of adoption of the rules, and of bringing behavior into conformity with the preconditions for EU membership. This had been initiated in the economic sphere with the transformation of ownership rights; it was carried on in the social sphere with the transformation of welfare systems. Unlike the two preceding policies, largely impacted upon by the dynamic of globalization, this reform of the regions can be said to have shown up the central role of the EU. The modernization of the state, or, in other words, the adaptation of the central and decentralized administrations to the demands of rationality, will thus have brought to a close the great dynamic of the formation of the post-Communist states, by putting bureaucratization at the heart of the institutions and of the behavior of the public actors. It has taken over a number of the elements we saw in passing when we examined privatization in chapter two. These elements related, on the one hand, to institutionalization, to specialization and to networking; on the other hand, they assumed human freedom and produced a situation where the notion of choice was based on an understanding of the principles of action, the combining of means to achieve an optimal end, and the acceptance of responsibility for consequences. In this respect, systemic change was effected, right throughout the 1990s, on the same basis: modernization, resting, on the one hand, on the rationality of the actors and, on the other, on institutions embodying behaviors whose collective rules enable—singular or societal—equilibria to be adjusted productively. The latter reflect social consensuses. It remains for us to find out how the local actors reacted to the domination of a set of formal rules, by recomposing their own resources—whether that set of rules depended on the opening up of borders and the domination of markets, or was linked, rather, to EU intervention. This is the aim of the next part of this book.

PART 2

Societies and Markets

Workers, Peasants, Labor Unions, Associations, Community Organizations

The first part of this work has brought out the differential effects of the pressure of European rules on the formation of states after 1989, based on an examination of the forms of transformation of public property, welfare systems and public administration. Though sometimes reduced to playing only a limited role alongside certain international bodies, the EU has managed to appear as the central actor on several occasions: when it has been able to provide the missing references and the corresponding action repertoires (e.g., where some privatization institutions are concerned); when it has been able to function to safeguard the continuity of exchanges, particularly in terms of providing legal safeguards; and when it has imposed its rules as the condition for membership (by reference to the *Acquis Communautaire*). In this way, the EU has played an active part in the redistribution of powers and the establishment of new forms of governance. These conclusions are in keeping, overall, with those that emerge from examining the processes of the EU15, which very much give pride of place to public policies, with the specific difference here that, in the cases we examine, *polities* have also been impacted to a great extent by the EU.

There then remains the question that has also received little attention in the West, which relates to fields other than policies: this concerns the Europeanization of intermediate actors such as labor unions, associations and parties. Do we see a redistribution of powers at this level, and the reinforcement of labor union, associative, and political behaviors? The findings of the literature on EU15 are ambivalent on this point.[1] The originality of the East European situations lies in the fact that it is not a question either of examining the formation of social or political networks on a Union-wide scale or of assessing the possible retroactive impact of such networks on national organizations. It is much more a question of identifying how the European challenge determined the formation and functioning of these intermediate organizations or, in other words, how the former actors adopted and adapted the new constraints upon them, and how the new contexts enabled "new" actors to emerge, whether in phase with the new types of pressure or not.

Before examining the organizations, it is appropriate to look into the occupational groups that traditionally make them up: workers and peasants. This approach is all the more justifiable for the fact that the analysis of institutions is inadequate for accounting for local behaviors. It is one thing to adopt a set of rules and sectoral regulations, another to deduce from it the coordination and adjustment of behavior at the base of organizations. In other words, European Union pressure had massive effects on states, since they were expected to submit to common regulation by adopting it legislatively. This was the minimum condition for aspiring to membership of the EU. But the process of Europeanization cannot be reduced to a "top-down" dynamic that merely expresses the basically juridical pressure exerted on national states by the Union. Alongside the examination of the impact procedures of the European rules, we have at the same time to examine the modalities of their acceptance or rejection on the part of the different social groups, which were able to exploit various registers of resources the better to take advantage of—or, at times, forearm themselves against—them. Though history counts, it does not simply have effects advantageous to states or territories. The *longue durée* is registered in occupational practices, in the skills and informal rules which structure societal equilibria, just as much as do the formal rules. In this regard, the strategies of recomposition, defence and negotiation were very different between the industrial enterprise (chapter five) and the agricultural concern (chapter six), or between social organizations (chapter seven), citizen groups (chapter eight) and parties (chapter nine).

Workers and Managers. Local Compromises and the End of the Working Classes

The transformation of industrial enterprises was a major issue in the post-1989 transformation because, under the Communist regime, the enterprise functioned as the balancing point of economic, political, and social dynamics. In chapter one we stressed the very high level of homogeneity of the structure of production and its close interdependence with local territories. For this reason, the process of enterprise rationalization after 1989 was based on the autonomization of property rights and on identifying efficient component parts, defining the functions of units and actors, and recomposing the relations between them both within and outside companies. This process was accompanied by the general diffusion of the notion of control. It involved the adoption of radically new behaviors on the part of the various actors. It would seem that at local enterprise level, as previously in the higher reaches of the politicoeconomic field, the dynamics of change entailed broadly identical strategies. These strategies were initially made up of secrecy, alliances, clannishness, and scheming, the whole being directed toward an enormous misappropriation of local resources. The scope of this misappropriation made it possible both to secure these resources by lending them a new legal basis and by excluding several categories of—the most deprived—actors. Unlike what happened in agriculture or administration, which we shall see below, it was seldom possible in enterprises acquired by foreign buyers for the intermediate actors or the workers to convert their resources. Political or technological change forced them to adapt, often without any possibility of negotiation, or to leave the enterprise. But these strategies, which differed depending on the status of the buyer, were also produced by adopting the same standards of rationality. For this reason, the final adjustment was carried out under the auspices of the rationalization of managerial behavior, in which the large-scale use of flexibility entailed the exclusion of a significant number of employees. The aim of this chapter is to show this, highlighting first the different forms of enterprise, then the strategies for change, and, finally, the different actors.

Formal Property Rights and Effective
Control of Enterprises

The Terms of a Debate

The new rules put in place at the time of transition in 1989–1990 enabled individuals in posts of responsibility massively to reinvest the resources they had previously acquired and to do so entirely legally. What we were able to identify at the macro-economic level where privatization is concerned is very largely confirmed at the enterprise level. At this level, the former managers of the production units found themselves able to cushion the effects associated with the changes of regulation that, for them, translated into the need to function without subsidies, cover their liabilities from their profits alone or find partners to share costs. The first widely accepted finding produced the hypothesis that a mere modification of the rules of the game is not sufficient to promote a significant change in behavior. "Hard budget constraints" may be decreed at the top of the edifice, with the abolition of subsidies and the insistence that the enterprise make profits, but such an exhortation may, in reality, be cushioned by opportunist behavior at the base, in the enterprises. To paraphrase Michel Crozier, "You don't get from plan to market by decree." The illusion of 1990 was to think that the mere decreeing of macro stabilization rules from the top would necessarily produce appropriately adjusted micro behaviors. The reader will recall that this was the link between the different levels of intervention that the Balcerowicz Plan assumed to be necessary for systemic change to take place.

The second finding from the observation of the opportunism of the agents—which sociologists have expressed as "defense" on the part of the actors and as "resource recomposition"—led to the conclusion that a change in property rights may not bring about increased efficiency, if control cannot be exercised mainly on managers. By contrast with the theory of property rights, which confines itself to looking at the formal context of operation alone, the theory of agency stresses the notion of control and foregrounds the concept of incentives. It postulates that management by executives must remain under the external control of rights holders, or there is a risk that all capacity of constraint will be lost. Otherwise, one runs the danger of seeing particular forms of agreement emerge between the various actors within the enterprise. This theory is in direct line of descent from Weberian thought, according to which the emergence of the capitalist enterprise is concomitant with the distinction between owner and manager. Whereas the domestic economy privileges the "household," the basis of patriarchal domination and nonmonetary exchange, the capitalist economy is characterized by the rationally managed enterprise. It is accompanied by the distinction between owner and manager, the domination of rational legal rules and of a monetary economy. Between these two extremes of economic units, there are a large number of intermediate cases. These constitute "hybrid" forms of the enterprise and attest to a rationality often dominated by other than strictly formal considerations, such as values.[1]

After 1990, a sizeable literature strove to show that if there is no external oversight, the individuals in place tend to exploit their former contacts.[2] Bargaining with employees tends, then, to be about the maintenance of employment levels, in exchange for keeping the managers in their posts, all of this at the expense of investors. Several economists have, moreover, managed to show that only an external controller, in the form, for example, of a direct foreign investor, is capable of reducing transaction costs. Only such oversight makes access to capital, markets, training, and technologies possible. By contrast, the absence of such a figure can only lead to an absence of development, given the impossibility of settling the debts inherited from the old regime, restructuring companies or expanding local levels of trade. These considerations, widely reflected in public and specialist opinion, have been reinforced by the results from quantitative surveys relating to the volume of restructurings effected, the numbers of jobs created, the extent of product innovation, or the improvement of product quality. All these findings, communicated with great fanfare, have tended to demonstrate the superiority of a form of enterprise—acquisition by a foreign buyer—over the enterprise acquired by its employees. "A consensus on the negative role of mass privatization" has thus developed.[3]

However, despite these remarks, the sale of enterprises to their employees has often been the only possible solution available to the authorities. In the absence of an external buyer, ownership rights have had to be restructured among the available personnel. For this reason, privatization has often been carried out in post-Communist Europe without the mediation of foreign capital. All the more so as foreign capital was very reticent in the early years of the process and highly selective thereafter. In other words, privatizations took place with those within the companies as its only partners. In most cases, management buyout (MBO) was a fallback solution in the absence of an external buyer. Within this context, two forms of MBO emerged. The first was based on majority shareholding by employees and management, in accordance with very varied principles of distribution: seniority, salary level, or a mix of the two. The principles of association were equally diverse, since the managers may or may not have received the majority of shares, and that majority may have been equally divided between employees and outsiders (possibly financial institutions). Alternative forms appeared, such as "Employee Stock Ownership Plans" (ESOP), in which case several external actors—partners from banking or government—took over the financing of the company against income from future products. The second form of internal buyout involved an absence of control on the part of the employees, who in this case held a minority of the shares. The transfers were identical to the preceding case, but share distribution followed one of many courses. In Hungary, 10% of the capital was handed over to the managers. In Poland, the figure was as high as 20%, to which was added 15% in the name of mass privatization. In Bulgaria and Estonia, the managers profited from 33% of all transactions, and some received a further 20% at a discount. The legislation was, consequently, very varied between one country and another.[4] There were a great many management buyouts in Poland, Romania, Hungary, and Slovenia. These were, then, one of the favored forms of enterprise transformation, once corporatization had been achieved. Though Hungary greatly favored direct foreign investors, MBOs were nonetheless the most widespread form. Romania opted almost exclusively for this type of management throughout the decade. In 1995, 95% of enterprises were management buyouts, while, in the case of Lithuania, the figure stood at 70%.[5] This just shows the variety of types of enterprise and of corporates, and hence the complexity of local situations. It was only by caricaturing MBOs and depicting them entirely as corrupt units that the merits of foreign direct investment (FDI) could be vaunted, by contrast, as a clear, simple solution. However, because of the interests in play, such a caricature was often presented. The specialist literature systematically denigrated MBOs in order to show FDI enterprises in a better light.

The Limits of a Form of Ownership

The MBO solution was disadvantageous for many reasons: the emergence of compromises favorable to employees rather than to investors; the absence of a financial horizon and the risks of "moral hazard," particularly associated with debts; the blocking of foreign investment; corruption; and the risk of subversion by a well-organized minority operating against a dispersed majority. Practice largely confirmed the fears of the economists, who were not in any case inclined to look favorably on forms of collective governance, such as self-management. They roundly denounced situations in which employees were favored, on the grounds that their short-term interests ran contrary to the pursuit of profit and, hence, to the interests of the enterprise. Large-scale corruption was the price to be paid.

Table 5.1   Distribution of Enterprises as a Function of Privatization Methods, 1997 (%)

	Sales to Foreign Investors	Sales to Domestic Investors	Equal Access Voucher	Insider	Other	Still State Property
Czech Rep	10	10	40	5	5	30
Hungary	45	12	—	3	20	20
Lithuania	12	2	43	9	—	43
Poland	10	—	6	—	44	40
Romania	5	5	20	10	—	60
Slovakia	7	3	25	30	5	30
Slovenia	1	8	18	27	21	25

Source: This table is based on figures taken from Djankov, S., and G Pohl, "The Restructuring of Large firms in the Slovak Republic," *Economics of Transition*, 6 (1), 1998, pp. 67–85.

In the conditions that prevailed in 1990 and subsequently, when the need to transform collective into private property found itself combined with legal uncertainties, an absence of capital and the maintenance of most economic executives in their posts, the path was certainly wide open for internal arrangements. It was all the more open for the fact that the new governments, as we saw in chapter two, were concerned to ground their legitimacy and their assets on the basis of the chosen modes of privatization. In some countries, employee buyouts were more of a response to internal relations of force, whether it was the unions that were involved, as was the case in the great Polish industrial centers, or interest groups formed by managers, as in the Hungarian example. Alongside the path of spontaneous privatization at the very beginning of the transformation, which was akin to barely disguised theft, the management buyout path was the most likely to be attended by corruption, for reasons of the slowness of the procedure, the power of the civil service, the absence of an independent oversight body, and the lack of transparency of the transactions.

Arrangements and Compromises

The fears expressed about abuses in the case of employee buyouts have been shown to be justified by many survey findings. Internal "arrangements" between employees and "schemes" hatched by officials within the hierarchy were to blame for this. The fall in industrial production levels in the first years of the 1990s did not correlate with a fall in employment levels. Whereas there were marked reductions in the former, levels of employment were able, in some places, to remain stable. This can be accounted for by the adjustments found within enterprises either in terms of reduced wages or working hours. Enterprise directors often found an answer to the ending of subsidies or to the collapse of former markets by reducing working hours.[6] Hence the idea that the compromises previously established between management and workforce on the basis of loyalty and paternalistic domination can be said to have been revamped after 1990 under cover of an understanding to keep everyone in a job, albeit at the expense of overall efficiency. The preservation of employment levels was also built on an absence of wage claims. At the beginning of the processes—that is to say, until 1994–1995—it was not unusual to see employment curves rising in certain protected public sectors, such as mining, steel, or the mechanical industries. These practices expressed the response capacity of local actors, who were confronted with unprecedented situations in environments where hardly any redeployment of labor was possible. Given the previous economic structure, which had led to a high degree of autarky on the part of firms and territories, no alternative in terms of external labor markets was, in fact, available in crisis-ridden environments. In these conditions, the only rational response consisted in reallocating forces and inventing solutions to totally unprecedented problems. Far from corresponding to preconceived plans or "backward" mentalities, these responses were effectively solutions cobbled together in an emergency. The labor unions, which were now present only in public enterprises, sought, in these conditions, to promote employment at all costs.

Moreover, though many "compromises" were found, they did not reflect any sizeable degree of power on the part of employees. On the contrary, many transformations merely had the effect of temporarily preserving previous employment levels. The processes of "internal privatization" were led by the former managers, who had remained in post. They involved the transformation of all or parts of enterprises into autonomous private companies. This was the requirement for transforming ownership rights, first of all, and for moving from a regime of public property to a private (or "commercialized") regime. This had to be done, moreover, if one were to hope to sell off the potentially saleable parts of the enterprises in the best financial conditions. This movement of "internal privatization" applied, then, to a large number of production units and led to the break-up of departments and services, most of which remained on the same sites. In most cases, this process of break-up was effected with the retention of the same machines and workforce. But far from having merely given expression to consensuses between the parties involved, these changes to the rules of the game were often made without consulting the employees. The latter were kept in ignorance of the—very often temporary—clauses relating to their departure. On several occasions, managers strove to present their enterprises in the worst possible light, so as not to have them privatized and, hence, to acquire them cheaply. In many cases, the agreements ceding enterprises to their managers turned out to be contrary to the interests of the workers. Once the executives had achieved their aims of pillage, or once they had been obliged to renegotiate the initial contracts with buyers whom they had themselves most often approached, the workers were regarded as a "liability." To retain their own advantages, enterprise directors of this kind did not hesitate to make their employees redundant in very large numbers. Several studies have shown that the labor union officials colluded with the directors in these negotiations, seeking thereby to safeguard their own futures. In other cases, also very numerous, ownership rights were on many occasions ceded to individuals who were solely interested in realizing an immediate profit on the basis of a drastic reduction in the workforce. In that case, the public authority in charge of privatization sometimes had to take over the mishandled enterprise in question, but to do so with a reduced workforce, the better to attract a new investor. On each occasion, the workers were the ones to suffer from these practices.

Embezzlement and Corruption

Cases of embezzlement were legion. Some enterprise directors managed to turn internal "privatizations" to their advantage by creating third companies from scratch or by facilitating contracts with the former mother companies, which were the main debtors of the new shareholders. In a Polish enterprise analyzed in 1997, a dust-extraction company was created to supply the rotary ovens of the mother company, the cement works, with cold ashes. The shareholders of this third-party company were the chief executives of the cement works and of maintenance companies that had already been "privatized" along the lines outlined above. Thanks to this coalition, dividends were paid in proportion to the profits gained from the cement works, thanks to high levels of orders placed by these companies and fulfilled by the cement works.[7] Everywhere in Central and Eastern Europe, individual interest groups were able to gain control of the circuits upstream and downstream from public enterprises and, consequently, sell products very dear to the public enterprise, which the director of that enterprise then sold on to another dealer at a loss, the three managing directors being effectively in league. These examples extended the phenomena of fraudulent seizure to the creation of networks of subcontractors around mother companies, by which the latter were opened up for exploitation. On many occasions, the large public enterprise collapsed, while all around the small firms that were formerly dependent upon it flourished, enjoying favorable contracts that contributed to its ruin. What happened at the local level to the detriment of the workers reflects what happened at the national and international levels to the large-scale detriment of the citizens, with the Gudzowaty case in Poland or the instance of Multigroup in Bulgaria.[8]

Corresponding to these processes of internal "privatization" between directors who once belonged to the same enterprise were external alliances evidencing the strength of the previous networks between the leading figures in the enterprises and the higher central administrative levels. This is particularly clear in the case of the external trade administrations that were, before 1989, exclusive partners to the foreign clients in their sector. In this regard, the possession of an address book full of Western partners was, after 1989, an unparalleled item of "economic capital." It was all the easier for the officials who were formerly members of these public bodies to set up in business for themselves after 1990 for the fact that their set-up costs involved only the hire of a room for the installation of a telephone. They were easily able to trade on their network of contacts by rebranding themselves as intermediaries for the enterprises of which they had previously been heads of sales. These external alliances often brought the banks into play, since they had every interest in the state continuing to support as yet unprivatized enterprises on account of the debts they had accumulated. Insofar as the banks were associated very early on with the capital of the enterprises, they had to take on the liabilities of their portfolios. Only uninterrupted state aid to enterprises could lighten the burden of the banking institutes, all the more so as, with the concentration of banks playing its part here, the state had a financial interest in several of them. The fall of a single bank could have threatened the entire banking edifice and undermined confidence in the state.

For all these reasons, in a period that, in reality, extended throughout the 1990s, the privatization of assets enabled the same individuals to
remain in their jobs, insofar as they were able to exploit the resources and
activate the contacts formed under the previous regime. Like the maintenance of the former leaders in place, the continuance of certain other
behaviors after 1990 can be explained by the complexity of the modes of
governance, which in turn generated the reproduction of forms of dependency within the enterprise. The introduction of the privatization laws,
far from entailing the contractualization of labor relations, tightened,
rather, the bonds of patronage. These bonds functioned between directors, consolidated in their clientelist status, and employees who were even
more powerless as a result of the elimination of intermediary elements, be
it overseer jobs in the workplace, the old labor unions, or even the party.

In the face of massive embezzlement, detrimental in the first instance
to the employees, some economists argued for the protection of the workers, who were not infrequently victims of their managers in the case of
buyouts.[9] Aoki proposed coupling insider control with monitoring by the
banking system, once the latter was put on a sound footing and placed in
a position of direct oversight.[10] For his part, Stiglitz suggested granting
monitoring rights to employees and hence instituting a system of shared
governance.[11] Sociologists have argued for taking social logic into account
in the various transactions in order to be more able to enforce account-
ability.[12] However, despite all the pathological phenomena relating to
management buyouts, other work has been able to show the advantages
of the enterprises formed in this way by comparison with enterprises sold
off to foreigners.

Obscure Governance

Economic theory extols the superiority of foreign investment over
employee buyouts for one fundamental reason: the external control that
is supposed to be exerted over agents thanks to the panoply of incentives
at the disposal of the principal. Once again, practice has shown this to be
correct. However, by concentrating solely on outcomes in terms of profit,
the theory does not take into account other phenomena that nonetheless
ensure the stability of the enterprise and provide a basis for trust. These
advantages can be measured in terms of maintenance of social peace,
reduction of social conflict, and employees' attachment to their enterprise. Involved here, then, is motivation, which is indicative of increasing
productivity. Several works (most often East European in origin) have
shown that there were more conflicts where direct foreign investment
was involved, and that anxieties were more diffuse. These were linked to
the new working conditions and to the behavior of the new hierarchies.[13]
Other writers have concluded that, far from giving rise to continuous
ransackings of enterprises, management buyouts have been characterized
by strict respect for the principles of financial discipline.[14] The findings

of these studies have led to assertions that these enterprises have achieved high profits and that the results in terms of rationalization of employment have been real. Consequently, processes of restructuring genuinely did take place in these cases. It has also been shown, for example, that, though reductions in the workforce tended to be avoided in Estonian and Latvian buyouts, the same did not apply in Romania or Poland.[15]

Moreover, the considerable advantages ascribed to direct foreign investment over management buyouts, in terms of clarity of decision making based on a more exact knowledge of the reality of the work units, have often been found not to pertain. Several studies have exposed the irrationality of decisions taken in the field of the private management of employment by direct foreign investors. Decisions to reduce the workforce were based on prejudice about "over manning," assessed crudely by the buyer without any prior examination of the state of the works. Such "rough" assessments, consequently, ran up against the hidden realities of the inequalities in the volume of employment in Soviet-type enterprises, which, as we saw in chapter one, are often characterized by a bloatedness of the maintenance sectors. To facilitate the achievement of the objectives of workforce reduction, foreign buyers often resorted to redundancy programs. And this practice was resorted to on a large scale by the public directors of politically important sectors, such as mining and iron and steel. The implementation of these programs depended on the payment of a substantial sum of money in exchange for the voluntary departure of the individuals concerned. A similar strategy was sometimes carried out without any precise idea either of the criteria for entitlement to voluntary redundancy or of the ultimate target figure for the workforce. The argument of the uncertainty pertaining in markets and on the political scene poorly concealed ignorance of the real state of the enterprise by buyers who were concerned only to reduce their costs and "prune down" the operation.

In East Germany, the irrationality of certain decisions arrived at on the basis of formal rationality led, for example—under cover of the rationalization of the workforce—to drastic reductions, the collapse of certain "combines," and their replacement by a myriad of small units, a large number of which turned out to be incapable of surviving in the short term—only for it to be admitted a few years later that these cuts had cut too heavily into the productive environments and that the trend now had to be reversed. Things moved, in this way, from a vision in which the "very large," condemned without any genuine examination, was dominant, to a second vision in which the "very small" gained the upper hand without any serious justification. The structural funds were then called upon publicly to revive what private management had largely contributed to destroying. In Poland, redundancy programs appeared, without any clear objective regarding the targets to be achieved either in the private sector first or, subsequently, in the public sector (mainly mines and steelworks). In all cases, the only consideration was the desire to radically and very rapidly reduce the volume of employment. In some enterprises, up to 40% of the workforce was cut in a period of 18 months or less. How did the buyers operate? By implementing on a grand scale methods commonly used in Western Europe, with the difference that there the issues are understood and the results are sometimes negotiated with the labor unions. In Eastern Europe, it was on a basis of the concealment of information that these practices emerged, greatly facilitated by the weakness of the labor unions and the position of strength acquired by the buyers. The capacity to master uncertainty and, even more, to disseminate it, was one of the guarantees of success. To reinforce the incentive character of the proposed programs, the managers of the enterprises concerned linked the payout figures to the speed with which employees made up their minds. If they chose to leave within 6 months, they would pocket twice as much as those who needed 12 months to decide, and 3 times as much as those who felt they needed 18 months. The fact that these redundancy programs were set up to circumvent an undertaking signed with the public officials on acquisition of the company suggests that the alleged practices of trust and openness were little better in this type of company than in the others where the previous managers were still in post. The undertaking in question stipulated that the buyer committed himself to maintaining levels of employment in the three years following acquisition. After those three years—that is, in the fourth year—a reduction of 10% could take place. In the fifth year, the buyers were at liberty legally to reduce the workforce as they wished. The signing of such undertakings was done in the conviction that they would be violated at the earliest opportunity and in the certainty that they would in no way lead to a break between the former managers and the local officials. Why was this? Because it served the interest of all the actors in the chain of decision making leading to the sell-off, beginning with the managers in place. They were able to make a substantial profit from the sell-off of these enterprises, if only by the assurance, which they had been able to negotiate, that they would retain their jobs. It was the same with the labor unions, which were associated in some circumstances with the support procedures put in place by the buyer, when they too were given guarantees that they would be the last to be affected by redundancies. As for the workforce, they were at first happy to receive such large sums of money, if only in some cases to regret it later, given the shortage of employment in the immediate surrounding areas. The last beneficiaries were the local public authorities, who saw the foreign buyer taking on costs they would otherwise have had to shoulder. However, none of these different actors was concerned with the medium or long term. These redundancy programs were elaborated without any consultation with the environing public sector. The municipalities had no part in a situation that suddenly saw a large number of individuals both thrown out of the local labor market and in possession of significant sums of money. Only in exceptional cases were these programs accompanied by the enterprises setting up advisory units. The municipalities, to whom that particular collective prerogative fell, were, in actual fact, often hostile to the big enterprises—which already decided their employment policies without consultation—aspiring to encroach on their territory in such a high-handed way. In the end, local employment seldom profited from this windfall from redundancy programs, with the exception of the consumption sector—mainly automobile franchises and bars.

Actors in the Enterprise

Rationalization

In the 1990s, direct foreign investment enterprises were ranked ahead of any other form of enterprise because they promoted access to what had previously been missing: financial resources, technologies, and skills. In reality, toward the end of the decade several studies showed that an adjustment had taken place between the various forms of enterprises, in that MBOs had been forced, in order to survive, to adopt the same logic of rationalization as those involving direct foreign investment.[16] In the end, the same mechanisms of economic efficiency came into play everywhere. They involved a specialization of functions as a result of primacy being restored to the formal purpose of action and, as a consequence, to the pursuit of high performance. They led to the individualization of tasks and functions thanks to training, and the redefinition of everyone's place. They gave rise, in the end, to the coordination of action through the introduction of flexible forms of organization guaranteed over time by control procedures. In Central and Eastern Europe, this process of the intense modernization of work units formed part of the dynamics of rationalization of working environments, which, in the West in the 1980s, were radically modified under the effect of the domination of flexibility-based management models mainly of Japanese origin. In this respect, the opening up of East European enterprises seems to have represented an unrivalled opportunity to recycle certain modes of managerial thinking that had already been much criticized for their excesses before 1990. Based on the encouragement of "lean production," these models involved the flattening of hierarchies and the reduction of stock. Primacy was accorded to quality, conceived in terms of reducing to the extreme the time spent on production, delivery, and repair.[17] Within this schema, which dominated the last quarter of the twentieth century, innovation was promoted by a set of incentives that reinforced individual commitment by more flexible working conditions, a thoroughgoing individualization of the employment contract and, consequently, less use of collective agreements. However, before 1989 many studies had shown the limits of such organizations of labor when they were accompanied by increased stress, a high pace of work, a sense of alienation, and decreased individual satisfaction. No lessons were drawn from these studies in the following decade in Central and Eastern Europe. Worse, the negative effects experienced were legion, merely because these methods were imposed in total isolation from the organizational and cultural context in which they had been developed.

Changes in Organization

In Central and Eastern Europe, organizational changes involved, first, the restructuring of hierarchies, which were denounced as obsolete, the elimination of strictly political departments, and the reorganization of the technical sectors, such as maintenance departments. The latter had over time risen to considerable proportions by dint of the very nature of the shortage economy, which made continuous supply of materials difficult. The repair departments were bloated for the sole reason that the smooth functioning of workshops had to be ensured, whatever the operating faults of the moment. Once these flows were assured, these maintenance sections lost their importance. Their functions were redistributed within each department. Rather than forming a separate department, all-powerful on account of the essential services it was able to render, they were now incorporated into the different departments, with each departmental manager responsible for their costs. Other departments were created from scratch, such as commercial and sales sections. The functional equivalents of these departments did, admittedly, exist before, but they were not properly resourced, on account of the nature of the economy in which the enterprises operated. The Soviet-type economy was a command economy and hence a supplier's economy. It implied that consumers worked out their choices not on the basis of their preferences, but as a function of the available supply. Quality was correspondingly devalued and marketing activity was reduced to a very low level. With attention now being focused on quality, all the elements of the enterprise were reoriented.

In this way, rational calculation descended to the level of the elementary work units. Generally, the process of rationalization expressed itself in all the factors entering into the industrial process being taken into account. Each intervention was specifically measured and registered in a continuous chain, the control function being there to ensure necessary adjustments. The form of control that previously applied, which was in keeping with the vertical organization of units, gave way after 1990 to the establishment of decentralized intermediaries in charge of the circulation of relevant information and the reporting of that information at every stage. In a general way, reporting and control services were thus designated to ensure the coordination, monitoring, and control of the industrial process, not the gathering of data, which was now left to the decentralized levels. In the method of calculation, the balances that previously enabled results to be related to previous forecasts gave way to the adoption of continuous monitoring criteria and modifications as a consequence. Balance sheets were now most often quarterly, not annual. The securing of flows at the level of production and budgetary monitoring became a priority of an entirely revamped sector, that of quality. For this reason, control became the guarantee of development, based on the coordination of individualized operations and actions. The real change by comparison with the previous form of organization, defined in terms of "exogenous" ideological control, was based on this dynamic of the "endogenization" of social control, that control being taken upon themselves by each individual, now assumed to be a free, responsible actor. The "great transformation" in organizational terms within enterprises may be said to have consisted in imposing the notion of control as a precondition for collective development at all stages of activity—from the most elementary action to production, and to the recording of that production in the accounts.[18] In this regard, what happened at the local level in the modernized enterprise prefigured what was demanded at the general level in these countries when they had to adopt rules of external control (in the control of their frontiers or in health and plant-health monitoring) in order to ensure they receive development aid. More broadly, the ensuring of collective safety by the new member countries has been the guarantee of each country's right to development. In the enterprise, the control of each element of the process has been the basis on which everyone's activity has rested.

Jobs

In terms of job content, one might have expected a degree of enrichment following the opening up of economies and enterprises. There were very great expectations in this direction. A great number of engineers and technicians had been thwarted in the exercise of their skills under the former regime and the absence of any modernization of equipment before 1989 had led to their being sidelined, whatever plans they may have formed. Having played a large part in the fall of the Communist regime, from which they had turned away because it did not prize their professional contribution, their expectations of the foreign buyers were very high, both regarding technological investment and the punishment of those responsible for the economic debacle. Their hopes were dashed to a very great extent, and employees were only too seldom involved in the processes of change. Some foreign buyers were even less inclined to satisfy these expectations, because the state of the markets was difficult to assess and they were largely unfamiliar with the enterprises they had just acquired. In these conditions, rather than take the reins of the company, it was better in their view to keep the existing managers on, even if it meant shadowing that management with teams of expatriates, to whom they would entrust the key sectors of financial control and commerce. This also explained their concern not to state their social and technological investment strategies, which were not, in any event, particularly firm. Their capacity to play on uncertainty also reflected their profound ignorance of local realities, of languages and, more generally, the balances of forces on the shopfloor. For all these reasons, the continuation of existing methods, even if they were outdated in the West, seemed to offer greater security.

Several studies have reported the intense dynamic of re-Taylorization of workshops, either in a "soft," insidious form, with the importation of Japanese Kaizen type methods, or in much harsher form in other contexts with the "disciplining" of employees, forced at times to submit to harassment. In some places, "yellow lines" were drawn on the ground in the factories to indicate a boundary that should on no account be overstepped. In East Germany, the distinct prevalence of assembly workshops was accompanied by a large-scale lowering of required skill levels.[19] Instead of an intelligent management based on valuing the resources accumulated and skills acquired in the workplace, a type of intervention came to predominate that was based on emitting stimuli and expecting standardized responses. The whole was based on the most archaic conception of social development. The call for a stiffening of discipline was accompanied by a strict monitoring of working hours. This was badly received, not least because these decisions formed part of endlessly repeated campaigns criticizing the disorganization of workshops under the former regime and the alleged "idleness" of East German workers. The Soviet-type economy was constantly depicted as an overmanned economy with many "hidey-holes" for laziness and shirking on the part of individuals who were "naturally" inclined to idleness.

So far as occupational status goes, qualifications were largely downgraded, and the workers were often overqualified for the jobs assigned to them. Unskilled jobs were the first to be affected by employment restructuring measures. Czech observers add that the same applied to skilled workers. Only one-fifth of skilled workers in the Czech Republic were of the opinion that their skills were used better after 1989.[20] Some modifications to factory hierarchies were uncomfortable for certain workers. This was the case, for example, with the abolition of the post of overseer. The employees in question, who derived their prestige before 1989 from having been singled out among the skilled workers, were now reduced to the ranks. The foremen, who were often seen as first in rank in the world of production, were transformed into the lowest rank of management, in charge of discipline and, to an even greater extent, of bureaucratic control. The German sociologists Voskamp and Wittke have highlighted the particularity of the "pact of execution" that linked them both to their management and their workers, in which they fulfilled a function of professional mediation that was recognized by all.[21] They were, in this way, the real negotiators in the department and the workshop and formed the basis on which what one sociologist termed a "culture of cooperation"[22] was built. In breaking these links of proximity, the upheavals that came out of 1989 deprived them of their status. A number of surveys of engineers and technicians have revealed the intense frustration that gripped them when they came to understand that all the innovative solutions they had developed within the previous economy were to be discarded as mere tinkering. As for management posts, many of these were taken by expatriates in the companies acquired by foreigners. This applied to the posts of general manager and director of finance, strategy, quality, and production. By contrast, responsibility for human resources was systematically left to local employees. This enabled the foreign buyers to distance themselves from the very unpopular measures relating to redundancies and the implementation of redundancy programs, leaving the responsibility for these to locals.

A Mixed Assessment

These radical changes to organization, function, and status generated both satisfaction and concern. We shall take the cases of satisfaction first. For those able to take advantage of the dynamic of the raising of skill levels and to hitch their wagons to the West, they were intense. Young, highly qualified, dynamic employees were the ones who most often benefited here. It was they who mostly received the training. This brought with it both job enrichment and wider recognition. Working in a foreign company undoubtedly represented experience that could be put to good use individually and was widely envied in the broader community, on account of the massive destruction of jobs all around. We should also add that significant improvements to health and safety were made everywhere and were well-received.[23]

The concerns were felt by many categories of workers—sometimes the same categories as before. Many engineers or technicians complained that their skills, already neglected under the old regime, were no more highly regarded by the new owners, who were concerned only with selling off the whole of the industrial heritage. Where they had been hoping for a change that would bring recognition of individual capacities, it actually took the form of a collective rupture. Sweeping judgments were pronounced with no concern for particular situations. Decisions to overturn the organization of workshops were taken with no regard for equilibria arrived at over the long term. And all this was done in the name of principles whose introduction merely increased the disorder. Thus, a number of employees criticized the stiffening of disciplinary measures, the increased pace of work, and the higher levels of stress and competition—all things unlikely to promote efficient rationalization of the workplace. Others highlighted unexplained management decisions, which consisted in leaving those responsible for the previous economic debacle in their jobs or dismissing the most experienced on the grounds of their advanced age.

In the end, the very rationality of action was questioned. This led to the two systems being compared. At times preference went to the old regime over the new, on the grounds that human environments were better respected subjectively. This meant that workplace camaraderie and relational closeness came to be viewed with renewed regard—as indeed was a whole social system that was irreducible to the political system with which the newcomers had sought to equate it, the better to ignore it and impose their own view of matters. In the previous system, appeals against decisions were possible through the guardian figure of the foreman/overseer or even the party representative (or, much more rarely, the union representative). In the rationalized work environment that pertained in the following period, nothing could be set against the abstract measurement of time. Rational calculation, measured and mathematized, won out over workplace relations. No one could appeal against the stopwatch when it came in the form of digital technology, with measurement and control effected by everyone. As a result, the compensatory function of the imagination found solace in regretting not so much the past political order as the ability to circumvent the norm, to temper the rule, to slow or speed up the pace of work—in a word, to gain mastery over time.[24]

Contracts and Networks

Just as the macro-economic policy of the transformation of property ownership led to a general redistribution of relations between the center and the periphery of the industrial groups, at the local level enterprises redefined their relations with their immediate environment. It was in East Germany, apparently, that contractualization was most intense. That was where contracts became the most widespread form of exchange: the wage contract in the enterprise was made with each individual to set individual tasks, and also when enterprises were restructured. When certain departments were separated from the mother company—often the maintenance shops or the "social" departments—the contracts established between the managers stipulated not just the retention of all the employees, but also the maintenance of permanent relations between the mother company and the unit that had now become a subsidiary. However, unlike the contracts characteristic of the previous regime, these were set within circumscribed time limits, rarely stretching beyond one year. Beyond this, there were many accounts of failure. Outside of the enterprise, contracts of the same type were struck between the different partners. The opportunity for this was provided by the establishment of employment companies (*Beschäftigungsgeselleschaften*). These brought together the managers of enterprises that were facing restructuring, public partners from the local authorities, the *Treuhandanstalt* privatization agency, and the labor unions. These companies of a new type, created on a pattern established in the West in the 1960s at the time of mining crises, had the object of providing transition in employment by creating a "second labor market." They took it upon themselves to pay the employee a wage, consisting in part of the individual's unemployment benefit payment, while in exchange employees committed themselves to retraining. They were also to carry out public works, in the interval when the enterprise was being restructured. At the end of the process, individuals should be able to find employment in a new enterprise or create their own job.[25] In this way, the adjustment of East Germany to West German demands, painful as it may have been, was nonetheless carried out in a highly rule-governed way. A great number of apprenticeships were created. This involved local, regional, and national partners, all of them bent on providing retraining within the firm and revitalizing its environments. Moreover, even though decentralization won out in Germany and dealt a severe blow to collective bargaining, the social actors retained significant room for maneuver. Collective agreements were signed despite the powerful deregulatory dynamic affecting the joint industrial institutions. Levels of public aid were massive during this period. A substantial training effort was undertaken and carried through. More than half of the East German labor force was involved. The contract, on which statuses—and hence possibilities of choice—were founded, carried the day.

This process of contractualization—and hence of rationalization—was of much smaller scope in Eastern Europe, if only because of the lower number of foreign takeovers. For this reason, the social partners were less able to control the transformations, particularly as there was little experience in this regard. The labor unions were barely able to influence change, both because they were few in number and also because of the strategy of the other public and private partners who pushed them aside. The asymmetry of resources in favor of the employers showed itself in a high level of use of redundancy programs in companies acquired by foreign interests. According to some sources, 25% of Polish companies saw such programs implemented,[26] and we have stressed above the nature of the relations of force that such "contracts" revealed. The significant deregulation of labor law encouraged an Anglo-Saxon style of management in which self-employment was widely promoted.[27] Though the rules of contractualization were more implicit, this does not mean a lower intensity of change. Reductions in staffing levels were on the same scale as those carried out in the former GDR over time periods that were barely longer. This lesser internal regulation led, in the same way, to reduced exchanges with local environments. Accounts of cooperation between work units and public authorities are rare, though this could have attenuated the effects of an unemployment that was highly concentrated in certain areas. A number of instances of support units being created by foreign enterprises are reported. Similarly, a number of cooperation programs between municipalities and enterprises appeared. These were the exception. This low degree of regulation had its counterpart in a high degree of informal regulation that took several forms. In his studies of working conditions in Polish enterprises, Portet has brought out the importance of informal relations or, more exactly, of collusion between managers and employees. The former permitted the latter to use some elements of enterprise property for private ends outside of working hours. For example, the works driver was able to use the company vehicle for a second job outside the enterprise; the mechanic was able to borrow company tools for work carried out in his garage, and so on. The revenue earned in this way provided its beneficiary with an indispensable supplementary income and assured the employer of social peace, enabling him also to maintain quite low wages.[28]

These forms of implicit agreement between the workplace actors did, indeed, guarantee the maintenance of the consensuses built before 1989—all the more so, as the public authorities were not to be outdone themselves. By turning a blind eye to the activities linked to the "gray" economy, they accepted the need for such safety-valves in local situations of economic devastation. Something similar applied not simply to so-called informal activities, but also to jobs found abroad outside of the centrally set quotas and, more generally, to cross-border exchanges. These various jobs were indispensable in supplementing difficult individual situations. They ensured the survival of local milieus and the continuity of human environments. The overall economic damage was certainly high, since, beyond the losses in tax revenues to the community, it expressed itself in the spread of an enormous informal economy that helped to foster dependence among the weakest in the community and to freeze situations that were not subsequently able to evolve. In agriculture, micro-holdings continued to exist, thereby blocking the formation of a coherent market in land prices. However, on the other hand, such practices performed an irreplaceable social function that, if it had been subject to diligent public oversight, would have forced individuals to migrate, with the danger that even greater disorder would ensue as the life was squeezed out of the small towns. This is one of the aspects of the range of issues around agriculture that we shall have to examine in the next chapter.

Conclusion

One of the main lessons of the 1990s lies no doubt in the finding, established very early on, that merely changing the form of ownership is not sufficient to ensure that enterprises perform well. Only effective control exerted on the new owners from outside can be efficacious. Where independent individuals external to the enterprise are not able to modulate incentives as a function of results, it seems we have to stand by and watch the persistence of behavior that was, under the previous regime, seen as a set of lame compromises. These compromises were characterized by collusion and corruption. The decentralization of management procedures has thus led in some cases to the continuance of past relations and old compromises. What had been observed at the macro level of the privatization of economies repeated itself at the micro level of enterprises. Corruption was widespread. The period of post-Communism—in other words, the period of the privatization of formerly public assets—was characterized by the duality of forms of regulation, exogenous, and endogenous. Borne by actors who were either "outsiders" or "insiders," the rules, strategies, and consensuses pertaining within these forms of regulation have been quite distinct from one another. Though MBOs enabled more previous resources to be reinvested and the reproduction of certain local consensuses between management and employees, this has led to enormous dependency and the exclusion of workers, particularly the unskilled. If, on the other hand, we have noted the superiority in technical, financial, and qualification terms of direct foreign investment enterprises, we have pointed out how much of these latter could provide scope for some shady strategies. A number of strategies developed by Western managements, in cahoots with certain actors internal and external to enterprises, led to significant processes of exclusion. We may conclude, more broadly, that the rules of hierarchical control seem to have won out to a great extent over the rules of autonomy forged by the workers in the workplace. Managerial staff, either working internally with their pre-1989 counterparts or externally when they found themselves linked up with foreign partners, came out very much on top over the shopfloor workers. The latter found themselves with barely any resources of their own to draw on. The solutions they had accumulated previously now scarcely had any impact. The informal compromises fell apart in the face of the new technological orders. The new technologies were adopted without any local compromises; there was simply a strict adjustment to them. A great number of individuals were kept out of the process of change within the enterprise or even removed from it.

Moreover, far from the contrasts hardening, the various forms of enterprise—whether they were sold off to their managers/employees or to a foreign buyer—demonstrated, in the long term, the same adjustment dynamics. At the end of the decade, observers agreed that those enterprises of the former type that managed to survive had, in reality, adopted the same standards of management and efficiency as direct foreign investment enterprises. By comparison with the other forms of ownership and viewed from the angle of economic performance, they were ranked behind enterprises acquired by foreign investors but ahead of those that had remained under the control of the public authorities.[29] We may go further and say that private enterprises tended to become clearly distinguishable from those remaining under state control, on the grounds that there was, in reality, little between enterprises acquired by their managers and those acquired by foreign buyers, even if everyone agreed that the best performances were achieved by direct foreign investment enterprises. These are all arguments that speak in favor of caution where ranking is concerned, and at least demand that we cease to think in terms of strict laws in this area. As for the enterprises that remained under public control, there is hardly anything to say, except that they drew on a broad consensus among their economic and professional managers to delay decisions on transformation. The technical ministries, particularly the Industry Ministry, sought to retain whole swathes of their old power and were more confrontational with the Budget Ministry. These are all behaviors that have increasingly come to be seen as ineffective and expected to be modified with membership of the European Union, insofar as the success of the impact of structural funds is linked, above all, to the reallocation of public resources and budgetary discipline.

It is at this point that we may bring in the concept of "Europeanization." The European Union has helped to promote the fulfillment of a dynamic that was initiated in its absence, under the auspices of free-market liberalism and globalization. Modernization finally came about on an identical pattern, in which privatized enterprises adopted the same behaviors over time. The European Union played even less of a role since it had nothing to offer in terms of social policy. Chapter Thirteen of the *Acquis Communautaire* confines itself to support measures for the mobility of workers in a European space characterized as the "large single market." Free-market logic won out in its harshest aspects in Eastern Europe, without giving rise to a strengthening either of the cobargaining organizations or the assisted labor-market institutions. The Western part of Europe has complained about the company relocations it may have suffered, but not about the foreign investment it promoted, the substantial profits amassed in that way, or the local disruption occasioned thereby.

CHAPTER SIX

The Agricultural Question. Public Laissez-faire and the Recomposition of Individual Strategies

The question of the relations between globalization, Europeanization, and national sovereignty deserves special attention for two reasons when it comes to the area of agriculture: as regards modernization, there has barely been any, if, by that term, we understand a rise in the norms of productivity and efficiency that Western European and North American agricultures can claim, on the basis of the size of land-holdings, agricultural employment, specialization of production, new technologies, and institutions. Faced with the enormous range of age-old problems associated with East European agriculture, characterized by deficits in all the areas just mentioned, *laissez-faire* policies—or in other words, sovereignties—prevailed in the 1990s. By contrast, the European Union played a preponderant role in imposing (sanitary and phytosanitary) standards as prerequisites for integration. In this way, they forced enterprises to adjust to European requirements. Moreover, the union played a decisive role in terms of preparing the administrations that were destined to manage the European funds of the agricultural policy. In the face of these two types of constraints—the first relating to the modernization of what were particularly backward agricultures, the second to the normative security imperatives of the European Union—national sovereignties adopted a "low profile" where their own strategies were concerned. In other words, the public elites contented themselves with land restitution policies, the application of which gave rise to many instances of disorder and much resistance to change on the part of many farmers. In this essential stage in the transformation of economies after 1989, recompositions largely won out, contributing at the same time to engendering marked continuities with the past.

The aim of this chapter is to stress the particularity of agricultural situations before 1990 in terms of land holding and village compromises, in order to understand three original features after 1990: the precariousness of the renewed consensuses, by virtue of their very fragile foundations that were under pressure to be modified profoundly; the discrepancies between—both domestic and European—representations of change, and local realities; and the great variety of rural and agricultural situations.

The Historic Issues

If we confine ourselves solely to the question of property rights, the range of issues for agriculture is not so different from that pertaining in industry. In effect, the whole range of juridical forms specific to the statized economy were overturned from 1990 onward and so, as a consequence, were all social statuses. However, as we stressed in the foregoing chapter, the transformation of legal forms is not sufficient to explain the real changes, given the inequality of resources available to the actors involved. Some groups of individuals are more able than others to exploit the new rules of the game. In this respect, there is, however, a major difference between the industrial and agricultural sectors: the industrial sector was largely restructured under the impact of direct foreign investment—directly by financial inflows and indirectly by the spread of models of management and rational conduct. The agricultural sector did not actually see the same influx of outsiders as identified in the foregoing pages in the form of foreign investors, except in the agribusiness sector and in Hungary. For this reason, the examination of the transformations of agricultural and rural milieus shows actors ranged against one another who were previously concentrated in an identical type of holding and local environment, namely the collective farm, though there is again one notable exception here: Poland. Moreover, most importantly, though industrial transformation was a massive focus of interest for the national and international public authorities from the early part of the decade, this was not the case with agriculture. Why not? First, because of the lack of interest of agribusiness investors, at one here with the interests of the national public authorities, who were resolved not to raise problems relating to land, the symbol of sovereignty. The social and national consensuses ran deep on this question and everyone realized that, in challenging them, the remedy may turn out to be worse than the disease. But what was that disease? It was identified very early on as excess employment—there was talk of concealed unemployment on an unimagined scale and employment volumes exceeding requirements by 20%—followed by an absence of specialization, as shown by the all-pervasive presence of mixed farming with stock rearing and by the land question. In several countries, 50% of East European holdings were less than five hectares in size. In other words, excess employment, the absence of specialization, and the size of holdings were the elements on which the historical backwardness of East European societies and economies were based; these were problems that had been identified long ago, but never properly solved.[1] For this reason, the size of the task discouraged the public authorities, which preferred in the 1990s not to elaborate genuine agricultural policies, the implementation of which would have led to radical upheavals. Central *laissez-faire* policies were the order of the day. They were justified by the policy of restitution of property seized during the Communist period, while locally the actors rejigged their strategies with largely unexpected results. Far from leading to the liquidation of corporate forms, the transformation initiated in 1990 led in fact in several places to the reproduction of the great cooperative holdings, while small, if not indeed very small, holdings proliferated in rural environments. The policies of the European Union seemed ill-prepared to deal with this dualism, which more or less reproduced the archaic character of the historic structures and had a hand in the exclusion of a large number of individuals.

Legacies. Forms of Agricultural Holding and Social Compromises before 1989

The impact of the policy of collectivization left a profound mark on the East European countryside from 1948 onward, when it came under Communist domination. It generated powerful local consensuses that, in large measure, ensured the stability of the Communist regimes. These are worthy of recall, if we are to understand the strength of the resistance to change after 1989.

East European Varieties of the Soviet-Type Model of Collective Farming

Between 1950 and 1989, agricultural structures were profoundly revolutionized in Central and Eastern Europe following the application of the policy of land collectivization directly inspired by the Soviet collectivization model of the 1930s. There were, however, three substantial differences between the Soviet model and its East European applications.

The first difference relates to the agrarian reform implemented in the years 1944–1945 by the Communist governments even before their absolute seizure of power. By carrying out these reforms, the Communist authorities realized part of the program of the prewar reformers. Thanks to them, the new elites acquired a certain legitimacy within what were massively rural populations. The aim pursued was to strengthen the position of the small peasants, eliminate the big landholders, and, above all, to avoid presenting themselves as mere "copies" of their Soviet model. The watchword in 1944 was defense of the image of a national Communism, which entailed the defense of private agriculture, parliamentary democracy, and pluralism; these were all policies that would be dismantled in the three years after the war. However, the reform of 1944–1945, just like that of 30 years before, was incomplete.[2] Once again, farmers were restricted to holdings that were too small. The redistribution was limited, often to 20 or 30 hectares, with the majority often receiving fewer than 5.

All in all, the reform involved 12 million hectares of land expropriated for 3 million families. In Romania, 1.5 million hectares were distributed to some 800,000 farmers. In 1918–1921, the figure had been four million. In Bulgaria the historic fragmentation of holdings was reinforced by the measures adopted by the Communist government, which had been partially at the helm since 1944 and was definitively so after December 1945. But in that country, only 136,000 hectares were involved in the redistribution for 128,000 families, each of which received little more than a hectare. This again explains the renewed fragmentation of land once the Communist period came to an end. However, the effects of this reform were largely unexpected. After 1989, when it came to restituting lands seized in the collectivization policy, the legislators would often base themselves on land registers drawn up 45 years earlier. The former beneficiaries of the postwar reforms would then be able to claim and obtain their property as constituted at that time. This partially explains the constitution of a fringe of farmers who would, subsequently by other means, be able to build up large holdings.

The second difference relates to the Polish exception. Beyond its numerical importance, it is its historic importance that should retain our attention.[3] Quite exceptionally in the Soviet bloc, Poland managed to preserve the private dimension of its agriculture under the protection of the compromise struck by Gomulka. Recalled to power in October 1956 following the bloody demonstrations at Poznan in June of the same year, the former Communist official, denounced in 1948 for "nationalist activities," had made his return six years later conditional upon official recognition of the church and private agriculture. So as not to aggravate what was already a very tense situation in the East European bloc on account of the unanticipated effects of the de-Stalinization policy, the high point of which would come with the outbreak of the Hungarian revolt in November 1956, the Soviets were forced to accept this fundamental deviation from Leninist orthodoxy. Having been forced in the 1950s to submit to enforced integration into cooperative farms, the Polish farmers left them in droves from the end of 1956 and thus kept the farming of small private family holdings in existence. However, although they conceded the principle of private agriculture, the Polish authorities never stopped combating it, regarding it as a form rendered obsolete by historical progress. During the 1960s and 1970s, there was no let-up in the discrimination against private farmers. Between 1950 and 1980, the share of cultivable land taken by private agriculture was to fall from 89.6% to 74.5%. Yet, a quarter of a century later, the decision to retain private agriculture throughout the Communist period would be identified as one of the basic causes of the Polish crisis in 1980. Small agricultural holdings were the more able to silently contest Communist power because they had the powerful backing of the Catholic church that was dominant in rural areas. In 1989, 78% of Polish farms were private. This figure was roughly the inverse of the other countries, where 80%, if not indeed 90%, of holdings were state-owned. The average size of private holdings was barely larger than 6 hectares in Poland at that date and more than 20% of the Polish working population were involved in agriculture.

The third essential difference by comparison with the Soviet model of the collectivization of land relates to the presence of a significant amount of cooperative property, based on a radically different legal principle from state ownership. It differed from state ownership in so far as the members of the cooperative remained owners of the property they had contributed at the point of entering the cooperative, unlike state farms, which belonged entirely to the public authorities. This distinction was of no importance before 1989. Legal forms were all merged at that point in the notion of collective property, formally indistinct, but in fact very significant. The distinction would turn out to be crucial after 1990 when the former members would be able to assert their rights of ownership and recover their assets. This policy of redistribution, which is not complete in some countries 20 years after it was initiated, clearly became very tricky for several reasons. First, on account of the development undergone by the property that was initially contributed, since the state of the land has not remained as it was for 40 years. This substantially complicated procedures for the restitution of a single piece of land to several owners. Second, on account of the impossibility at times of providing proof of titles to property, given the fact that the Communist authorities were constantly eliminating them, either in the form of boundary markers or written documents. Some public authorities did not hesitate, after 1990, to put bureaucratic obstacles in the way of the process of restitution, mainly for electoral reasons. Various modes of restitution were employed.[4] The aim everywhere was to favor the small private owner or farmer against the cooperative. Now, as we shall see, the outcomes did not greatly correspond to expectations.

After 1989, these exceptions to the Soviet rule represented notable resources in the hands of the local actors, be it the legal dispositions of 1944–1945, Polish private agriculture, or the cooperatives. In each case, these resources can be measured in terms of legal defense capacities or of networks of actors whose mobilization made it possible to cushion the effects of new political decisions or, more generally, the impact of regulatory changes.

Village Consensuses

During the collectivization process of the 1950s, the social classes that traditionally characterized the East European countryside experienced a radical upheaval. The great latifundist owners were eliminated or expropriated. The small farmers lost the right to work the land individually. The group of middle-ranging farmers, historically small in number, found themselves very quickly forced to join the agricultural cooperatives. The circuits supplying agricultural production and supplied by it were taken over by the state. Wage labor became the dominant form of relations of production, and the organization of work developed along industrial lines. This led to the establishment of hierarchical relations within the work teams, who were under the authority of foremen, whose position represented the lowest rung in the managerial hierarchy. At the top of that hierarchy were the farm management, the union representative, and, overseeing everything, the party secretary. In this respect, agricultural organization was entirely in step with the centralized principle of industrial organization. For this reason, some observers have spoken of "depeasantization" to underline the fact that, under socialism, the peasantry was eliminated, with the exception of Poland, so that where there had been peasants there were now agricultural *workers*. Collectivization reached its apogee in the GDR and Bulgaria when, in the 1960s and 1970s, agricultural combines were set up. These gathered entire villages into a single unit and went so far as to employ several tens of thousands of individuals.[5] A strict division of labor emerged between the activities of raising crops and stock rearing. These combines, extending over tens of thousands of hectares, controlled herds numbering several tens of thousands of head of cattle. The marginal position in which private agriculture was kept in Poland led to similar results. After 1990, some spoke of the farmers as an "obsolete class" and even as a "hangover," reviving the argument—though it is a retrograde one—of the "end of the farming class."[6]

However, despite these radical transformations of ancestral traditions, in a sense the Communist period did not affect certain traditional elements of the East European countryside. This was particularly the case with the agrarian dualism that underlay social relations, both formal and informal. Historically, this dualism represented a split between the great latifundist agricultural concerns and the tiny plots of land, ranging the great landowners against the little farmers and the "landless." The latter, very numerous in Hungary and Galicia, were also to be found in Central Poland, in the valleys of Dobrudza, in Romania, and, to a much lesser extent, in Bulgaria. The various reform efforts devised in the early twentieth century and largely implemented after the First World War failed everywhere, mainly on account of the "Great Terror" induced among the landowners by the Bolshevik Revolution in the USSR.[7] In this context, agrarianism, which was a very powerful political current throughout Central and Eastern Europe, particularly in Bulgaria, Poland, Romania, and Hungary, stood up for small private property and agricultural cooperatives as the basis for modern society, against the two dominant currents of capitalism and Communism. After 1945, the dualism that had intensified in the previous period was both thrown over and completely redefined. Thrown over, first, following the agrarian reform of the immediate postwar years, as we mentioned above. The scope of that reform was considerable, both in terms of the elimination of the large landholdings and the constitution of a class of farmers who at last owned their own land, even if it was partial and ultimately ineffective. Moreover, the dualism was set on an entirely new footing once the collectivization of land became the only agricultural policy, permitting use of the little patch of land at the margins. However, this margin would in fact make all the difference, since, over the long term, economic efficiency very often seemed to be in inverse proportion to the size of units. This new opposition between the great collective farm and the small plot enabled social relations between the various actors to reform. The size of the plot did, admittedly, vary with the various "hardenings" of the political line. For example, at the beginning of collectivization the Bulgarian authorities permitted private holdings of 0.2 hectares in areas of intensive cultivation and 0.5 hectares elsewhere. In the late 1950s, these limits were arbitrarily lowered to 0.1 hectares and 0.2 hectares, then set back to the initial level at the end of the next decade. As evidence of the essential character of the plot, the statistics in that same country show that between 1975 and 1983 production in the cooperatives fell by 26%, whereas vegetable production on the small plots rose by 92%.[8]

Within the framework of this dualism, significant social compromises occurred. Several observers have stressed that these revolved, in each case, around the division of labor and the renting of land. From the 1950s onward, a division arose in respect both of crops and farms as a function of the type of workforce. It fell to the collective farms to make extensive use of the widely available labor for growing grain and for large stock-rearing operations; they also had a monopoly on machinery. The small plot holders occupied themselves, by contrast, with growing fruit and vegetables and with intensive stock farming with the use of a family labor force. The negotiation between the two forms of—collective and private—farmers revolved around the products that the family obtained from the exploitation of the lands belonging to the collective farm, first very informally, then, over time, increasingly in the form of contracts. In the 1950s, for example, the small holders were permitted to divert part of their collective work time into exploiting their own plot, but they then had to remit part of their produce to the cooperative. In Bulgaria, this took place at first without the use of the collective machines. Later, negotiation was to bear on the "renting" of that machinery. These widespread forms of tolerance and informal exchange received more widespread official recognition in the 1980s. In Poland, the collective farms were authorized, in a sense, to "privatize" collective property by allowing the cooperators to farm large parts of the collective concern under contract. This is identical to what was implemented by the Hungarian industrial managers in the form of internal subcontracting through "VGMKs." Thanks to these "privatization" contracts, department or workshop managers were able to fulfill public orders through the use of machines outside official working hours and for substantially higher rates of remuneration. Similarly, in Bulgaria, but earlier, from 1982 onward, the Ministerial Council had authorized the establishment of long-term leases. After 1990, the length of these leases would represent a decisive advantage for the building of large agricultural concerns. Even before 1989, mixed forms of ownership were seen. This made it possible for Verdury to write, in connection with East European agriculture, of "fuzzy property rights."[9]

The Political Representations of Social Change after 1990

The Crises of 1989

However—and this is the paradox of this key episode in post-1989 agricultural transformation—though the statuses, ways of life and working, forms of organization of the farms and villages, and networks of exchange and relations with the town were remodeled from top to bottom during the Communist period, the shortcomings of the East European countryside before 1945 once again became glaring when the collective framework disappeared after 1989. All the more so as the first measures taken as part of the restitution of properties and the privatization of farms were adopted in the profoundest ignorance of the realities to which they applied. "Decollectivization" was carried out on the basis of a visceral rejection of the collective forms that had structured the rural and agricultural world for half a century. It fitted into a set of ideological representations, in response to particular interests, without any regard either for the needs or expectations of the countrysides. Agricultural transformation was in fact carried out on the basis of the idea that time could be turned back, that the socialist period had ultimately been of no consequence, and that it was merely a question of restoring the conditions that applied before collectivization for everything to work again. A broad policy of property restitution ensued, without any concern for the social realities that might have emerged in the rural areas in the meantime. It was accompanied by a *laissez-faire* policy in keeping with the ideological representations of a neoliberalism based on the brutal removal of subsidies, "freedom" for the producer, and the family farm model. As in the case of industrial privatization, the detailed forms of redistribution were highly ideological. The scheme adopted by the Czech Republic was, as one observer put it, "full and direct," while redistribution was implemented in Hungary on the basis of vouchers.[10] The two solutions encountered a substantial number of conflicts between cooperatives and villages. These were settled by the courts in the Czech Republic and on the basis of informal rulings in Hungary. In the end, to quote Giordano and Kostova, the *paysannerie pensée* won out over the *paysannerie vécue.*[11]

The modernization, if we must adopt this term—though it is doubtless inappropriate here—found expression in a considerable regression in standards of living that is not solely attributable to the state of agriculture in 1989. It cannot merely be put down to the opening of markets, to the collapse of trade within the Soviet-type market, and to the crisis that affected the other—mainly industrial—sectors. The fall-off in agricultural activities is also to be ascribed to the incompetence of the political officials after

1989, who proved incapable in the 1990s of articulating transformation plans that both respected human environments and met the demands for modernization that had been called for over several decades. Once again in the twentieth century, a great number of agricultural workers found themselves expelled from their living space and jobs on purely ideological grounds. They were left with barely any resources of their own, except their "resourcefulness" both as individuals and as families.

Local Recompositions

Confronted with this destructuring of their frame of action, individuals responded by recomposing the resources at their disposal, whether land, capital, or labor. The policy of land restitution, on the one hand, and *laissez-faire*, on the other, permitted of different strategies of appropriation and delegation, the most unexpected effect of which was doubtless the reproduction in many places of the former structures of farming. The cooperatives and the big collective farms, which the reformers had sworn in 1990 to eliminate once and for all, reappeared with a vengeance. Why was this? Quite simply because there was no other way out for the small landowners, who were incapable of finding their way around the new labyrinth of regulations, and because the newcomers knew how to exploit their skills. By the end of the 1990s, in some countries like the Czech Republic and Slovakia, these big corporate structures had won out over private ownership so far as extent of cultivable land was concerned. Moreover, in Poland the level of concealed unemployment was estimated at 900,000, then in the National Development Plan for 2007 at almost 2 million.[12] Elsewhere the statistics are unreliable.

So, unlike the transformation of industrial ownership that took place largely under the impact of an influx of foreign investors and external resources, agriculture displayed an original form of development and a wide range of forms of farming were seen. The unexpected character of this transformation process related to the fact that, though it was centered mainly on local actors and the recomposition of family and occupational networks, it also led to the continuance of previous situations. In so doing, it blocked some avenues of development and froze situations that had long been thought outmoded. For many individuals, the return to the land represented the failure of a life-choice adopted many decades before, but at the same time a solution that enabled them to cushion the effects of the social crisis. Already in the 1960s, the land had proved incapable of ensuring the survival of those who worked it. A number of peasants had migrated to the towns and cities where there were jobs. These "peasant-workers" represented a numerically and sociologically significant category, particularly in Poland and Slovakia. Several sociological studies carried out in the 1960s and 1970s were devoted to them. They showed how difficult it was for factory managers to plan activities, particularly in summer, when these individuals, who had remained peasants, returned, most often without warning, to their plots of land to perform necessary work in the fields. Disciplinary campaigns contributed to the socialization of these groups, without ever entirely integrating them into industrial life. This ability to leave their industrial jobs to perform their agricultural work represented a substantial element in favor of the peasants in negotiations within the villages. Now, the crisis that began in 1990 hit the secondary sector. The mono-industrial centers that had located in large numbers in rural sites, the better to take advantage of the available labor, were the first to close. The workers—many of them unskilled—withdrew, then, to their plot of land. But this had already failed to provide them with a living several years before, which was largely why they had left it. Part of the explanation for surplus employment or "concealed unemployment" has its source here. Another explanation relates to the destructuring of the collective farms themselves, particularly the great state farms mentioned above. For the agricultural workers who had been suddenly thrown out of work, the individual plot remained the only available resource. One last explanation lies in the absence of rationalization of employment on some of the big corporate farms. These were "recomposed" on the basis of the preservation of employment levels, reproducing more or less the compromises identified in the industrial enterprise in the previous chapter. Iliev speaks in the Bulgarian case of the extension of certain elements of the compromise struck before 1989 between the cooperative managers and individuals who were masters of their small plots. After that date, it would seem that there had been a trade-off between their successors, in so far as the big companies hesitated to acquire land on account of the fragility of the leases. They preferred to invest in the purchase of equipment, while the small farmers retained their negotiating power by allowing them to rent land and keeping control of the villages.[13] Agrarian dualism, on the one hand, the permanence of certain networks, on the other, and reciprocal dependencies thus ensured continuity from one period to the next. In Bulgaria, Gerald Creed has been able to show how the Bulgarian peasantry were able to mobilize the resources accumulated under socialism to forearm themselves against the effects of the new policy after 1990, which was perceived as a grave risk of "repeasantization," when they had managed to free themselves from peasant life in the 1950s and subsequently, particularly thanks to the combining of several jobs.[14]

The question of agricultural excess employment is linked to the issue of the land market and multiactivity. We can understand, for the reasons outlined above, that, in the absence of alternative local employment, individuals who were previously employed in industry and found that their only means of survival lay in their household plot, tended to hang on to that plot for as long as possible. More exactly, in order to survive, they had to find additional means, and it is these alternatives to a situation that is already economically unviable that account for the absence of a market in land. In this connection, income from working abroad has generally represented the most advantageous solution. There are many cases where one spouse, often the wife, goes off for several months to work in a Western country. The opening of internal EU borders in 2004 facilitated these temporary migrations. Added to this are supplementary forms of work of all kinds, whether it be the spouse having a service job in the local administration or in a local shop or the grandparents being able to supplement the family income thanks to a pension. Finally, the proximity of Eastern frontiers bordering on very deprived countries provided the opportunity for all kinds of "dealings," producing rapid, but irregular, gains, the most extreme having undoubtedly been the evasion of the embargo imposed on Serbia. One way or another, a whole range of resources of the order of individual "resourcefulness" ensured the survival of microholdings. However, this has correspondingly restricted the modernization of land use, shackling the efforts of those who, for want of land, are unable to specialize. Thus a semisubsistence agriculture emerged, admittedly safeguarding the existence of a very great number of individuals, but doing so at the expense of the rationalization of agriculture. Agricultural modernization also suffered from the desires of the public authorities, which, in wishing to protect themselves against any undue risk, favored leases that are commonly regarded as too short and a policy of very prohibitive loans. Both young people trying to enter the market and farmers who wished to expand their holdings found themselves penalized as a result.

In Romania, the public authorities put considerable obstacles in the way of the restitution process, in order to hold on to the better part of state lands.[15] They made wide use of bureaucratic means by limiting the time period for claims to 90 days, with an obligation to provide the original of titles to land, together with a copy. Even if this time period represented an increase over the one initially laid down, the process of property recovery was substantially hindered by it. Obviously, few individuals were able to assert their rights within the time periods and in the terms laid down. Moreover, the burden of proving what had befallen them lay with the victims of the Communist regime's exactions, yet they were prevented from consulting the archives of the Securitate; 80,000 peasant farmers presented themselves as victims, but most were denied the means of proving the political character of their past fate. Similarly, it was extremely difficult to prove that the "donations" by which the peasants were forced to give up their lands in the 1950s and 1960s were extorted from them by force. Moreover, these restitutions involved no more than 10 hectares in the hills, though not in the plains, and the law passed in February 1991 stipulated that restitution was an ideal to be pursued, but one that could not be achieved in every case. Finally, the former driving forces in the villages, in particular the church and its parishes, were not able to recover their prewar possessions and, as a consequence, by contrast with what had happened in the aftermath of the 1918–1921 reform, they did not play the expected leverage role. In that earlier period, the parishes had assumed a decisively important role in the rebirth of agriculture. The post-1990 restitutions actually met the wishes of the very small peasants, but in no way contributed to a restructuring of land-holding or agriculture.

In Bulgaria, the inheritor party to the Communist Party (the Bulgarian Socialist Party) and the Liberal Party engaged in continuous competition, which led to endless reversals of policy and, at the end of the day, a thoroughgoing destruction of the world of agriculture.[16] The quantity of land redistributed was very small by comparison with other countries. The average amount of land recovered was 1.3 hectares. Hence the dispersion of agricultural holdings and the reappearance of the land question, since the law had not provided for any form of obligatory consolidation of plots. Many individuals living in the towns recovered their land on one basis or another, but did not for all that return to the countryside, hence giving rise to a high degree of speculation in land. To this may be added the aging of the new owners. In 1995, 60.5% of them were already over 60. Only 5% of those who were able to recover land were aged under 40. As of the end of August 1995, there were 2,389 cooperatives possessing, on average, 771 hectares (40% of the land in cultivation) and 585,400 members. Though very rare in the mountainous regions of the southwest (where land holdings are fragmented and not very extensive), there were many such cooperatives in the Danubian Plain and the Thracian Basin. Where private structures are concerned, 1,777,000 holdings have emerged, covering altogether 2,391,000 hectares. The overwhelming majority of these are microholdings; 87% of those working them have less than one hectare of land; 69% cultivate less than 0.5 hectare.[17] In all the countries, redistribution policies were in the end supported in a most irregular fashion; agricultural policies were lacking; and the modernization of the countryside was held back. For example, between 1989 and 2004, the Polish land market saw little development, with the average size of holdings rising only from 6.9 to 8.1 hectares. In Romania in the same period, it barely rose above 3.5 and in Bulgaria scarcely exceeded 3 hectares.

Actor Dynamics

There have been considerable changes in status among those in agriculture, in so far as, under the impact of the collapse of the collective structures, land restitution, sales and leases, together with the emergence of associations, the dynamics of transformation have thrown up new actors, while others have disappeared into unemployment and exclusion. Landowners, small and large (though rarely medium-sized), agricultural workers, the unemployed and intermediaries in the agribusiness chain have each had very different resources, both between and within each of the groups mentioned. Does the distinction between "winners" and "losers" in the transformation also apply to agriculture? Certainly it does, but not in the same way as in industry. Between the two sectors, the availability of previously acquired resources turned out to be a decisive factor.

In industry, the implementation of new technologies or the modernization of production units rendered the knowledge accumulated before 1989
entirely obsolete. The "do–it–yourself" approach was of no use whatever
in forearming oneself or in adapting the new technologies. In agriculture,
by contrast, accumulated knowledge was reinvested to a much greater
extent.[18] These resources were, first, family resources. This applies in the
case of those who returned to farming, which turned out to be a fiasco
when their parents had left agriculture many years before. By contrast,
there was success for those who, on account of the size of their holdings
and also networks of contacts, took over holdings. The resources were,
second, power resources. This was true for the whole group of technical
directors or engineers, and also of bureaucrats in the central and regional
administrations, who were able to orient themselves in contexts that had
undergone overwhelming change as a result of the privatization of their
previous jobs. Alongside a substantial fall-off in agricultural employment,
which differs from one country to the next, we find the development of
three joint dynamics that apply in all the countries.

The Absence of a Return of Inheritors

The first dynamic concerns the absence of any return of the former prewar landowners. They met with a general refusal to return their property
to them after 1990. This marked both a desire not to reproduce the antagonisms that had been vehicles of such painful class conflicts and a concern
not to see certain populations come to the fore again, such as churches or
Jewish emigrant populations. The desire of certain Jewish communities to
have their rights recognized in respect of what they regarded as despoil-
ment verging on pure and simple theft and not an expropriation more or
less grounded in the law, as in the case of the old nobility or the churches,
is a concern that was given short shrift. The question of Jewish property
was once again subject to a broad taboo. By contrast, negotiations and
partial agreements did occur with some ecclesiastical hierarchies, with the
churches recovering some of their property. For these reasons, the pros-
perous landowners who emerged after 1990 derived their wealth mainly
from the immediately preceding period, that of Communism, and sometimes from the conditions associated with the forms of land ownership at
that time. In this regard, the Communist period definitely represented a
break with the past and a considerable opportunity for some individuals.

Conflicts

The second dynamic concerns the tremendous conflicts of interest that set
distinct social categories against each other in the East European countryside by virtue of the particular resources they were able—or unable—to
mobilize. This involved, on the one hand, historic resources relating to the
postwar agrarian reforms or to the Communist period and, on the other,

networks of relations arising as part of family trajectories or occupational milieus. Here the bonds formed in technical or intermediate jobs, in sales or supply, or, alternatively, as engineers turned out to be decisive—jobs that were legion on the collective farms and in the commercial circuits surrounding agricultural holdings. Among those normally referred to as the post-1990 winners, we find those people who managed to take skillful advantage of the new rules of the game, thanks to technical competence acquired on the state farms or the cooperatives. They were able to profit from the cheap sell-off of machinery when state farm equipment was dispersed, and they knew, above all, how to lease or buy land to constitute what were, often, efficient farms. In the same way, the former directors of the cooperatives or the state farms managed to adapt by converting their political and economic resources. There were people able to exploit ambiguities in the law, retard the process of restitution, and retain control of farms whose intimate workings they understood. They were largely backed in this by local intermediate trading companies (dairies, wholesalers, and abattoirs). Examples of embezzlement, corruption, and extortion are legion here again. As for the newcomers from the West, they were mostly in cahoots with the big distribution centers. They may be referred to as agricultural capitalists. Endowed with great technical skills, knowing Western markets well and assisted by powerful connections, they contributed to rapidly modernizing the rural areas, with the inequalities and dependencies that brought. Also, Poland is a paradox in that the considerable advantage it derived before 1989 from the presence of a massively private agriculture transformed itself into a major shortcoming once the Communist structure disappeared. On the one hand, the characteristic of private agriculture, made up of resistance to Communism and individual resourcefulness showed itself to be sadly powerless in coping with the market constraints harshly imposed in 1990. On the other hand, the absence (or lesser presence) of collective farms resulted in the lesser availability of engineers and technicians who, by contrast, in the other countries, have turned out to be one of the engines of modernization and of land recomposition.

Continuities and Discontinuities

The third dynamic involves both continuity and discontinuity where the categories of actors dominating the East European countryside are concerned. It has on several occasions been interpreted in terms of a revival of the agrarian dualism that specifically characterized this European zone, at least until 2000. Thereafter one finds a decline of collective forms on account of market constraints. However, the collective farms have continued to be powerful actors in some countries. They attest, in part, to the permanence of state power and, in part, to the capacity of certain individuals, particularly the former managers, to reorder, on a different legal basis, units providing employment for a large number of individuals. This is particularly the case in the Czech Republic, Romania, and Eastern

Germany. In Poland, the abolition of the collective farms led to a generalized impoverishment of the populations concerned. The collapse of the collective state farm left significant groups of people entirely without resources, and they are now vegetating in territorial "pockets" of unemployment and social exclusion. Whereas state farms employed 450,000 people in 1990, 10 years later the figure had fallen to below 100,000. These groups seem all the more abandoned for the fact that the previous regime had strongly favored them, and their dependence on the state is widely stigmatized. These people came from impoverished agricultural regions before the Second World War, most often in the Eastern border areas, and they had come to find not only possibilities of employment, but also housing. The collective farm had put a roof over their heads; it had provided them with an income, a working environment, and, most often, a home—in short, an identity. However, even before 1989, studies had highlighted their low level of social cohesion and the significant presence of pathologies, including alcoholism and, often, illiteracy.

However, if for several agricultural directors, the reformulation of corporate forms kept their accumulated capital in being, for many former small landowners, forced into cooperatives before 1989, the recovery of their lands after this date did not spell an increase in their standards of living. On the contrary. By dint of the erosion of their purchasing power in the 1990s and very harsh economic difficulties associated with the obsolescence of equipment and its nonrenewal, their level of wealth fell. Recriminations over the new rules were everywhere accompanied by the observation that "though in the past there was money and no machines, now there are machines but no money to acquire them with." Often aged, these former cooperative members now hold a few thousand square meters or, at best, a few hectares. They have had neither the skills nor the knowledge to adapt to the new economic circumstances, which required knowledge of the market and direct access to distributors. As a result, some have been forced to lease their lands to the former managers of the collective farms.

In this way they have contributed, sometimes against their will, but sometimes to their satisfaction, to reproducing collective forms of organization. The fact that the beneficiaries of such operations have most often been the former managers of the collective farms have made their regrets the more bitter. The great majority of these small—or very small—farmers have also felt the need to find additional resources, which have proved essential to the survival of their farms. This has largely involved dual activity, a common phenomenon in Western Europe, but not at all on the scale experienced in the East. It has also involved drawing on the pensions of grandparents living under the same roof on the shared farm. This has contributed to keeping the extended family model in being, since three generations often coexist in a single house.

After 15 years of transformations, the differences between countries are great. Observers agree that two patterns are distinguishable here. The first embraces the Czech Republic, the former GDR, Slovakia, Estonia, and Hungary. There the agricultural population has declined substantially; during the first decade, corporate farms on the cooperative model held their own, and then declined, while agribusiness's share has grown. The second group covers those countries where agriculture remains a large-scale activity: Lithuania and Latvia, Poland, and the two Balkan states. Whereas in all the other countries of the zone employment in the primary sector is declining sharply, it is maintaining its level in Poland and growing substantially in Romania and Bulgaria. Moreover, the average size of holdings is small in these countries (in 2000, it stood at 3.5 hectares in Romania, 6.7 in Bulgaria, and 8.1 in Poland). The share of agriculture in the GNP is in steep decline. If we take just the figures for Poland and Bulgaria, then between 1989 and 1997 it fell from 15% to 6% in Poland and from 26.6% to 17.3% in Bulgaria; it is estimated that 77% of Bulgarian farms sell almost nothing on the market, while the figure is 45% in Poland.[19] The data below indicate that there are often significant interconnections between phenomena of high agricultural employment, high unemployment, and weak purchasing power by comparison with that applying in EU15 at the time of enlargement.

The European Challenges

With regard to the exigencies and capacities of the European Union, the agricultural and rural situations of the East European countries posed difficulties that were all the greater for the fact that the timescales of the interventions were radically different in the different parts of the

Table 6.1   Agriculture and Unemployment

	Agricultural Employment (2002)	Agriculture as a % of GDP (2002)	Unemployment (2003)	Purchasing power as a % of EU Average	Spending on Food as a % of Income 1999
Romania	35.2	20.2	7.7	—	60
Bulgaria	21.2	10	18.7	—	48
Poland	19.6	2.5	19.2	38.0	30
Lithuania	18.6	2.1	12.7	29.3	58
Latvia	15.3	2.9	10.5	29.3	45
Slovenia	9.7	2.1	6.5	71.6	28
Slovakia	6.6	2.1	17.1	48.0	38
Estonia	6.5	2.9	10.1	37.3	39
Hungary	6.0	3.1	5.8	52.0	31
Czech Republic	4.9	1.2	7.8	58.7	32
EU 15	4.0	1.6	8.0		22

Source: This table is based on data found in Rieger, Elmar, "Wohlfahrt für Bauern? Die Osterweiterung der Agrarpolitik," *Osteuropa*, 54 (5–6), 2004, p. 298, and Segrè A. and Swinnen J.F.M., "Agricultural Transition and European Integration," *MOCT-MOST: Economic Policy in Transitional Economies*, 9 (3), 1999, pp. 215–228.

continent. Several countries in Western Europe, including France, saw agricultural labor force participation rates in the 1950s and 1960s that were comparable to those in Central and Eastern Europe 40 years later. In Western Europe, the dynamics of restructuring had depended on migrations from the countryside to the towns and cities, thus effecting transfers of population from the primary sector toward the industrial and, eventually, tertiary sectors. Now, in Eastern Europe, this virtuous circle proved strictly impossible to achieve. Why was this? First, because of the massive crisis besetting small and medium-sized towns, as highlighted above. Migratory dynamics had to be impeded, so as not to promote the formation of zones of unemployment and exclusion on the perimeters of the urban areas. Second, because the crisis in the industrial sector was not over; there was a need for the dynamics of restructuring to accelerate and no prospects for large-scale recruitment emerged clearly in this sector. As for job openings in the tertiary sector, it would take time for these to be credible and time was what was lacking.

The second defective element where time was concerned related to the pace of transformations. What occurred in Western Europe through separate interventions needed to be carried out simultaneously in Eastern Europe. We are referring here to the rural development policies that were outlined in Western Europe after the agricultural development policies had borne fruit—or, rather, revealed their excesses. The questions of environmental "conditionality," of quality, and later of "sustainable development" were posed after the errors of extreme agricultural development were recognized and admitted. They led in the 1980s to food scares and, more generally, to crises of confidence about the entire agribusiness sector. This is not how things were in Eastern Europe. The question of quality arose all at once, and it did so, moreover, out of a sense that it was lacking. Furthermore, the concentration and simultaneity of agricultural and rural development interventions had the effect of singularly raising the level of conformity with standards that was demanded, and to that degree accelerating the enforced adaptation procedures. The nonnegotiable imposition of sanitary and phytosanitary checks, carried out to Western standards, eliminated any alternative course that could have been taken in the East European countryside. From the outset, notions of quality were gauged by Western criteria. From this standpoint, Eastern Europe was assumed to have everything still to learn in this area. For this reason, local realities were largely ignored and only Western equilibria prevailed. In other words, the economic interests of Western Europe remained, for their part, unaltered.

How, then, was a response to be found to the problems mentioned above of excess employment and the absence of a land market and specialization, solutions to which had been needed in some cases for centuries, if we take the case of Poland, for example? In the view of the French agronomist Alain Pouliquen, the question of employment—or, more exactly, of excess employment—represents the most important challenge post-2004. If this were not to be resolved in the coming years, it would threaten the entire transformation of certain countries—Poland, Romania, and Bulgaria— with failure.[20] The social measures adopted to meet this major challenge have been massive. They draw largely on what was done in the West. By the use of early retirement schemes, they aim to tie individuals to the land by granting them the means of subsistence in exchange for putting the largest part of their holdings on the market. There is a threefold objective here: to enable individuals to have a decent life, to boost the land market, and to increase the size of medium-scale farms. Where the absence of specialization is concerned, we have noted the large-scale retention of mixed farming with stockbreeding in response to the risks associated with market fluctuations on the part of individuals who are not, as it happens, highly qualified. By preventing any specialization, this behavior has contributed to keeping traditional situations in being. This does not mean there has been no specialization. On the contrary, in some places ingenious farmers have managed to tailor their activities to labor-intensive segments of the economy. They are, however, the exception. But in the absence of a genuine public policy, such initiatives can only be individual ones, all the more so as the credit required for the basic outlay has been subject to very high interest rates. Proposals aimed at taking advantage of the rural heritage have emerged in the form of agritourism projects, but these ran up first against the crisis in agriculture, then against the question of standards. For such a policy to emerge, agriculture will undoubtedly have to be first assured of its continued existence. It is only on this condition that the farm can be assured of its main income stream, and tourism considered thereafter as a viable activity. This is what is at stake in the measures contained in the SAPARD Preaccession Program, which prefigured the Agricultural Guidance and Guarantee Fund (EAGGF Guidance). These measures are directed toward farm modernization, the training of young farmers, and the development of the working environment. Having said this, two factors have contributed since 2004 to the achievement of these objectives: the growth in purchasing power made possible by the specialization of agriculture, and the satisfaction derived from obtaining European funds as part of the CAP. Not only have incomes greatly increased, but land prices have also risen, thus enabling the market in land to begin to move.

Finally, for all these development measures to function correctly, it seems necessary, above all, that the workers in agriculture should be organized. Now, on this point there are still glaring deficiencies. The notion of comanagement of reform by the professional actors in agriculture became taboo in the 1990s and institutional actors were also sadly lacking. The question of institutional partners had not arisen in the Communist period, insofar as the agricultural world had its own representative agricultural organizations. These were admittedly beholden to the Communist party, but they were nevertheless largely integrated into the decision-making forums so far as the primary sector was concerned. After 1990, the farmers' organizations largely failed to support change for a whole series of reasons ranging from their disappearance or absence to their being not very much involved by the authorities in public decision making or their having developed into political organizations. As in the case of declining labor unionism and a dialogue between employers and unions that was, as we shall see in the next chapter, most often merely formal, the agricultural trade unions did not want to assume responsibility for the conduct of reform. The torpedoing by the Samoobrona Party in 2000 of the policy of "concertation" proposed by the Polish authorities speaks volumes. Rather than engage in a policy of the comanagement of reform that would force it to cooperate over long years, assuring it of great professional legitimacy, that party set conditions on its participation that would inevitably be rejected.[21] The agricultural advice organizations, which were present before 1989 in all the countries and recognized for their competence, often limited their field of activity after that date to the large farms. As a result, they abandoned the ones that had greatest need of their assistance, namely the farms of less than 20 hectares. It also seems doubtful, in this connection, whether the preparation period for administrations for the management of European funds actually fostered the emergence of competent social and occupational partners in agriculture. This is one of the major issues in the new European programming exercise (2007–2013), at a point when competitive pressure from the OECD countries is increasing.

Conclusion

Investigating the historical realities of East German agriculture, the anthropologist Michel Streith concluded that the land was not uniform and a variety of forms of farming were employed.[22] Extending his analysis to the Czech case of Bohemia-Moravia, the geographer Violette Rey argued in 1996 that "there is a danger that the dualism of agrarian structures will impose itself as the dominant signature of post-socialism,"[23] with a number of special cases like the former GDR and Bohemia-Moravia where large units win out alongside vulnerable small holdings. Some years later, this judgment is also shared by Christian Giordano, who takes the view that the return of dualism marks the end, in the short term, both of microholdings, given their very low chances of survival, and corporate forms, on account of the constraints associated with the competition rules involved in integration into the EU market. In this scenario, only three forms of holding would, in the medium term, remain: large family farms, agribusiness farms, which European integration will strengthen, and medium-sized farms sustained largely by the structural funds. Alain Pouliquen backs up this view, foreseeing a substantial transformation of the actors involved, announcing the short-term disappearance of nonprofitable farms, the reduction of the number of jobs on the corporate-type farms, the introduction of mechanization and advanced technologies, and the modernization of the processing chains and industries. The equilibrium of the countryside is thus going to be thoroughly upset on account of radical changes to be expected at the level of the landownership structure and following the setting aside of very large areas of land, while in some places not working will bring in more revenue than working. Having said this, the period that began in 2004 has brought to light a situation that few observers had envisaged before that date, namely the bolstering of micro-ownership thanks to subsidies from the CAP and the structural funds, which, far from being targeted at modernization, have been much more oriented toward individual consumption. It is the major paradox of the new situation that it sustains in Eastern Europe a type of farming that the entire tradition of Western Europe impugns, having almost wiped it out. In a context in which incomes are still low and alternatives exist in terms of migration, it is conceivable that this reality will last for some time yet, largely supported by the European Union.

CHAPTER SEVEN

Labor Relations. The Weakness of the Social Dialogue

For a while in the early 1990s, as Communism collapsed, it was possible to take the view that the labor unions would be among the main beneficiaries of regime change and, like Solidarnosc in Poland, would be the driving forces of the civil society that was expected to emerge. The possibility of making collective agreements and the right to strike, which were granted to them from the outset, alongside their inclusion in the tripartite decision-making forums that emerged at the time, seemed a guarantee of their effectiveness. Very soon, however, two dynamics played their part in wrecking these prospects. The first of these was the way negotiation at company level took precedence over industry-wide bargaining in the 1980s in Western Europe. The East German transformation accentuated this trend toward the decentralization of collective bargaining and the opening up of companies to Eastern Europe amplified it further, on the back of the widespread argument that extrication from Communism could not mean a tightening of the external constraints imposed on enterprises. The latter should, it was said, operate in legislative and occupational environments freed from all collective obligations. Central and Eastern Europe thus presented itself as the long-awaited opportunity for executives in all camps, West and East, who were eager to extend a type of "flexible management," without opposition from arguments that were easily ascribable to the preceding Communist period and, on that basis, widely condemned. From the outset, collective action and the protection of jobs were denounced as relics of the past. In the opinion of Václav Klaus, then prime minister of the Czech Republic, the labor unions and the employers' organizations seemed like "residues of socialism" (*Lidove Noviny,* 5 November 1993, cited in Myant).[1] The second dynamic was that of the European Union, whose neoliberal strategy promoted market liberalization and reduced social policy to merely ensuring the mobility of workers. This is why social policies were relegated to the national policy sphere, if indeed they existed at all. Within this framework, the employers' organizations had little interest in playing the game of cooperation and negotiation. The state was thus the better able to promote privatization policies. As for foreign investors, they had little incentive to play the social development card, in so far as labor law deregulation, a low-wage policy, and the absence of constraints with regard to labor relations were key assets in sustaining the dynamic of direct foreign investment. For these reasons, it seems difficult to speak of a "system of industrial relations" in Central and Eastern Europe after 1989 in terms of the model devised by the sociologist J.T. Dunlop.[2] It seems more legitimate to emphasize "localized arrangements" as a function of particular situations, along the lines that we have seen in the last two chapters. The aim of this chapter is to understand how the disorganized state of the social partners makes it possible to explain the two weaknesses that affected Central Europe during the period of this study: low levels of conflictuality and of sectoral regulation. Rather than social dialogue, this twofold weakness left room only for the two opposing poles: tripartism at the national level and enterprise bargaining. At these various levels, the results were very mixed. With a view to accession to the European Union, which drove the action of governments throughout this period, the adjustment of economic policies alone prevailed. Europeanization was there none.

The Social Partners

The first partner that has to be mentioned here is the state. Throughout the period, it remained a privileged one, if only because it remained a large-scale employer and, having charge of collective affairs, it enjoyed substantial prerogatives, chiefly of the legislative kind. We shall examine tripartite policy after first dealing with the partner organizations.

The Labor Unions

The end of the monopoly of Soviet-style trade unionism cleared the path for an enormous pluralism in Central and Eastern Europe. In the first case we shall examine two ideologically opposed labor union confederations that were pitted against each other, surrounded by sectoral unions of little importance. The first confederation was heir to the old Soviet-type unions, while its adversary inherited the aspirations of 1989. Instances of this type of opposition are found in Poland and Bulgaria, with OPZZ (the All-Poland Alliance of Trade Unions) and CITUB (the Confederation of Independent Trade Unions) on one side, and Solidarnosc and Podkrepa on the other. A polarization of the labor union field of this kind does not, however, exclude alliances formed at the grassroots level within companies. The second type of unionization is found in the Czech Republic, Slovakia, and Slovenia, countries where a confederation uniting the great majority of industry unions operates. The last case is that of Hungary and Romania, which are characterized by an enormous pluralism of labor unions. At the end of 2000, Central and Eastern Europe had an average rate of unionization of around 30%. The highest rates were in the Czech Republic, Slovakia, and Slovenia. In these countries, collective labor agreements are mandatory. By contrast, the rates were 18% in Hungary and Estonia. Clear criteria of representativeness were often lacking, as in Poland, while in Latvia, the LBAS union was the only one officially recognized within the National Tripartite Cooperation Council. In Slovenia, it was the Chamber of Commerce and Trades, a key actor in economic life that fulfilled this role.

Given the absence of a law on the criteria of representativeness for employers' and workers' organizations, the various organizations claiming representative status were able to gain membership of the tripartite commissions, and decentralized negotiations expanded as a consequence. For collective agreements to be seen as legitimate, Poland, the Czech Republic, and Slovakia decided that the unions would need to have the support of 50% of the employees. For the other countries a threshold of 10% of employee support was generally regarded as sufficient. What has been called the "Czech model" was based on the choice between a company union and an elected employee council. Only if there is no union do works councils exist. On the other hand, this "model" failed in Slovakia in 2003. More than 15 years after 1989, there are, then, 3 forms of representation of interests structuring the labor union field in Central and Eastern Europe. The first is based solely on the company union. This model covers Estonia, Latvia, Lithuania, and Poland (here the union enjoys a legal monopoly, except in state enterprises). The second model is based on the choice between a union and a works council. This is the case in the Czech Republic and in Slovakia between 2002 and 2004. The third model is based on dual representation on the basis of a labor union and a works council. This has applied in Hungary since 1992, in Slovenia after 1993, and in Latvia, where it was possible from 2002 onwards.[3]

The Employers

The employers' organizations have been very weak since the beginning of the 1990s. This can be explained, initially, by a lack of tradition. The maintenance of several state enterprises encouraged sustained relationships and networks. Thus, the "clubs" where members of the old industrial structures meet have predominated. There are said to be as many as 80 in some countries, and even 90 in Romania and Hungary. These clubs have enabled the bonds between the economic and political sectors to be reinforced, bonds that, as we saw in chapter two, underpinned the process of property transformation. For "spheres" or "networks" of this kind, collective bargaining could only be seen as an undesirable constraint. One of the underlying dynamics of post-1989 transformation has, indeed, been based on secrecy of decision making, both at central and local levels. In many cases, the key to success turned out to be acting

Table 7.1   Levels of Organizational Membership on the Part of the Social Partners and Coverage of Agreements (as a Percentage of Employees)

	Unions	Employers	Coverage by Collective Agreements	Works Councils?
Slovenia	42	50	98	Yes (widely found)
Slovakia	35	50	48	Yes (low coverage)
Hungary	25	40	42	Yes (medium coverage)
Czech Republic	30	30	35	Only in exceptional cases
Poland	18	19	30	Only in state enterprises
Latvia	19	30	20	Few as yet
Estonia	15	30	20	No
Lithuania	14	20	13	Planned

Source: This table is based on data found in Kohl, Herbert, "Arbeitsbeziehungen in den neuen EU Mitgiedstländern und ihre Implikation für das europäische Sozialmodell," in Timm Beichelt and Jan Wierlgohs (eds.), *Perspektiven der europäischen Integration nach der EU—Osterweiterung*, Workshop Documentation, FIUT Viadrina, 2005, pp. 51–71.

quickly and without witnesses. Moreover, one of the ways of ransacking public enterprises was to work under cover of the creation of subcontractor networks (see chapter six). The choice of the market, regarded as more lucrative than state socialism, did not in any way imply a dimension of negotiation or redistribution, but a process of silent seizure and appropriation. The creation of chambers of industry followed this same pattern. One of the objectives was, if not to keep enterprises state-run, then at least to extract the greatest possible profit from them where they had to be sold off. This mainly involved the extortion of bribes and the maintenance of the former managers in their jobs. The same goes for a large number of labor unions that were in positions of strength in certain enterprises. All in all, almost 20 years after the fall of Communism, employers' organizations do not exist as fully fledged partners in dialogue in Eastern Europe; in 2005, they represented between 30 and 40% of industrial companies or, in other words, between 2 and 5% of the total number of enterprises.

Low Levels of Social Conflict

Given the substantial changes to occupational statuses and modes of life, we might have expected an explosion of discontent and, consequently, the formation of social movements. The theory of democratic transitions postulates that the new regimes resulting from the collapse of an authoritarian or dictatorial regime are often confronted with outbreaks of conflict.[4] Why should this be? Because such periods are conducive to the accumulation of recovered freedom, the disappearance of fear, and the decentralization of decision-making processes. As a result, demonstrations and strikes increase in number. This hypothesis is confirmed in practice by the Latin

American experiences, which were characterized by a large number of violent, if not indeed lethal, conflicts. As early as 1990 in Eastern Europe, a number of observers feared the return of the military,[5] the destabilization of democracies, civil violence, and an escalation of protest, or even anomic movements.[6] In 1991, Adam Przeworski suddenly announced that "the East has become the South."[7]

Two Interpretations

In reality, conflicts in Central and Eastern Europe have not been extensive. The national average has been relatively low, even if we must stress at the outset the lack of statistical information, particularly in the early post-1989 years. At that time, strikes in fact came to be organized only within official trade union circles. Over the period, conflict was concentrated mainly in certain sectors, and in those sectors conflicts were numerous, frequent, and on a significant scale. This was particularly the case in the public sector, in the fields of health, education, the civil service, and the justice system. Here the main claims related to wages, which were constantly indexed to minimum wage scales. Two other sectors were involved: public transport—mainly railroads and aviation—where the big public companies were undergoing restructuring and privatization, and the agricultural sector, where hostility to the abolition of public subsidies combined with fears relating to enlargement to bring the farmers out on to the streets. Two radically opposing schools of thought have emerged in Eastern Europe to explain this state of affairs. The first of these contends that there was a high level of conflict, while the second sees the scope of such conflict as being, in the end, rather limited.

Examining the data available for the brief period 1989–1993, Ekiert and Kubik have argued that there was a significant level of conflict in the aftermath of Communism.[8] The repertoire of the actors in struggle was often nonviolent, street demonstrations were large, and some labor stoppages led to hunger strikes. These actions involved all social groups, though farmers, industrial workers, public sector employees, and the young were to the fore. Poland is the country that saw most demonstrations of this type in that period. If we take number of days lost as a guide, then the scale of the protests increased over time. The figure for Poland is still the highest, at 14,881 in total, as opposed to 6,071 in the former GDR, 2,878 in Hungary, and 2,419 in Slovakia. The high level of conflict in East Germany was a surprising phenomenon, considering the absence of strikes since 1933 and the abolition at that date of labor unions. It is, however, understandable given the supremacy of West German trade unionists in the East German structures. An important conclusion of the two authors cited relates to the identification of the old organizations as engines of protest—this is particularly the case in Poland—and, above all, to the fact that they were resolutely reformist. They were not driven by any intention of changing the system, but by the concern to defend employees' interests, particularly in terms of employment. Other studies, based on the same findings, have concluded that union strategies on the ground within enterprises were similar even when the national organizations were unyieldingly opposed to one another at the top. This goes both for Poland and Bulgaria. In the latter country, however, we must stress that unity between the unions underlay the general strike of late December 1996 that led directly to the fall of the Videnov government.[9] Concentrating their attention more specifically on Poland,[10] the two writers conclude that civil society was strengthened in that country by conflict, but by conflict that was, above all, nonviolent, generally not opposed to the existing system, and directed toward the economic sphere. For his part, Kirov has shown that the conflicts were particularly large in scale in the period preceding the introduction of the Currency Board in 1997. From that date onward, there was far less industrial strife.

On the other hand, using these same data, Vanhuysse has attempted to show that, whether taken in themselves or related to the same phenomena in other countries, they attest to a very low level of conflict in Central Europe. Of the 1,476 protests that occurred in Poland, only 8% were violent; in Hungary, the figure was 23% out of 699 protest actions and in Slovakia 2% out of 295 actions. There were only a small number of strikers: in the period 1990–1995, the figure for Hungary was 6.6 strikers per thousand workers, while for Poland it was 11.3, the Czech Republic 2.8, Slovakia 1.1, and Romania 2.2. Comparison shows these figures to be much lower than those for Western Europe. In the same period, the figure for France was 0.5 strikers per 1000 employees (but this does not take into account the actions in the Juppé period in 1995), for Sweden 7.5, for Great Britain 13.7, and for the United States 1.6. They are also much lower by comparison with Latin America, where, though the figure is 1 per thousand in Columbia, it is 8.5 in Venezuela, 33 in Peru, and 93 in Brazil. With regard to the numbers of days lost, we arrive at identical findings. In Hungary, during this period, the figure is 8.7 days per thousand workers, while it is 28.2 for Poland, 0.7 for the Czech Republic, 10 for Slovakia, and 11.3 for Romania. The figure for France is 12.7, for Sweden 46.9, for Denmark 25.7, for Great Britain 19.9, and for the United States 28.5, while in Latin America the number of days lost in Venezuela is 39, in Brazil 144, and in Peru 134. For all these reasons, Ekiert and Kubik's approach needs to be put into perspective, even though it is widely reflected in the specialized literature. The available data neither allow us to conclude that there was "widespread instability," nor that democracy was in danger. In 1991, less than 1% of Polish workers participated in strikes. Moreover, we have to distinguish between the number of strikes and the number of strikers. In 1993 in Poland, for example, though there are more strikes (reflecting the peak reported by Ekiert), it is in fact in the previous year, 1992, that the largest number of strikers is found.

A Low Level of Institutionalization

How, then, are we to explain this apparent paradox of a lull in labor protest in such a troubled period? The Hungarian sociologist Gerkovits cites the size of the rural population, the absence of extreme inequalities in wages, and the growth of social expenditure as a percentage of GDP. We may counter this argument by pointing out that the rural population in Romania at times engaged in more strike actions than occurred elsewhere, and that farmers' demonstrations in Poland were among the biggest. Furthermore, though social expenditure was rising, this varied from country to country and the phenomenon has to be seen in terms of a very low starting point. The targeting of this expenditure was more toward pensions than employment and, moreover, the number of beneficiaries was falling over the period, as we saw in chapter three. And several studies, notably by Olsen, have successfully demonstrated that there is no direct link between material situation and a response in terms of protest action. The last argument comes from Tocqueville, who pointed out that it is not the most downtrodden individuals who protest and lead revolutions, but those who have a certain margin of freedom.

Are the variables that reflect typically national factors more credible? In Vanhuysse's view, mention must be made of the recognition in Hungary before 1989 of the right of association and the right to strike. Such a rapprochement between the parties before the fall of the Communist regimes had, he argues, fostered dialogue between the social partners. Similarly, Kubik and Ekiert suggest that the tripartism created in Hungary in 1988 led to a reduction in tension. This certainly did occur in that country. We also have to acknowledge that this right to social dialogue was already contained in the Polish law of 1984 creating the trade unions, and that an expanded social organization, PRON, had been created from scratch in Poland in 1986 to get around the acknowledged failure of the "new" labor unions. None of these measures in any way reduced the levels of conflict in that country during the period concerned. Still in Poland, the former dissident Jacek Kuroń, who became minister of labor in 1990, had created forums for discussion and social dialogue. However, tripartism very quickly came to look like a façade and was abandoned. More broadly in Central and Eastern Europe, tripartism seems to have succeeded in imposing peace wherever negotiations took place at levels higher than the enterprise (with regard to social minima). By contrast, where company-level agreements prevailed, tripartite agreements were not established or, if they were, they had little effect. In conclusion, the "corporatism" hypothesis, introduced to account for the low level of conflict, barely seems pertinent, given the weakness of the institutions of social dialogue. It does not seem possible to establish a correlation between the institutional forms of social dialogue and the number of agreements struck, either industry-wide or at company level. In Hungary the number of industry-wide agreements fell from 24 in 1992 to 7 in 1995, while the number of company agreements rose in the same period from 391 to 816. In Poland, 10 agreements were signed at a level above that of the company (industry-wide or regional) in 1996, as against more than 6,000 at company level, but in 1994, this figure had fallen below 4,000. In 1996, 65% of local union branches stated that wages were negotiated at industry level, with figures of 72% for the Czech Republic and 97% for Poland.[11]

In response, then, to the question of why this revolutionary period of the post-1989 years saw so few strikes in Eastern Europe, when the situation was largely one of instability and institutional openness, it is tempting to distinguish between the aspect of the individualization of behavior and that of the institutionalization process. The increasing individualization of behavior was based on the possibility now for everyone to refuse to join a trade union on grounds of personal freedom. Simultaneously, the collective organizations were freed from all constraints with regard to their members. Such a valorization of individual and collective freedom cleared the way for an enormous policy of *laissez-faire*, which was admittedly harmful to the interests of the most deprived and the least organized—in the event, most of the workers—but welcome to the interest groups and other structured organizations. The latter were able to exploit their former resources. In Bulgaria, in particular, this led to an enormous degree of predation on public property by the unions, and their private enrichment. Combined with the unions' difficulty to hold other than defensive positions, on account of growing unemployment and an uncertainty manipulated to an enormous extent by economic and political leaders, the decision to shift collective bargaining to enterprise level considerably reduced the prospects of successful protest action. In the view of Kubik and Ekiert, the later low level of conflict after 1995 can be explained, among other things, by the openness of action structures, and by institutional weakness with regard to the organization of protest.[12] We no doubt have to stress the distinction between individual and collective perceptions, as shown in many opinion survey findings both in East Germany and Poland. Though individual situations were in many cases assessed rather positively, the situation of others and of society more generally were negatively evaluated. Spread out over time, a negative evaluation at time T was positively corrected at T+1, thus showing up the enormous hope on the part of the surveyed individuals of individual improvement in the short term. These are all elements that can be drawn on to support the "individualization of behavior" argument, which is compatible to a great extent with the thesis of a consensus surrounding the decisions taken in the early stages and their expected outcomes. Over the period, in all countries and for some categories of people, the conviction prevailed that the reforms were the surest way of arriving at the hoped-for standards, since they were based on the freedom of the individual, an absence of collective constraints, and an opportunity for everyone to develop his or her skills.

What System of Industrial Relations?

It is only for the sake of convenience that the term "system," referring to Dunlop's writings, is used here, since no level of collective bargaining actually corresponds to it, and neither do the actors involved or the agreements struck. The question remains, nevertheless, of what level of agreement was arrived at on the different planes of collective, national, sectoral, or local bargaining.

The National Level: Tripartite Bargaining

In Eastern Europe, the most widespread form of social dialogue has been paritarism, though this is relatively rare in Western Europe.[13] This can be explained by the fact that there was no tradition of bargaining there, but, on the other hand, a high degree of state influence in economic affairs. Hence the natural form inherited from democratization after decades of centralism. In the period of intense crisis that was the early 1990s, tripartism was seen as the basis of the social pact founded on a division of responsibilities—beginning with the responsibility of the state. In this sense, paritarism was a condition of survival for governments that were called upon to have their populations swallow the bitter pill of reforms. The employment situation and the very low level of wages played a crucial role in the formation of social compromises. The aim was to find an equilibrium between a minimum level of security and essential reform of the economic and social systems. Hence, the essentially political character of the compromises arrived at through tripartism. In the absence of traditions of sectoral or company bargaining, it was ILO regulations that prevailed. This is very often recognized as having had the virtue of enabling major conflicts to be avoided while achieving some social gains, mainly in terms of setting social minima.[14] Tripartism first took shape in Hungary in 1988, then in Czechoslovakia in 1990, giving rise in 1993 to Czech and Slovakian National Councils. In 1993, Bulgaria and Romania created tripartite national bodies, followed the next year by Poland and Slovenia. In Bulgaria, the signing of the Association Agreement enabled the unions to impose social dialogue as a precondition (the same applied in Romania). In 1997, when the Currency Board was established under the aegis of the IMF, the unions played a major role, being brought in because of the need for consent on the part of the population. In most of the countries, tripartite councils worked on the basis of a triangular agreement that gradually acquired a basis in law: in Romania in 1997, in Slovakia and Estonia a year later, and in Poland in 2001.

The Limits of Tripartism

Despite efforts and expectations in 1989, tripartism came up against some very significant limits that gradually emptied it of its meaning. First, the tripartite decisions taken were never about subjects like the budget, privatization, incomes, or European negotiations, which were the major political issues of the period. During the 1990s, the paritary bodies had very little room for maneuver. Ultimately, they found themselves confined to carrying on within the strict limits of what had been adopted in 1990: namely, the negotiation of social minima and the minimum wage. Over time, with the exception of Hungary, they had little or no involvement in the field of social security. Moreover, no link was established between national negotiation and collective industry-wide negotiations. Tripartism had barely any influence over regional questions, where forums may have been set up by law, but in practice met little.[15] In reality, the state remained the main actor. As political fortunes fluctuated, it considerably reduced the scope of tripartism, and tripartite bodies were in fact abolished in Bulgaria and the Czech Republic without consultation with the social partners. In the early stages of the transformation process, social peace was the main objective. Governments were under pressure and agreements were signed as a result. Later, this need to associate the partners in decisions proved to be less crucial for governments, even though more agreements were signed as integration approached in 2004. Even so, the period of preparatory work for the programming of structural funds was not grasped by the various governments as an opportunity to involve the unions. Hence the trend here that is opposite to that in the West, where tripartite agreements are gaining renewed legitimacy and their numbers are growing.

Formalism seems to have largely predominated in Eastern Europe, with agreements having been drawn up either to conform to the—much reduced—demands of the European Union or to reflect the domination of flexibility rules. In 2002, the Hungarian Labor Code ratified a collective decision to raise the working day from 8 hours to 12 and the extent of permissible overtime to 200 hours per annum. Some observers of the Hungarian situation conclude from this that it opened up considerable scope for negotiation between the various parties. But the whole question is whether relations between them are balanced and agreements respected. The foregoing pages have shown that these relations are largely asymmetrical. Salary categories have been fixed, reference periods for negotiation have been extended, and rights of appeal to the labor inspectorate for nonpayment of overtime hours have been granted,[16] but the question remains to what extent these arrangements will be properly monitored, particularly as there has been a distinct weakening of union apparatuses in Hungary. Similarly, in 2005, an appeals commission was established in Bulgaria, but it has only a dozen members.

The Social Dialogue at Industry Level

National bilateral or tripartite relations have not been supported by an extensive sectoral structure. There have been few industry-wide agreements. In 1995, there were 35 such agreements in the Czech Republic, but the figure was only 12 in 2001. In Hungary, there were 24 in 1992, but 14 in 1998. These agreements were, therefore, exceptions. By comparison, 600 agreements are signed each year in France and 400 in Belgium. The absence of sectoral dialogue is an important indicator of the lack of a system of industrial relations. Moreover, this low number of agreements combines with a low level of coverage, since only around 10% of employees are concerned. The figure is 50% in Germany. Moreover, the Eastern European agreements are very general documents, which often content themselves merely with reproducing the law, without dealing with matters specific to the enterprise, namely questions of wages, jobs, and working conditions. The possibility of having these agreements apply to unrepresented employers (the extension rule) has not been utilized. The scope for this has even diminished in the Czech Republic.

Why have there been no industry-wide agreements? First because of the way public assets were restructured. Restructuring gave rise to an extreme diversity of companies in a single sector, to a proliferation of SMEs and to very low levels of unionization. Foreign companies have, for their part, confined their efforts to the economic and financial conditions of the firm, not of the sector. To this must be added the absence of intermediate levels, as we saw in the case of the administration in chapter four. The absence of a tradition and culture of negotiation have prevailed. Most importantly, as we have noted, it is difficult to impose a binding system on all enterprises at a time of many economic difficulties and when the emphasis is on individual freedom. This was the central argument used in East Germany to limit the scope of the institutional transfer of West German collective bargaining and relegate negotiation to enterprise level. Economic arguments were largely advanced to justify the exemption of companies declared incapable of financing very expensive procedures. "Exemption clauses" (*Öffnungsklausel*) were introduced and very rapidly became the norm. In Central and Eastern Europe, organizations do not have authority over those mandating them and are denied the right to sign agreements in their name. Moreover, since tripartism functioned a great deal at the centralized level, this contributed to hampering the decentralized level.

Company Level

Given the above-mentioned limitations at the national and sectoral level, one might have expected that the enterprise would fill the vacant place when it came to striking agreements. This has not been the case. How is this to be explained? Doubtless, first, by reference to the policy of privatizing the economy and the ensuing economic structure. On the one hand, a host of—sometimes intermingled—forms of ownership appeared, so that enterprises acquired by foreigners and those taken over by "insiders" coexisted with joint stock companies, whose shares were most often held by national investment funds, and with other companies that were

Table 7.2 Synoptic Table of Coverage by Sectoral Collective Agreements in the New Member States

	Number of multiemployer agreements	*Number of sectoral collective agreements*	*Extension Procedures*	*Number of workers covered*
Bulgaria		14 industry sectoral agreements and 46 branch collective agreements, most of them in the public sector (2000), but not complete coverage.	Yes, under ministerial decision (Labor Code, April 2001)	20%
Czech Republic	1998: 25	1997: 17 2001: 12		—
Estonia	2001: 10 subsector agreements	1999: 14 2000: 16 2001: 7	Yes, since act of June 2000	Fewer than 10%
Hungary	1998: 48 1999: 52	1998: 14 1999: 19	Yes, applicable according to article 34 of the Labor Code, but not used.	11% (in 1999)
Latvia		1999: 10		Fewer than 10%
Lithuania	—	—		Fewer than 10%
Poland	2000: 136	2000: 20	Yes, by decision of the Minister of Labor upon request of the social partners and under the new legislation in 2000.	Fewer than 10%
Romania	—	2001: 19	Yes, provisions apply to all workers in the sector.	
Slovakia	—	1993: 39 1998: 55 2000: 29	Possible when decided by the Ministry of Labor	Up to 60%
Slovenia	—	2000: 38 100% (mandatory)	Yes, when decided by the Ministry of Labor	100%

Source: European Union, *Industrial Relations in Europe* (DG Employment, 2002), p. 111; Daniel Vaughan-Whitehead, *EU Enlargement versus Social Europe? The Uncertain Future of the European Social Model*, Cheltenham: Edward Elgar, 2003, p. 245.

joint ventures. Hence the difficulty of grouping them in a single category. It was, ultimately, left to the directors to decide alone whether or not they treated the local partners as interlocutors. On the other hand, the big state enterprises went into decline, bringing the bastions of state trade unionism down with them. At the same time, the SME sector, which emerged powerfully, was not able to make up the difference, for at least two reasons. First, because only with difficulty did unionism take root in the private sector, and, second, because the structure of the SMEs often prevented it. Unlike small companies in the EU 15, which have on average nine employees and often employ highly skilled individuals in high-performance market segments, East European SMEs have between three (Poland) and five (Slovakia) employees, with low levels of skill, working more within the commercial, repair, or local services sectors and only rarely in highly developed services. The very high number of self-employed workers accounts for the low rate of unionization, particularly as foreign investors did not view unionization favorably either. The reasons most often cited by the latter for moving to Eastern Europe do not include a desire to develop social relations. On the contrary, alongside such factors as size of markets, wage costs, and individual skills, it is the absence of social "constraints" that attracts investors. The argument is rendered all the more explicit by the fact that the local public authorities compete fiercely with one another to attract investment, as we mentioned in chapter two. To the fore among their arguments are the cheapness of labor and the absence of any restrictive social agreements.

What are we to make, then, of the hypothesis that foreign investors can be said to have introduced strong social regulation, and that they are responsible for social as well as economic development? This does not necessarily contradict the foregoing, provided that three arguments are accepted. The first is that we are speaking here exclusively of big companies; in other words, large multinational enterprises with a strong partnership profile of the type some term "Rhenish," in reference to the pioneering work of Michel Albert.[17] It is certain that the big companies— and we are speaking here exclusively of big companies—are the drivers of social relations in Western Europe. Even if comanagement is less on the agenda in Europe as a whole, the social partners are nonetheless influential in strategic decisions over development in Eastern Europe. How are they to do this, other than by making their agreement conditional on the management's commitment to transfer the type of partnership in force within the mother company? The aim is to act so that the "less socially demanding" East European enterprise does not gain the upper hand and diminish a West European level of regulation that has been dented already. The exemplary case of this was provided by the IG Metall union in the negotiations carried out by Volkswagen to acquire Skoda in the early 1990s. Yet we should not be misled by this endlessly cited case. There is other evidence to show the poor level of working conditions imposed on the workers in companies acquired by foreign capital. We have examined this in chapter six. In Poland, some multinational companies make massive use of temporary (seven–eight months) contracts. Portet is particularly critical of how women are treated in that country, and not merely in the clothing sector, which is well-known for making use of so-called flexible forms of organization. These are characterized by limited contracts against a background of low wages and overtime working, not to mention what are at times degrading working conditions.[18]

East Germany had already provided what we might term the negative archetype of this type of transfer. The imposition of West German regulation had contributed to ruining East German companies by the excessively high cost of implementation, a lack of understanding of the rules by the East German actors, and, perhaps most importantly, discrepant expectations between the two sides. While West German organizations were fully involved in bargaining on skill levels, working hours, and wages, following a strategy that was more than a decade old, the East German workers and their representatives had only one aim in mind: preserving jobs, in a situation where, in a period of less than two years, almost three million were going to disappear out of the eight million recorded in 1990. For a whole series of reasons, which have to do with the initial conditions pertaining in the former GDR and also with the conditions laid down in the Monetary Unification Treaty, the relative maintenance of employment levels in East Germany was achieved on the basis of a deep imbalance in terms of working hours and wage conditions. These imbalances were still not rectified 15 years after unification, even though an agreement made in 1990 stipulated that equality of working conditions and wages between the two parts of Germany would be arrived at in the three years following unification. This example may stand for Eastern Europe as a whole: without prejudging the generous determination of the West European labor unions to play their part in the development of Eastern Europe, we have to admit that what was initially involved here was a desire to defend social gains that were greatly endangered by the new candidate states. All the more so—and this is the last argument—as the European Union makes it mandatory for multinational companies to elect a so-called European committee, whose presence is indicative, if not of a harmonization of behavior, then at least of operating rules within the Union. Now, on the eve of integration in 2004, fewer than one-fifth of the European works councils of companies active in the candidate countries had locals on them even as observers, never mind as members. It is thus a considerable exaggeration to see in this anything more than the very fragile beginnings of a social Europe, the reality of which is indeed belied by too many actual interventions by the Brussels authorities.

Failing Social Europe and Absent Social Dialogue

The basic reason why social partnership was not regarded as a key element in the dynamics of integration lies in the political will of the commission and, more generally, of the member states. The specialist literature makes a distinction between the "soft *Acquis*," which leaves the member states some scope for adaptation, and the "hard *Acquis*," which imposes community obligations using the threat of sanctions. Rather than make social dialogue a necessary condition for entry into the union with penalties in case of noncompliance, the EU left it as an option that the candidates might decide to choose. Some of them chose to apply it; others eschewed it, leaving states and employers untrammeled in their use of power. We have already seen how the labor unions were eased out of the dialogue in Hungary, and even how the paritary bodies were purely and simply abolished in some countries. Far from imposing a directive on this subject, EU legislation relied on recommendations, green or white "papers," and reports. In short, there were no binding arrangements. This lack of pressure was accompanied by the absence of any legal basis in the *Acquis* for collective bargaining. For this reason, two fundamental social freedoms—the possibility of drawing up collective agreements and of engaging in collective action in the form of strikes—were not safeguarded.[19]

The Absence of a Project for a Social Europe

When we were examining the structural funds and the policy of decentralization in the conclusion to chapter four, we noted how the commission's approach could be driven more by formal considerations than by concern for policy content. It did not, ultimately, raise the question of the relevance to Eastern Europe of certain development tools forged in the West. Clearly this was because priority was given to the dynamic that favored competitiveness and adjustment.[20] Admittedly, as with what happened in the countries of Southern Europe in the 1980s, there was some thinking on development tools. It led, among other things, to the doubling of the funds allotted for structural aid measures. Moreover, the commission was very innovative, at the time of the reshaping of the PHARE program (originally created as "Poland and Hungary: Assistance for Restructuring their Economies"), in granting greater room for maneuver to the candidate countries,[21] to the point where it has been possible to describe enlargement to the East as a model of its kind.[22] However, important criticisms have been leveled against the commission, and more generally against the member states, on the grounds that they did not respond to three challenges posed by the new members. The first of these relates to the dynamic of market liberalization, in the wake of the initial decisions adopted under pressure from the IMF. That dynamic simultaneously generated low wages, the deregulation of forms of employment, and an intensified pace of working. To this may be added a low level of collective agreements and a low level of social expenditure, when expressed as a percentage of GDP. The difference in the size of social budgets in the two parts of the continent is significant, since expenditure on employment policies is less than 1% of GDP in Eastern Europe, while it stands at 2.5% in the Western half of the continent. Such differentials imply a lower level of expenditure on active employment policies in general, and on vocational education or training in particular. The second challenge relates to the institutional differential between the two parts of Europe, given the way each has developed. Where the directing of aid as part of the European Social Fund (ESF) is concerned, the complexity of the various regulations has been criticized, together with the fact that local institutions were for a long time absent. The third issue relates to the refusal of the old members to take serious account of inequalities between the different parts of the union. "The social," to borrow Vaughan-Whitehead's expression, "was the poor relation in the negotiations."[23] The commission initially conceived its action on the basis of the Washington Consensus, which simply meant liberalizing the former Soviet-style economies without any accompanying social support measures, except to argue for the adoption of appropriate procedures and institutions. In other words, it refrained from pressing on the new members the demands in terms of employment policy and, more generally, of social solidarity that are normally associated with its name—demands it could have imposed as part of its assistance programs. Comparison of the lengths of time spent on negotiating the various chapters of the *Acquis Communautaire* leaves no doubt on this point. The chapter on social policy was among the quickest to be settled, which demonstrates how few regulations were to be adopted, or, if one prefers, shows the marked preferences of the East European governments for not assuming the task of imposing social constraints.

The allocation of structural funds could have reflected a desire to correct these differences, by taking better account of the realities of employment and prompting a reorientation of public budgets. In the event, the pursuit of competitiveness won out over all other considerations, all the more so as there were many economists in Eastern Europe who regarded social protection costs as unwelcome for emergent economies. As Vladmir

Table 7.3   Length of Negotiations (in Months) for Various Chapters of the *Acquis Communautaire*

	Bulgaria	Czech Republic	Estonia	Hungary	Latvia	Lithuania	Poland	Romania	Slov.	Slovak.
Freedom of movement	8	17	24	13	0	5	19	21	0	19
Competition	39	41	30	43	18	18	43	49	29	30
Agriculture	33	30	30	30	18	18	30	25	18	30
Taxation	10	25	31	19	13	10	28	20	9	25
Employment and social policy	6	20	13	14	16	4	18	6	3	14
Regional Policy	31	24	26	27	15	15	32	29	15	27
Environment	23	18	18	18	6	7	22	31	8	16
Justice and International Affairs	28	19	23	18	12	10	14	32	12	19

Source: This table is based on data found in Bönker, Frank, "Konsequenzen des EU-Beitritts für die Sozialpolitik in den neuen Mitgliedstaaten," in Amelie Kutter and Vera Trappmann, *Das Erbe des Beitritts. Europäisierung in Mittel- und Os Europa*. Baden-Baden: Nomos, 2006, p. 259.

Rys wrote, "to the extent that social criteria [were] not taken into account alongside the political and economic criteria, social protection questions [were] reduced to their economic aspects only."[24] Though the European Union greatly stresses consideration of human resources, in reality the commission does not concern itself with them. For the latter body, social support policies fall within the sphere of national policy.[25] According to Vaughan-Whitehead, the reason for this discrepancy between the union's stated intent and the actual absence of a European social policy is the fear that "enlargement may bring serious risks for social Europe," on account of inequalities between the various parts of the European Union, with the East having an underdeveloped level of social protection, general problems of social cohesion, and developments in many social fields running counter to the West. In the neoliberal agenda, argues Zusza Ferge, "there is no recommendation to attempt to approach full employment, while indirect pressure for privatization of pensions and health care is apparent in all accession reports."[26] In the view of the Hungarian sociologist, basing her opinion on the reading of 10 monitoring reports, social issues do not have an important place in the thinking here. Questions of poverty and exclusion receive scant treatment. In this respect, the dynamic of neoliberal globalization can be said to have prevailed very distinctly over that of Europeanization. To put it another way, the European project was barely distinct from the project of globalized liberalism, even though the exceptional situation in which Eastern Europe found itself called for other conceptions of support.

The Limits of a European Strategy

The issue of employment in its connection with enlargement was posed in a variety of different ways at Community level. First—and too often—in terms of the impact of enlargement on employment and labor markets in the member states. Some observers took the view that production would be transferred abroad at a faster rate than before, whereas others feared an influx of workers, skilled or unskilled, but prepared in any event to work for substantially lower wages. The second aspect considered was that of the free circulation of labor, as guaranteed by the EU Treaty. This became a subject of topical discussion from the point when the question arose of identical social entitlements on European soil for all European nationals. The better endowed, old member states found themselves obliged to provide cover for their employees, while the candidate states rightly feared a massive exodus of their most highly skilled individuals. The third aspect was preparation for the European Social Fund (ESF), which is extremely complex for the new entrants. The ESF is based, in fact, on a strategic document, the European Employment Strategy (EES), which calls on each member state to draw up a National Employment Action Plan, respecting several imperatives mentioned in chapter four above, such as lifelong learning, gender equality, the social dialogue, and so on. Combining these various documents—the European Employment Strategy, the Joint Assessment Paper, Sectoral Plans for Human Resources and Employment, and the Regional Program involving the Training Dimension—proved very difficult, on account of the obligation the candidate states were under to adopt all these documents simultaneously and link them together.[27]

The obstacles the candidate countries came up against were associated, first and foremost, with the imperatives linked to the strategy we have just mentioned. The notion of equality of opportunity between the sexes—which is a recurrent theme of the employment policies of the European Commission—is an unfamiliar problem for the new member states. Before 1989, they could—rightly—claim significant advances in terms of female employment by comparison with the West: it was of the order of 90% in the best countries of the Eastern bloc, with Bulgaria and the GDR in the lead. They were particularly able to claim this because social policies had encouraged parental leave, guaranteed return to work for young mothers, and developed sizeable daycare facilities within enterprises (see chapter one). However, long before the fall of Communism, several Polish and Hungarian studies had shown a deep inequality both in hierarchical responsibilities and in the division of domestic tasks. In each case, women were treated worse than men, and this was sharply reflected in wage differentials. This inequality between the sexes was accentuated after 1990 for several reasons. Women were made redundant in enormous numbers for the simple reason that they were less well qualified. Over the decade, and with the notable exception of Hungary, female unemployment was much greater than male. Moreover, this discrimination was intensified by conversion aid policies that systematically favored male jobs, whether in skills programs or in the public works projects set up in the municipalities. We shall see this in the final chapter. From 1990 onward, levels of social benefit diminished, limiting women's independence even more. In this scenario of exclusion, Roma women without doubt suffered most, as has been shown by some important studies, particularly those carried out in Bulgaria, by virtue of their status as recipients—as mothers—of social funds before 1989. During the 1990s, the woman question received no attention in any country, other debates having dominated, if not monopolized, the public arena.

A second strand of the European Strategy that was barely incorporated into policy—or only incorporated with great difficulty—was that relating to "initial" and "continuing" training. The question of educational dropout was only seldom taken into account. The same was true of illiteracy, which the previous regimes had prided themselves on having eradicated, but which reappeared in certain rural "pockets." We do not have statistics on this. The dimension of workplace-based (or "sandwich-course") training was ignored by many of the new candidate states, on the grounds that large numbers of the enterprises in which such training could have taken place had disappeared. Though very prevalent before 1989, particularly in the countries where German influence was strong, it was absent after that date. Here again, statistical data are lacking. As for lifelong learning, this was an entirely new concept that was difficult to incorporate into national or regional strategies. National schemes and funding were often directed solely toward the unemployed. For its part, the private training market was merely embryonic. Though language schools abounded in the capitals, there were very few elsewhere. Hence the question arises not merely of funding, but of access to training centers across the whole territory. This is one of the issues for the coming years; the response to it will have to combine consolidation of growth centers and access for the greatest number to public provision.

Conclusion

A triple convergence of interests seems to have contributed to reinforcing the neoliberal dimension of the European Union and to squeezing social considerations out of enlargement policy. The first line of convergence is the one that can be drawn between the acknowledgment of the major social underdevelopment of the Eastern half of Europe and the neoliberalism of the Commission that, on the one hand, does not favor an extended European social policy and, on the other, intends to preserve Western Europe's established social rights. Given that it was impossible for the new member states to incorporate the institutional and budgetary constraints attaching to a high level of social regulation, the former countries of the EU15 had no interest in seeking to impose them.[28] This is explained by the commission's lack of interest in declaring its social vision and its inability to say what "good" social institutions are. All the more so—and this is the second line of convergence—as foreign direct investment companies were the main winners in this social dumping contest. If what justifies foreign direct investment in these countries is the size of markets, then labor costs are certainly the other benefit to be gained. When these two factors are combined with high levels of skill and qualifications, then the enlightened self-interest of the parties concerned calls for social legislation to be limited to nonrestrictive generalities.[29] We have seen the strength of certain employers brought together to reduce the scope of social legislation. The third line of convergence is the one that exploits the collusion between the central and local public authorities, all of which are bent upon attracting investors. Their promotional campaigns depend on highlighting the presence of an undemanding labor force and unrestrictive social legislation. Some observers conclude from this that there is here a minimal understanding on limited standards and, particularly, on collective disregard for inequalities.

Yet should we conclude from this acknowledgment of the sorry state of labor relations that there is a total absence of rules in Central and Eastern Europe? Are the low numbers of unionized workers and the weak capacity

for mobilization indicators of an "anomie" of social regulation? It would
be an exaggeration to assert this for several reasons. First, there is conflict
at times, and collective bargaining does take place. Agreements are signed,
despite there being few of them. And indeed a social system, of whatever
nature, cannot function without a minimum of stability. Equilibria in
external markets cannot guarantee the stability of the enterprise's internal
markets, and for this reason trust is necessary, if only to thwart oppor-
tunistic behavior, stabilize the labor force, and ensure continuity. More
broadly, though power is expressive of hierarchical control, nevertheless it
can be applied only if it is accepted by those subjected to it. The legitimation of order is a precondition of its durability. For this reason, it would be
illusory to think that management can do whatever it likes when it comes
to managing the labor force in Central and Eastern Europe. In smashing
collectivism and expelling individuals from their traditional milieus, the
end of Communism cannot be said to have promoted a strengthening of
collective regulation. "Flexibility" seems to be the watchword everywhere
and the European Union has given its blessing to it. This is a fact. But in
spite of this, social consensuses seem broadly established, as is attested by
decisions on public policies, which no party—or almost no party—seeks
to challenge. The broad policy outlines adopted in 1990 and thereafter
are matters of majority consensus, and EU accession has been the objective pursued by all governments since 1998. Here the notion of "cognitive
Europeanization," which may characterize the whole of the processes of
enlargement, also goes for the social field. It rests on the adoption of a
similar pattern by the different candidate countries (and member states),
based on the exchange of "best practices," experience, and, to a lesser
extent, common organizations, which the European councils—in places
where they actually function—are able to be. All in all, the institutions
of democracy, and the market, on the one hand, and shared cognitive
references and common experiences, on the other, have been the pillars
on which the countries of Central and Eastern Europe have developed
solidly.

CHAPTER EIGHT

Civil Societies. Networks of Sociability, Associations, and Public Debates

The final dimension relating to the capacity of the local actors to meet the demands of the modernization initiated in 1989—to which the European Union is firmly committed—is that of civil societies. At issue here are the foundations of democracy. The underlying hypothesis is the one expressed in the introduction of this book that Europeanization may play a role of cushioning global economic pressures. By promoting majority participation and social control, the aim is to limit possible encroachments on the rights of the citizen, to assure the bureaucracy of a legitimate base for its action and to reduce the negative effects of an uncontrolled neoliberalism that, in the end, merely strengthens the position of the powerful. In the history of ideas, and in the West, a very extensive school of thought has defined civil society as the bulwark of the citizens in the ceaseless struggle to assert individual rights against the state's endeavor to hold uncontested sway over public and private space. Civil society has thus seen itself endowed with various functions of defense and protection (Locke), intermediation (Montesquieu), socialization (Tocqueville), and, more recently, integration (Putnam) and communication (Habermas). As the safeguard, successively, of natural, civil, and political rights, civil society has been advanced as the pillar of democracy, without which neither men, citizens, nor the middle classes would exist.[1] This is the heritage of the European Union and the reason why it is committed to valorizing the decentralized levels, grassroots initiatives, and local allegiances.

Now, as during the debate on decentralization, the debate on civil society has shown up the discrepancy between a program driven by an ideal type of democracy, devised to fit Western European societies, and local realities characterized by specific traditions and unyielding demands on the part of the political centers. An examination of the formation of civil societies in Eastern Europe after 1989 reveals an entirely different reality from that of Western Europe. There has not so much been an adjustment between modernization and civil societies as a decoupling of the two. It seems difficult, for example, to speak of the emergence of a public space by virtue of which representations and actions shared by the associative actors would be constructed. And yet this acknowledgment of the weakness of civil society does not mean we can conclude that democracy has been weak in the new member states. In these countries modernization, Europeanization, and social change are not necessarily linked.

This chapter examines three arenas productive of civil society, after first clarifying the multiple meanings of this term by relating it to what it meant before 1989. The first arena is that of voluntary organizations or associations, a large number of which have survived from the earlier period, without, however, being comparable, either in volume or content, with their counterparts in the West. The relationship with the state is, therefore, different. A second arena is that of the Euroregions. The European Union has attempted to promote transborder cooperation throughout Central Europe so as to overcome historic oppositions and even hatreds, and to promote decentralized exchange. The third arena is that of the public debates concerning the position to be taken with regard to the past, particularly by way of "lustration" policies.

The Issues. Civil Society and the State

How Is Civil Society to Be Defined?

The problematic of civil society has run through all the periods analyzed in this work, beginning with the pre-1989 period. "Civil society," as we saw in chapter one, had taken two distinct paths. In the first of these, the reference was to the nonpolitical society of daily life and of primary groups; in the second, it was to what is normally called "dissidence," though this only applied in certain countries. The latter conception had pitted against the Soviet-type state a system of values radically different in content, if not in orientation, from the values advocated by the Communists. After 1990, economic modernization was often carried out in a manner contrary to the interests of the actors of the earlier social mobilization, as examination of the forms of privatization has often shown. Does this mean that, from this point on, civil society was pushed aside and the formation of the political center was the only concern? Certainly not. There was a very high degree of tension between the two poles that structured public action, depending on whether the focus was on centralization or decentralization. The two major figures of post-1990 transformation in the Czech Republic expressed this in exemplary fashion: the first of them, Václav Havel, by giving statesmen the duty of protecting individuals from state encroachment by reinforcing the intermediate institutions; the second, Václav Klaus, by eliminating any public debate if it meant further questioning the major choices that had been overwhelmingly resolved upon and challenging them.[2] However fierce the clashes may have been, involving, as we saw in part 1, various coalitions of actors, the constitutions of the new states force us to acknowledge that the problematic of civil society has been at the heart of public debate, since all of them mention it. In the view of the German political scientist Klaus von Beyme, it was in respect of civil society that the constitutional texts were most innovative.[3] There is reference to the Anglo-Saxon conception of civil society in Lithuania, the Czech Republic, and Slovenia. And the concept is closely associated everywhere with the notion of citizenship, which is not confined to the holding of a passport, but includes a set of rights, among which is the right to be deprived of one's citizenship only by decision of the president operating under parliamentary oversight. Constitutional texts frequently open with important references to the past, either in the form of "Many centuries ago" (as in the preamble to the Lithuanian constitution) or the Slovak constitution's reference to the heritage of Cyril and Methodius and "of the great Moravian empire." It is the paradox of this strong constitutional affirmation and the weak reality of civil societies after 1990 that needs to be explained.

If viewpoints have varied widely since 1990 so far as the definition of civil society is concerned, this is because more or less everyone has accepted that the concept referred to two orders that are not necessarily compatible: the order of primary groups and the political order. In the former case, the notion of social capital, taken from Putnam, has often been mobilized to stress the density of the bonds of trust and the strength of the commitments that ground social learning.[4] These represent resources reinforcing the reciprocity and foresightedness of public action. On this basis, several levels of social interaction can be identified after 1989. They account both for the continuing existence of the earlier bonds and the emergence of new relations, in terms of a growing dynamic of institutionalization in which the European Union has had an important place. The latter, as we shall see when we look at the Euroregions, has in fact attempted to overcome situations of historical opposition between different national communities by spreading a model of cooperation based on trust and networks. In the second case, that of the political order, the notion of civil society seems, by contrast, to be the vehicle of democratic consolidation, in so far as it is based on citizen participation and tolerance. It is the crucible in which the new elites are formed. It thus appears to maintain a close relationship with the legal bureaucracy, in so far as the rule of law proper to the democratic state guarantees freedom in all its collective forms to individuals, who, in return, ensure the legitimacy of the democratic institutions.[5] Despite the opposition between these two approaches—which has to do with the difference between the "amorphous" character of social capital and the institutional aspect of civil society—both raise the question of the relationship of the state to civil society. How does the post-Communist state foster democracy by ensuring trust and solidarity? How, indeed, do individuals keep democracy alive through their relationships and public debates? Within this framework, what role does the European Union play?

The Explanations Provided for a Social Deficit in Eastern Europe

There have been several conflicting theses on the status to be accorded to the term "civil society" after 1990. All highlight the effects of Communist Party domination before 1989, but go on to make two mutually exclusive points with regard to the following decade. The first argument is that the Communist Party caused the emergence of a homogeneous social movement, which then blocked any concrete initiative in the following decade. An entire school of thought emerged after 1990 that criticized the "social movement"—the reference was chiefly to Solidarnosc, but also to other social groups—for its lack of concrete political engagement before that date and, ultimately, its "antipolitical" stance that, it is claimed, fostered not only a withdrawal of citizens into the private sphere, but also the appearance of undemocratic dynamics.[6] The absence of civil society would, in this way, be explained by an excess of "idealism" before 1989—an idealism ranging the values of individual morality against the *Realpolitik* of the state. On this view, "antipolitics" can be said to have devalued public action by reducing it to a thing of base compromise. This is said to have led, in the following decade, to contempt for politics and to a disengagement on the part of the citizenry that, in some cases, produced barbarism. This idealism imbued with "fundamentalism" is not to be dissociated from the equally "fundamentalist" stance that consists in signing up to any decision taken by the United States, particularly in foreign policy. A similar posture has led many representatives of the old social movements unquestioningly to defend the American engagement in Iraq on the grounds that it is a question of the survival of the "free world" against "barbarism"; in the eyes of a number of observers, these slogans have discredited those who in the 2000s subscribed to the nonviolent, "antipolitical" ideals of the 1970s and 1980s.[7] The second unexpected consequence of this absolute domination on the part of the Communist Party before 1989 is said, conversely, to relate to the very absence of any social movement, and this is credited with generating the anomie of the 1990s. Since it rested on a combination of nationalism and individualism, Communist-type modernization is said to have generated a profound misunderstanding, after 1989, of the nature of social and political commitment.[8] This is also the position adopted by the Hungarian sociologists Cox and Vass when they argue that Hungary transformed itself during the Kádárist period into a soft authoritarianism, ill-suited to fostering powerful social organizations.[9] This second line of interpretation relates also to the domination by parties after 1989, which is explained by the social vacuum from which they are said to have emerged, a vacuum whose effect was to hinder the emergence of social initiatives. For the Hungarian sociologist Agh, who employs the terms "overparticization" and "overparlementarization," the specifically East European pathology after 1989 consisted in leaving the field entirely free for parties and politics, to the detriment of any free expression of civil society.[10] In Agh's view, as previously in Lewis's, civil society is perceived as a "spontaneous" vehicle of development and it was this "grassroots" spontaneity that was expected to appear in 1989. According to the Berlin sociologist Wiesenthal, its nonemergence produced disappointment and bitterness. Others argue that the intellectuals did not match up to the situation and accuse them of betraying their noble calling.[11]

In one of the very rare works devoted exclusively to the question of civil society—alongside the two other major references[12]—three factors are identified to explain its weakness after 1989.[13] The first has to do with individuals' experience of the illegitimacy of collective rules under socialism and their widely shared distrust of any form of obligatory association. The second relates to the persistence after 1989 of private networks with bonds so strong as to render the new organizations irrelevant. These include the family and friendship groups. These networks, it is argued, act as substitutes for organized civil society. Disappointment at certain post-Communist developments and capitalism are said to have induced individuals to disengage from society and withdraw into the private sphere. For Morjé Howard, as for other sociologists, the direct legacy of Communism can be said to be—through liberalism—the valorization of individualism at the expense of collective action.

Critique of a Eurocentric Position

By contrast with these positions, which argue overwhelmingly that civil societies were absent after 1989, several anthropologists have contested the very possibility of applying this concept of civil society to East European situations in the same way as it is applied in the West. Burawoy and Verdury, Creed, and Hann have taken this position, as have many other scholars, most of them anthropologists.[14] After 1989, the price to be paid for such a usage would, in their view, be neglect of the specificities of Communism and of its capacity to build a society on the basis of social relations that cannot be reduced to the terms of classical Western philosophy. To refer to the latter would condemn one to making comparisons that result only in denigrating the element being compared, which is always seen as presenting pathological factors, weakness, lateness, or lack. For this reason, modernization is, according to these anthropologists, a useless category. It is, in fact, based on ideas of historical progress that compare various societies against one another in order to establish a hierarchy among them. In this evaluation of advanced or backward development, civil society is perceived as a stage leading toward democracy. Conversely, its absence is the sign of a lack of democracy and hence of a totalitarian state. The rejection of this Eurocentrism entails the rejection of three important theses that were, nonetheless, widely advanced both before and after 1989.

The first of these concerns dissidence. For its defenders, this represented the "true" societies of Eastern Europe, because it articulated the defense of autonomous values against the state. According to the authors we have just cited, however, such a position leaves out of account that a vast tissue of social relations was based on specific values—the values of everyday life—which we attempted to cover in chapter one by stressing the importance of nonpolitical references. The acceptance of the political framework of regimes by various social networks did not signify acceptance of the forms of Communist domination on their part, nor did it indicate their own alienation. The second thesis is the so-called refrigerator theory. This says that the Communist period froze the "true" relations and imposed violence and artifice in their place. On this view, the course of history can freeze at a particular moment and resume its development at a later point. As a consequence, the reverse of this illusion would justify another unleashing of violence, but a legitimate one this time, since it would consist in smashing everything to recover the origin of a historical flow that had remained unchanged. The elimination of all the legacies of the Communist period would enable us to recover the "true" societies that were, ultimately, totally unaffected by Communism. The third erroneous thesis is the one that consists in concluding—in the wake of the foregoing theories, which in the end retain nothing whatever from the Communist period—that social relations were, after 1989, characterized by anomie. Anomie and the "everything is political" of the pre-1989 years could only lead, in the following period, to the same phenomena, since only nothing can come out of nothing.

Running counter to these interpretations, Chris Hann sees civil society as the phenomenon attested to by the regrets and nostalgia expressed by the various actors once the old form of political regulation by the Communist parties is destroyed and replaced by the new form of regulation by the market. In other words, "civil society" could be said to refer before 1989 to varied social connections, local understandings, and circles of restricted sociability that existed in large quantities and that, after that date, individuals attempt to revive. These connections related to the existence of clubs, circles, associations, and networks, all based on voluntary endeavor and local, neighborly relations—and also on tradition, solidarity, mutual aid, and assistance. The social bonds in question have nothing whatever to do with the "associations" Locke writes of, nor, even less, with the Hegelian vision of stages preliminary to the rational state. Nor do they fit with Marx's view of civil society as, ultimately, a mystification on the part of the bourgeois with the aim of masking their exploitation of the proletarians. In Hann's view, civil society is of the order of the affective and primary; it is about community solidarity that is founded and fuelled by the *longue durée*. Katherine Verdury adopts the same stance when she argues that it is not (formal) property rights that regulate relations between individuals in their relationship with the land, but the relationships human beings maintain among themselves. Michael Streith, Christian Giordano, and Gerald Creed adopt the same posture when they examine the rural worlds of East Germany and Bulgaria. Michael Burawoy extends this line of thinking to the enterprise. Chapters five and six of this work are equally concerned to identify the local recomposition dynamics opposing the central constraints bearing down from outside. The important difference separating the industrial fields, on the one hand, from the agricultural or administrative worlds, on the other, relates to the introduction into the former case of a nonnegotiable element (new technologies), whose implementation calls for adjustment of a kind that brooks no possible "arrangement." The introduction of new technologies into the enterprise strictly excluded the reproduction of the former social ties. It entailed the development of technical training sessions involving strict respect for procedures and the construction of workshop relations on that basis. Learning was programmed "from the top down." By contrast with this dynamic of the imposition of an abstract measurement of time, other occupational milieus were able to draw on "arrangements" based on experience, and on a learning of the new contexts, on the basis of individual and collective repertoires of skills. The individualized contract did not impose itself as the sole form of relationship. A space for negotiation was found, leading to a shared set of rules.

Analyzing the above-mentioned work by Morjé Howard, Jan Kubik takes over the anthropologists' criticism of the Westernizing orientation of much of the writing on civil society.[15] Stressing the absence of connections between modernization, on the one hand, and democracy on the other, he insists that there can be no correlation between civil society and modernization if we consider, for example, the high number of civil associations in Germany in the later nineteenth century and the fact that they did not prevent that modernized country from sliding into the catastrophe of Nazism in the 1930s. As Hirschmann has written in a number of crucial works, what may appear an advantage in the development of one country may play no role in another. This is the case with the mobilization of the labor force in the United States in the nineteenth century, a nonexistent factor in Japanese development. Modernization relates, then, to quantitative factors, while civil society relates to bonds of tolerance between groups. If modernization is in no way correlated with civil society, the absence of the latter is consequently no indicator of a lack of modernization. Hence the possible disjunction between modernization and democracy. If civil society may exist without states being developed on the basis of rational bureaucracies, states may, conversely, play merely a limited role in the formation of civil societies. The traditional correlation between the presence of a civil society and a strong state here runs up against its limits. Qualitative notions of tolerance seem to be much more important, particularly the tolerance that may emerge between the different political elites, as do the links between the various domains of public life, and the transparency and responsibility of elites toward their electors. Conversely, the absence of civil society rests on clientelism, secrecy, and corruption. In these conditions, how are we to assess the voluntary organizations and associations that emerged in Central and Eastern Europe and how are we to evaluate EU action in their favor?

Associations, NGOs, and Expanded Cooperation

Associations Old and New

The first level of sociability indicative of civil society refers to the situation of the old associations after 1989.[16] A very large number of these disappeared, carried off by the fall of the Communism that had sustained them. This is the case with those that catered for groups targeted by the previous regime in one form or another, such as young people, women, and pensioners. More generally, all the organizations of political mobilization were affected, particularly neighborhood associations. Occupational organizations often disappeared too, corresponding to the elimination of the public sphere, and very often also tenants' associations and the housing management unions. Those associations whose existence derived from the very nature of the regime and provided its corporatist base also went under, labor unions foremost among them. The aims and purposes of these have now radically changed, as we saw in the previous chapter. Other groups, the most numerous, have remained in existence, such as the two largest in each country: the sporting and recreational associations. These are said to contain more than one-third of all members of voluntary organizations in Central and Eastern Europe. Then come the associations devoted to cultural pursuits and religious activities.[17] Others have transformed themselves in response to new situations, such as the associations that now deal with questions of homelessness, AIDS, drugs, and social exclusion. These social—and sometimes societal—problems are often entirely left to organizations of the Caritas type, which have little experience in the field. Assistance from the state and, more particularly, from the municipalities, is very limited. These organizations have several features in common: they are more widespread in urban than in rural areas; they are able to mobilize only a small number of voluntary workers (by comparison with the figures for Western Europe); they are particularly short of funds, as purchasing power declined in many places in the 1990s; and their relations with the public authorities are often difficult.

According to several observers, these organizations are, in fact, evidence of the deficiencies of the state. They are not defined as partners of the public authorities, like the German "third sector,"[18] but more as service providers relatively unintegrated into public decision making. Their loose relations with the state reflect the weak relationship between bureaucratization and democracy. Moreover, those whose activity is defined by social issues are few in number. Whereas the "third sector" covering the social field is said to represent up to 50% of voluntary associations in Western Europe, the figure would be barely 20% in Central Europe. The size of associative networks and other similar movements seem to be in inverse proportion to the state's capacity to co-opt partners and build the third sector as a decisive ally in the management of certain fields. This mistrust grew over the decade, not so much because of a "natural" weakening of the mobilization of the early years, but of a more hard-line stance on the part of the various governments, which were uninclined to share their prerogatives. It would seem that the labor unions and political parties also fell victim to this. In terms of local political involvement, few studies indicate the permanence of strong networks or the emergence of new bonds of sociability. On the basis of surveys carried out in small Czech towns, Zdenka Vajdova found a low level of local involvement.[19] During the 1990s, local politics was found to have declined greatly as a focus for the activity of citizens, while their own sense of powerlessness had increased, despite a positive evaluation of the post-1989 changes. The very low sense of participation was more marked in the small municipalities than in the largest cities, as though paradoxically the anonymous character of the latter was more favorable to participation. The members of the social movement of 1989 have lost their importance and few studies conclude that rural associations have been strengthened; the finding, rather, is of an enormous destruction of the old rural equilibria.

In the early 1990s it seems that associations saw considerable growth everywhere, followed by decline. However, this growth is said to have been less pronounced in Hungary. The difference in that country by comparison with Poland or the Czech Republic would seem to be that civic involvement was lower at the moment of transition, given the greater degree of tolerance before 1989. However, Cox and Vass point out that, though associations in Hungary numbered 6,570 in 1982 (including labor unions), there were 24,051 of them 10 years later and 47,963 in 1997. Conversely, in Romania it seems that the surge of the early years came to a standstill in 1995 following an "institutionalization" of the relations between the voluntary and the public sectors, and the associations developing a greater realism.[20] This was also the case in the Czech Republic and Poland, where in the early 1990s charitable associations gave way to associations concerned largely with environmental protection. The European funds doubtless played a large part in this, in so far as the European Union sees it as part of its role to participate in the structuring of local milieus. To this end, the commission distributed 36.5 million euros to assist 19 national programs in 6 countries and gave 157 million euros to the LIEN program that covers several countries.

These various forms of aid sought, first of all, to support national initiatives on the environment, media organization, public finance, and training. Then, in 1996–1997, they were targeted at groups of women and the underprivileged; support for democracy followed and, from 1999 onward, aid for community-based organizations. Through this targeted support, it is the aim of the European Union to strengthen the management capacity of NGOs, in order to build associative partnership networks in preparation for the implementation of the structural funds. The intention here, as elsewhere, has been to participate in establishing favorable conditions for collective action, at the risk of producing a feeling within the associations of sometimes being used for the purposes of others.[21] In this way it is

expected that European Social Fund (ESF) monies will bring many training and social support associations into being and, similarly, that there will
be many producers' and consumers' associations created through deploy-
ment of the European Regional Development Fund (ERDF). This policy
of incentives and support for associations seems to have borne some fruit,
even though many observers have highlighted the fact that a number of
associations of this type have merely promoted an ineffective bureaucratization and the enrichment of the Western partners. Ferge and Juhasz
point out that the EU allotted 5.5 million euros as part of the PHARE
program to consolidate Hungarian civil society and several associations
were created as part of this initiative. The two Hungarian sociologists do,
however, stress these associations' lack of resources of their own and point
out that the state favors certain groups that are in its pay. Until 2004, 16%
of the monies distributed to strengthen civil society were overseen by parliament, but 62% were distributed by the government alone.[22] In this way,
the state has remained in charge of the construction of civil organizations,
integrating them, as it saw fit, into the political game or removing them
from it on its own initiative. In Latvia, the law states that associations are
to be informed by the government of any law that may relate to them.
However, associations must first be officially approved before this happens. After 2004, everywhere in the region, the associations were notable
absentees from the projects supported by the structural funds, thus greatly
limiting the degree of public–private partnership.

The Euroregions, a Shared Social Capital?

Alongside the support provided to voluntary organizations, the European
Union has attempted to extend a type of networked cooperation that had
already proved its worth in Western Europe: namely, the Euroregion.
Through these bodies, the community attempted to strengthen civil and
political cooperation by restoring the trust that had so often been undermined by past history. The objective assigned to the Euroregions is to seek,
generally, to get beyond historical antagonisms and facilitate exchanges
between border populations that have been separated in the past—by,
among other things, wars. The fields of intervention are mainly economic
and cultural, in that their mission consists in consolidating economic cooperation, and in influencing infrastructure projects, municipal and regional
development, and the protection of the environment. The aim is to try to
develop a regional identity and, subsequently, promote the European idea.

   What emerges notably from these Euroregions that have thrived in all
the border areas of the new states? Mainly, two key ideas: the idea of a
new local governance, which would enable the failure of the transnational
institutions to be offset, and the idea of social capital, thanks to the development of networks and access to resources and to local public decision
making.[23] This is particularly clear in the case of the Baltic Euroregion,
which includes all those countries fringing the Baltic.[24] And even more so

in the most complex of all the Euroregions, the Carpathian Euroregion.[25] When it was created in 1993, there were 10 million inhabitants in that region, spread out over 5 Polish voivodships, 13 Slovakian districts, 5 Ukrainian oblasts, 3 Hungarian counties, and 6 Romanian regions. Its declared aim was to transcend ethnic exclusivism by fostering a vast reconciliation between ethnic groups torn apart by history and by promoting a Transcarpathian regional identity. However noble and ambitious these objectives may have been, they all ran into a number of difficulties relating both to enduring cross-border hatreds and institutional differences. The latter differences separated the decentralized states, such as Hungary, Slovakia, and Poland, from those that had remained tightly centralized, such as Ukraine and Belarus. The regions were thus endowed with asymmetric powers that hampered cooperation. Worse, when the new European border legislation came in, it heavily penalized local exchanges, reducing almost to nothing the projects framed within the Euroregions and the partnerships with the noncandidate states.[26] If, in the West, the exchanges between Poles and Czechs, on the one hand, and Germans, on the other, were decidedly successful, there were barely any successful exchanges with Eastern partners. Within the Carpathian Euroregion, such exchanges were quite simply absent. The Ruthenian question remained a source of major tensions between the different partner countries, since none wished to recognize it: the Romanians and Slovaks feared Hungarian irredentism, while Kiev feared the separatism of its own province and all of them were afraid the Poles and Hungarians would profit from the situation. Limited from above by the much better endowed *Interreg* projects, the Euroregions seem limited from below, local communities having their own cooperation agenda that may or may not coincide with the Euroregions. Beyond noting the festive and cultural exchanges between young people, folk groups and students that foster communication and, hence, certainly reinforce trust, it is difficult to accord a significant role to these forums, which carried great hopes in the 1990s. In some critical areas, the Euroregions have not fulfilled their role, as when the Tisza was heavily polluted, following a spillage of waste from a Romanian mine into that Hungarian river. Ultimately, the aim of promoting transregional networks by overcoming historic divisions seems to run up against the weight of traditions and rivalries. The new European instrument of transborder cooperation (EGTC) for the period 2007–2013 has, however, set itself the task of meeting this challenge by strengthening local powers both financially and in terms of legal powers of intervention.

A Public Debate. Lustration

A third element drawn upon in the examination of civil societies concerns the kinds of public discussions that have developed around the treatment of former Communist officials. This was one of the great societal issues of the 1990s.[27] The question is whether this debate, which in most cases unleashed the fiercest passions, actually produced a democratic public space, indicating the emergence of a civil society. The policy known as lustration refers to a form of "clean-up" action, aimed at purging the new state of the elites who may have held on to their posts in the new period and who had previously been guilty of offenses against the citizenry. The term "de-Communization," which is sometimes coupled with it, refers to the policy aimed at debarring former Communist Party officials from public office. That policy was not implemented, unlike the lustration policy, though the latter clearly poses the problem of defining offenses, establishing relevant procedures and then laying down corresponding penalties. For this reason, the debate was of fundamental importance, since the capacity of all the actors involved was at issue: the capacity of public opinion to grasp the question, which brings previous social consensuses into play, and propose solutions acceptable to the widest majority; the capacity of the new institutions, particularly the legal institutions, to have their viewpoint prevail and hence meet the demand for justice underlying the 1989 revolutions; the capacity of the bureaucracy to lay down procedural rules validated by the majority; and the capacity of the parties themselves to propose laws and obey them. In other words, the debate on lustration was crucial, since it raised the question of the vigor of democracy at its very foundations—the negotiations that developed at the point when the Communist regimes collapsed in 1989. There was, in this regard, constant suspicion in Poland that the "Round Table" negotiations had amounted to an enormous act of skullduggery between the exiting elites (Jaruzelski and his associates) and those of the opposition (Walesa et al.). Hence the need to know whether the parties "shielded" groups or individuals who were guilty of reprehensible actions. The major risk democracy runs when it undertakes such a policy of confronting its past is, clearly, one of either doing serious injustice or stifling debate; in both cases there is a risk that all politicians will be condemned as equally corrupt.

A Skewed Debate

Outside of any national context, those arguing for a policy of lustration may seem to have an unanswerable case. The first and most fundamental argument was the need to do justice to the victims of Communist regimes that in 1989 were everywhere justly condemned as illegitimate. Granting justice to the victims and performing what has come to be called "the duty of memory" was one of the primordial tasks expected of the new institutional bodies. The individuals known to be guilty of crimes were very quickly imprisoned, such as Erich Honecker's successor Egon Krenz, who was known to be guilty of issuing an order to fire on individuals crossing the border illegally. However, though these cases were cut-and-dried, all the other relating to the daily activities of spying, snooping, betrayal, and immorality were much more difficult to define, particularly as the debate was everywhere conducted in conditions not conducive to calm deliberation. First from lack of experience. It was not possible to draw on any previous legislation. The rare precedents were taken either from the resistance movements in 1945—though in that case the facts were acknowledged and summary justice prevailed—or from the tribunals set up after 1945—though these were the work of the occupying powers, in particular the Americans. Hence the wealth of arguments immediately raised against such a debate, on the grounds that such a tribunal would have infringed the national sovereignty that had now been regained. The complexity of such a debate had a great many aspects to it, beginning with the fact that the secret police had operated by lies, threats, blackmail, the extortion of confessions, and manipulation on a grand scale. In these conditions, there was every possibility that, far from revealing the identity of informers, the police files would deliberately complicate the task of any later, external examination, since the individuals concerned were capable of manipulating and compromising other individuals than the genuine informers—people who actually had nothing to do with such activities. For this reason, it was argued that the secret police organizations, even when destroyed, were still capable of great harm and that, in reopening these files, there was a serious risk of handing an unexpected victory to the enemies of democracy. This was what inspired the declaration of Polish Prime Minister Tadeusz Mazowiecki, when he came into office in August 1989, that a line should be drawn under the previous period, and citizens should not be excluded at the very moment when the new democracy was seeking to produce social cohesion. By this declaration, long resented because it lent credence to the suspicion that deals had been struck among the elites at the time of the Round Table, Mazowiecki, whose integrity was beyond question, was trying to warn against opening an apparent Pandora's box, at the risk of acting just like those exposed to public condemnation. By contrast, Pastor Joachim Gauck, who chaired the Commission on the Stasi Files in East Germany, argued from the same assumptions regarding the possible manipulation of the documents by the former security services, that an efficient assessment machinery should be set up to enable information to be cross-checked. The ambition at least was to put the victims—and, more broadly, the citizens—at the center of the system. Citizen rights against the arbitrary power of the state, on the one hand, social peace against justice to individuals, on the other—these were the often skewed terms in which public debates became entangled, at the expense of the citizens. In fact, Germany, aided, admittedly, by an efficient bureaucracy, managed to develop an unrivalled machinery, to satisfy a number of its citizens, and meet the demands of justice until 2007, even though the institution was criticized for many dysfunctions. By contrast, the other East European democracies, riven by powerful internal conflicts and lacking an arbiter "above the fray," worked out more or less rickety—and largely unsatisfactory—compromises. However, even through these, it was the sovereignty of the states and, to an even greater extent, of the societies that expressed themselves. For, during the 1990s, the proofs adduced were random, the assessment tools fragile, and the tribunals' experience nonexistent. The risk of shaking confidence in the new institutions was, on the other hand, considerable, on account of the judicial system's incapacity to respond to what was demanded of it. In what promised to become a maelstrom of the most disreputable popular passions—based on anonymous accusations and the "poison-pen" spirit—who could hope to escape? All the more so as the organs of state security had behaved less criminally in the two decades preceding the fall of the regime and there was broad social tolerance. If, moreover, it was easy to identify the GDR border guards who had fired on and killed the individuals who had got through the barbed wire, and if it was similarly easy to hold the Politburo official to account, it was not the same in the other countries. Kádár could clearly be held responsible for the repression that hit Hungary after 4 November 1956. But it was in fact the same man who had managed to "open up" his country's economy and, in this respect, he was the only person to make positive provision for the future, as the post-1990 period has shown. Everywhere the chain of command had diluted into extensive compromises. There had rarely been killings after de-Stalinization and the Gulag murderers had transformed themselves into the servile bureaucrats of "socialist legality." Moreover, which individual profile were the investigative measures to target? The answer was easy in the case of all the agents of state security who were identified as such. It was everywhere accepted that none of them could seek to hold a post in the new public institutions. But what was to be done with the higher officials of the party? How was the full extent of responsibilities to be assessed for those who had had some contact with the state security bodies? The same went for the military brigades in the enterprises. And for the individuals in the research centers and industrial units who had an open monitoring role. Moreover, time had passed. Individuals might have changed their attitudes and ideas. Behavior, which was reprehensible long ago and adopted in what might be exceptional circumstances, could have been redeemed by subsequent acts. How, moreover, was one to assess the behavior of those who had believed in these regimes and had, for example, used their pens to support them? Here, too, declarations "on the individual's honor" were demanded almost everywhere of those applying for responsible positions in the public services. Beyond this, little more was done, except where individualized files revealed blatant offenses.

By making the contents of the files public, together with the names in them, the greatest danger was definitely that of undermining the confidence that had previously assured social relations of their continuity, breaking up families, destroying reputations, and provoking irremediable dissensions for a gain that would mainly accrue to Western public opinion, which would thereby have its already hostile conception of the entire East European heritage confirmed. A similar opinion could in fact justify considerations of a colonial type, to the effect that nothing of the past should be preserved, everyone being suspected of having compromised themselves—if not, indeed, done deals—with a dictatorial regime. Particularly as the handover of the funds that had belonged to the secret police services had been tainted by much double-dealing. Even in the case of the GDR, where the Stasi archives were seized as early as January 1990, acts of concealment had taken place from the previous autumn onward. Files had been burned. In the other countries of the Soviet bloc, officials spread out over the national territory had time to discard a large number of compromising documents. In Poland, there are said to have been negotiations over the removal of files that could sully the reputation of the Catholic church. According to some sources, 40–50% of files disappeared in this way. Yet this did not prevent the Catholic hierarchy from becoming embroiled in a number of scandals, the most important of which forced the resignation of the prospective Metropolitan of Warsaw in the early days of January 2007. Also in Poland, in spring 2007, the Kaczynski government stirred up feelings nationally and internationally when it introduced a law aimed at forcing up to 700,000 individuals to reveal the nature of their activities under the old regime. Because it was not directed only against applicants to the public services, as previous such laws had been, but against professionals in the health, education, media sectors, and so on, the government was criticized by the Constitutional Court for jeopardizing the foundations of the constitutional state. The main clauses of the law were annulled. In the case of the Baltic states, the Russians are thought to have repatriated the files, leaving behind only those that compromised the new national elites. In Romania, where the reform Communists won out at the time of regime change, the safeguarding of the archives is said to have been quickly attended to. The last argument advanced for not opening up the files was that of efficiency: it was said that the new regimes would suffer from the loss of so many experienced individuals. It seems this argument was used to justify a great deal of concealment in the Czech Republic.

In the end, the effects of the actions undertaken as part of lustration operations were very limited; 250,000 individuals were assessed by the Gauck Commission on the basis of the opening of more than 2 million Stasi files. Elsewhere, the figures show the difficulties encountered. In the Czech Republic, 15,000 individuals were involved, comprising all the agents of the secret services identified, together with the officials of the Communist Party, beginning at district level. In Poland, 20,000 individuals were involved (*Rzeczpospolita*, 29 October 1998); unlike their counterparts in the other countries, they were not dismissed from their jobs, unless they had given false testimony. The law kept the officials of the radio and television stations and the information agencies in their posts. Elsewhere, the effect was even slighter: in Hungary 600 people fell foul of the law, while in Lithuania it was only 80 and in Bulgaria no more than 25 (up to 1998). In most cases, the exposure of their former activities entailed no penalty. Ten years later, the figures have changed little.

Table 8.1 The Consequences of the Lustration Laws Adopted in the Countries of Central and Eastern Europe

Country	Legislative Measures	Situation of the Archives and Effects of the Measures Taken
Czechoslovakia	Lustration law in 1991	Access to the civil service and to elective office was restricted. 10,000 individuals were disqualified in 1999 in the Czech Republic
Germany (East)	Lustration law in 1990	110 000 individuals were investigated, 1,100 were found guilty (mainly of electoral fraud or murder at the borders), after the archives were partially destroyed before January 1990.
Poland	Lustration law in 1997, stiffened in 2006, then rendered partly invalid in 2007.	No prohibition on office, but a requirement to acknowledge one's involvement publicly. High level of tension regarding access to archives, particularly as many files were destroyed.
Hungary	Lustration law in 1994	Destruction of 100,000 out of 110,000 files in 1989. 540 persons affected by the measures on restricted access to some parliamentary or ministerial posts.
Baltic States	Estonia: law in 1992; Latvia: law in 1993; Lithuania: law in 1999	Access to archives made difficult by their repatriation by the KGB before 1991. The laws are damaging to citizenship, as they discriminate heavily against Russian individuals.
Bulgaria	Lustration law in 1992, repealed in 1995, but reintroduced a year later.	Failure of this policy on account of the massive destruction in 1990 involving 46% of the files, the lack of access to the archives and a highly charged political situation.
Romania	Law Opening the Securitate Archives in 1999, but no lustration law.	Large number of archives destroyed. High level of political tension. No results. In 2006, the opening of the archives was declared unconstitutional.

Conclusion

Examination of the foregoing shows that there are democracies that are not necessarily backed up by strong civil societies, but that one cannot infer from this a correlation between weak civil society and weak democracy. We have noted the same absence of correlation between modernization and civil society. Networks of sociability exist that are not reducible to what is understood by this term in Western Europe. It seems to be one of the central elements of the liberalism of the states emerging from Communism after 20 years of transformation that they are founded on strong bonds based on primary groups that cannot be equated with an active society, but that weak democracies do not necessarily ensue. The advantage of the approach in terms of social capital is that emphasis is put on relations within networks of sociability that only research of an anthropological type is capable of revealing. Relations of trust may develop in local (or even micro-) milieus, but without giving rise to interpretations in civil society terms. In this sense, the anthropologists are no doubt right to stress the difference of the relationship with the state, which is not conceived as opposition, but is distinguishable more by notions of governance, solidarity, and altruism that apply to what are most often rural—but sometimes also urban—milieus. The whole question is how they will manage to exploit their resources over the long term, in the face of the process of bureaucratization indicative of the growing modernization and Europeanization of these societies.

Thus, whether we are speaking of designating intermediate units between individuals and the state or organized forms of civil collective action, it seems civil societies are a terrain that is largely absent in Central and Eastern Europe after 1989, at least in the Western sense of the term. The quantitative or qualitative examination of the associative sector leaves no doubt on this point, despite the large number of NGOs, which do not necessarily have local roots. Moreover, the previous chapters have stressed the low level of collective social regulation, the deep disaffection with the labor unions, and, in addition, in many cases, incomplete decentralization. For all these reasons, we are justified in querying the reality of citizen participation in the public arena, given the lack of any social mobilization concomitant with the modernization of the economies, and the absence of Europeanization. However, germs of such participation are present. They herald a degree of structuring in the near future, particularly as a result of constitutional provisions, on the one hand, and of the structural funds, on the other. Just as political and economic actors—most often central ones—have seized on legal pressures from the European Union as so many opportunities to reinforce their position, so constitutional provisions and European funds are a resource available to the citizens to ensure civil societies of stability.

CHAPTER NINE

The Development of the Social Structures and the Formation of New Cleavages

In order to grasp the interactions of the exogenous constraints of the type exerted by the EU and trade globalization with those of endogenous change, the last area we have to analyze is that of developments in the social structures. These developments reflect both a major adjustment to specifically Western dynamics and the maintenance of many traditional components. The elements involved may be the size of the primary sector in certain countries or the strengthening of religiosity in others. These are important factors that lead us to conclude that the processes of modernization are complex, that there are divergent trajectories in the two halves of Europe and that social interests slowly become structured during this period. They are so many elements that enable us to specify the nature of the social divides underlying partisan orientations in this part of Europe that, in this respect also, differs from the Western half. On the basis of this analysis, the typology of "cleavages" drawn up by Rokkan and Lipset is thrown substantially into question. The reference to recent history has been used to highlight the decisive impact of the Communist period on partisan positionings. The new inequalities that emerged in the post-1989 period, together with the European Union, have appeared to be powerful factors influencing the formation of political cleavages.

The Diversification of the Social Structures

Trends in Wages and the Increasing Preeminence of Educational Qualifications

Wage inequalities have increased everywhere since 1989, leading to the fragmentation of social structures.[1] During the Communist period, the wage spread was rather narrow, on account of the high level of social expenditure and a low-wage policy. Egalitarianism was real, given the low magnitude of salary differentials and people's attachment to it. Moreover, two factors seem crucial in determining the wage level: whether the job is in the production or consumption sector, and the gender of the worker. The studies carried out in the 1980s show sectoral differences to be highest in Eastern Europe. Workers in the mines and steelworks were much better paid than their equivalents in other sectors. Added to this were the facilities afforded in terms of housing, shopping, and leisure. By contrast, it was common knowledge that wages were lower in the intellectual, education, and health professions. There was often an inverse relation between the income and the prestige attaching to a particular social status. Many of these features have continued in being from one period to the other, as witness the high wages paid in the mining sector, particularly in Poland and Bulgaria, and the low salaries that still apply in education, health, and the social services, especially in Poland, Hungary, Bulgaria, and the Czech Republic. The differential between males and females is reportedly still significant, though no greater than it is in Western Europe, and the relationship between income level and prestige is tending to become harmonized.[2] However, there are more differences than similarities.

The first reason for this is the emergence of a vast private sector in which wages are generally higher, at least for certain (foreign) firms and certain (managerial) jobs. With the exception of Hungary, where the difference by comparison with the public sector appears to be only 6%, this is the case everywhere. In the 1990s, the differential was reportedly close to 30%. The second, fundamental element relates to the close link that now exists between income and educational level. From 1990 onward, educational qualifications became the main factor in social position, evidence that belonging to the old nomenklatura was no longer the privileged route to becoming a manager. In other words, "meritocracy" has supplanted party allegiance. While sociological studies have shown that in 1993 possession of a managerial post depended on membership of the old power networks,[3] from 1998 onward other trends were just as strongly visible. Michaly Laki has demonstrated that most individuals occupying leading posts who remained party members until 1989 acquired ownership rights to their companies. Over the decade, however, the dynamic of enterprise-creation by individuals with no links to the previous regime was in the ascendant, while that former group declined.[4] In his work on enterprises in 1998, Jacek Wasilewski reinforces this finding and concludes that things are distinctly different from how they were in 1993. By the end of the 1990s, educational qualifications were by far more important for obtaining a managerial post than the old forms of loyalty to the political authorities. On the basis of a survey of 178 executives, the Krakow sociologist concludes that the elites had been depoliticized.[5]

The other effect of the strengthening of the correlation between jobs and educational qualifications can be gauged by the inequality of treatment between different types of students. During the period 1990–2004, the number of Polish university students more than tripled, rising from almost 13% to 43.6% of a cohort.[6] This growth paralleled that of the private university institutions. In 2002, there were 221 private institutes out of a total of 344 university institutions. Since the public universities remained the most prestigious, they were also the most difficult to get into. Hence, they favored the children of highly qualified individuals over the children of other categories, such as workers or peasants. Almost 60% of the students in the private institutes have to pay fees that exceed a month's gross minimum wage, while the income of a manager or a university teacher is three times the income of a blue-collar worker. It is to be noted, however, that despite this deepening of the differential between the different occupational categories, we do not see any particular change in the relative scale of jobs or prestige. Ten years on, CEOs and higher civil servants are still at the top of the list and, conversely, blue-collar workers, skilled and unskilled, in industry and agriculture are still at the bottom. Similarly, we do not find any profound changes in values surveys, with the exception of employment in public political office, which has declined appreciably in prestige and is now at the bottom of the scale. The intellectual professions are still appreciated as much as ever, as are the health professions, though the same is also true of occupations in the mining sector—evidence of the permanence of a "worker ethos" that may be ascribed directly to a continuance of the values of the previous period.

Trends in the Economic Sectors and Employment

Sectoral Changes

During the 1990s, three trends are identifiable where sectoral change is concerned. The first is a significant reduction in the primary sector in the Czech, Hungarian, Slovak, Estonian, and Slovenian cases, but not elsewhere: Poland more or less stabilized its agricultural population at 20% in 2004, as did Lithuania. In Latvia, the primary sector has passed the 15% mark. As for Bulgaria and Romania, they passed the 30% and 40% thresholds respectively. In those countries, substantial groups of individuals laid off from the industrial sector returned to their little patch of land in the country, where they contributed to aggravating the phenomenon of excess employment, thus swelling the figures for concealed unemployment. A second dynamic is that of deindustrialization, which has varied widely from one country to another. While intense in Hungary, it was less so in Poland. Overall, the fall in industrial production over 10 years was 33% in Bulgaria, 27% in Poland and Slovakia, 14% in the Czech Republic, 25% in Romania, and 10% in Hungary. The third dynamic is the tertiarization of all these economies, with the exception of the Czech Republic and Romania, as a result of the significant increase in services, particularly consultancy, financial services (especially insurance), and, in certain countries, tourism.[7] These three trends attest to the significant modernization of the post-Soviet economies, though this again varies widely from one country to another, since the "back-to-the-land" phenomenon may be interpreted as one of demodernization and increased peripheralization.

It would, however, be a mistake to read this as a regression. The maintenance of agricultural and rural traditions may also be an opportunity to assert an identity, even though no one denies that there will have to be profound upheavals if these economies are to "catch up."

With the exception of the Czech Republic, employment rates are particularly low in Central and Eastern Europe. In 2004, the average was 58.8%. This is well below the EU15 figure of 63.9% and very far from the ambitions of the commission, which wants to raise it above 70%. The rate in Poland is barely higher than 51%. The fall can, admittedly, be explained by the redundancies and restructurings in the early part of the decade and, to a much greater degree, by three phenomena: unemployment, the informal economy, and, to a lesser degree, migration. However, given the fact that part-time employment is much lower in Central and Eastern Europe, the full-time comparison is not so unfavorable to the region. The female employment rate is higher than in the West, except in Poland, Slovakia, and Hungary. Movements in activity rates by age group between 1990 and 1999 show, primarily, a substantial decline. Two groups in particular suffered over the decade: young people aged between 15 and 24 and individuals between 50 and 65. In 2002, the employment rate for young people was 15 points lower than in the EU.

The first age group covers those who are often the least qualified individuals, who have not managed to enter the labor market. In late 2001, the unemployment rate in Poland was 40% for the 20–24 age group, and over 50% for 18/19-year-olds. All in all, one-third of the unemployed are in the 15–24 age bracket. The employment rate for this same category is 27% in Eastern and 45% in Western Europe.[8] Throughout the zone, a large number of young people can be added to these two categories who are either receiving university education and are therefore delayed in entering the working population, who are undergoing various forms of training, or who are faced with a situation in which they are overqualified for the jobs that are on offer. The years 1999–2003 saw a shift in favor of the most highly educated and away from the least educated.[9] The second age group contains individuals who have either been forced out of the labor market or granted early retirement. However, because of the low

Table 9.1 Employment Trends between 1995 and 2000 (in Thousands)

	Industry	*Agriculture*	*Services*	*Balance*
Czech Republic	−208	−85	+62	−230
Hungary	+100	−43	+114	+170
Poland	−245	−630	+605	−270
Romania	−636	+101	+146	−388
Slovakia	−51	−57	+62	−45
Slovenia	−39	−1	+54	+15

Source: This table was elaborated using data taken from Based on United Nations Economic Commission for Europe, *Economic Survey of Europe*. Geneva, 2003, p. 77.

Table 9.2 Activity Rates by Age Group, 1990 and 1999

	1990			1999		
	15–24	*25–49*	*50–64*	*15–24*	*25–49*	*50–64*
Bulgaria	51.9	95.1	55.3	—	—	—
Czech Rep.	57.7	96.0	55.7	48.7	89.3	59.4
Estonia	53.0	95.6	68.5	43.5	88.2	62.2
Hungary	51.5	86.0	36.0	40.7	79.0	37.9
Latvia	56.1	95.1	67.4	41.6	87.0	53.1
Lithuania	49.5	93.9	61.9	39.8	92.6	59.8
Poland	44.3	87.3	60.6	37.3	85.0	47.8
Romania	59.8	87.7	42.9	45.8	84.8	58.1
Slovakia	58.8	95.6	55.3	45.6	89.5	45.6
Slovenia	50.4	93.1	42.0	41.8	91.3	38.2

Source: This table has been made on the basis of data found in International Labour Office, *Pension Reform in Central and Eastern Europe*. Volume 1: *Restructuring with Privatization. Case Studies of Hungary and Poland*. Geneva: ILO, 2000.

level of pension provision, the individuals concerned seek employment in what are, most often, low-skilled jobs.

Employment has polarized around educational qualifications; those without any were the first victims of the industrial and agricultural restructurings. Where state farm employees are concerned, the agricultural workers have experienced enormous change. They were only very seldom employed to work on the new agricultural concerns and hence contributed to the formation of pockets of poverty or even social exclusion. In industry, it was also the unskilled workers who were the first to be excluded from the restructuring processes. As has been said, this often affected entire industrial areas, in which the central city had managed to furnish employment where agriculture was unable to provide people with a living. The Polish sociologist Adamski believes that 20% of Polish workers lost their jobs in this way.[10]

Forms of Employment. Private Employment,
Public Employment, Self-Employment

Forms of employment have undergone major changes. The private sector covers two categories. The first is that of firms with direct foreign investment: it is often difficult to see any job creation in these companies in the first decade, since their purchase generally led to intense restructuring and substantial reductions in levels of employment. In this respect, the hopes vested in direct foreign investment at the very beginning of the transformation processes have scarcely been fulfilled. The second category is that of the SMEs: this has grown considerably since 1990, as can be seen from the growth of the service sector. Market liberalization actually enabled both the big combines to be dismantled and some previously integrated sectors to be "privatized," service companies of all kinds emerging in the wake of that development. It also made possible a creative flowering of commercial activities in rural areas, the market for such activities rapidly becoming saturated. It enabled SMEs in the new technology, consultancy, finance, and insurance sectors to emerge and grow very rapidly in urban areas. It is these companies, much more than the restructured firms, that have been responsible for growth.[11]

Within this dynamic of SME development, we should mention the— very widespread—form of "self-employment." In Central and Eastern Europe, this term covers some very varied realities. Excluding farming, these run from company creation to work in the public services, not forgetting ordinary freelance work. Self-employment is characterized by the prevalence of the so-called civil contract, which here replaces the employment contract governed by the labor code. As a result, the individual becomes responsible for paying his or her social security contributions. This is the main advantage of this type of strictly individualized contract, based on the performance of a task in exchange for a fixed remuneration.[12] As a result, the company avoids the obligations it would have to meet under a collective agreement. At the moment of integration in 2004, around 500,000 people were working on contracts of this type in Poland. However, far from seeing this absence of a contract as an asymmetric arrangement that works to their detriment, many regard it as further proof of their freedom. To have responsibility for paying one's own social security contributions is to be able to break the contract at will and to have one's employment bound only by one's own desires.

Having said this, we have to note the considerable deregulation of labor that has occurred since 1990.[13] This has been based on an increase in overtime working, self-employment, freelance contracts, and piece working. The consequence, in most cases, has been the loss of a de facto right to strike and of social benefits, and also of the attendant employment conditions. An enormous delocalization of economic activities to Eastern Europe has occurred. This has entailed a thoroughgoing redefinition of relations within companies, on the basis of a general implementation of flexible organization and of a Taylorization that has, in some cases, assumed extreme forms, as we saw in chapter six. Flexibility has found expression in part-time and temporary contracts. As for working hours, they are generally much higher than in Western Europe. In the EU15, working hours at the end of 2004 stood at 40 per week.[14] In the new member states, the figure was 42.4 for Latvia, 41.8 for Slovenia, 41.5 for Poland, 41.4 for the Czech Republic, and 41.3 for Estonia. On average, 20% of employees work more than 50 hours per week (as against 10% in the EU15). These data do not take account of overtime, which has increased to a great extent, as, for example, in Hungary, where 200 hours may be negotiated.[15] We have, in short, seen the imposition of all kinds of flexibility, conducive to enormous informality, and to a vast tolerance of social marginality. Part-time working is, however, less used than in Western Europe, which can perhaps be explained by the respective legacies. In 2003, the proportion of part-time working ranged from 2%

Table 9.3 Self-Employment as a Percentage of Total Employment between 1993 and 2000

	1993			2000		
	Males	Females	Total	Males	Females	Total
Poland	32.2	29.9	31.2	25.9	18.4	22.5
Hungary	17.4	11.3	14.6	18.7	9.6	14.6
Czech Republic	15.8	9.4	12.8	18	9.0	14.5
Slovakia	9.0	3.5	6.6	10.9	4.1	7.8
Lithuania	21.5	14.6	18.3	19.2	12.7	15.9
Estonia	10.4	6.2	8.4	9.7	6.4	8.1
Latvia	12.4	6.9	9.8	12.5	8.4	10.5
Bulgaria	12.9	9.2	11.2	18.3	10.6	14.7
Romania	24.4	19.4	22.1	32.6	17.4	25.4

Source: This table is based on data found in International Labour Office, *Pension Reform in Central and Eastern Europe*. Volume 1: *Restructuring with Privatization. Case Studies of Hungary and Poland.* Geneva: ILO, 2000.

in Slovakia to 11% in Poland. The relatively high proportion in Latvia, Lithuania, and Poland may be explained by the size of the agricultural sector.[16]

Unemployment

Between 1990 and 2008, the dynamic of unemployment can be divided into four periods.[17] The first has largely been analyzed in terms of a purging of the inefficient structures of the Soviet-type economy. In other words, it was more of a transitional period (1990–1993) that enabled an adjustment to occur, conceived in terms of systemic recession. The second period (1994–1999) has been seen more in terms of company restructuring and the adaptation to market conditions. It was accompanied by a substantial suppression of jobs and hence significant upheaval in the various economic sectors, but at the same time a profound upsurge in job creation. The SMEs were the vehicles of this particular dynamic. The third period, which began in 2000, deepened the differences between national trajectories. Though some countries, such as Slovakia, Bulgaria, and Poland, passed the 15% unemployment threshold, other countries reduced it to less than 10%. The high rate of unemployment in Slovakia particularly hit the Roma population. For its part, Poland was faced with a sizeable task of industrial restructuring at the very moment when, between then and 2006, more than 600,000 young people were arriving on the labor market. From EU accession in 2004 onward, a general decrease in unemployment is observable, since in January 2005 Poland had a rate of 17.8%, Slovakia 16.3% (falling by almost 3 points in less than a year), and Lithuania 8.3%. Two years later, these figures either fell to below the 10% mark, to 4.3% for Lithuania and 11.1% for Slovakia.[18] All in all, the shock of 1990–1992 was of exceptional intensity for all the countries except Czechoslovakia (where so-called mass privatization was based on a vast social consensus that depended on keeping individuals in their jobs). The decline of unemployment from 1995 onward, then its further take-off in certain countries after 1999–2000 (Poland, Slovakia) and its gentle decrease after EU accession attest to short and very intense cycles that mainly reflect the staggered intensification of restructuring. The most important difference from the 1990s is that, after 2004, shortages of labor were experienced, mainly due to very strong employment and wage growth in the new member states.

How are we to characterize unemployment in the countries of Central and Eastern Europe over the 20 years that have now elapsed? Despite substantial variations over 20 years, the structure of unemployment has hardly varied at all.[19] There is, first, a long-term unemployment, which in 2003 affected more than 40% of the unemployed. Calculated on the basis of 11 workless months, the long-term unemployed represent 60% and more in Romania, Bulgaria, and Slovakia, and almost 50% in Poland and the Czech Republic.[20] The 1955 studies carried out by Zecchini very early revealed a feature that has persisted over almost two decades: those who "fall" into the pool of the unemployed have little chance of refinding work, for the rates of return to employment are very low.[21] Thus the OECD economist spoke of a "stagnant pool" to indicate that job creation was not achieved through the employment agencies, but by the passage of workers directly from public to private enterprises. The latter did not absorb the unemployed. Why was this? Probably because information on individuals was deficient; because a bad image of the individual who has lost his job became solidly rooted—stigmatization relegates him to the rank of idler who, in a way, deserves his fate; because there is a loss of skills associated with long-term unemployment; and because the regions where there is unemployment are not those where other jobs are on offer. This remark also applies to the different sectors. Despite the creation of jobs in the private sector, an unemployed person has little chance of finding employment. We should add to this general picture the finding that public aid has proved very ineffective, particularly "public works programs," which have only in rare cases produced a return to employment.[22]

Table 9.4 Unemployment Rate, 1998–2007

	1998	2000	2004	2007
Bulgaria	NC	16.4	12.1	6.9
Czech Republic	6.4	8.8	8.3	5.3
Estonia	9.2	12.8	9.7	4.7
Hungary	8.4	6.4	6.1	7.4
Latvia	14.3	13.7	10.4	6.0
Lithuania	13.2	16.4	11.4	4.3
Poland	10.2	16.1	20.0	9.6
Romania	NC	7.3	8.1	6.4
Slovakia	12.6	18.8	18.2	11.1
Slovenia	7.4	6.7	6.3	4.9

Source: These figures were taken from Eurostat statistics, available online: http://epp.eurostat.ec.europa.eu

The longer workers have been out of a job, the less chance there is of them obtaining employment. For this reason, the phenomena around "unemployability," widely analyzed in the West, have found confirmation in Central and Eastern Europe.

Unemployment affected young people in huge numbers, particularly school-leavers. Since the young were regarded by entrepreneurs as too expensive or too unskilled, older people and those in employment had more chance of retaining their jobs. Moreover, women were in a majority in the unemployment statistics in the first half of the decade, as they were after 1998 in Hungary, Poland, and Bulgaria, where female unemployment exceeded the West European average of 52%. With women's jobs underpaid, a large number of females left the labor market. Though very much in the majority in the industrial and agricultural unemployment statistics, women have benefited from the growth of the tertiary sector. However, being penalized by the nature of the available public employment (particularly in public works) and by a high level of discrimination at the point of recruitment, they have been more affected than men by long-term unemployment and for that reason have been readier to take— less well-paid—part-time jobs. Phenomena of "multiple social disadvantage" have, to a large degree, brought stigmatization for women working in industry or agriculture, unskilled women, the disabled and members of minorities. The supply of jobs has fallen far short of the demand, particularly in the countryside.

Unemployment has been largely territorialized. The town/country split has been reinforced by the very low level of mobility, made even more acute by problems relating to transport, the housing shortage, and behavioral customs. Where the town/country split is concerned, we should stress that in many places the map of unemployment does not show rural areas among those with the highest levels. However, this is because concealed unemployment largely prevails in the rural areas, greatly distorting the statistics. This is the case in Poland, Romania, and Bulgaria, and also in the Eastern parts of Hungary and Slovakia. A last element concerns unregistered unemployment. It is assumed in Poland that 20–30% of individuals who could claim unemployment benefit are not found on the register, but a similar number are thought to be on the lists while actually working. Here questions of poverty, "moonlighting," and migration come into play.

Poverty

As calculated by the World Bank, poverty means earning less than 2.15$ per day.[23] On this basis in 2003, 6.4% of Bulgarians, 6.6% of Lithuanians, and 6.8% of Romanians may be termed poor. If we take a base of 4.2$ per day, for which there are more solid grounds, we would have to multiply these figures by a factor of four or five. There would then be fewer than 1% of Czechs and Slovenes who were poor, but 15.4% of Hungarians, 18.4% of Poles and Bulgarians, 34.1% of Latvians, and 44.5% of Romanians.[24] As a

general rule, poverty increased after 1989, particularly the phenomenon
of the "working poor," irrespective of the fact that most of the countries
either returned to, or surpassed, their 1990 levels.[25] Inequalities of income
increased everywhere between 1989 and 2001. Vaughan-Whitehead has
suggested that working poverty in Eastern Europe affected 40% of the
population, with spikes of over 70% in the case of Poland and Lithuania.[26]
According to the data in the 2003 Development Report and on the basis
of an income of less than 5$ per day (PPA), 5.8 million individuals in
Poland (15.1% of the population) are poor; 8.1% are living at a level below
the subsistence minimum (the figure was 4.3% in 1996). These figures
largely represent unemployed, unskilled individuals living in rural areas
with a large number of children. Some 5.4% of children suffer from mal-
nutrition (2.9% in 1990). The Fourth Cohesion Report indicates that
poverty affects children in Poland (29%), Lithuania (27%), and Romania
(25%) worst. However, since 2004, poverty is said to have diminished
appreciably.[27]

Generally, agricultural producers not producing for the market are
affected by poverty. In some countries this is a very substantial group. It is
estimated that in Poland, around 50% of peasant farmers with one or two
hectares of land do not produce for the market and are living in poverty.
Minorities are more subject to exclusion and poverty than majority populations. Several studies have shown that among these groups the Roma
suffer most, given their massive exclusion from the workplaces where the
requisite qualifications are lowest. With men having lost their jobs and
having barely any hope of finding new work, it falls to the women, who
are still as active as mothers as they were before—even though social benefits have virtually disappeared—to be the breadwinners in the toughest
of conditions. Urban poverty is distinct from rural poverty, since the latter affects particular populations. Urban poverty has reinforced the traditional features of certain cities. For example, Lodz in Poland has always
had insalubrious districts with high levels of poverty. These have now
become areas of confirmed social exclusion. Urban poverty has increased
thanks to resourceless populations living outside of occupational or famil-
ial milieus. The term "social disqualification," signifying loss of the reference markers linked to employment, the family, and the symbolic register,
can appropriately be attached to such cases. Rural poverty is different,
as it afflicts a well-identified population in enormous numbers. Those
concerned are often former employees of the state farms, who lost their
jobs in the wake of the abolition of the collective state enterprises. Today,
these groups, involving entire families that were in the past assisted by the
public authorities in respect of housing, work, childcare, and education,
do not have the educational qualifications to find employment elsewhere.
Their unemployability is attributable to their low level—or even total
lack—of qualifications. It is reinforced by their lack of mobility, given the
fact that the local municipalities have left them their apartments in the
former farm, but now without any amenities or comfort.

The Informal Economy, Moonlighting, and Migration

The foregoing data help to explain the size of the "gray" or informal economy, which is a very important economic and social reality in Central and Eastern Europe. The informal economy is, in fact, the product of a situation in which lifeless labor markets are combined with low wages and poverty, and also with deficits in public institutions. When the latter are incapable of providing welfare benefits that enable people to meet their minimum needs, "individual resourcefulness" is often the only way out with, as its "dark" side, the maintenance of a type of local regulation that locks individuals into dependence on employers.

Informal economy phenomena did not simply appear after the fall of Communism. They were very often found in the old Soviet-type economies, figuring in the analysis of two phenomena: the absence of certain goods on the market and "individual resourcefulness." In this sense, they were closely associated with the shortage economy, and indeed smoothed its operation. After 1990 these so-called phenomena of "social pathology" related more to misappropriation (the informal economy), and also to a contraction in the labor market and in incomes ("moonlighting"). Mention must be made here of the border regions, particularly in the East. After seeing an unprecedented collapse of the collective agricultural structures and of trade with the neighboring former Soviet republics, these effects were not offset by the arrival of foreign investors, as happened on the Western borders. For these reasons, these regions were a significant arena for "gray dealings," whether in the form of local "bazaars" or mobile small markets. In the 2000s, the imposition of the so-called Schengen legislation penalized these areas a second time by forcing the authorities to implement very strict border control procedures. This significantly reduced the level of such "makeshift" forms of trade and of other little dealings of all kinds, which had fulfilled a crucial social function of cushioning the effects of change. The scale of the misappropriation that falls under the heading of the informal economy is substantial. Official Polish assessments (drawn up by the Statistical Office's research institute) speak of a figure equivalent to 100 billion dollars for the year 1994, which is 20% of GDP. Some have suggested a range between 20 and 40% of GDP. It would seem there were some positive developments over the decade, even though the informal economy remained very sizeable in 2004. It was said to represent even more than 40% of GDP in Latvia/Estonia, 35% in Bulgaria and Romania, 30% in Poland and Lithuania, 25% in Hungary and Slovenia, and 20% in Slovakia.[28] According to a report submitted to the Brussels Commission at enlargement in 2004, three groups may be distinguished among the new members. The first involves those in which the volume of transactions in the "gray" economy corresponded to between 8 and 13% of GDP (Czech Republic, Slovakia, and Estonia). The middle group (between 14 and 20% of GDP) concerns Poland, Slovenia, Hungary, Lithuania, and Latvia. The last group, allegedly between 21 and 22%, includes Bulgaria and Romania.[29] The main activities concerned are said to be those associated with hotels and catering, repair, agriculture, and, to a much lesser extent, manufacturing. Professional services are also very much involved. The Bulgarian specialists add that this relates to activities extending over at least 10 hours per week, for which the income received is higher than the average wage. Men are more involved than women, and people in urban areas more often than those in rural parts. More than one-third of these individuals would seem to be unemployed and these activities provide three quarters of their income (the rest being made up by their unemployment benefit). They are mostly (more than 60%) without professional qualifications, even though one finds a nonnegligible number of highly qualified individuals among them. One-fifth of such activities consist in agriculture and gardening, followed by building work, domestic work, caretaking, and repair. Foreign workers are said to be involved in greater numbers in the rural areas, particularly at harvest time. There is massive recourse to the informal economy by the unemployed.

Finally, if "moonlighting" may be interpreted as an implementation of strategies for circumventing the economic situation internally, migration is, in a sense, its external equivalent. Outside the Communist period, the countries of Central and Eastern Europe have always been lands of emigration. Between 1945 and 1989, the waves of emigration corresponded in fact to the periods of repression, known as "normalization" that followed the Hungarian uprising of 1956, the Czech uprising of 1968, and the various periods of revolt in Poland in 1968 and 1981 in particular. From 1990 onward, forces for migratory mobility reemerged. These dynamics were continuous until 2004, either in permanent or temporary forms, particularly to keep farms functioning or to provide additional incomes in ways connected with the proximity of borders. The main destinations were Germany and Austria, as well as the United States. After 2004, these dynamics changed in nature. They came to public attention, particularly in the Polish case, though subsequently also in that of Romania and Bulgaria, on account of fears aroused in the West of population movements that were seen as excessively large and uncontrollable. This is why, with the exception of three countries (Great Britain, Ireland, and Sweden), the former member states negotiated transitional periods and limited access to their labor markets. As a result, the three countries cited above received more immigrants than the old continental nations from the new accession countries. Above all, however, it was the profiles of the migrants that were surprising, since, far from concerning unskilled individuals, as was the case before 1939, these dynamics involved qualified people (working in the sectors of health and medicine, as well as building or catering). The impact was so great that it contributed to reversing historic dynamics and making Poland since that date a country of immigration. Another substantial effect is the impact on labor markets and jobseeker figures, which have fallen, particularly in Poland. The number of emigrants is thought to have risen to two million between 2004 and 2007, 65% of these to Great Britain.

How Valid Is the Theory of Cleavages?

Given our understanding of these various component features of the growing differentiation of interests after 1989, how are we to evaluate their impact on the polarization into parties? This is to ask the question of the assessment of the typology of political cleavages drawn up by Rokkan and Lipset, and hence, more widely, to enquire into the structuring of the modernization dynamics of the European states.[30] That approach, which has been widely drawn on since 1989 for the analysis of parties in Central and Eastern Europe,[31] has been subjected to many criticisms, mainly on the grounds that it is inappropriate to transfer an evolutionary development model based on cleavages to a reality characterized by different legacies.[32] In other words, the two pairs of social divides analyzed by Rokkan would apply to the West only and not to Eastern Europe. What cleavages are significant, then, in the analysis of Central and Eastern Europe?

A Critique of the Cleavages Approach

Several observers have highlighted the thoroughgoing changes brought about by Communist domination over more than 40 years. To begin with, the peasantry can be said to have disappeared, leaving behind a group of agricultural wage earners who no longer share the specific interests of the peasants of yesteryear. Similarly, the working classes can be said to have undergone a total transformation, on account of the industrialization process that left them largely disorganized, without trade unions worthy of the name, and also without employers standing against them. To this may be added the crucial absence of an active urban middle class. For these three basic reasons, which show up the decisive impact of the Communist period, not only may the parties be said to be differently constructed after 1989, but they are in no sense mass parties or parties with an activist membership. They are, fundamentally, elite parties, operating, in the words of the Berlin political scientist Gert-Joachim Glaessner, as "political organizations made up of new and old elites in pursuit of electors and a social base."[33] Sharing these criticisms, the Czech political scientist Machonin has highlighted the five original cleavages that structure the post-1989 political scenes.[34] The first of these concerns the opposition between the privileged individuals of the old system and the new rising class, based on the observation that the former were a group of individuals without high skills or qualifications in the 1960s and 1970s, at the point of their recruitment, but were heavily favored by the authorities before 1989 in exchange for their unfailing support for the Communist regime. Given an increase in income inequalities, the second cleavage is the one between rich and poor: 18–25% of wage earners have allegedly been "winners" in the great post-1989 transformation, but at the bottom of the scale there are 25–30% who are poor or excluded. Egalitarianism, the basis of pre-1989 social equilibria, has seemingly been shattered since that date, leaving behind deep income inequalities. The third cleavage concerns the opposition between the advocates of civil society, who incline toward the "libertarian," and those individuals favoring authoritarianism and bureaucracy. Jean Michel de Waele and Alain Sellier see the cleavage between authoritarian and democratic behavior as reproducing that between traditionalism and Westernism.[35] Authoritarianism can be equated with nationalism, a role for the state in history, and an antiabortion, proreligion stance. In the view of all the authors just cited, it is this basic opposition that seems to have been most significant after 1990. The fourth cleavage is between the advocates of the European Union and the Eurosceptics. The former are, for the most part, qualified individuals supporting postmodern dynamics of development (and the environment). The latter are more attached to the pre–1989 values of egalitarianism. Finally, the last cleavage refers to the relations between the centers and the minorities. We shall return to this point below.

All in all, it would seem that the absence of cleavages in Central and Eastern Europe after 1989 can be chiefly explained by the low degree of social stratification at the end of almost half a century of Communism. The dominant egalitarianism can be said to have produced an absence of differentiations of status, education, and property—a feature reinforced by the absence of civil society noted in the last chapter. For these reasons, what may be true of Western Europe can be said not to apply in the East. In this context, it would be interesting to examine the subsequent structuring of this opposition, enabling Rokkan's various cleavages to be questioned. Let us examine the validity of the different pairs stated above, with the clear understanding that a cleavage is not simply a recognition of one of the poles mentioned, but the recognition of a conflict that differentiates interests, this cleavage then being taken up by opposing parties. Communist or socialist parties, agrarian parties, liberal parties, conservative parties, or confessional parties can be distinguished on this socio-economico-cultural basis, it being also understood that several cleavages may overlap and the various issues involved may be taken up by a single party. This may lead to coalitions around particular issues. The analysis of these coalitions and, more generally, of the development of the political scenes, is not the aim of this work. We shall confine ourselves to examining the validity of the Rokannian cleavages in the light of the findings established in the foregoing chapters.

Class Conflict

The first cleavage is the one relating to class conflict, which, according to some writers, has singularly diminished in Western Europe. This can be explained both by the way working-class influence has diminished and by the change in status of the employers, following the introduction of new forms of governance of enterprises. In Eastern Europe, the conclusions we drew from chapter six confirm this thoroughgoing change in the working classes, but for other reasons. It follows the massive deindustrialization that has occurred since 1989 and the deep changes in modes of representation, particularly labor union representation. The notion of *Facharbeitergesellschaft* (skilled workers' society), which was used to describe the GDR,[36] became obsolete after 1989, on account of the dynamics of training running through the whole of East German society. These dynamics modified social statuses from top to bottom. This remark goes for the whole of Eastern Europe, confronted, as it was, with an enormous deindustrialization. Unskilled workers were the big "losers" in the transformation of the industrial world, as we have seen. The defeat of the engineers and technicians, who could have found a place in the new order but did not, found no resonance in trade union milieus. There was no white-collar union. As for the blue-collar unions, their substantially decreased levels of representation and mobilization contributed to dismantling a working-class identity that was, in fact, widely differentiated by sector before 1990. Some observers saw the class consciousness among Polish workers in 1980 as one of the features of Solidarnosc's exceptionalism, such a thing being nonexistent in the other Eastern bloc countries.

The most important point is doubtless the fundamental change affecting the employers, given the radical changes in rights of ownership and the lack of professional organizations. As a social category, these employers are not interested in sharing their prerogatives either at the central level in tripartite forums or at the local level within enterprises. On the contrary, the employers' social predominance expressed itself in the weakening of workers' power, the reinforcement of discipline, the imposition of strict norms, and the abandonment of collective forums for negotiation. As in Western Europe, the forms of governance radically modified identities and the nature of conflicts.

In chapter seven we identified the low level of conflictuality for a whole set of reasons relating both to the development of ownership structures and to the fall in union membership, but also to levels of consensus about the paths being followed. The high degree of individualization consecutive upon the process of modernization seems to have swept away everything that could remotely resemble class conflict. The individualization of contracts, which presents itself as one of the great innovations of the post–Communist period, is based on calculation and the measurement of time, whether the worker who is party to the contract is an employee or a subcontractor. Such an arrangement is not conducive to collective action. Self-employment is the extreme form of this. Though we would not wish to assert that there are no oppositions of interest between employers and employee, we have at least to admit that some of those oppositions are only weakly articulated to procedures of conflict and negotiation, and that they are not in any way reflected in party programs. Hence the references for this cleavage now seem very weak.

Urban/Rural Conflict

What validity are we to accord to the cleavage between the urban world and the rural? This too is very much weakened in Western Europe on account of the considerable fall in the numbers working in agriculture over the past 30 years. An agricultural country like France, which, at the turn of the 1950s, had 45% of its workforce in agriculture and 10 years later 25%, had barely 2% working in that sector in 2007 and the number of farms has gone on falling. The same dynamic is at work in Eastern Europe, under the combined impact of the collapse of collective agricultural structures and the accelerated tertiarization of activities, while the old agricultural populations have been hit by a significant level of unemployment (particularly in the form of "concealed unemployment"). Yet the situation is highly differentiated. Five countries, highlighted in chapter six, reveal opposite dynamics: Latvia and Lithuania with 15% of workers in agriculture, Poland, where the rate has leveled out since 1990 at around 20%, Bulgaria where it has risen to 30%, and Romania where, since 2002, it has passed the 40% mark. The question here is whether such differences in social structure foster conflicts between urban and rural milieus in such a way as to account for the emergence of agrarian parties in opposition to urban ones. The answer is complex. On the one hand, it must take account of the upheaval in the structure of farms and the fall in agricultural incomes, especially in the first years. On this point, it seems appropriate to speak of an "agrarian question" in Poland, Slovenia, Hungary, Latvia, Lithuania, Bulgaria, and Romania, as is confirmed by the existence of peasant parties, some of them powerful (Rieger, 2004). For this reason, some observers take the view that the urban/rural cleavage is pertinent. The answer must, however, take account of the other countries, which have seen falls in agricultural employment or incomes and that do not have powerful agrarian parties. The influence of the Slovakian agrarian party is significant, even though agricultural workers make up less than 10% of the workforce, whereas the Bulgarian agrarian party has less of an influence, even though the proportion of agricultural workers is much higher.

The Bulgarian agrarian party, UAPB, has split into several smaller parties and has had to combine with the PSB (the reformed ex-Communists), which seems far more capable of defending agricultural interests, or at least did so until 1997. The Bulgarian case is particularly important here, since that was the only country that had, before the war, been led by an agrarian party, Stambolijski's Agrarian Union, which was in power from 1919 to 1923. The fact that its heirs were incapable of reviving its program after 1990 proves the thoroughgoing nature of the transformation wrought by Communism, the weakness of the—mostly urban—opponents after 1990, the diminution of tensions between the urban and rural worlds after land redistribution, and the very weak actuality of the rural/urban cleavage in that country. The key element here seems to be the evolution of peasant

identities on the part of individuals who do not now think of themselves
as peasants, on account of the opportunities found for work outside agriculture before 1989. According to Gerald Creed, this is what explains
the rural population's rejection after 1990 of liberal policies aimed at dismantling the cooperatives, the aim of which was to "repeasantize" them,
but this time without the peasants having sufficient resources to make a
living. Their decision to support the successor to the Communist Party,
the PSB, is to be explained not by any ideological commitment to the
Communist cause, but by the concern to preserve some elements of the
traditional cooperative spirit, the legacy of which Communist collectivization had partly taken over.[37]

Agrarianism was a mainstream current in interwar politics. There
was a point when the formation of a "Green International" was contem-
plated that would have brought together the agrarian parties of Bulgaria,
Hungary, Poland, and Lithuania. Though, admittedly, it came to nothing,
it nonetheless attempted to unite various East European countries around
a program for the defense of small property against urban capitalism and,
beyond this, against the Communist and fascist ideologies. Agrarianism
did not, however, have any real resonance in Central and Eastern Europe
after 1990. For several reasons, the reformed ex-Communist parties, such
as the Bulgarian PSB, seemed more able than the others to take up peasant demands. First, because, like the representatives of the old socialist or
social-democratic parties, those who remembered political agrarianism
were advanced in age in 1990 and, 10 years later, they had more or less
disappeared. Second, because the pre-1989 transformations of agriculture
had provided rural populations with an identity and means of resistance
to the post-1990 upheavals, and because the other parties that tried to
reform agriculture were liberal, urban parties, whose ignorance of rural
conditions contributed in large part to hastening the devastation of the
countryside. To the arguments relating to the socioeconomic dynamics of change, we have doubtless to add the influence of the Common
Agricultural Policy (CAP). From 2004 onward, the CAP was massively
supported by East European farmers and by the small peasants, even when
they expressed anti-European positions at election times, and also by the
other parties. The support given to the CAP eliminated a massive source
of the opposition that could have anchored itself in the defense of a strictly
national agriculture, representing interests largely separated from those
taken up by the other parties. In reality, all parties defended the European
mechanism, which was conceived in terms of financial aid. As for the
occasional anti-European declarations on the part of some peasant parties,
these involved considerations that had nothing to do with agriculture, but
concerned the sovereignism they shared with other parties on the Right
and extreme Right that were also attached to the defense of the "values
of the soil."

Given the success of the agricultural policy among the farmers, less
than a year after Poland joined the European Union, the Samoobrona

Party had radically changed its stance. It no longer called for Poland to leave the EU, but actively sought a more advantageous renegotiation of the accession treaty. In so doing, it was attempting to combine two opposing postures: support for European aid and constant criticism of Brussels. Though it was still a member of the Law and Justice (PiS) government in 2006—alongside the extreme Right-wing League of Polish Families (LPR)—it disappeared completely from the political scene in October 2007 when it failed to gain 5% of the vote, even though it had been bowling along at twice that figure only three years before. It had neither been able to claim credit for the success of the CAP among the peasants—who saw it at that point as a dangerously disruptive force—nor develop a genuine sovereignist policy or defense of sectional interests, as its partner/competitor the PiS had done. Ultimately, its longstanding competitor, the Polish Peasants' Party (PSL), even though it remained in the Diet and participated actively in the government produced by the elections of 2007, barely profited at all from its disappearance. This is proof, if any were needed, that agricultural interests were better articulated within the other parties, namely those of the liberal (Civic Platform or PO) and sovereignist (PiS) Right.

The Conflict between Secularism and Religion

Examination of the secularization/religion cleavage in Central and Eastern Europe reveals a deeply unbalanced situation in favor of secularization, with the exception of Poland, Romania, and Bulgaria, but for very different reasons in each case. Moreover, this feature of secularization is also noted in Western Europe by the authors cited above. Yves Mény and Yves Surel find that religious practice has diminished, but that religious institutions are nonetheless maintained. Religious education remains widespread in Italy, France, and Germany. They conclude that this cleavage still has enduring influence, mainly because religious values are very important. It is on this count that a distinction with the Eastern part of the continent has to be drawn, since diversity predominates there. The Communist period contributed very greatly to reducing the influence of the churches, in so far as they were put under constant surveillance and were continuously being infiltrated by internal security organizations. The Communist parties saw the churches as one of their most influential enemies, if not indeed the most dangerous, and they had to be kept down, if not indeed wiped out, for the parties to retain full control of behavior. With the exception of Poland and, to a certain degree, the GDR and Hungary,[38] the Communist authorities achieved their goals. The churches were subordinated, some were abolished and their priests, when they were not executed in the 1950s, were put in prison. In the Bulgarian case, the dependence of the Orthodox church on the Communist authorities was extreme. In such conditions, the question after 1989 was not simply what would happen to religion within populations for whom religious practice had represented a constant danger, but what positions would be adopted on societally significant subjects that brought the controlling moral influence of the churches into play. In this connection, the various debates on abortion have shown the influence of secularization, revealing a majority stance based on secular rather than religious frames of reference. History seems to have had an enormous effect, in the sense that the period of Communist domination seems to have been far more significant than that which preceded it. As the German sociologist Detlev Pollack points out, in no other country does one find such a low rate of religious belief as in the Czech Republic or the GDR.[39]

Even in the case of Poland, with its very marked Catholicism, a distinction has to be made between the massive adherence of the citizenry to religion and their proabortion stance. This observation puts the influence of immediate past history firmly on the agenda. Post-1989 choices fit into a tradition that saw the Communist authorities tolerate, and in some cases encourage, abortion on the grounds that it was, in their view, proof of women's liberation and a mark of progress over capitalism. History seems to have the decisive impact here, despite a "return" of religion in the form of a very appreciable increase in those claiming membership of a religion. Hence a clear distinction between the declaration of a religious faith, which may in some cases be written off as social conformism, and espousal of modern, secular social choices.

Taking up issues linked to the membership of one church or another often appears to political parties as a way of reinterpreting the past in the light of their ideological positioning. Poland is unusual in that, although the Right-wing parties present themselves clearly as the defenders of religion, the social-democratic party does not advocate antireligious positions. More than 90% of Poles surveyed claim to be Catholics, an allegiance that greatly transcends any political divisions. John Paul II was a "father figure" to the nation, even managing to bring together at his funeral in Rome in 2005 those sworn enemies Walesa and Kwasniewski, successive presidents of the Polish third republic. As for the defense of the Orthodox church by the Bulgarian Socialist Party, this was largely a way of contesting the pro-European orientation of its opponent, the UDF, whose support for the "schismatic" church was essentially a challenge to the Communist hold over religion. For all concerned, it is a question of reinterpreting past history in the name of opposing values. If there is a divide or "cleavage," it is not, then, between religion and secularism, since all the actors claim to support one church or another, but between partisan prisms of which religion is one facet. The clear separation observed between membership of a church and adherence to a particular form of social behavior it calls for suggests a thoroughgoing secularization. This is reinforced by the significant reduction in the number of churchgoers registered over the decade, with the exception of Poland and, to a lesser extent, Bulgaria and Romania. Fifteen years after the fall of Communism, the churches find themselves very much shorn of power and resources and with very little purchase on the behavior—or even convictions—of their believers. Pollack ends by saying that they took quite a long time to realize that their controlling moral influence over society was a thing of the past.

The Center/Periphery Cleavage

There remains the cleavage between center and periphery. Many observers see this as the key factor that explains how East European political scenes are structured.[40] This work falls in with that position. It does so because some form of this cleavage has been the historic lot of all our countries without exception, allowing it to be reformulated in relation to many different political and economic issues. In highlighting its pertinence, we are able also to include several dimensions of the three preceding cleavages. The analysis of the center/periphery cleavage allows us, in fact, to identify the peripheral position of these states as a consequence, in all the cases cited, of the loss of national sovereignty over several centuries and also of the weakness of the state between 1919 and 1939, and its liquidation as such between 1945 and 1989 as a result of Soviet domination, not forgetting its weakness in the 1990s. The aim of this work has been to analyze the consequences of the reappropriation of national sovereignty in the face of adaptive pressures emanating first from globalization and, to an even greater extent, from the EU. On each occasion, this basic context generated tensions and conflicts that gave rise to partisan divides. These pitted supporters of the center against advocates of the periphery, each of these two poles developing in response to—domestic and international—circumstances. In this regard, the center/periphery cleavage overlaps with the very important cleavage of geopolitics. The latter pits those parties favoring stronger alliances with the West, themselves differentiated between a pole favoring the United States and a more European pole, against those that have no intention of sacrificing the past or, in more extreme terms, the "Slavic community." Each of these positions is conditioned by the idea of sovereignty or, in other words, of nation-state centrality, alliances being supposed to strengthen or diminish its influence.

In each case, "center" refers here to the occupying powers of the nineteenth and twentieth centuries, while "periphery" means the national cultures. Once sovereignty is acquired, the periphery becomes the center once again and the old center becomes the main threat. The concrete applications of this center-periphery axis have, thus, been different depending on the relationship to national sovereignty. For some, it is a question of the relationship with minorities (hence variations in the way regional divisions are established; see chapter four), for others it relates to which nationals are "in" or "out" (as in Hungary), in others it is seen in language terms (in the Baltic states) but, paradoxically, less in oppositions around religion (which have largely faded in Poland). Two categories of country can be distinguished: the first relates the center/periphery divide to the relationship with unitary national history; the second updates the center/periphery cleavage in a conception of the relation to national minorities, particularly those minorities with a degree of economic power. For all, however, this center/periphery cleavage has been reformulated with regard to representations of what the sovereign Nation should be, when confronted with the EU and with opening up its domestic markets, or when oriented more toward the nation-state and full, undivided sovereignty.

For this reason, center and periphery are the two structuring poles that enable a number of previously established findings to be reinterpreted. It was the variable of national sovereignty that was decisive in understanding a number of public policies, as it polarized the various parties, depending on whether they had formed coalitions with external partners or refocused themselves on what in other, earlier historical configurations constituted the periphery, that is, the national dimension. The former showed their support for international institutions, the EU and foreign investors; the latter set greater store by their own resources, while simultaneously denouncing the "sell-off" of their sovereignty.

This notion of center and periphery is crucial, then, for understanding the treatment of history, which is recomposed period by period—a distinction being made between the immediate past and the present—in such a way that we may say the political landscapes are structured on the basis of post-1990 opportunities, as a function either of positionings with regard to the immediate past or of new alliances. During the first decade, the interpretation of the past mainly polarized opinion and behavior through a clear distinction between pro- and anti-Communists. This initial divide was then subsumed in the pro- and anti-EU division, it being understood that in the countries of Central Europe (with the exception of Slovakia) no party really contested the decision to submit to the political conditionality exerted by the EU, while elsewhere anti-EU opinion prevailed. Vachudova coined the interesting concept of "illiberal democracy" to characterize political landscapes of the Slovak, Romanian, and Bulgarian type, which in 1989 and subsequently were made up of political parties that were clearly resolved not to go down the road of breaking down borders, economic reform, civil society, and pluralism, setting more store by a sovereignty in which past elements were left out of account—that is to say, a sovereignty reduced to the "old/new" leaders. The EU can be said to have exerted influence on them by way of the support it gave to voluntary organizations, and to liberal parties that were able, in the circumstances, to gain power and then sign up resolutely to the accession process. The counterexample is provided by the Yugoslav case and, in a different way, by Ukraine, where these democratic forces were not able to reverse the initial dynamic of authoritarianism and of "illiberal" regimes.[41] This is why it is useful to analyze the reform carried out internally by the old Communist parties and whether they became social-democratic parties of the Western European type or remained unreconstructed.[42]

Conclusion

Following Vachudova, then, it is of interest to distinguish partisan positions in terms, on the one hand, of their support for authoritarianism or liberalism, and, on the other, of their promotion of state interventionism or the market. One then acquires a better understanding of the nature of the alliances that may emerge between liberal parties and former Communists in opting for the EU and, conversely, between sovereignists and religious fundamentalists for the defense of national values. This is why, in criticizing their opponents, extreme Right parties or some so-called "populist" parties freely associate liberalism, cosmopolitanism, the European Union, and on occasion—as in the case of Poland—the new social-democratic parties that, for their part advocate the various themes of the economic opening up of markets, a political preference for the European Union and the defense of the underprivileged. But what is true of Poland does not necessarily apply to Bulgaria in this precise way, nor, even more, to the Czech Republic, where other configurations prevail, depending on whether the former Communist Party is allied with the advocates of Orthodoxy (as in the Bulgarian case) or takes an unreconstructed, anti-European stance (as in the Czech example). One can see from this the decisive influence of the EU dimension in the divisions between parties, the latter being largely dominated by the opposition between the "winners" and "losers" of the post-Communist transformation. But this process of Europeanization—for this is what it is at the political level—can be understood only in the light of domestic situations, characterized definitively by the demand for national sovereignty. In other words, the Europeanization of the East European political landscapes—in the event, the impact of the European "question" and of European rules, procedures and exigencies on domestic scenes—was able to emerge only on condition that these rules were reformulated in the long-term strategies of the parties, which, for their part, articulated differently orientated visions of national sovereignty.

CHAPTER TEN

General Conclusion

It has been the aim of this work to give an account of the application, scope, and limits of the approach in terms of Europeanization to the candidate countries of Central and Eastern Europe after 1989, and to do so from several standpoints. The first of these is an approach in terms of legacies, particularly the legacies associated with the Communist period and, less frequently, with the periods preceding the Second World War. We have seen the impact of the representations, of the interests, and even of the historical territories that ensued from this for the period that began in 1989. This has enabled us to understand the strength of certain groups in the period of post-Communism. But these legacies were the more able to shape events because certain rules specific to the post-1989 period turned out themselves to be obstacles to progress, thus strengthening the hands of many actors as "veto players." To the legacies of the Communist period must be added the instances of resistance to change produced by the excessively violent impact of exogenous rules, as, for example, within enterprises, where skills were wiped out without serious evaluation, in agriculture, where forms of collective organization were swept away at a stroke, in the administrations, where inappropriate methods were applied without discernment and, more generally, in all areas of work, with over-hasty assessments of human resources that took no account of individual experience or of group projects. The way human environments were brutally swept aside enables us to understand why, in certain areas and for certain groups, the old settings of action and working relations have come to seem attractive once again and a whole period has been subject to cognitive readjustment, despite in other respects being massively rejected.

Another angle of approach consisted in examining the nature of the EU rules that were strong or weak depending on the sector, and led to processes of adjustment involving various degrees of constraint, each with particular modes of oversight and control. These forms of control proved inescapable when collective security was at stake or, in other words, when matters were entirely the prerogative of the EU. On the other hand, controls were gentler when public policy depended more on the nation-state. The strict adaptation that applied in the former case, which characterized sanitary and phytosanitary control, for example, or the control of external borders, contrasted with the open coordination method that, in the area of employment policy, offered greater flexibility for adaptation.

This led on to an analysis of the various types of impact of European rules, particularly by highlighting the field of representation—particularly in the case of privatization or social policies—and the field of "adaptive" pressure, depending on the existence or absence of particular groups (e.g., "policy advocates" in the case of privatization policies or welfare state reform), and, finally, the field of strategies, which were the guiding thread of all the analyses, be it a question of alliances formed internally with central or local actors (in cases of privatization or regionalization) or externally with foreign partners, be these international institutions or direct foreign investors. This shows the extent to which the Europeanization of the countries of Central and Eastern Europe can be said to have impacted not only the public policy field (with privatization policies), but also the fields of state organizations (with the flagship reforms of regionalization) and political exchanges (with, inter alia, the examination of social divides). However, by studying certain occupational groups, we have seen why the EU could in the end have little influence, leaving it up to local actors to carry out their own transformation. What often won out, in combination, were groups endowed with sizeable previous resources and foreign actors.

At the end of this work, Europeanization may be defined, in the East European case, as the process of adaptation of European Union rules by groups equipped with varied resources, largely borrowed from the immediate period or acquired over the course of the 1990s thanks to various alliances, which underwent a cognitive, normative, and practical adjustment as a result of the premium put on the value most highly esteemed by states during negotiations with the EU: namely, national sovereignty, and its pendant, where individual strategies are concerned, individual freedom.

For this reason, Europeanization is not reducible to the mere process of the extension of EU regulation, as is argued in several Western analyses, which see it as a mere exercise in the transference of norms. Nor can it be equated with convergence. Rather, what we have shown is that there is no rule that has not been adapted to fit with national heritages, on the one hand, and with the new operating contexts that emerged out of 1989, on the other, and ultimately "recomposed" as a function of the various strategies of alliances. In the end, states remained sovereign in the conduct of their internal transformations. For this reason, Europeanization is much more a thing of institutional diversity and, at times, the indicator of a failure of certain expected behaviors to materialize, than the mark of a homogeneity that is nowhere on the horizon today. Whether or not this process of Europeanization can lead, after the last enlargement of 2007, to convergence dynamics on the scale of the 27 member countries, is something the next few years will reveal. The rise of sovereignisms and populisms against a background of acute Euroscepticism after 2004 would tend, rather, to indicate that Europeanization may be combined to a great extent with a divergence in political practices between Western and Eastern Europe. This unexpected strengthening of national reflexes as a result of EU pressure is not, in the end, at odds with the very history of European construction. With the new members, the EU is more than ever a union of sovereign states, not a federation.

If the East European cases have one specific characteristic, it is to be found in this demand for state sovereignty. We have seen that this was all the stronger for the fact of its having been crushed or denied for long periods. This explains the initial convergence of thinking with the West European elites in the expression of a genuine "collective European identity,"[1] since that national sovereignty was conceptualized within the European framework, in either its pre-1939 or post-1989 form. For this reason, the "return to Europe" was the obvious course for East European elites at that date. Vachudova is right to stress the fact that this concerned the elites of the "liberal democracies," for when the bearers of this identity were political actors united in the idea of construing the benefits of membership as the general interest, there was a match between representations and interests. But when this general interest of membership was not shared as such by all the components of the political scenes (the "illiberal democracies"), then accession was rejected.[2] What the cases of the East European countries that entered the EU in 2004 and 2007 show is that they all, at different speeds, took this sharing of a common interest—and hence a unified collective strategy—on board, and for this reason were integrated into the EU. Furthermore, it is because they did so that reforms were launched so much more quickly, setting off a virtuous cycle that linked domestic reforms to the final objective.[3] But if they did so, this was also because there was an advantage attached to the substantial costs that accompanied the transformation of their economies and societies. From these remarks, we shall draw two final conclusions.

The first concerns the validation of the approach in terms of Europeanization for the understanding of the transformation in Eastern Europe and, hence, the connection of that approach with currents of analysis in the West. This represents a very important gain and, by opening up the vast field of comparison of the different processes of change in Eastern and Western Europe, it puts an end once and for all to the brief interlude of "Sovietological" approaches. Whether one stresses the "constructivist" dimension by granting primacy to "ideas" and the strategies that ensue from them[4] or adopts the "realist" approach that is concerned primarily with interests and the combinations of costs and benefits that they reveal,[5] Europeanization is a pertinent approach for understanding Eastern Europe. However, it is so only on condition that the particular weight of history is taken into account: the demands of identity, the impact of national sovereignty, and the strategies that ensue from it—in other words, "path dependency."

The second conclusion is of a practical order. It relates to the understanding of the phenomena of Europeanization in Eastern Europe so
far as the new policies established with regard to the "new neighbors"
(ENP—European Neighbourhood Policy) are concerned. It is clear today
that when the anticipated benefit (integration) fails to materialize, the
grounds for adjustment are largely inoperative.[6] The new members of the
EU27 agreed to carry out their difficult process of transformation for
two major reasons: first, because it was a question of giving body to that
European unity that, once accepted, led to certain choices and excluded
others; second because the EU15 was "credible" in linking the ensured
benefit of integration and financial assistance to the costs of the internal
transformations required.[7] This is what is to be understood by the notion
of "political conditionality," which definitely forced candidate countries
into adjustment by making the adoption of the *Acquis Communautaire* the
ultimate criterion of membership, but which equally forced the EU itself
to indicate very precisely the date from which, with all the chapters of the
Acquis closed, membership would be effective. In this regard, the period
of adjustment—another term for Europeanization—did indeed unfold
according to the terms of a contract, a contract admittedly made between
unequal partners with asymmetric resources, but partners who were
"bound" reciprocally by rights and duties freely consented to. With the
"new neighbors policy," however, not only is it not certain that the idea of
a European "collective identity" preexists that policy, but it is clear, at least
up to the present, that these countries will not have the benefit of integration at the end of their efforts to incorporate the *Acquis*. With the framework of negotiations set in this way, it is hard to see what would induce
them to undertake such expensive and politically uncertain reforms. On
the other hand, one can clearly grasp the risks of instability and growing
uncertainty on the borders of the EU. It is these same elements that lay at
the basis of European construction 60 years ago, and then of its extraordi-
nary extension for the benefit of the vast majority.

NOTES

Introduction: Modernization, Europeanization, and Path Dependency

1. Berendt, Ivan T., *Decades of Crisis. Central and Eastern Europe before World War II*. Berkeley/London/Los Angeles: University of California, 1996; Janos, Andrew, *East Central Europe in the Modern World: The Politics of the Borderland from the Pre- to the Post-Communist System*. San Francisco: Stanford University Press, 2000.
2. Schimmelfenning, Frank and Ulrich Sedelmeier, *Conceptualizing the Europeanization of Eastern and Central Europe*. Ithaca NY: Cornell University Press, 2005.
3. Habermas, Jürgen, *Die nachholende Revolution*. Frankfurt am Main: Surkhamp, 1990.
4. Ash, Garton, *We the People*. London: Granta, 1990.
5. Weber, Max, *Economy and Society*. Berkeley: University of California Press, 1978.
6. Lepsius, Rainer Maria, "Die Institutionenordnung als Rahmenbedingungen der Sozialgeschichte der DDR," in Hartmut Kaelbe, Jürgen Kocka, and Hartmut Zwahr (eds.). *Sozialgeschichte der DDR*. Stuttgart: Klett Kotta, 1994, pp. 17–30.
7. Parsons, Talcott, *Societies: Evolutionary and Comparative Perspectives*. Englewood Cliffs NJ: Prentice Hall, 1966.
8. Zapf, Wolfgang, *Modernisierung, Wohlfahrtentwicklung und Transformation*. Berlin: Editions Sigma, 1994 and "Die Transformation in der ehemaligen DDR und die soziologische Theorie der Modernisierung," *Berliner Journal für Soziologie*, 3, 1994, pp. 295–305.
9. Calculated in dollars (base 1960), the GNP of Central Europe, by comparison with that of Western Europe, stood at 56% in 1860, 57% in 1913, 61% in 1938, and 82% in 1982 (figures from Berendt, *Decades of Crisis. Central and Eastern Europe before World War II*, p. 188).
10. Mises, Ludwig von, *Socialism: An Economic and Social Analysis*. Liberty Fund, 1981 (sixth edition).
11. Lepsius, Rainer Maria, "Die Institutionenordnung als Rahmenbedingungen der Sozialgeschichte der DDR," in Hartmut Kaelbe, Jürgen Kocka, and Hartmut Zwahr (eds.), *Sozialgeschichte der DDR*. Stuttgart: Klett Kotta, 1994, pp. 17–30. See also Meuschel, Sigrid, *Legitimation und Parteiherrschaft, Zum Paradox vom Stabilität und Revolution in der DDR*. Frankfurt am Main: Surkhamp, 1992.
12. Glaessner, Gert-Joachim (ed.), *Der lange Weg zur Einheit*. Berlin: Dietz Verlag, 1993; Kollmorgen, Raj, "Auf der Suche nach Theorien der Transformation. Überlegungen zu Begriff und Theoretisierung der postsozialistischen Transformationen," *Berliner Journal für Soziologie*, 4, 4, 1994, pp. 381–399.
13. Dobry, Michel, *Democratic and Capitalist Transition in Eastern Europe. Lessons for the Social Sciences*. Dordrecht/Boston: Kluwer Academic, 2000.
14. Lutz, B. and R. Schmidt, *Chancen und Risiken der industriellen Restrukturierung in Ostdeutschland*. Berlin: Akademie Verlag, 1995.
15. Bibo, István, *Misère des petits états d'Europe de l'Est*. Paris: Albin Michel, 1984.
16. Evans, Peter B., Dietrich Rueschemeyer, and Theda Skokpol, *Bringing the State Back in*. Cambridge: Cambridge University Press, 1984; Rueschemeyer, Dietrich, Evelyn Stephen, and John D. Stephens, *Capitalism, Development and Democracy*. Oxford: Polity Press, 1992.

17. Kutter, A. and V. Trappmann (eds.), *Das Erbe des Beitritts. Europäisierung in Mittel- und Osteuropa. Europäische Schriften.* Baden-Baden: Nomos, 2006.
18. We need cite only Grotz, Florian, *Politische Institutionen und Post-sozialistische Parteiensysteme in Ostmitteleuropa.* Opladen: Leske und Budrich, 2000; Green Cowles, Maria, James Caporaso, and Thomas Risse (eds.), *Transforming Europe: Europeanization and Domestic Change.* Ithaca NY: Cornell University Press, 2001; Tanja, Börzel and Thomas Risse, "When Europe Hits Home: Europeanization and Domestic Change." European Intergration Online Papers, 2000. http:// eiop.or.at/eiop/text/2000-015a.htm; Featherstone, K. and C. M. Radaelli (eds.), *The Politics of Europeanization.* Oxford: Oxford University Press, 2003; and, in French, Palier, Bruno and Yves Surel, *L'Europe en action, l'européanisation dans une perspective comparée.* Paris: L'Harmattan, 2007; Baisnée, Olivier and Romain Pasquier, *L'Europe telle qu'elle se fait. Européanisation et sociétés politiques nationales.* Paris: CNRS Éditions, 2007.
19. Lippert, B. and G. Umbach, *The Pressure of Europeanization: From Post-Communist State Administrations to Normal Players in the EU System.* Baden-Baden: Nomos, 2005; Schimmelfenning, Frank and Ulrich Sedelmeier, *Conceptualizing the Europeanization of Eastern and Central Europe.* Ithaca NY: Cornell University Press, 2005.
20. Kutter, A. and V. Trappmann (eds.), *Das Erbe des Beitritts. Europäisierung in Mittel- und Osteuropa. Europäische Schriften.* Baden-Baden: Nomos, 2006; Saurugger, S. and Yves Surel, "L'européanisation comme processus de transfert de politique publique," *Revue Internationale de Politique Comparée,* 13, 2, 2006, pp. 179–211; Bafoil, François and Timm Beichelt (eds.), *L'Européanisation d'Ouest en Est.* Paris: L'Harmattan, 2008.
21. Palier and Surel, *L'Europe en action, l'européanisation dans une perspective comparée,* and Baisnée and Pasquier, *L'Europe telle qu'elle se fait. Européanisation et sociétés politiques nationales.*
22. O'Donnell, Guillermo and Philippe Schmitter, *Transition from Authoritarian Rules: Prospects for Democracy.* Baltimore: Johns Hopkins University Press, 1986; Przeworski, Adam, *Democracy and the Market, Political and Economic Reforms in Eastern Europe and Latin America.* New York: Cambridge University Press, 1991.
23. Cf. Roland, Gérard, *Transition and Economics: Politics, Markets, and Firms.* Cambridge MA: MIT Press, 2000; Major, Istvan, *Privatization and Economic Peformance in Central and Eastern Europe. Lessons to Be Learnt from Western Europe.* Cheltenham: Edward Elgar, 1999; Lavigne, Marie, *The Economics of Transition. From Socialist Economy to Market Economy.* London: Macmillan, 1999; Orenstein, Mitchell A., *Out of the Red. Building Capitalism and Democracy in Post-Communist Europe.* Ann Arbor: University of Michigan Press, 2000; White, Stephen, Judy Batt, and Paul G. Lewis (eds.), *Developments in Central and Eastern European Politics.* Basingstoke: Palgrave, 2003; Winiecki, Jan, "Determinants of Catching Up or Falling Behind: Interaction of Formal and Informal Institutions," *Post-Communist Economies,* 16, 2, June 2004, pp. 137–152.; Zielonka, Jan and Alex Pravda (eds.), *Democratic Consolidation in Eastern Europe. Vol. 1: Institutional Engineering. Vol. 2: Institutional and Transnational Factors.* Oxford: Oxford University Press, 2003.
24. Caporaso, James, Maria Green Cowles, and Thomas Risse (eds.), *Transforming Europe. Europeanization and Domestic Change.* Ithaca NY: Cornell University Press, 2001; Börzel, Tanja, *Pace-Setting, Foot-Dragging and Fence-Sitting. Member State Responses to Europeanization.* Queen's Papers on Europeanization, 4/2001. http://www.qub.ac.uk/ies/onlinepapers/poe4-01.pdf. And from the same authors, "Shaping and Taking EU Policies: Member State Responses to Europeanization." Queen's Papers on Europeanization, 2/2003. http://ideas.repec.org/p/ erp/queens/p0035.html and "Deep Impact? Europeanization and Eastern Enlargement," in Kutter, A. and V. Trappmann (eds.), *Das Erbe des Beitritts. Europäisierung in Mittel- und Osteuropa. Europäische Schriften.* Baden-Baden: Nomos, 2006, pp. 99–115.
25. Schimmelfennig, Frank, "Strategic Calculations and International Socialization: Memberships, Incentives, Party Constellations, and Sustained Compliance in Central and Eastern Europe," *International Organization,* 59, Fall 2005, pp. 827–860.
26. Börzel, Tanja, "Deep Impact? Europeanization and Eastern Enlargement," in Kutter and Trappmann (eds.), *Das Erbe des Beitritts. Europäisierung in Mittel- und Osteuropa. Europäische Schriften,* pp. 99–115.
27. Kutter and Trappmann, *Das Erbe des Beitritts. Europäisierung in Mittel- und Os Europa,* pp. 257–269.
28. Radaelli, Claudio, "The Domestic Impact of European Union Public Policy: Notes on Concepts, Methods, and the Challenge of Empirical Research," *Politique européenne,* 5, 2001; Palier, Bruno and Yves Surel, *L'Europe en action, l'européanisation dans une perspective comparée.*

Paris: L'Harmattan, 2007; Bafoil, François and Timm Beichelt (eds.), *L'Européanisation d'Ouest en Est*. Paris: L'Harmattan, 2008.

29. Sedelmeier, Ulrich, "Eastern Enlargement: Towards a European EU?" in Helen Wallace and William Wallace, *Policy-Making in the European Union*. Fifth Edition. Oxford: Oxford University Press, 2005, pp. 402–428.

30. Lippert, Barbara, "Teilhabe statt Mitgliedschaft. Die EU und Ihre Nachbarn im Osten," *Osteuropa*, 57, 2–3, 2006, pp. 69–94.

31. Garton Ash, Timothy, *We the People*. London: Granta, 1990 and Tismaneanu, Vladimir, *Between Past and Future. The Revolutions of 1989 and Their Aftermath*. Budapest: Central University Press, 2000.

32. March, James and Jan Olsen, *Rediscovering Institutions. The Organizational Basis of Politics*. New York: Free Press, 1989.

33. North, Douglas C., "Economic Performance through Time," *American Economic Review*, June 1994, pp. 359–368.

34. Stark, David, "Recombinant Property in Eastern European Capitalism," *American Journal of Sociology*, 4, 1996, pp. 993–1027.

35. Dobry Michel, *Democratic and Capitalist Transition in Eastern Europe. Lessons for the Social Sciences*.

36. Beyer, Joachim and Jan Wielgohs, "On the Limits of Path Dependency Approaches for Explaining Post-Socialist Institution Building: Critical Response to David Stark," *East European Politics and Societies*, 2001, 2, pp. 356–388.

37. Bafoil, François. "L'entreprise polonaise. Entre ruptures et continuités," *Sociologie du Travail*, June 2006, pp. 240–256.

38. Kitschelt, Herbert, Zdenska Mansfeldova, Radoslav Markowski, and Gabor Toka, *Post-Communist Party Systems. Competition, Representation and Inter-Party Cooperation*. Cambridge: Cambridge University Press, 1999.

39. North, "Economic Performance through Time," *American Economic Review*, pp. 359–368; Chavance, Bernard and Olivier Magnin, "The Emergence of Various Path-Dependant Mixed Economies in Post-Socialist Central Europe," *Emergo*, Autumn 1995, pp. 55–74; Delorme, Robert, *A l'Est du nouveau?* Paris: L'Harmattan (Collection "Pays de l'Est"), 1996; McDermott, G.A., "Renegotiating the Ties That Bind. The Limit of Privatization in the Czech Republic," in Gernot Grabher and David Stark (eds.). *Restructuring Networks in Post-socialism*. Oxford University Press, Oxford, pp. 70–106.

40. Stark, David, "Recombinant Property in Eastern European Capitalism," *American Journal of Sociology*, 4, 1996, pp. 993–1027; Stark, David and Laszlo Bruszt, *Postsocialist Pathways. Transforming Politics and Property in East Central Europe*. Cambridge: Cambridge University Press, 1998; Tas, Rona Anton, *The Great Surprise of the Small Transformation. The Demise of Communism and the Rise of the Private Sector in Hungary*. Ann Arbor: University of Michigan Press, 1997.

41. Regional Studies, 2001.

42. Creed, Gerald W., *Domesticating Revolution: From Socialist Reform to Ambivalent Transition in a Bulgarian Village*. University Park: Transylvania State University Press, 1998; Hann, Chris and Elisabeth Dunn (eds.), *Civil Society: Challenging Western Models*. London: Routledge, 1994.

43. Cf. chapter three on the reform of the welfare states.

44. Cf. chapter four on decentralization.

45. Cf. chapter five on industrial entreprises and chapter six on agricultural concerns.

46. Stark, David, "Recombinant Property in Eastern European Capitalism," *American Journal of Sociology*, 4, 1996, pp. 993–1027.

47. Stark, David and Gernot Grabbher, *Restructuring Networks in Post-Socialism: Legacies, Linkages, Localities*. London: Oxford University Press, 1997.

One   The Legacies. Picture of a Political Economy of Soviet-Style Socialism

1. Stark, David and Laszlo Bruszt, *Postsocialist Pathways. Transforming Politics and Property in East Central Europe*. Cambridge: Cambridge University Press, 1998.

2. Brus, Wlodzimierz, *The Economic History of Eastern Europe 1919–1975*. Oxford: Clarendon Press, 1985.

3. Voslenski, M., *La Nomenklatura, les privilégiés en URSS*. Paris: Belfond, 1980; Lowit, Thomas, "Y a-t-il des Etats en Europe de l'Est," *Revue Française de Sociologie*, 20, 1980, pp. 431–466.
4. Granick, David, *Enterprise Guidance in Eastern Europe. A Comparison of Four Socialist Economies*. Princeton NJ: Princeton University Press, 1975; Nove, Alec, *The Soviet Economy: An Introduction*. London: George Allen and Unwin, 1961; Kornai, Janos, *Economics of Shortage*. Amsterdam: North-Holland, 1980; and, in French, Kerblay, Basile, *La Société soviétique contemporaine*. Paris: Armand Colin, 1977; Asselain, Jean-Charles, *Plan et profit en économie socialiste*. Paris: Presses Nationales de Sciences Po, 1981; and Andreff, Wladimir, *La crise des économies de type soviétique*. Grenoble: Presses Universitaires de Grenoble, 1993.
5. Haraszti, Miklos. *Worker in a Workers' State*. New York: Universe Books, 1978.
6. Kornai, Janos, *Economics of Shortage*. Amsterdam: North-Holland, 1980.
7. Stark, David and Victor Nee (eds.), *Remaking the Economic Institutions of Socialism: China and Eastern Europe*. Stanford: Stanford University Press, 1989.
8. Katsenelinboingen, Aron, "Coloured Markets in the Soviet Union," *Soviet Studies*, 29, 1, 1977, pp. 62–85.
9. Bafoil, François, "La classe ouvrière post-communiste. Des 'héros au pouvoir' à l'exclusion des 'petites gens,'" *Genèses*, 37, 2000, pp. 74–97.
10. Duchêne, Gérard, *L'économie de l'URSS*. Paris: La Découverte, 1989.
11. Offe, Claus, *Varieties of Transition. The East European and East German Experience*. Cambridge: Polity Press, 1996.
12. Barbu, Daniel, "Du parti unique à la particratie," in Waele, Jean Michel De (ed.), *Partis politiques et démocraties en Europe centrale et orientale*. Brussels: Éditions de l'Université de Bruxelles, 2004.
13. Verdury, Katherine, "What Was Communism and What Comes Next," in Tismaneanu (ed.), *Between Past and Future*, 1999, pp. 63–85.
14. See Pomian, Krzysztof, *Pologne, défi à l'impossible*. Paris: Editions ouvrières, 1983.
15. Zaremba, Marcin, *"Pologne 1956–1980. Le socialisme du Bigos,"* in F. Bafoil (ed.), *La Pologne*. Paris: Fayard, 2007, pp. 198–222.
16. Esping Anderson, G., *The Three Worlds of Welfare Capitalism*. Cambridge: Polity Press, 1990.
17. Kaelbe, Hartmut and Günther Schmidt (eds.), *Das europäische Sozialmodell. Auf dem Weg zum transnationalen Sozialstaat*. WZB Jahrbuch, 2004.
18. Tomka, Béla, "Wohlfahrtsstaatliche Entwicklung in Ostmitteleuropa and das europäische Sozialmodell, 1945–1990," in Hartmut Kaelbe and Günther Schmidt (eds.), *Das europäische Modell. Aud dem Weg zum transnationalen*. WZB Jahrbuch, 2004, pp. 107–139.
19. Vortman, Heinz, "Die soziale Sicherheit in der DDR," in Werner Weidenfeld and Hartmut Zimmermann (eds.), *Deutschland Handbuch. Eine doppelte Bilanz 1949–1989*, Bundeszentrale für politische Bildung, 1989, pp. 326–341.
20. Michel, Patrick, *La société retrouvée—Politique et religion dans l'Europe soviétisée*. Paris: Fayard, 1988.
21. Hann, Chris and Elisabeth Dunn (eds.), *Civil Society: Challenging Western Models*. London: Routledge, 1994.
22. Zapf, Wolfgang and Meinolf Dierkes (eds.), *Institutionsvergleich und Institutionsdynamik*. WZB Jahrbuch, 1994.
23. Bafoil,"La classe ouvrière post-communiste. Des 'héros au pouvoir' à l'exclusion des 'petites gens,'"; Kott, Sandrine, *Le communisme au quotidien, l'entreprise est-allemande*. Paris: Belin, 2001.
24. Creed, Gerald W., *Domesticating Revolution: From Socialist Reform to Ambivalent Transition in a Bulgarian Village*. University Park: Transylvania State University Press, 1998.
25. Rychard, Andrzej, *Reforms, Adaptation and Breakthrough*. Warsaw: IFIS-Pan, 1993.
26. Berendt, Ivan T., *Decades of Crisis. Central and Eastern Europe before World War II*. Berkeley/London/Los Angeles: University of California, 1996; Janos, Andrew, *East Central Europe in the Modern World: The Politics of the Borderland from the Pre- to the Post-Communist System*. San Francisco: Stanford University Press, 2000; Aleksum, Natalia, Daniel Beauvois, Marie-Elisabeth Ducreux, and Jerzy Kloczowski, *L'histoire de l'Europe de l'Est*. Paris: PUF, 2004.
27. Mantran, Robert (ed.), *Histoire de l'empire Ottoman*. Paris: Fayard, 1989; Castellan, Georges, *Histoire des Balkans, XIV–XXème siècle*. Paris: Fayard, 1991; Dimitrov, Vesselin, *Bulgaria, the Uneven Transition*. London: Routledge, 2001.
28. Creed, Gerald W., *Domesticating Revolution: From Socialist Reform to Ambivalent Transition in a Bulgarian Village*. University Park: Transylvania State University Press, 1998.

29. Rupnik, Jacques, "Dissent in Poland, 1968–1978: The End of Revisionism and the Rebirth of Civil Society," in Rudolf, Tokes L. (ed.), *Opposition in Eastern Europe*. London: Macmillan, 1979, pp. 60–111.

30. Mlynar Z., W. Brus, and P. Kende (eds.), *La crise des systèmes de type soviétique*. Étude no. 13. Cologne, 1986.

31. Kende, Pierre, *Le défi hongrois, de Trianon à Bruxelles*. Paris: Buchet Chastel, 2003.

32. Gordon Skilling, Harold, *Czechoslovakia's Interrupted Revolution*. Princeton NJ: Princeton University Press, 1976; Marie, Jean-Jacques and Balasz Nagy (eds.), *1956, Pologne–Hongrie, ou le Printemps en Octobre*. Paris: Études et Documentation internationales, 1966; Garton Ash, *We the People*. London: Granta, 1990.

33. Davies, Norman, *God's Playground: A History of Poland*. Oxford: Clarendon Press, 2 vols., 1981; Pomian, Krzysztof, *Pologne, défi à l'impossible*. Paris: Editions ouvrières, 1983; Rollet, Henry, *La Pologne au XXe siècle*. Paris: Pedone, 1984; Bühler, Pierre, *Histoire de la Pologne communiste. Autopsie d'une imposture*. Paris: Karthala (Collection "Hommes et sociétés"), 1997; Bafoil, Françoil (ed.), *La Pologne*. Paris: Fayard, 2007.

34. Babeau, André, *Les conseils ouvriers polonais*. Paris: FNSP, 1960.

35. Pomian, Krzysztof, *Pologne, défi à l'impossible*. Paris: Editions ouvrières, 1983.

36. Touraine, Alain, François Dubet, Michel Wiewiorka, and Jan Strzelecki, *Solidarity. Poland 1980–81*. Cambridge: Cambridge University Press, 1983.

37. Adamski, Wladyslaw, *Societal Conflict and Systemic Change*. Warsaw: IFIS, 1993.

38. Rychard, Andrzej, *Reforms, Adaptation and Breakthrough*. Warsaw: IFIS-Pan, 1993.

39. Several authors have argued, however, that the subsequent option in favor of the market had its roots in 1980–1981, when the workers concluded that public enterprise was not the answer and formed a positive view of private initiative; in their view, nonalienated labor—and hence, by extension, the private economy—was to be preferred. See Bafoil (ed.), *La Pologne*.

40. Aron, Raymond, *Democracy and Totalitarianism*. Ann Arbor: University of Michigan Press, 1990.

41. Linz, Juan J. and Adam Stepan, *Problems of Democratic Transition and Consolidation, Southern Europe, South America, and Post-communist Europe*. Baltimore and London: Johns Hopkins University Press, 1996.

42. Kitschelt, Herbert, Zdenska Mansfeldova, Radoslav Markowski, and Gabor Toka, *Post-Communist Party Systems. Competition, Representation and Inter-Party Cooperation*. Cambridge: Cambridge University Press, 1999.

43. Linz and Stepan, *Problems of Democratic Transition and Consolidation, Southern Europe, South America, and Post-communist Europe*.

44. Perron, Catherine, *Les Pionniers de la démocratie*. Paris: Gallimard/Le Monde, 2003.

45. Sugar, Peter, "Continuity and Change in Eastern Europe. Authoritarism, Autocracy, Fascism and Communism," *East European Quarterly*, 1984, pp. 1–23.

46. Bozoki, Andras and John T. Ishiyama (eds.), *The Communist Successor Parties of Central and Eastern Europe*. Armonk NY: M.E. Sharp, 2002, pp. 287–302.

Two   Privatization and the Formation of East European States

1. Lavigne, Marie, *The Economics of Transition. From Socialist Economy to Market Economy*. London: Macmillan, 1999.

2. Myant, Martin, *The Rise and Fall of Czech Capitalism: Economic Development in the Czech Republic since 1989*. Cheltenham: Edward Elgar, 2003, p. 19.

3. "The beneficiary of a monopoly by a status group restricts, and maintains his power against, the market, while the rational-economic monopolist rules through the market" and "These capitalistic monopolies differ from monopolies of status groups by their purely economic and rational character." Weber, Max, *Economy and Society*. Berkeley: University of California Press, 1978, vol. 1, p. 639.

4. Ziblatt, Daniel and Nick Biziouras, 1999, "Communist Successor Parties in East Central Europe," in Bozoki, Andras and John T. Ishiyama (eds.), *The Communist Successor Parties of Central and Eastern Europe*. Armonk NY: M.E. Sharp, 2002, pp. 287–302.

5. Staniszkis, Jadwiga, *The Dynamics of Breakthrough in Eastern Europe: The Polish Experience.* Berkeley: University of California Press, 1991; Hankis, Elemer, *East European Alternatives.* Oxford: Clarendon Press, 1990.

6. Holmes, Lesley and Wojcieh Roszkowski, *Changing Rules.* Warsaw: ISP-Pan, 1995.

7. Kirov, Vassil, "Facing EU Accession: Bulgarian Trade Unions at the Crossroads," in Dimitrova, D. and J. Vilrokx (eds.), *Trade Union Strategies in Central and Eastern Europe: Toward Decent Work.* Budapest: ILO, 2005, pp. 111–151.

8. Ganev, Venelin, "The Dorian Gray Effect: Winners as State Breakers in Postcommunism," *Communist and Post-Communist Studies,* 34, 2001, pp. 1–25.

9. Bruszt Stark, "From System Identity to Organizational Diversity: Analyzing Social Change in Eastern Europe," *Contemporary Sociology,* 21, 1992, pp. 299–304; Stark, David, "Recombinant Property in Eastern European Capitalism," *American Journal of Sociology,* 4, 1996, pp. 993–1027; Stark, 1998; Tas, Rona Anton, *The Great Surprise of the Small Transformation: The Demise of Communism and the Rise of the Private Sector in Hungary.* Ann Arbor: University of Michigan Press, 1997.

10. Domanski, Henryk, *On the Verge of the Convergence. Social Stratification in Eastern Europe.* Budapest: Central Europe University Press, 2000; Jasinska–Kania, A., Melvin L. Kohn, and K. Slomczynski, *Power and Social Structure (Essays in Honour of Wlodziemierz Wesolowski).* Warsaw: Wydawnictwa Uniwerstytu Warszawskeigo, 1999; Szelenyi, Ivan and Szonja Szelenyi, "Circulation or Reproduction of Elites during the Post-Communist Transformation of Eastern Europe," *Theory and Society,* 24, 1995, pp. 613–628; Vecernik, Jan and Petr Mateju, *Ten Years of Rebuilding Capitalism: Czech Society after 1989.* Prague: Academia, 1999; Machos, Csilla, "Eliten in postsozialistischen Ungarns," in Höpiken, Wolfgang and Holm Sundhausen (eds.), *Eliten in Südosteuropa. Rolle, Kontinuitäten, Brüche in Geschichte und Gegenwart.* Munich, 1998; Sterbling, Anton, "Eliten in Sudosteuropea, Rolle, Kontinuitäten, Brüche," *Aus Politik und Zeitgeschichte,* B10–11, 2003, pp. 10–17; Gabanyi, Anneli Ute, and Anton Sterbling (eds.), "Sozialstruktureller Wandel, soziale Probleme und soziale Sicherung in Südosteuropa." *Südosteuropa-Studien* 65, Südosteuropa-Gesellschaft, München 2000; Mink, Georges and Jean-Charles Szurek, "1989: une révolution sociale? Acteurs, structures et représentations à l'Est," *Revue d'Etudes Comparatives Est/Ouest,* 25, 4, December, 1994, pp. 5–228.

11. Sterbling, Anton, "Eliten in Sudosteuropea, Rolle, Kontinuitäten, Brüche," *Aus Politik und Zeitgeschichte,* B10–11, 2003, pp. 10–17.

12. Ragaru, Nadège, *Apprivoiser les transformations post–communistes en Bulgarie: la fabrique du politique (1989–2004).* Doctoral thesis, 2 vols., 2005.

13. Schoeneman, Richard, "Captains or Pirates? State Business Relations in Post-Communist Poland," *East European Politics and Society,* 19, 1, 2005, pp. 40–75.

14. McMenamin, Ian, "Parties, Promiscuity and Politicization: Business-political networks in Poland," *European Journal of Political Research,* 43, 2004, pp. 657–676; Wasilewski, Jacek, "Polish Post-Transitional Elites," in Zagorska, J. Frentzel and J. Wasilewski (eds.), *The Second Generation of Democratic Elites.* Warsaw: IPS, 2000, pp. 197–216.

15. Ragaru, Nadège, *Apprivoiser les transformations post–communistes en Bulgarie: la fabrique du politique (1989–2004).*

16. Kirov, Vassil, "Facing EU Accession: Bulgarian Trade Unions at the Crossroads," in Dimitrova, D. and J. Vilrokx (eds.), *Trade Union Strategies in Central and Eastern Europe: Toward Decent Work.* Budapest: ILO, 2005, pp. 111–151.

17. The *Kommerzielle Koordinierung* had total control over 223 companies within and outside the GDR. It was involved in scandals over weapons embargo evasion, money-laundering, and the bribery of officials.

18. Fischer, Wolfram, Herbert Hax, Hans Karl Schneider, and Wolfgang Seibel (eds.), *Treuhandanstalt. Das Unmögliche wagen* (Forschungsberichte). Berlin: Akademie Verlag, 1993.

19. Myant, Martin, "Civil Society and Political Parties in the Czech Republic," in Simon Smith (ed.), *Communities and Post-Communist Transformation. Czechoslovakia, Czech Republic and Slovakia.* London, Routledge, 2003.

20. Surdej, Alexander, "Political Corruption in Post-Communist Poland," *Forschungstelle Osteuropa Bremen,* 65, 2005, pp. 5–20.

21. Agh, Attila, "Die neuen politischen Eliten in Mitteleuropa," *Leviathan,* 15, 1996, pp. 422–436.

22. Linz, Juan J. and Adam Stepan, *Problems of Democratic Transition and Consolidation, Southern Europe, South America, and Post-communist Europe.* Baltimore and London: Johns Hopkins University

Press, 1996; Kitschelt, Herbert, Zdenska Mansfeldova, Radoslav Markowski, and Gabor Toka, *Post-Communist Party Systems. Competition, Representation and Inter-Party Cooperation*. Cambridge: Cambridge University Press, 1999.

23. Glaessner, Gert-Joachim, "Le pouvoir bureaucratique! solution des conflits en RDA," in Mlynar Z., W. Brus, and P. Kende (eds.), *La crise des systèmes de type soviétique*. Étude no. 13. Cologne, 1986; Werth, Nicolas, *La terreur et le désarroi. Staline et son système*. Paris: Perrin, 2007.
24. Bartlett, W., "Industrial Policy and Industrial Restructuring in Slovenia," *Journal of Southern Europe and the Balkans*, 2000, 2, 1, pp. 11–23.
25. McMaster, Irene, and Martin Ferry. 2005, "Implementing Structural Funds in Polish and Czech Regions: Convergence, Variations, Empowerment?' *Regional and Federal Studies*, 15 (1), March: 19–39.
26. Hirschman, Albert O., "Obstacles to Development: A Classification and a Quasi-Vanishing Act," *Economic Development and Cultural Change*, 13, 4, pp. 385–393.
27. Dexia, *Sub-national Governments in the European Union: Responsibilities, Organisation and Finances*. Paris: Dexia Editions, 2008.
28. Evans, Peter B., Dietrich Rueschemeyer, and Theda Skokpol, *Bringing the State Back in*. Cambridge: Cambridge University Press, 1985.
29. Schoenman, "Captains or Pirates? State Business Relations in Post-Communist Poland," pp. 40–75.
30. Ahrend, Rudiger and Joachim Oliveira Martins, "Creative Destruction or Destructive Perpetuation. The Role of the State-Owned Enterprises and SMEs in Romania during the Transition," *Post-communist Economies*, 15, 3, 2003, pp. 331–356.
31. OECD, *Business Clusters. Promoting Enterprises in Central Europe*. LEED, 2006.
32. OECD, *Poland, Territorial Review*, 2008.
33. Batt, Judit, "Transcarpathia: Peripheral Region at the 'Centre of Europe,'" in ESRC, *"One Europe or Several."* Working Paper 27/01, 2001; Lepesant, 2004.
34. Lepesant, Gilles, "La Pologne, et son voisinage oriental," in F. Bafoil (ed.), *La Pologne*. Paris: Fayard, 2007, pp. 497–501.
35. Bafoil, François and Timm Beichelt (eds.), *L'Européanisation d'Ouest en Est*. Paris: L'Harmattan, 2008.
36. Winiecki, Jan, "Determinants of Catching Up or Falling Behind: Interaction of Formal and Informal Institutions," *Post-Communist Economies*, 16, 2, June 2004, pp. 137–152.

Three   The Reforms of the Welfare States

1. Esping Anderson, G., *The Three Worlds of Welfare Capitalism*. Cambridge: Polity Press, 1990.
2. Kornai, Janos, "The Citizen and the State: Reform of the Welfare System," *Emergo*, Winter, 1998, pp. 2–14.
3. Kaufman, Robert R., "Market Reforms and Social Protection: Lessons from the Czech Republic, Hungary and Poland," *East European Politics and Societies*, 21, 1, 2007, pp. 1111–1125.
4. Lendvai, Noémi, "The Weakest Link? EU Accession and Enlargement: Dialoguing EU and Post-communist Social Policy," *Journal of European Social Policy*, 14, 3, 2004, pp. 319–333.
5. Ringlod, Dena, "Social Policy in Post-Communist Europe. Legacies and Transition," in Linda J. Cook, Mitchell A. Orenstein, and Marilyn Rueschmeyer (eds.), *Left Parties and Social Policy in Post-Communist Europe*. Boulder: Westview Press, 1999, pp. 11–46.
6. Rusin, Philippe, "Économie politique de la transition polonaise," in F. Bafoil (ed.). *La Pologne*, 2007, pp. 281–302.
7. Orenstein in Cook, Orenstein, and Rueschmeyer (eds.), *Left Parties and Social Policy in Post-Communist Europe*.
8. Orenstein, Mitchell A. and Martine R. Haas, *Globalization and the Development of Welfare States in Post-Communist Europe*, International Security Program, Belfer Center for Science and International Affairs, February 2002; Ringlod, Dena, "Social Policy in Post-Communist Europe. Legacies and Transition," in Cook, Orenstein, and Rueschmeyer (eds.), *Left Parties and Social Policy in Post-Communist Europe*, pp. 11–46; Guilén, Ann M., and Bruno Palier, "Does Europe matter?" *Journal of European Social Policy*, 14, 3, 2004, pp. 203–209; Holzmann, Robert,

Mitchell A. Orenstein, and Michael Rutkowski (eds.), *Pension Reform in Europe: Process and Progress*. Washington DC: World Bank, 2003.

9. Holzmann, Robert, Mitchell A. Orenstein, and Michael Rutkowski (eds.). *Pension Reform in Europe: Process and Progress*. Washington DC: World Bank, 2003.

10. OECD, *Economic Survey Poland n°8*, 2004.

11. Kornai, Janos, "The Citizen and the State: Reform of the Welfare System," *Emergo*, Winter, 1998, pp. 2–14 and Kornai, Janos and Karen Egglestone, *Welfare, Choice and Solidarity in Transition: Reforming the Health Sector in Eastern Europe*. Cambridge: Cambridge University Press, 2001.

12. Tomka, Béla, "Wohlfahrtsstaatliche Entwicklung in Ostmitteleuropa and das europäische Sozialmodell, 1945–1990," in Hartmut Kaelbe and Günther Schmidt (eds.), *Das europäische Modell. Aud dem Weg zum transnationalen*. WZB Jahrbuch, 2004, pp. 107–139.

13. Ferge, Zsusza and Gabor Juhasz, "Accession and Social Policy: The Case of Hungary," *Journal of European Social Policy*, 14, 3, August 2004, pp. 233–251.

14. In Tomka, "Wohlfahrtsstaatliche Entwicklung in Ostmitteleuropa and das europäische Sozialmodell, 1945–1990," p. 129.

15. Schülpetz A., "Policy Transfer and Pre-accession. Europeanizaiton of Czech Employment Policy," *WZB-Paper*, SP III. 2004–201E; Beaumelou, Fabienne, "Le fonds social européen (FSE): un outil d'adaptation des compétences?" *Réalités Industrielles, Les Annales des Mines*, November 2004, pp. 68–71.

16. International Labour Office, *Pension Reform in Central and Eastern Europe*. Vol. 1: *Restructuring with Privatization. Case Studies of Hungary and Poland*. Geneva: ILO, 2000.

17. MIRE, *Comparer les système de protection sociale en Europe du Sud* (Rencontres et Recherches), vol. 3, Rencontres de Florence, Ministère du Travail, 1997.

18. Tomka, "Wohlfahrtsstaatliche Entwicklung in Ostmitteleuropa and das europäische Sozialmodell, 1945–1990," p. 132.

Four   Regionalization Reforms and the Redistribution of Powers between Central and Regional Actors

1. Benz, Artur, Dieter Fürst, Kilpert, H., and D. Rehfeld, *Regionalisation. Theory, Practice and Prospects in Germany*. Östersund: SIR, 2005; Benz, Artur, "Comments on Bafoil's Contribution," in Christian Lequesne and Monika MacDonagh-Pajerova (eds.), *La citoyenneté démocratique dans l'Europe des vingt-sept*. Paris: L'Harmattan, 2007, pp. 251–256.

2. Lepesant, Gilles, *Géopolitique des frontières de l'Allemagne*. Paris: L'Harmattan, 2000.

3. Wollmann, Hellmut, "Institution Building, and Decentralization in Formerly Socialist Countries: The Cases of Poland, Hungary, and East Germany," *Environment and Planning, Government and Policy*, 15, 1997, pp. 463–480.

4. Violette Rey, L. Coudroy de Lille, and Emmanuelle Boulineau, *L'Élargissement de l'Union Européenne: réformes territoriales en Europe centrale et orientale*. Paris: L'Harmattan, 2004, pp. 153–168.

5. Lhomel, 1998; Lhomel, 2002, "Le développement régional dans les pays candidats à l'Union Européenne," in La Documentation Française, *Le Courrier des Pays de l'Est*, 2002, 1026; Lhomel, Edith, "Régions, territoires et administrations," in F. Bafoil (ed.), *La Pologne*, 2007, pp. 347–366.

6. Perron, Catherine, *Les Pionniers de la démocratie. Elites politiques locales tchèques et est-allemandes, 1989–1998*. Paris: PUF, 2004.

7. Lozac'h, Valérie, *Le transfert du gouvernement local ouest-allemand dans les nouveaux Länder. Une comparaison entre Eisenhüttensatdt et Hoyerswerda*. Doctoral thesis, IEP Paris, 1999.

8. Myant, Martin, "Civil Society and Political Parties in the Czech Republic," in Simon Smith (ed.), *Communities and Post-Communist Transformation. Czechoslovakia, Czech Republic and Slovakia*. London, Routledge, 2003.

9. Horvath, Tomasz (ed.), *Decentralization: Experiments and Reforms*. Vol. 1: *Local Governments in Central Eastern Europe*, Budapest: IGI Books, 2000.

10. Lozac'h, Valérie, *Le transfert du gouvernement local ouest-allemand dans les nouveaux Länder. Une comparaison entre Eisenhüttensatdt et Hoyerswerda*.

11. Gorzelak, Grzegorz, *Regional Dimension of Transformation in Central Europe.* London: Jessica Kingsley, 1996.

12. Boulineau, in Rey, Violette, L. Coudroy de Lille, and Emmanuelle Boulineau, *L'Élargissement de l'Union Européenne: réformes territoriales en Europe centrale et orientale.* Paris: L'Harmattan, 2004.

13. Illner, Michael, "Réformes sur la voie de la décentralisation dans trois pays d'Europe centrale et orientale candidats à l'adhésion: Hongrie, Pologne, République tchèque," *Notre Europe, Etudes et recherches,* 17, June 2002.

14. Glaessner, Gert-Joachim (ed.), *Der lange Weg zur Einheit.* Berlin: Dietz Verlag, 1993.

15. Grabher, Gernot, "The Elegance of Incoherence: Economic Transformation in East Germany and Hungary," in Eckard Dittrich, Gert Schmid, and R. Whitley (eds.), *Industrial Transformation in Europe: Process and Context.* London: Sage, 1995, pp. 33–54.

16. Wiesenthal, Wiener (ed.), *Einheit als Interessenpolitik. Studien zur sektoralen Transformation Ostdeutschland.* Frankfurt am Main: Campus Verlag, 1995.

17. Rey, Coudroy de Lille, and Boulineau, *L'Élargissement de l'Union Européenne: réformes territoriales en Europe centrale et orientale.*

18. Horvath, *Decentralization: Experiments and Reforms*; Illner, Michael, "Réformes sur la voie de la décentralisation dans trois pays d'Europe centrale et orientale candidats à l'adhésion: Hongrie, Pologne, République tchèque," *Notre Europe, Etudes et recherches,* 17, June 2002.

19. Dexia, *Sub-national Governments in the European Union: Responsibilities, Organisation and Finances.* Paris: Dexia Editions, 2008.

20. Bryson, Philip J. and Gary C. Cornia, "Public Sector Transition Economics: The Struggle for Fiscal Decentralization in the Czech and Slovak Republics," *Post-communist Economies,* 16, 3, September 2004, pp. 263–283.

21. Wollmann, Hellmut, "Institutionenbildung in Ostdeutschland: Rezeption, Eigenentwicklung oder Innvation," in Eisen, Andreas and Helmut Wollmann (eds.), *Institutionenbildung in Ostdeutschland. Zwischer exoegener Steuerung und Eigendynamik.* Opladen: Leske und Budrich, 1996; and by the same author: "Institution Building, and Decentralization in Formerly Socialist Countries: The Cases of Poland, Hungary, and East Germany," *Environment and Planning, Government and Policy,* 15, 1997, pp. 463–480.

22. Lehmbruch, Gerhardt, "Institutionstransfer im Prozess der Vereinigung: zur politischen Logik der Verwaltungsintegration in Deutschland," in Benz, Artur, Hartmut Mäding, and Wolfgang Seibel (eds.), *Verwaltungsreform und Verwaltungspolitik im Prozess der deutschen Einigung.* Baden-Baden: Nomos, 1992, pp. 41–66.

23. Lozac'h, Valérie, *Le transfert du gouvernement local ouest-allemand dans les nouveaux Länder. Une comparaison entre Eisenhüttensatdt et Hoyerswerda.*

24. Perron, Catherine, *Les Pionniers de la démocratie. Elites politiques locales tchèques et est-allemandes, 1989–1998.* Paris: PUF, 2004.

25. Guyet, Rachel, *Innovations et limites des politiques de l'emploi dans les nouveaux Länder, Le cas de Leipzig, 1990–1999.* Doctoral thesis, IEP Grenoble, 2 vols., 2000.

26. Lorenz, Sabine and Kai Wegrich, "Lokale Ebene im Umbruch: Aufbau und Modernisierung der Kommunalverwaltung in Ostdeutschland," *Aus Politik und Zeitgeschichte,* B5/1998, Das Parlament.

27. Wollmann, Hellmut, "Institution Building, and Decentralization in Formerly Socialist Countries: The Cases of Poland, Hungary, and East Germany," *Environment and Planning, Government and Policy,* 15, 1997, pp. 463–480; Illner, Michal, "Réformes sur la voie de la décentralisation dans trois pays d'Europe centrale et orientale candidats à l'adhésion: Hongrie, Pologne, République tchèque," *Notre Europe, Etudes et recherches,* 17, June 2002; Yoder, Jennifer, "Decentralization and Regionalization after Communism, Administrative and Territorial Reforms in Poland and the Czech Republic," *Europe-Asia Studies,* 55, 2, March 2003, pp. 263–286; Ferry, Martin, "The EU and the Recent Regional Reform in Poland," *Europe-Asia Studies,* 55, 7, 2003, pp. 1097–1116; Perron, Catherine, *Les Pionniers de la démocratie. Elites politiques locales tchèques et est-allemandes, 1989–1998.*

28. Fowler, Brigid, "Hungary: Patterns of Political Conflict over Territorial Administrative Reform." *Regional Studies* (Special Issue on "Region, State, and Identity in Central/Eastern Europe") (2001): 15–37.

29. Beaumelou, Fabienne, "Le fonds social européen (FSE): un outil d'adaptation des compétences?" *Réalités Industrielles, Les Annales des Mines,* November 2004, pp. 68–71.

30. European Commission, *Growing Regions, Growing Europe, Fourth Report on Economic and Social Cohesion.* Brussels: European Commission, 2007; European Commission, *Territorial Agenda of the European Union, towards a More Competitive Europe of Diverse Regions.* Brussels: European Commission, 2007.

31. Illner, Michal, "Réformes sur la voie de la décentralisation dans trois pays d'Europe centrale et orientale candidats à l'adhésion: Hongrie, Pologne, République tchèque."

32. Bafoil, François and Edith Lhomel, "La préparation aux Fonds structurels de l'UE. Les exemples de la Pologne," *Le Courrier des Pays de l'Est,* March 2003, pp. 28–38; Bafoil, François, Fabienne Beaumelou, Rachel Guyet, Gilles Lepesant, and Catherine Perron, *Critique Internationale,* Special Issue: "Les instruments de l'élargissement de l'Union européenne," 25, 2004, pp. 109–182; Papadimitriou, Dimitris and David Phinemore, "Les jumelages institutionnels: les leçons du cas roumain," *Revue d'Etudes Comparatives Est Ouest,* 34, 3, 2003, pp. 37–64.

33. Hughes, James, Gwendolyn Sasse, and Claire Gordon, "EU Enlargement and Power Asymmetries: Conditionality and the Commission's Role in Regionalization in Central and Eastern Europe," in *One Europe or Several?* (Working Paper, 49/04), University of Sussex, 2004.

34. Bafoil, Beaumelou, Guyet, Lepesant, and Perron, *Critique Internationale,* Special Issue: "Les instruments de l'élargissement de l'Union européenne," pp. 109–182.

35. Hughes, James, Gwendolyn Sasse, and Claire Gordon, "EU Enlargement and Power Asymmetries: Conditionality and the Commission's Role in Regionalization in Central and Eastern Europe."

36. These conclusions are drawn from the personal experience of the author, who was in charge in Warsaw in 2002–2003 of the ex ante assessment of the programming documents, then in post in the Department for the Programming and Management of Funds in the Mazovia region. They were largely corroborated by other EU experts in a study published in 2004 (Bafoil, Beaumelou, Guyet, Lepesant, and Perron, *Critique Internationale,* Special Issue: "Les instruments de l'élargissement de l'Union européenne"). Four years later (2007–2008), the author, acting on this occasion as "Special Adviser" to the OECD on the production of the Territorial Review of Poland drafted by Dorothée Allain-Dupré, was able once again to confirm the persistent mistrust and misunderstanding between the Ministry of Regional Development and many regional actors, who feel themselves to be largely misunderstood, if not indeed treated with contempt, by the Centre (OECD, *Poland, Territorial Review,* 2008).

37. Dimitrova, Alexandra, "Enlargement, Institution Building and the EU's Administrative Capacity Requirement," *West European Politics,* October 2002, pp. 171–190.

38. Council Regulation (EC) No 1260/1999 of 21 June 1999 laying down general provisions on the Structural Funds.

39. Dabrowski, Marcin, "Structural funds as a Driver for Institutional Change in Poland," *Europe-Asia Studies,* 60, 2, March 2008, pp. 227–248; Grosse, Tomasz G., "Save Public Assets. Monitoring Corruption Threats in the Distribution of Structural Funds. The Case of IROP in Poland," Institute of Public Affairs, February 2007.

40. Bafoil, François and Timm Beichelt (eds.), *L'Européanisation d'Ouest en Est.* Paris: L'Harmattan, 2008.

Part 2   Societies and Markets

1. Surel, Palier, 2007; Baisée, Pasquier, 2007; Bafoil, Beichelt, 2008.

Five   Workers and Managers. Local Compromises and the End of the Working Classes

1. Weber, Max, *Economy and Society.* Berkeley: University of California Press, 1978.

2. McDermott Gerald. A. 1997 "Renegotiating the ties that bind: the limits of privatisation in the Czech Republic," in Gernot Grabher and David Stark (eds.). *Restructuring Networks in Post-socialism.* Oxford University Press, Oxford: 70–106; Earle, J.S., and S. Estrin, "Employee Ownership in Transition," in R. Frydman, C.W. Gray, and A. Rapaczynski, *Corporate Governance in Central Europe and Russia.* Vol. 2: *Insiders and the State.* Budapest/London/New York: 1996; Kogut B., "Direct Investments. Experimentation and Corporate Governance in Transition Economies," in Frydman, Gray, and Rapaczynski (eds.), *Corporate Governance in Central Europe and Russia,* vol. 1, pp. 293–332; Coffe, R., "Institutions and Investors: The

Czech Republic," in Frydman, Gray, and Rapaczynski (eds.), *Corporate Governance in Central Europe and Russia*, vol. 1, pp. 111–186; Djankov, S. and G. Pohl, "The Restructuring of Large Firms in the Slovak Republic," *Economics of Transition*, 6, 1, 1998, pp. 67–85; Major, Istvan, *Privatization and Economic Peformance in Central and Eastern Europe. Lessons to Be Learnt from Western Europe*. Cheltenham: Edward Elgar, 1999.

3. Wild, Gérard, "Economie de la Transition: le dossier," in D. Colas (ed.), *L'Europe post-communiste*. Paris: PUF, 2002, pp. 257–389. Within this general picture, the Czech Republic certainly represents an exception, in so far as the choice of "voucher privatization" corresponded to Vaclav Klaus's desire to create a domestic mass capitalism by excluding any potential foreign buyers, even if this meant ruling out fruitful forms of cooperation. See Pavlinek, Petr, "The Role of Foreign Direct Investment in the Privatisation and Restructuring of the Czech Motor Industry," *Post-Communist Economies*, 14, 3, 2002, p. 363.

4. Uvalic, Milica, and Daniel Vaughan-Whitehead (eds.), *Privatization Surprises in Transition Economies, Employee-Ownership in Central and Eastern Europe*. Cheltenham: Edward Elgar, 1996.

5. Uvalic, Milica, and Daniel Vaughan-Whitehead (eds.), *Privatization Surprises in Transition Economies, Employee-Ownership in Central and Eastern Europe*.

6. Zecchini, Salvatore (ed.). *Lessons from the Economic Transition, Central and Eastern Europe in the 90s*. Dordrecht/Boston: Kluwer Academic, 1997.

7. Bafoil, François, "Post-Communist Borders and Territories: Conflicts, Learning and Rule Building in Poland," *International Journal of Urban and Regional Research*, September 1999, pp. 85–110.

8. Ganev, Venelin, "The Dorian Gray Effect: Winners as State Breakers in Postcommunism," *Communist and Post-Communist Studies*, 34, 2001, pp. 1–25.

9. Earle, 1996; Aghion and Carlin, 1997; Aghion, 1998.

10. Aoki, Masahiko and Hugh Patrick (ed.), *The Japanese Main Bank System*. Oxford: Clarendon Press, 1994.

11. Stiglitz, Joseph E., *Globalization and its Discontents*. London: Allen Lane, 2002.

12. Stark, David and Laszlo Bruszt. *Postsocialist Pathways. Transforming Politics and Property in East Central Europe*. Cambridge: Cambridge University Press, 1998.

13. Jarosz, Maria, *Foreign Owners and Polish Employees of Privatized Enterprises*. Warsaw: PIS-PAN, 1997; Maciaszek, J., K. Mikolajczyk, and B. Roberts, "Some Consequences of Eliminating Unprofitable Output: Evidence from Polish Enterprises," *Europe-Asia Studies*, 50, 1, 1998, pp. 141–152.

14. United Nations Economic Commission for Europe, *Economic Survey of Europe,* Geneva, 1998.

15. Vaughan-Whitehead, 1996.

16. United Nations Economic Commission for Europe, *Economic Survey of Europe*. Geneva, 1999.

17. Womack, J.P., D.T. Jones, and D. Roose, *The Machine That Changed the World*. New York: Rawson Associates, 1990.

18. Major, Istvan, *Privatization and Economic Peformance in Central and Eastern Europe. Lessons to Be Learnt from Western Europe*. Cheltenham: Edward Elgar, 1999.

19. Heidenreich, Martin, *Krise, Kader, Kombinate. Kontinuität und Wandel in ostdeutschen Betrieben*. Berlin: Editions Sigma, 1992; Lutz, B. and R. Schmidt, *Chancen und Risiken der industriellen Restrukturierung in Ostdeutschland*. Berlin: Akademie Verlag, 1995.

20. Vecernik, Jan and Petr Mateju, *Ten Years of Rebuilding Capitalism: Czech Society after 1989*. Prague: Academia, 1999.

21. Voskamp, Ulrich and V. Wittke, "Aus Modernisierungsblokkaden werden Abwärtspiralen. Zur Reorganization von Betrieben und Kombinaten der ehemaligen DDR," *Göttingen SFU Mitteilungen*, December 1991, pp. 12–30.

22. Durand, Claude, *Management et rationalisation. Les multinationales occidentales en Europe de l'Est*. Brussels: de Boeck University, 1997.

23. Bafoil, François, "L'entreprise polonaise. Entre ruptures et continuités," *Sociologie du Travail,* June 2006, pp. 240–256.

24. Vecernik, and Mateju, *Ten Years of Rebuilding Capitalism: Czech Society after 1989*; "La classe ouvrière post-communiste. Des 'héros au pouvoir' à l'exclusion des 'petites gens,'" *Genèses*, 2000, 37, pp. 74–97.

25. Guyet, Rachel, "Innovations et limites des politiques de l'emploi dans les nouveaux Länder, Le cas de Leipzig, 1990–1999." Doctoral thesis, IEP Grenoble, 2 vols., 2000.

26. Jarosz, Maria, *Foreign Owners and Polish Employees of Privatized Enterprises*. Warsaw: PIS-PAN, 1997.

27. Portet, Stéphane, "Poland: Circumventing the Law or Fully Deregulating?" in D. Vaughan-Whitehead (ed.), *Working Employment Conditions in New Members States*. Geneva: ILO, 2005, pp. 273–337.
28. Portet, "Poland: Circumventing the Law or Fully Deregulating?"
29. Djankov, S. and G Pohl, "The Restructuring of Large firms in the Slovak Republic," *Economics of Transition*, 6, 1, 1998, pp. 67–85.

Six   The Agricultural Question. Public *Laissez-faire* and the Recomposition of Individual Strategies

1. Berendt, Ivan T., *Decades of Crisis. Central and Eastern Europe before World War II*. Berkeley/London/Los Angeles: University of California, 1996; Roszkowski, Wojcieh, *Land Reforms in East Central Europe after World War II*. Warsaw: ISP-PAN, 1995; Pryor, Frederic, *The Red and the Green, the Rise and Fall of Collectivized Agricultures in Marxist Regimes*. Princeton NJ: Princeton University Press, 1993.
2. Agrarian dualism had not been broken down before 1939. In Poland, 64.1% of the population at that date held 16.3% of cultivable land, while 0.7% possessed 40.5%. "Agrarian reforms have not improved matters," writes François Fejtö; "they have in fact aggravated the problem besetting agriculture in that region: the extremely low level of agricultural productivity," vol. 1, p. 313.
3. Davies, Norman, *God's Playground: A History of Poland*, 2 vols. Oxford: Clarendon Press, 1981; Maurel, Marie-Claude, *Les paysans contre l'Etat*. Paris: L'Harmattan, 1998; Beauvois, Daniel, *La Pologne: histoire, société, culture*. Paris: La Martinière, 2005; Bafoil, François (ed.), *La Pologne*. Paris: Fayard, 2007, pp. 497–501.
4. Swain, Nigel, "Agricultural Restitution and Cooperative Transformation in the Czech Republic, Hungary and Slovakia," *Europe-Asia Studies*, 51, 7, 1999, pp. 1199–1219.
5. Giordano, Christian, Dobrinka Kostova, Evelyne Lohman-Minka (eds.), *Bulgaria, Social and Cultural Landscapes*. Fribourg: University Press, 2000; Wädekin, Klaus Eugen, "The Place of Agriculture in the European Communist Economies: A Statistical Essay," *Soviet Studies*, 29, August 1977.
6. See the works of the Polish sociologists and ruralists: Frenkel, Dzun, Mokrzycki, Halamska, Gorlach, Szafraniec, Wilkin; *La Pologne*. Paris: Fayard, 2007, pp. 327–345.
7. Roszkowski, *Land Reforms in East Central Europe after World War II*.
8. Ilia, Iliev, "Small Farms in Bulgaria, a Four-Decade Anomaly," in Janos Matyas Kovacs, Petia Kabakchieva, Roumen Avramov (eds.), *East-West Cultural Encounters, Entrepreneurship, Economic Knowledge*. Sofia: East-West, 2004.
9. Verdury, Katherine, "What Was Communism and What Comes Next," in Tismaneanu (ed.), *Between Past and Future*, 1999, pp. 63–85.
10. In the Czech Republic, the procedure assigned 15% to the members of the cooperatives and to retirees, after which 25% was earmarked for sale to individuals seeking to acquire property. The remainder was divided into three parts, 50% of which was to offset the contribution of land, 30% the contribution of capital and 20% the number of years worked. See Swain, Nigel, "Agricultural Restitution and Cooperative Transformation in the Czech Republic, Hungary and Slovakia," *Europe-Asia Studies*, 51, 7, 1999, pp. 1199–1219.
11. Giordano, Kostova, and Lohman-Minka (eds.), *Bulgaria, Social and Cultural Landscapes*, p. 106.
12. OECD, Poland, *Territorial Review*, 2008.
13. Ilia, "Small Farms in Bulgaria, a Four-Decade Anomaly," in Matyas Kovacs, Kabakchieva, and Avramov (eds.), *East-West Cultural Encounters, Enterpreneurship, Economic Knowledge*.
14. Creed, Gerald W., *Domesticating Revolution: From Socialist Reform to Ambivalent Transition in a Bulgarian Village*. University Park: Transylvania State University Press, 1998.
15. Hirschhausen, Béatrice von, *Les nouvelles campagnes roumaines: paradoxes d'un retour paysan*. Paris: Belin, 1997.
16. Giordano, Kostova, and Lohman-Minka, *Bulgaria, Social and Cultural Landscapes*; Creed, *Domesticating Revolution: From Socialist Reform to Ambivalent Transition in a Bulgarian Village*.
17. Sedik, David J., Fock Karin, and Dudwick Nora, *Land Reform and Farm Restructuring in Transition Countries: The Experience of Bulgaria, Moldova, Azerbaijan, and Kazakhstan*. World Bank Report, 2007.

18. Rey, Violette (Studies Coordinated By), *Les nouvelles campagnes de l'Europe Centrale et Orientale.* Paris: CNRS, 1996; Streith, Michael, *Dynamiques paysannes en Mecklenburg, survie d'un savoir-faire.* Münster: LIT Verlag, 2005.
19. Bafoil, François and Vassil Kirov, "Comparing Sapard Preadherence Policies in Poland and Bulgaria," *Revue de sociologie bulgare* (in Bulgarian), 2003, pp. 12–24.
20. Pouliquen, Alain, *Compétitivité et revenus agricoles dans les secteurs agro-alimentaires des Peco, implications avant et après adhésion pour les marchés et les politiques de l'UE.* Rapport UE, 2000.
21. Bafoil, François (ed.), *La Pologne.* Paris: Fayard, 2007, pp. 327–346.
22. Streith, *Dynamiques paysannes en Mecklenburg, survie d'un savoir-faire.*
23. Rey, *Les nouvelles campagnes de l'Europe Centrale et Orientale.*

Seven   Labor Relations. The Weakness of the Social Dialogue

1. Myant, Martin, *The Rise and Fall of Czech Capitalism: Economic Development in the Czech Republic since 1989.* Cheltenham: Edward Elgar, 2003, p. 37.
2. Reynaud, Jean-Daniel, Catherine Paradeise, and Jean Saglio, *Le système des relations professionnelles.* Paris: CNRS, 1988.
3. Kohl, Herbert, "Arbeitsbeziehungen in den neuen EU Mitgiedstländern und ihre Implikation für das europäische Sozialmodell," in Timm Beichelt and Jan Wierlgohs (eds.), *Perspektiven der europäischen Integration nach der EU – Osterweiterung,* Workshop Documentation, FIUT Viadrina, 2005, pp. 51–71.
4. O'Donnell, Guillermo and Philippe Schmitter, *Transition from Authoritarian Rules: Prospects for Democracy.* Baltimore: Johns Hopkins University Press, 1986.
5. Offe, Claus, *Varieties of Transition. The East European and East German Experience.* Cambridge: Polity Press, 1996.
6. Agh, Attila, "Die neuen politischen Eliten in Mitteleuropa," *Leviathan,* 15, 1996, pp. 422–436.
7. Przeworski, Adam, *Democracy and the Market, Political and Economic Reforms in Eastern Europe and Latin America.* New York: Cambridge University Press, 1991.
8. Ekiert, Georg and Jan Kubik, "Contentious Politics in New Democracies. East Germany, Hungary, Poland and Slovakia, 1989–1993," *World Politics,* 50, July 1998, pp. 547–581.
9. Kirov, Vassil, "Facing EU Accession: Bulgarian Trade Unions at the Crossroads," in Dimitrova, D. and J. Vilrokx (eds.), *Trade Union Strategies in Central and Eastern Europe: Toward Decent Work.* Budapest: ILO, 2005, pp. 111–151.
10. Ekiert and Kubik, "Contentious Politics in New Democracies. East Germany, Hungary, Poland and Slovakia, 1989–1993"; Kubik, Jan, "How to Study Civil Society: The State of the Art and What to Do Next?" *East European Politics and Society,* 19, 1, 2005, pp. 105–120.
11. International Labour Office, *Pension Reform in Central and Eastern Europe.* Vol. 1: *Restructuring with Privatization. Case Studies of Hungary and Poland.* Geneva: ILO, 2000.
12. Ekiert and Kubik, "Contentious Politics in New Democracies. East Germany, Hungary, Poland and Slovakia, 1989–1993."
13. Lado, Maria, "Industrial Relations in the Candidate Countries," *European Foundation for the Improvement of Living and Working Conditions.* Budapest: ILO, 2004.
14. Vaughan-Whitehead, Daniel, *Working Employment Conditions in New Member States.* Geneva: ILO, 2005.
15. Vaughan-Whitehead, *Working Employment Conditions in New Member States,* p. 37.
16. Lado, cited by Vaughan-Whitehead, *Working Employment Conditions in New Member States,* p. 38.
17. Albert, Michel, *Capitalisme contre capitalisme.* Paris: Albin Michel, 1991.
18. Portet, Stéphane, "Poland: Circumventing the Law or Fully Deregulating?" in D. Vaughan-Whitehead (ed.), *Working Employment Conditions in New Members States,* pp. 273–337.
19. Vaughan-Whitehead, Daniel, *EU Enlargement versus Social Europe? The Uncertain Future of the European Social Model.* Cheltenham: Edward Elgar, 2003.
20. Bafoil, François, Fabienne Beaumelou, Rachel Guyet, Gilles Lepesant, and Catherine Perron, *Critique Internationale,* Special Issue: "Les instruments de l'élargissement de l'Union européenne," 25, 2004, pp. 109–182.

21. Papadimitriou, Dimitris and David Phinemore, "Les jumelages institutionnels: les leçons du cas roumain," *Revue d'Etudes Comparatives Est Ouest*, 34, 3, 2003, pp. 37–64.
22. d'Haussonville, Jean, "Les processus d'adhésion: cet élargissement est-il le mieux préparé de l'histoire de l'UE?" *Pouvoir*, 2003, pp. 5–39.
23. Vaughan-Whitehead, *EU Enlargement versus Social Europe? The Uncertain Future of the European Social Model*.
24. Rys, Vladimir, "Transition Countries of Central Europe Entering the European Union: Some Social Protection Issues," *International Social Security Review*, 54, 2–3, 2000, p. 185.
25. Lendvai, Noémi, "The Weakest Link? EU Accession and Enlargement: Dialoguing EU and Post-communist Social Policy," *Journal of European Social Policy*, 14, 3, 2004, pp. 319–333.
26. Ferge, Zsusza and Gabor Juhasz, "Accession and Social Policy: The Case of Hungary," *Journal of European Social Policy*, 14, 3, August 2004, pp. 233–251.
27. Beaumelou, Fabienne, "Le fonds social européen (FSE): un outil d'adaptation des compétences?" *Réalités Industrielles, Les Annales des Mines*, November 2004, pp. 68–71.
28. Lendvai, "The Weakest Link? EU Accession and Enlargement: Dialoguing EU and Post-communist Social Policy"; Deacon, B., "Eastern European Welfare States: the Impacts of Politics of Globalization," *Journal of European Social Policy*, 10, 2, 2000, pp. 146–161.
29. Bohle, Dorothea and Bela Greskovits, "Ein Sozialmodell an der Grenze. Kapitalismus ohne Kompromiss," *Osteuropa*, 54, 5–6, 2004, pp. 372–386.

Eight   Civil Societies. Networks of Sociability, Associations, and Public Debates

1. Croissant, Aurel, Wolfgang Merkel, and Hans Joachim Lauth, "Zivilgesellschaft und Transformation: ein internationales Vergleich," in Wolfgang Merkel (ed.), *Zivilgesellschaft und Transformation* 5. Opladen: Leske und Budrich, 2000, pp. 9–49.
2. Myant, Martin, "Civil Society and Political Parties in the Czech Republic," in Simon Smith (ed.), *Communities and Post-Communist Transformation. Czechoslovakia, Czech Republic and Slovakia*. London: Routledge, 2003, and *The Rise and Fall of Czech Capitalism: Economic Development in the Czech Republic since 1989*. Cheltenham: Edward Elgar, 2003.
3. Beyme, Klaus von, "Auf dem Weg zur Wettbewerbsdemokratie? Der Aufbau politischer Konfliktstrukturen in Osteuropa," in Beata Kohler Koch (ed.), *Staat und Demokratie*. Baden-Baden: Nomos, 1992, pp. 149–167.
4. Putnam, Robert, *Democracies in Flux: The Evolution of Social Capital in Contemporary Society*. New York: Oxford University Press, 2002.
5. Morjé, Marc, *The Weakness of Civil Society in Post-Communist Europe*. Cambridge: Cambridge University Press, 2003.
6. Smolar, Alexander, "Civil Society after Communism: From Opposition to Atomization," *Journal of Democracy*, 1, 1996, pp. 24–38.
7. Rupnik, Jacques, "De l'antipolitique à la crise de la démocratie: que reste-t-il de l'héritage de la dissidence?" in Lequesne, Christian and Monika MacDonagh-Pajerova (eds.), *La citoyenneté démocratique dans l'Europe des vingt-sept*. Paris: L'Harmattan, 2008, pp. 101–125.
8. Barbu, Daniel. 2004. "Du parti unique à la particratie," in Jean Michel De Waele (ed.). *Partis politiques et démocraties en Europe centrale et orientale*. Brussels: Éditions de l'Université de Bruxelles.
9. Cox, Terry and Laszlo Vass, "Government-Interest Group Relations in Hungarian Politics since 1989," *Europe-Asia Studies*, 2000, pp. 1095–1114.
10. Agh, Attila, "Die neuen politischen Eliten in Mitteleuropa," *Leviathan*, 15, 1996, pp. 422–436.
11. Lomax, Bill, "'The Strange Death of the Civil Society' in Post-Communist Hungary," *Journal of Communist Studies and Transition Politic*, 3, 1, 1997, pp. 41–63.
12. Zimmer, Annette and Eckhart Priller (eds.), *Future of Civil Society, Making Central European Nonprofit-Organizations Work*. Wiesbaden: VS Verlag für Sozialwissenschaften, 2004; Marc Morjé Howard, *The Weakness of Civil Society in Post-Communist Europe*. Cambridge: Cambridge University Press, 2003.
13. Morjé Howard, *The Weakness of Civil Society in Post-Communist Europe*.
14. Creed, Gerald W., *Domesticating Revolution: From Socialist Reform to Ambivalent Transition in a Bulgarian Village*. University Park: Transylvania State University Press, 1998; Hann, Chris

and Elisabeth Dunn (eds.), *Civil Society: Challenging Western Models*. London: Routledge, 1994.

15. Zimmer and Priller (eds.), *Future of Civil Society, Making Central European Nonprofit-Organizations Work*.

16. Kubik, Jan, "How to Study Civil Society: The State of the Art and What to Do Next?" *East European Politics and Society* 19 (1) (2005): 105–120.

17. Manfelsdova, Zdenka, Slawomir Nalecz, Eckhart Priller, and Annette Zimmer, "Civil Society in Transition: Civic Engagement and Nonprofit Organizations in Central and Eastern Europe," in Zimmer and Priller (eds.), *Future of Civil Society, Making Central European Nonprofit-Organizations Work*, pp. 99–119.

18. Lutz, B. and R. Schmidt, *Chancen und Risiken der industriellen Restrukturierung in Ostdeutschland*. Berlin: Akademie Verlag, 1995.

19. Vajdova, Zdenka, "Local Community Transformation. The Czech Republic 1990–2000," in Smith, Simon (ed.), *Local Communities in Contemporary Eastern Europe*. London: Routledge, 2003.

20. Cox, Terry and Laszlo Vass, "Government-Interest Group Relations in Hungarian Politics since 1989," *Europe-Asia Studies*, 2000, pp. 1095–1114.

21. Olcarius, Axel J., "Zwischen Empowerment und Instrumentalisierung: Nichtstaatliche Akteure der Umweltpolitik während des Beitrittsprozesses," in Amelie Kutter and Vera Trappmann (eds.), *Das Erbe des Beitritts. Europäisierung in Mittel- und Os Europa*. Baden-Baden: Nomos, 2006, pp. 339–358.

22. Ferge, Zsusza, and Gabor Juhasz, "Accession and Social Policy: The Case of Hungary," *Journal of European Social Policy*, 14, 3, August 2004, pp. 233–251.

23. Grix, Jim and Wanda Knowles, "The Euroregion as a Social Capital Maximizer: The German Polish Euroregion Pro-Europa Viadrina," *Regional and Federal Studies*, 12, 4, Winter 2002, pp. 154–176.

24. Westley-Scott, James, "Crossborder Governance in the Baltic Sea Region," *Regional and Federal Studies*, 12, 4, Winter 2002, pp. 135–153.

25. Batt, Judit, "Transcarpathia: Peripheral Region at the 'Centre of Europe,'" in ESRC, *"One Europe or Several."* Working Paper 27/01, 2001; OECD, *Poland, Territorial Review*, 2008.

26. In this regard, by imposing visas and strengthening border controls, the policy put in place to implement the Shengen legislation after 2004 greatly contributed to drying up the vast networks of informal exchange that had been present in ever greater numbers along the border zones in the 1990s and beyond (Bachmann, 2000).

27. Letki, Natalia, "Lustration and Democratization in East Central Europe," *Europe-Asia Studies*, 54, 4, 2002, pp. 529–552; Szczerbiak, Alex, "Dealing with the Communist Past or the Politics of the Present. Lustration in Post-Communist Poland," *Europe-Asia Studies*, 54, 4, 2002, pp. 553–572; Misztal, Barbara, "How Not to Deal with the Past: Lustration in Poland," *Archives Européennes de sociologie*, 48, 3, 1999, pp. 31–55.

Nine The Development of the Social Structures and the Formation of New Cleavages

1. United Nations Economic Commission for Europe, *Economic Survey of Europe*, 2004.

2. Domanski, Boleslaw, 2003, "Industrial Change and Foreign Direct Investment in the Post-Socialist Economy, The Case of Poland," *European Urban and Regional Studies*, 10, 2, pp. 99–118.

3. Szelenyi, Ivan and Szonja Szelenyi, "Circulation or Reproduction of Elites during the Post-Communist Transformation of Eastern Europe," *Theory and Society*, 24, 1995, pp. 613–628; Szelenyi, I., E. Wnuk Lipinski, and D. Treiman (eds.), "Circulation and Reproduction of Elites during the Post-Communist Transformation of East-Europe," *Theory and Society*, 24, 5, 1995; Mink, Georges and Jean-Charles Szurek, "1989: une révolution sociale? Acteurs, structures et représentations à l'Est," *Revue d'Etudes Comparatives Est/Ouest*, 25, 4, December, 1994, pp. 5–228.

4. Mihaly Laki, "Opportunities for Property Acquisition and Some Characteristics of Big Entrepreneurs in Post-Socialist Hungary," *Europe-Asia Studies*, 55, 5, July 2003, pp. 693–710.

5. Wasilewski, Jacek, "Polish Post-Transitional Elites," in J. Frentzel Zagorska and J. Wasilewski (eds.), *The Second Generation of Democratic Elites*. Warsaw: IPS, 2000, pp. 197–216.

6. Portet, Stéphane, "Poland: Circumventing the Law or Fully Deregulating?" in D. Vaughan-Whitehead (ed.), *Working Employment Conditions in New Members States*. Geneva: ILO, 2005, pp. 273–337.

7. Landesmann, Michael, Hermine Vidovic, and Terry Ward, "Economic Restructuring and Labour Market Developments in the New EU Member States," *WIIW Research reports*, 312, December 2004.

8. Sedik, David J., Fock Karin, and Dudwick Nora, *Land Reform and Farm Restructuring in Transition Countries: The Experience of Bulgaria, Moldova, Azerbaijan, and Kazakhstan*. World Bank Report, 2007.

9. Landesmann, Vidovic, and Ward, "Economic Restructuring and Labour Market Developments in the New EU Member States," p. 23.

10. Adamski, Wladyslaw, J. Buncak, Pavel Machonin, and Dominique Martin, *System Change and Modernization*. Warsaw: IFIS, 1999.

11. Rusin, Philippe, "Économie politique de la transition polonaise," in F. Bafoil (ed.). *La Pologne*, pp. 281–302.

12. Portet, "Poland: Circumventing the Law or Fully Deregulating?"

13. Vaughan-Whitehead, Daniel, *Working Employment Conditions in New Member States*. Geneva: ILO, 2005.

14. Including 41.6 for Austria, 38.8 for the Netherlands, 38.9 for France, and 39.6 for Germany.

15. Lado, Maria, "Industrial Relations in the Candidate Countries," *European Foundation for the Improvement of Living and Working Conditions*. Budapest: ILO, 2004.

16. Landesmann, Vidovic, and Ward, "Economic Restructuring and Labour Market Developments in the New EU Member States," p. 8.

17. It was for a long time difficult to obtain reliable data on account of the weakness of the statistical tools. These were particularly ill-adapted to deal with atypical categories such as layoffs, the homeless, workers in the gray economy, and so on. Moreover, it was difficult to compare homogeneous series over time (1990–1996) and between countries (Romania/Poland). "Registered unemployment" could not be equated with "recorded unemployment," the difference between the two relating to the fact that some individuals do not register as unemployed, either because they can see no point in doing so or they have found another job.

18. These figures are available on Eurostat Web site: http://epp.eurostat.ec.europa.eu/portal/page?_pageid=1996,39140985&_dad=portal&_schema=PORTAL&screen=detailref&language=fr&product=REF_TB_labour_market&root=REF_TB_labour_market/t_labour/t_employ/t_lfsi/t_une/tsiem110.

19. Sedik, Karin, and Nora, *Land Reform and Farm Restructuring in Transition Countries: The Experience of Bulgaria, Moldova, Azerbaijan, and Kazakhstan*.

20. Landesmann, Vidovic, and Ward, "Economic Restructuring and Labour Market Developments in the New EU Member States," p. 11.

21. Zecchini, Salvatore (ed.), *Lessons from the Economic Transition, Central and Eastern Europe in the 90s*. Dordrecht/Boston: Kluwer Academic, 1997.

22. Sedik, Karin, and Nora, *Land Reform and Farm Restructuring in Transition Countries: The Experience of Bulgaria, Moldova, Azerbaijan, and Kazakhstan*.

23. World Bank. 2001. *Making Transition Work for Everyone, Poverty and Inequality in Europe and in Central Asia*. Washington DC: World Bank. The 1 dollar per day figure applied in the 1980s; that of 2.15$ was determined on the basis of climatic conditions that call for particular expenditures. Some argue that a figure of 4.30$ would be more adequate for Eastern Europe and 2.15$ for the CIS.

24. United Nations Economic Commission for Europe, "Poverty in Eastern Europe and in the CIS," *Economic Survey of Europe*, 1, 2004, p. 169.

25. Heyns, Barbara, "Emerging Inequalities in Central and Eastern Europe," *Annual Review of Sociology*, 2005, pp. 163–197.

26. Vaughan-Whitehead, Daniel, *EU Enlargement versus Social Europe? The Uncertain Future of the European Social Model*. Cheltenham, Edward Elgar, 2003.

27. European Union, *Growing Regions, Growing Europe. Fourth Report on Economic and Social Cohesion*, p. 29.

28. Vaughan-Whitehead, *EU Enlargement versus Social Europe? The Uncertain Future of the European Social Model*.

29. Renooy, Piete, Staffon Ivarson, Olga van der Wusten, and Remco Meijer, *Undeclared Work in an Enlarged Union. An Analysis of Undeclared Work: An In–Depth Study of Specific Items.* Final Report. European Commission, DG Employment and Social Affairs, 2004.

30. Lipset, Seymour M. and Stein Rokkan, *Party System and Voter Alignments: Cross-National Perspectives.* New York: Free Press, 1967.

31. Toole, James, "The Historical Foundations of Party Politics in Post-Communist East Central Europe," *Europe-Asia Studies*, 59, 4, June 2007, pp. 541–566.

32. Glaessner, Gert-Joachim (ed.), *Der lange Weg zur Einheit.* Berlin: Dietz Verlag, 1993, Agh, 1998.

33. Glaessner (ed.), *Der lange Weg zur Einheit.*

34. Vecernik, Jan and Petr Mateju, *Ten Years of Rebuilding Capitalism: Czech Society after 1989.* Prague: Academia, 1999.

35. Waele, Jean Michel De (ed.), *Partis politiques et démocraties en Europe centrale et orientale.* Brussels: Éditions de l'Université de Bruxelles, 2004.

36. Zapf, Wolfgang, *Modernisierung, Wohlfahrtentwicklung und Transformation.* Berlin: Editions Sigma, 1994; and "Die Transformation in der ehemaligen DDR und die soziologische Theorie der Modernisierung," *Berliner Journal für Soziologie*, 3, pp. 295–305.

37. Creed, Gerald W., *Domesticating Revolution: From Socialist Reform to Ambivalent Transition in a Bulgarian Village.* University Park: Transylvania State University Press, 1998.

38. Michel, Patrick, *La société retrouvée—Politique et religion dans l'Europe soviétisée.* Paris: Fayard, 1988.

39. Pollack, Detlev, "Religion und Politik in den postkommunjistischen Staaten Ostmittel- und Osteuropas," *Aus Politik und Zeitgeschichte*, B 42–43, 2002, pp. 15–22.

40. Zarycki, Tomasz, "Politics in the Periphery: Political Cleavages in Poland Interpreted in Their Historical and International Context," *Europe-Asia Studies*, 52, 5, 2000, pp. 851–873.

41. Vachudova, Milena Anna, *Europe Undivided. Democracy, Leverage and Integration after Communism.* Oxford: Oxford University Press, 2005.

42. Cook, Linda J., Mitchell A. Orenstein, and Marilyn Rueschmeyer (eds.), *Left Parties and Social Policy in Post-Communist Europe.* Boulder: Westview Press, 1999; Bunce, Valerie, *Subversive Institutions. The Design and the Destruction of Socialism and the State*, Cambridge: Cambridge University Press, 1999; Bafoil, François (ed.), *La Pologne.* Paris: Fayard, 2007.

Ten   General Conclusion

1. Sedelmeier, Ulrich, "Eastern Enlargement: Towards a European EU?" in: Helen Wallace and William Wallace, *Policy-Making in the European Union.* Fifth Edition. Oxford: Oxford University Press, 2005, pp. 402–428.

2. Vachudova, Milena Anna, *Europe Undivided. Democracy, Leverage and Integration after Communism.* Oxford: Oxford University Press, 2005.

3. Balcerowicz, Leszek, *Socialism, Capitalism, Transformation.* Budapest: Central European University Press, 1995.

4. Sedelmeier, "Eastern Enlargement: Towards a European EU?"

5. Schimmelfennig, Frank, "Strategic Calculations and International Socialization: Memberships, Incentives, Party Constellations, and Sustained Compliance in Central and Eastern Europe," *International Organization*, 59, Fall 2005, pp. 827–860.

6. O'Donnell, Clara M. and Richard G. Whitman, "Das Phantom-Zuckerbrot. Die Rekonstructionfehler der ENP," *Osteuropa*, 57, 2–3, pp. 95–104; Lippert, Barbara, "Erfolge und Grenzen der technokratischen EU–Erweiterungspolitik," in Kutter, A. and V. Trappmann (eds.), *Das Erbe des Beitritts. Europäisierung im Mittel- und Osteuropa.* Baden-Baden: Nomos, 2006, pp. 57–74.

7. Schimmelfenning, Frank, Stefan Engert, and Heiko Knobel, *International Socialisation in Europe. European Organisations, Political Conditionality and Democratic Change.* Basingstoke UK: Palgrave Macmillan, 2006.

BIBLIOGRAPHY

Adamski, Wladyslaw. 1993. *Societal Conflict and Systemic Change.* Warsaw: IFIS.

Adamski, Wladyslaw, J. Buncak, Pavel Machonin, and Dominique Martin. 1999. *System Change and Modernization.* Warsaw: IFIS.

Agh, Attila. 1996. "Die neuen politischen Eliten in Mitteleuropa." *Leviathan* 15: 422–436.

Aghion, Paul and Olivier Blanchard. 1998. "On Privatization Methods in Eastern Europe and Their Implications." *Economics of Transition* 6 (1): 87–100.

Aghion, Philippe and W. Carlin. 1997. "Restructuring Outcomes and the Evolution of Ownership Patterns in Central and Eastern Europe," in S. Zecchini (ed.). *Lessons from the Economic Transition.* OEC: 241–262.

Ahrend, Rudiger and Joachim Oliveira Martins. 2003. "Creative Destruction or Destructive Perpetuation. The Role of the State-Owned Enterprises and SMEs in Romania during the Transition." *Post-Communist Economies* 15 (3): 331–356.

Albert, Michel. 1991. *Capitalisme contre capitalisme.* Paris: Albin Michel.

Aleksum, Natalia, Daniel Beauvois, Marie-Elisabeth Ducreux, and Jerzy Kloczowski. 2004. *L'histoire de l'Europe de l'Est.* Paris: PUF.

Andreff, Wladimir. 1993. *La crise des économies de type soviétique.* Grenoble: Presses Universitaires de Grenoble.

Aoki, Masahiko and Hugh Patrick (ed.). 1994. *The Japanese Main Bank System.* Oxford: Clarendon Press.

Aron, Raymond. 1990. *Democracy and Totalitarianism.* Ann Arbor: University of Michigan Press.

Asselain, Jean-Charles, *Plan et profit en économie socialiste.* Paris: Presses Nationales de Sciences Po, 1981.

Auer, Stefan. 2004. "Das Erbe von 1989, Revolutionen für Europa." *Osteuropa* 54 (5–6): 31–46.

Babeau, André. 1960. *Les conseils ouvriers polonais.* Paris: FNSP.

Bachmann, Klaus. 2001. *Polens Uhren gehen anders. Warschau vor der Osterweiterung der Europäischen Union.* Stuttgart/Leipzig.

Badescu, Gabriel and Paul E. Sum. 2005. "Historical Legacies, Social Capital and Civil Society: Comparing Romania on a Regional Level." *Europe-Asia Studies* 57 (1): 117–133.

Bafoil, François (ed.). 1999a. *Chômage et exclusion en Europe post-communiste. Allemagne, Pologne.* Paris: L'Harmattan.

———. 1999b. "Post-Communist Borders and Territories: Conflicts, Learning and Rule Building in Poland." *International Journal of Urban and Regional Research* September: 85–110.

———. 2000. "La classe ouvrière post-communiste. Des 'héros au pouvoir' à l'exclusion des 'petites gens.'" *Genèses* 37: 74–97.

———. 2002. *Après le communisme. Faillite du système soviétique, invention d'un modèle économique et social en Europe de l'Est.* Paris: Armand Colin.

———. 2004. "From Corruption to Regulation. Post-Communist Enterprises in Poland." In Béatrice Hibou (ed.). *Privatizing the State.* London: Hurst: 48–76.

———. 2006. "L'entreprise polonaise. Entre ruptures et continuities." *Sociologie du Travail* June: 240–256.

———. (ed.). 2007. *La Pologne.* Paris: Fayard.

Bafoil, François and Edith Lhomel. 2003. "La préparation aux Fonds structurels de l'UE. Les exemples de la Pologne." *Le Courrier des Pays de l'Est* (March): 28–38.

Bafoil, François, Fabienne Beaumelou, Rachel Guyet, Gilles Lepesant, and Catherine Perron. 2004. *Critique Internationale* (Special issue: "Les instruments de l'élargissement de l'Union européenne") 25: 109–182.

Bafoil, François, Rachel Guyet, Vladimir Thardy, and Loïc L'haridon. 2003. "Pologne, Profils d'agriculteurs." *Le Courrier des Pays de l'Est* 1034: 28–45.

Bafoil, François and Timm Beichelt (eds.). 2008. *L'Européanisation d'Ouest en Est.* Paris: L'Harmattan.

Baisnée, Olivier and Romain Pasquier. 2007. *L'Europe telle qu'elle se fait. Européanisation et sociétés politiques nationales.* Paris: CNRS Éditions.

Balcerowicz, Leszek. 1995. *Socialism, Capitalism, Transformation.* Budapest: Central European University Press.

Barbu, Daniel. 2004. "Du parti unique à la particratie," in Jean Michel De Waele (ed.). *Partis politiques et démocraties en Europe centrale et orientale.* Brussels: Éditions de l'Université de Bruxelles.

Bartlett, Will. 2000. "Industrial Policy and Industrial Restructuring in Slovenia." *Journal of Southern Europe and the Balkans* 2 (1): 11–23.

Barysch, Katinka. 2006. "East versus West? The European Economic and Social Model after Enlargement," in Giddens, Patrick Diamond and Roger Liddle (eds.). *Global Europe, Social Europe.* Cambridge: Polity Press: 52–69.

Batt, Judit. 2001. "Transcarpathia: Peripheral Region at the 'Centre of Europe,'" in ESRC. *"One Europe or Several."* Working Paper 27/01.

Beaumelou, Fabienne. 2004. "Le fonds social européen (FSE): un outil d'adaptation des compétences?" *Réalités Industrielles, Les Annales des Mines* November: 68–71.

Beauvois, Daniel. 2005. *La Pologne: histoire, société, culture.* Paris: La Martinière.

Benz, Artur. 2007. "Comments on Bafoil's Contribution," in Christian Lequesne and Monika MacDonagh-Pajerova (eds.). *La citoyenneté démocratique dans l'Europe des vingt-sept.* Paris: L'Harmattan: 251–256.

Benz, Artur, Dieter Fürst, H. Kilpert, and D. Rehfeld. 2005. *Regionalisation. Theory, Practice and Prospects in Germany.* Östersund: SIR.

Berendt, Ivan T. 1996. *Decades of Crisis. Central and Eastern Europe before World War II.* Berkeley/ London/Los Angeles: University of California.

Beyer, Joachim and Jan Wielgohs. 2001. "On the Limits of Path Dependency Approaches for Explaining Post-Socialist Institution Building: Critical Response to David Stark." *East European Politics and Societies* 2: 356–388.

Beyme, Klaus von. 1992. "Auf dem Weg zur Wettbewerbsdemokratie? Der Aufbau politischer Konfliktstrukturen in Osteuropa," in Beata Kohler Koch (ed.). *Staat und Demokratie.* Baden-Baden: Nomos: 149–167.

Bibo, István. 1984. *Misère des petits états d'Europe de l'Est.* Paris: Albin Michel.

Bischoff Gabriele and Martin Heidenreich. 2008. "The Open Method of Coordination. A Way to the Europeanization of Social and Employment Policies?" *Journal of Common Market Studies* 46 (6): 497–532.

Bohle, Dorothea and Bela Greskovits. 2004. "Ein Sozialmodell an der Grenze. Kapitalismus ohne Kompromiss." *Osteuropa* 54 (5–6): 372–386.

Boillot, Jean-Jacques. *L'Union européenne, un défi économique pour tous.* Paris: La Documentation française. 2003.

Bönker, Frank. "Konsequenzen des EU-Beitritts für die Sozialpolitik in den neuen Mitgliedstaaten," in Amelie Kutter and Vera Trappmann (eds.). *Das Erbe des Beitritts. Europäisierung in Mittel- und Os Europa.* Baden-Baden: Nomos, 2006: 257–269.

Börzel, Tanja. 2001. *Pace-Setting, Foot-Dragging and Fence-Sitting. Member State Responses to Europeanization.* Queen's Papers on Europeanization 4.

———. 2003. "Shaping and Taking EU Policies: Member State Responses to Europeanization." Queen's Papers on Europeanization 2. http://ideas.repec.org/p/erp/queens/p0035.html (Accessed on 28 October 2008).

————. 2006. "Deep Impact? Europeanization and Eastern Enlargement," in A. Kutter and V. Trappmann (eds.). *Das Erbe des Beitritts. Europäisierung in Mittel- und Osteuropa. Europäische Schriften.* Baden-Baden: Nomos: 99–115.

Börzel Tanja and Thomas Risse. 2000. "When Europe Hits Home: Europeanization and Domestic Change." European Integration Online Papers. http://eiop.or.at/eiop/pdf/2000-015.pdf (Accessed on 28 October 2008).

————. 2003. "Conceptualizing the Domestic Impact of Europe," in K. Featherstone and C.M. Radaelli (eds.). *The Politics of Europeanization.* Oxford: Oxford University Press: 57–80.

Bozoki, Andras and John T. Ishiyama. 2002. *The Communist Successor Parties of Central and Eastern Europe.* Armonk NY: M.E. Sharpe.

Brus, Wlodzimierz. 1985. *The Economic History of Eastern Europe 1919–1975.* Oxford: Clarendon Press.

Bryson, Philip J. and Gary C. Cornia. 2004. "Public Sector Transition Economics: The Struggle for Fiscal Decentralization in the Czech and Slovak Republics." *Post-Communist Economies* 16 (3): 263–283.

Buchowski, Michal, Edouard Conte, and Carole Nagengast (eds.). 2001. *Poland beyond Communism. Transition in Critical Perspective.* Memphis: University of Memphis Press.

Bühler, Pierre. 1997. *Histoire de la Pologne communiste. Autopsie d'une imposture.* Paris: Karthala (Collection "Hommes et sociétés").

Bunce, Valerie. 1999. *Subversive Institutions. The Design and the Destruction of Socialism and the State.* Cambridge: Cambridge University Press.

Caporaso, James, Maria Green Cowles, and Thomas Risse (eds.). 2001. *Transforming Europe. Europeanization and Domestic Change.* Ithaca NY: Cornell University Press.

Castellan, Georges. 1991. *Histoire des Balkans, XIV–XXe siècle.* Paris: Fayard.

Cerami, Alfio. 2005. "Social Policy in Central and Eastern Europe. The Emergence of a New European Model of Solidarity?" Paper presented at the Thrid Annual ESPAnet Conference. "Making Social Policy in the Postindustrial Age." 22–24 September. University of Fribourg, Switzerland.

Chavance, Bernard. 1994. *La fin des systèmes socialistes. Crise, réformes et transformations.* Paris: L'Harmattan.

Chavance, Bernard and Olivier Magnin. 1995. "The Emergence of Various Path-Dependant Mixed Economies in Post-Socialist Central Europe." *Emergo* Autumn: 55–74.

Chirot, Denis. 1989. *The Origin of Backwardness in Eastern Europe: Economics and Politics from the Middle Age until the Early Twentieth Century.* Berkeley: University of California.

Coffe, R. 1996. "Institutions and Investors: The Czech Republic," in Roman Frydman, Cheryl W. Gray, and Andrzej Rapaczynski (eds.). *Corporate Governance in Central Europe and Russia* 1: 111–186.

Colomer, Josef. 1997. "Stratégies institutionnelles et transitions politiques en Europe centrale et orientale (Institutional strategies and political transitions in Central and Eastern Europe)." *L'Année Sociologique* 47 (2): 105–124.

Cook, Linda J., Mitchell A. Orenstein, and Marilyn Rueschmeyer (eds.). 1999. *Left Parties and Social Policy in Post-Communist Europe.* Boulder: Westview Press.

Cox, Terry and B. Masson. 2000. "Interest Groups and the Development of the Tripartism in East and Central Europe." *European Journal of Industrial Relations* 6 (3): 325–347.

Cox, Terry and Laszlo Vass. 2000. "Government-Interest Group Relations in Hungarian Politics since 1989." *Europe-Asia Studies* 52 (6): 1095–1114.

Creed, Gerald W. 1998. *Domesticating Revolution: From Socialist Reform to Ambivalent Transition in a Bulgarian Village.* University Park: Transylvania State University Press.

Croissant, Aurel, Wolfgang Merkel, and Hans Joachim Lauth. 2000. "Zivilgesellschaft und Transformation: ein internationales Vergleich," in Wolfgang Merkel (ed.). *Zivilgesellschaft und Transformation* 5. Opladen: Leske und Budrich: 9–49.

Dabrowski, Marcin. 2008. "Structural Funds as a Driver for Institutional Change in Poland." *Europe-Asia Studies* 60 (2): 227–248.

Dahrendorf, Ralf. 1990. *Betrachtungen über die Revolution in Europa in einem Brief der an einen Herrn in Warschau gerichtet ist.* Stuttgart: DVA.

Davies, Norman. 1981. *God's Playground: A History of Poland* (2 vols.). Oxford: Clarendon Press.

Day, Stefen. 2004. "Die Osterweiterung des europapartien. Ambivalenzen eines Familienzuwachs." *Osteuropa* 54 (5–6): 223–235.

Deacon, B. 2000. "Eastern European Welfare States: The Impacts of Politics of Globalization." *Journal of European Social Policy* 10 (2): 146–161.

De la Porte, Caroline, Philippe Pochet, and Graham Romm. 2001. "Social Benchmarking, Policy Making and New Governance in the EU." *Journal of European Social Policy* 11: 291–307.

Delorme, Robert. 1996. *A l'Est du nouveau?* Paris: L'Harmattan (Collection "Pays de l'Est").

Delsoldalo, Giorgia. 2002. "Eastward Enlargement by the European Union and Transnational Parties." *International Political Sciences Review* 3: 269–281.

Derlien, Hans Ulrich. 1998 "Elitezirkulation in Ostdeutschland, 1989–1995." *Politik und Zeitgeschichte* B5: 3–17.

Dexia. 2008. *Sub-national Governments in the European Union: Responsibilities, Organisation and Finances.* Paris: Dexia Editions.

d'Haussonville, Jean. 2003. "Les processus d'adhésion: cet élargissement est-il le mieux préparé de l'histoire de l'UE?" *Pouvoir*: 5–39.

Dimitrov, Vesselin. 2001. *Bulgaria, the Uneven Transition.* London: Routledge.

Dimitrova, Alexandra. 2002. "Enlargement, Institution Building and the EU's Administrative Capacity Requirement." *West European Politics* (October): 171–190.

Djankov S. and G Pohl. 1998. "The Restructuring of Large Firms in the Slovak Republic." *Economics of Transition* 6 (1): 67–85.

Dobry, Michel. 2000. *Democratic and Capitalist Transition in Eastern Europe. Lessons for the Social Sciences.* Dordrecht/Boston: Kulwer Academic.

Domanski, Boleslaw. 2003. "Industrial Change and Foreign Direct Investment in the Post-Socialist Economy. The Case of Poland." *European Urban and Regional Studies* 10 (2): 99–118.

Domanski, Henryk. 2000. *On the Verge of the Convergence. Social Stratification in Eastern Europe.* Budapest: Central Europe University Press.

Durand, Claude. 1997. *Management et rationalisation. Les multinationales occidentales en Europe de l'Est.* Brussels: de Boeck University.

Earle, J.S. and S. Estrin. 1996. "Employee Ownership in Transition," in R. Frydman, C.W. Gray, and A. Rapaczynski (eds.). *Corporate Governance in Central Europe and Russia.* Vol. 2: *Insiders and the State.* Budapest/London/New York.

Eisenstadt, Simon H. 1999. "The Exit from Communism." *Daedalus* 12 (2): 21–41. Reprinted in Vladimir Tismaneanu (ed.). *The Breakdown of Communist Regimes. The Revolutions of 1989.* London: Routledge.

Ekiert, Georg and Jan Kubik. 1998. "Contentious Politics in New Democracies. East Germany, Hungary, Poland and Slovakia, 1989–1993." *World Politics* 50 (July): 547–581.

Esping Anderson, G. 2004. *The Three Worlds of Welfare Capitalism.* Cambridge: Polity Press.

European Commission. 2005. *Third Progress Report on Economic and Social Cohesion.* Brussels: European Commission.

———. (2007a). *Growing Regions, Growing Europe, Fourth Report on Economic and Social Cohesion.* Brussels: European Commission.

———. (2007b). *Territorial Agenda of the European Union. Towards a More Competitive Europe of Diverse Regions.* Brussels: European Commission.

Evans Peter B., Dietrich Rueschemeyer, and Theda Skokpol. 1984. *Bringing the State Back in.* Cambridge: Cambridge University Press.

Featherstone, K. and C. Radaelli (eds.). 2003. *The Politics of Europeanization.* Oxford: Oxford University Press.

Fejtö, François. 1992 (First Published, 1969). *Histoire des démocraties populaires.* Vol. 1: *L'ère de Staline (1945–1952).* Paris: Seuil (Collection "Points histoire").

———. 1996. *La tragédie hongroise. 1956.* Paris: Horay.

Ferge, Zsusza and Gabor Juhasz. 2004. "Accession and Social Policy: The Case of Hungary." *Journal of European Social Policy* 14 (3): 233–251.

Ferry, Martin. 2003. "The EU and the Recent Regional Reform in Poland." *Europe-Asia Studies* 55 (7): 1097–1116.

———. 2007. *Policy Developments in Poland, Regional Policy Developments in Member States and Norway: Country Reviews in 2006–07.* Glasgow: EPRC European Policies Research Centre. University of Strathclyde.

Ferry, Martin and Irene McCaster. 2005. "Implementing Structural Funds in Polish and Czech Regions: Convergence, Variations, Empowerment?" *Regional and Federal Studies* 15 (1): 19–39.

Fischer, Wolfram, Herbert Hax, Hans Karl Schneider, and Wolfgang Seibel (eds.). 1993. *Treuhandanstalt. Das Unmögliche wagen* (Forschungsberichte). Berlin: Akademie Verlag.

Fisera, Vladimir. 1978. *Workers' Councils in Czechoslovakia (Documents and Essays, 1968–1969).* New York: St. Martin's Press.

Fowler, Brigid. 2001. "Hungary: Patterns of Political Conflict over Territorial Administrative Reform." *Regional Studies* (Special Issue on "Region, State, and Identity in Central/Eastern Europe"): 15–37.

Frentzel-Zagorska, Janina and Jacek Wasilewski (eds.). 2000. *The Second Generation of Democratic Elites in Central and Eastern Europe.* Warsaw: PAN–ISP.

Frydman, Roman, Kenneth Murphy, and Andrzej Rapaczynski. 1998. *Capitalism with a Comrade's Face: Studies in the Postcommunist Transition.* Budapest: Central European University Press.

Gabanyi, Anneli Ute and Anton Sterbling (eds.). 2000. "Sozialstruktureller Wandel, soziale Probleme und soziale Sicherung in Südosteuropa." *Sudosteuropa-Studien* 65, Südosteuropa-Gesellschaft, München.

Ganev, Venelin. 2001a. "The Dorian Gray Effect: Winners as State Breakers in Postcommunism." *Communist and Post-Communist Studies* 34: 1–25.

———. 2001b. "The Separation of Party and State as a Logical Problem: A Glance at the Causes of State Weakness in Post-Communism." *East European Politics and Societies* 15 (2): 389–420.

Garton Ash, Timothy. 1989. *The Uses of Adversity: Essays on the Fate of Central Europe.* New York: Random House.

———. 1990. *We the People.* London: Granta.

Gérard Duchêne. 1989. *L'économie de l'URSS.* Paris: La Découverte.

Giordano, Christian, Dobrinka Kostova, and Evelyne Lohman-Minka (eds.). 2000. *Bulgaria, Social and Cultural Landscapes.* Fribourg: University Press.

Glaessner, Gert-Joachim. 1986. "Le pouvoir bureaucratique! solution des conflits en RDA," in Zdenek Mlynar, W. Brus, and P. Kende (eds.). *Les crises des systèmes de type soviétique.* Study no. 13. Cologne.

———. (ed.). 1993. *Der lange Weg zur Einheit.* Berlin. Dietz Verlag.

Gordon Skilling, Harold. 1976. *Czechoslovakia's Interrupted Revolution.* Princeton NJ: Princeton University Press.

Gorzelak, Grzegorz. 1996. *Regional Dimension of Transformation in Central Europe.* London: Jessica Kingsley.

Grabher, Gernot. 1995. "The Elegance of Incoherence: Economic Transformation in East Germany and Hungary," in Eckard Dittrich, Gert Schmid, and R. Whitley (eds.). *Industrial Transformation in Europe: Process and Context.* London: Sage: 33–54.

Granick, David. 1975. *Enterprise Guidance in Eastern Europe. A Comparison of Four Socialist Economies.* Princeton NJ: Princeton University Press.

Green Cowles, Maria, James Caporaso, and Thomas Risse (eds.). 2001. *Transforming Europe: Europeanization and Domestic Change.* Ithaca NY: Cornell University Press.

Grix, Jim and Wanda Knowles. 2002. "The Euroregion as a Social Capital Maximizer: The German Polish Euroregion Pro Europa Viadrina." *Regional and Federal Studies* 12 (4): 154–176.

Grosse, Tomasz G. 2007. "Save Public Assets. Monitoring Corruption Threats in the Distribution of Structural Funds. The Case of IROP in Poland." Institute of Public Affairs, February.

Grotz, Florian. 2000. *Politische Institutionen und Post-sozialistische Parteiensysteme in Ostmitteleuropa.* Opladen: Leske und Budrich.

Guilén, Ann M. and Bruno Palier. 2004. "Does Europe Matter?" *Journal of European Social Policy* 14 (3): 203–209.

Guyet, Rachel. 2000. *Innovations et limites des politiques de l'emploi dans les nouveaux Länder, Le cas de Leipzig, 1990–1999.* Doctoral thesis, IEP Grenoble. 2 vols.

Guyet, Rachel. 2004. "Le transfert de la Stratégie Européenne pour l'Emploi aux nouveaux États membres." *Critique Internationale* 25: 157–167.

Habermas, Jürgen. 1990. *Die nachholende Revolution.* Frankfurt am Main: Surkhamp.

Hall, Peter and Rosemary C.R. Taylor. 1996. "Political Science and the Three New Institutionalisms." *Political Studies* 44: 936–957.

Hankis, Elemer. 1990. *East European Alternatives.* Oxford: Clarendon Press.

Hann, Chris and Elisabeth Dunn (eds.). 1994. *Civil Society: Challenging Western Models.* London: Routledge.

Haraszti, Miklos. 1978. *Worker in a Workers' State.* New York: Universe Books.

Heidenreich, Martin. 1992. *Krise, Kader, Kombinate. Kontinuität und Wandel in ostdeutschen Betrieben.* Berlin: Editions Sigma.

Heyns, Barbara. 2005. "Emerging Inequalities in Central and Eastern Europe." *Annual Review of Sociology*: 163–197.

Hirschhausen Béatrice von. 1997. *Les nouvelles campagnes roumaines: paradoxes d'un retour paysan.* Paris: Belin.

Hirschman, Albert O. 1965. "Obstacles to Development: A Classification and a Quasi-Vanishing Act." *Economic Development and Cultural Change* 13 (4): 385–393.

Holmes, Lesley and Wojcieh Roszkowski. 1995. *Changing Rules.* Warsaw: ISP-Pan.

Holzmann, Robert, Mitchell A. Orenstein, and Michael Rutkowski (eds.). 2003. *Pension Reform in Europe: Process and Progress.* Washington DC: World Bank.

Hornbostel, Stefan (ed.). 1999. *Sozialistische Eliten. Horizontale und vertikale Differenzierungsmuster in der DDR.* Opladen: Leske and Budrich.

Horvath, Tomasz (ed.). 2000. *Decentralization: Experiments and Reforms.* Vol. 1: *Local Governments in Central Eastern Europe.* Budapest: IGI Books Howard.

Hübner, Peter. 1994. "Die Zukunft war gestern: Soziale und Mentale Trends in der DDR—Industriearbeiterschaft," in Hartmut Kaelbe, Jürgen Kocka, and Hartmut Zwahr (eds.). *Sozialgeschichte der DDR.* Stuttgart: Klett Kotta: 171–187.

Hughes, James, Gwendolyn Sasse, and Claire Gordon. 2004. "EU Enlargement and Power Asymmetries: Conditionality and the Commission's Role in Regionalization in Central and Eastern Europe," in *One Europe or Several?* (Working Paper, 49/04), University of Sussex.

Iankova, Elena A. 2000. "Multi-Level Bargaining During Bulgaria's Return to Capitalism." *Industrial and Labor Relations Review* 54: 115–137.

Iliev Ilia. 2004. "Small Farms in Bulgaria, a Four-Decade Anomaly," in Janos Matyas Kovacs, Petia Kabakchieva, and Roumen Avramov (eds.). *East-West Cultural Encounters, Entrepreneurship, Economic Knowledge.* Sofia: East-West.

Illner, Michal. 2002. "Réformes sur la voie de la décentralisation dans trois pays d'Europe centrale et orientale candidats à l'adhésion (Hongrie, Pologne, Répubique tchèque)." *Notre Europe, Etudes et recherches* 17 (June): 1–39.

International Labour Office. 2000. *Pension Reform in Central and Eastern Europe.* Vol. 1: *Restructuring with Privatization. Case Studies of Hungary and Poland.* Geneva: ILO.

Janos, Andrew. 2000. *East Central Europe in the Modern World: The Politics of the Borderland from the Pre- to the Post-Communist System.* San Francisco: Stanford University Press.

Jarausch, Konrad H. and Martin Sabrow (eds.). 1999. *Weg in den Untergang. Der innere Zerfall der DDR.* Göttingen: Vandenhoeck & Ruprecht.

Jarosz, Maria. 1997. *Foreign Owners and Polish Employees of Privatized Enterprises.* Warsaw: PIS-PAN.

Jasinska–Kania, A., Melvin L. Kohn, and K. Slomczynski. 1999. *Power and Social Structure (Essays in Honour of Wlodziemierz Wesolowski).* Warsaw: Wydawnictwa Uniwerstytu Warszawskeigo.

Kaelbe, Hartmut and Günther Schmidt (eds.). 2004. *Das europäische Sozialmodell. Auf dem Weg zum transnationalen Sozialstaat.* WZB Jahrbuch, Edition Sigma: Berlin.

Kaelbe, Hartmut, Jürgen Kocka, and Hartmut Zwahr (eds.). 1994. *Sozialgeschichte der DDR.* Stuttgart: Klett Kotta.

Kasers, M.C. and E.A. Radice. 1984. *The Economic History of Eastern Europe, 1919–1975.* 2 vols. Oxford: Clarendon Press.

Katsenelinboingen, Aron. 1977. "Coloured Markets in the Soviet Union." *Soviet Studies* 29 (1): 62–85.

Kaufman, Robert R. 2007. "Market Reforms and Social Protection: Lessons from the Czech Republic, Hungary and Poland." *East European Politics and Societies* 21 (1): 11–25.

Keating, Michael. 2003. "Regionalisation in Central and Eastern Europe: The Diffusion of Western Model?" in Michael Keating and James Hughes (eds.). *The Regional Challenge in Central and Eastern Europe, Territorial Restructuring and European Integration*. Brussels: PIE Lang.

Kelly, Judith. 2006. "New Wine in Old Wineskin: Promoting Political Reforms through the New European Neighbourhood Policy." *Journal of Common Market Studies* 44 (1): 29–55.

Kende, Pierre. 2003. *Le défi hongrois, de Trianon à Bruxelles*. Paris: Buchet Chastel.

Kende, Pierre and Krzysztof Pomian. 1978. *Varsovie, Budapest, 1956*. Paris: Seuil.

———. 1984. *Egalité et inégalités en Europe centrale et orientale*. Paris: Presses de la FNSP.

Kerblay, Basile. 1977. *La Société soviétique contemporaine*. Paris: Armand Colin.

Keune, Michael. 2001. *Local Development, Institutions and Conflicts in Post-Socialist Hungary: An Overview*. Budapest: ILO.

Kirov, Vassil. 2005. "Facing EU Accession: Bulgarian Trade Unions at the Crossroads," in D. Dimitrova and J. Vilrokx (eds.). *Trade Union Strategies in Central and Eastern Europe: Toward Decent Work*. Budapest: ILO: 111–151.

Kitschelt, Herbert, Zdenska Mansfeldova, Radoslav Markowski, and Gabor Toka. 1999. *Post-Communist Party Systems. Competition, Representation and Inter-Party Cooperation*. Cambridge: Cambridge University Press.

Klingemann, Hans Dieter. 1994. "Die Entstehung wettbewerbsorientierten Partiensysteme in Osteuropa," in Wolfgang Zapf and Meinolf Dierkes (eds.). *Institutionsvergleich und Institutionsdynamik*. WZB Jahrbuch, Berlin.

Kogut B. 1996. "Direct Investments. Experimentation and Corporate Governance in Transition Economies," in R. Frydman, C.W. Gray, and A. Rapaczynski (eds.). *Corporate Governance in Central Europe and Russia* 1: 293–332.

Kohl, Herbert. 2005. "Arbeitsbeziehungen in den neuen EU Mitgiedstländern und ihre Implikation für das europäische Sozialmodell," in Timm Beichelt and Jan Wielgohs (eds.). *Perspektiven der europäischen Integration nach der EU—Osterweiterung*, Workshop Documentation, FIUT Viadrina: 51–71.

Kollmorgen, Raj. 1994. "Auf der Suche nach Theorien der Transformation. Überlegungen zu Begriff und Theoretisierung der postsozialistischen Transformationen." *Berliner Journal für Soziologie* 4 (4): 381–399.

Kornai, Janos. 1980. *Economics of Shortage*. Amsterdam: North-Holland.

———. 1990. *The Road to a Free Economy. Shifting from a Socialist System: The Example of Hungary*. New York: W.W. Norton and Budapest: HVG Kiadó,

———. 1992. "The Postsocialist Transition and the State: Reflections in the Light of Hungarian Fiscal Problems." *American Economic Review, Papers and Proceedings* 82 (2): 1–21.

———. 1998. "The Citizen and the State: Reform of the Welfare System." *Emergo* Winter: 2–14.

———. 2000. "What the Change of the System from Socialism to Capitalism Does and Does Not Mean." *Journal of Economic Perspectives* Winter 14 (1): 27–42.

Kornai, Janos and Karen Egglestone. 2001. *Welfare, Choice and Solidarity in Transition: Reforming the Health Sector in Eastern Europe*. Cambridge: Cambridge University Press.

Kott, Sandrine. *Le communisme au quotidien, l'entreprise est-allemande*. Paris: Belin. 2001.

Kubik, Jan. 2005. "How to Study Civil Society: The State of the Art and What to Do Next?" *East European Politics and Society* 19 (1): 105–120.

Kutter, Amelie and Vera Trappmann. 2006. *Das Erbe des Beitritts. Europäisierung in Mittel- und Ost-Europa*. Baden-Baden: Nomos.

Kydd, Jonathan. Sophia Davidova, Miranda Mackay, and Thea Mech (eds.). 1999. "The Role of Agriculture in the Transition Process towards a Market Economy. Proceedings of a symposium conducted in association with the Südost Institute and the Thyssen Foundation (Economic Studies [ECE]). 1014–4994, no. 9)." Geneva, United Nations.

Lado, Maria. 2004. "Industrial Relations in the Candidate Countries." *European Foundation for the Improvement of Living and Working Conditions*. Budapest: ILO.

Landesmann, Michael, Hermine Vidovic, and Terry Ward. 2004. "Economic Restructuring and Labour Market Developments in the New EU Member States." *WIIW Research reports* 312, December.

Lavigne, Marie. 1974. *The Socialist Economies of the Soviet Union and Europe*. Translated by T.G. Waywell. London: M. Robertson.
———. 1999. *The Economics of Transition. From Socialist Economy to Market Economy*. London: Macmillan.
Lehmbruch, Gerhardt. 1992. "Institutionstransfer im Prozess der Vereinigung: zur politischen Logik der Verwaltungsintegration in Deutschland," in Artur Benz, Hartmut Mäding, and Wolfgang Seibel (eds.). *Verwaltungsreform und Verwaltungspolitik im Prozess der deutschen Einigung*. Baden-Baden: Nomos: 41–66.
Lendvai, Noémi. 2004. "The Weakest Link? EU Accession and Enlargement: Dialoguing EU and Post-Communist Social Policy." *Journal of European Social Policy* 14 (3): 319–333.
Lepesant, Gilles. 2000. *Géopolitique des frontières de l'Allemagne*. Paris: L'Harmattan.
———. 2007. "La Pologne, et son voisinage oriental," in F. Bafoil (ed.). *La Pologne*. Paris: Fayard: 497–501.
Lepsius, Rainer Maria. 1994. "Die Institutionenordnung als Rahmenbedingungen der Sozialgeschichte der DDR," in Hartmut Kaelbe, Jürgen Kocka, and Hartmut Zwahr (eds.). *Sozialgeschichte der DDR*. Stuttgart: Klett Kotta: 17–30.
Letki, Natalia. 2002. "Lustration and Democratization in East Central Europe." *Europe-Asia Studies* 54 (4): 529–552.
Lhomel, Edith. 2002. "Le développement régional dans les pays candidats à l'Union Européenne," in *Le Courrier des Pays de l'Est*. La Documentation Française. Doc n°1026.
———. 2007. "Régions, territoires et administrations," in Bafoil (ed.). *La Pologne*: 347–366.
Linz, Juan J. and Adam Stepan. 1996. *Problems of Democratic Transition and Consolidation, Southern Europe, South America, and Post-Communist Europe*. Baltimore and London: Johns Hopkins University Press.
Lipjard, Simon. 1992. "Democratization and Constitutional Choices in Czechoslovakia, Hungary and Poland, 1989–1991." *WZB-Paper*. FS III 92–203.
Lippert, Barbara. 2004. *Bilanz und Folgeprobleme der EU Erweiterung*. Baden-Baden: Nomos.
———. 2006a. "Erfolge und Grenzen der technokratischen EU–Erweiterungspolitik," in A. Kutter and V. Trappmann (eds.). *Das Erbe des Beitritts. Europäisierung im Mittel- und Osteuropa*. Baden-Baden: Nomos: 57–74.
———. 2006b. "Teilhabe statt Mitgliedschaft. Die EU und Ihre Nachbarn im Osten." *Osteuropa* 57 (2–3): 69–94.
Lippert, Barbara and G. Umbach. 2005. *The Pressure of Europeanization: From Post-Communist State Administrations to Normal Players in the EU System*. Baden-Baden: Nomos.
Lipset, Seymour M. and Stein Rokkan. 1967. *Party System and Voter Alignments: Cross-National Perspectives*. New York: Free Press.
Lomax, Bill. 1997. "'The Strange Death of the Civil Society' in Post-Communist Hungary." *Journal of Communist Studies and Transition Politic* 3 (1): 41–63.
Lorenz, Sabine and Kai Wegrich. "Lokale Ebene im Umbruch: Aufbau und Modernisierung der Kommunalverwaltung in Ostdeutschland." *Aus Politik und Zeitgeschichte* B5/1998. Das Parlament.
Lowenthal, Richard. 1979. "The Ruling Party in Mature Society," in M.G. Field (ed.). *The Social Consequences of Modernisation in Communist Systems*. Baltimore: Johns Hopkins University Press.
Lowit, Thomas. 1971. *Le syndicalisme de type soviétique*. Paris: Armand Colin.
———. 1979. "Y a-t-il des Etats en Europe de l'Est?" *Revue Française de Sociologie* 20: 431–466.
Lozac'h, Valérie. 1999. *Le transfert du gouvernement local ouest-allemand dans les nouveaux Länder. Une comparaison entre Eisenhüttensatdt et Hoyerswerda*. Doctoral thesis, IEP Paris.
Lüdke, Alf. 1994. "'Helden der Arbeit'—Mühen beim Arbeiten. Zur Missmutigen Loyalität von Industriearbeitrn in der DDR," in Hartmut Kaelbe, Jürgen Kocka, and Hartmut Zwahr (eds.). *Sozialgeschichte der DDR*. Stuttgart: Klett Kotta: 188–213.
Lutz, B. and R. Schmidt. 1995. *Chancen und Risiken der industriellen Restrukturierung in Ostdeutschland*. Berlin: Akademie Verlag.
Machos, Csilla. 1998. "Eliten in postsozialistischen Ungarns," in Wolfgang Höpiken and Holm Sundhausen (eds.). *Eliten in Südosteuropa. Rolle, Kontinuitäten, Brüche in Geschichte und Gegenwart*. Munich, Südosteuropa-Jahrbuch. 29.

Maciaszek, J., K. Mikolajczyk, and B. Roberts. 1998. "Some Consequences of Eliminating Unprofitable Output: Evidence from Polish Enterprises." *Europe-Asia Studies* 50 (1): 141–152.

Major, Istvan. 1999. *Privatization and Economic Peformance in Central and Eastern Europe. Lessons to Be Learnt from Western Europe*. Cheltenham: Edward Elgar.

Manfelsdova, Zdenka, Slawomir Nalecz, Eckhart Priller, and Annette Zimmer. 2004. "Civil Society in Transition: Civic Engagement and Nonprofit Organizations in Central and Eastern Europe," in Annette Zimmer and Eckhart Priller (eds.). *Future of Civil Society, Making Central European Nonprofit-Organizations Work*. Wiesbaden: VS Verlag für Sozialwissenschaften: 99–119.

Manning, Nick. 2004. "Diversity and Change in Pre-Accession Central and Eastern Europe Since 1989." *Journal of European Social Policy*: 211–232.

Mantran, Robert (ed.). 1989. *Histoire de l'empire Ottoman*. Paris: Fayard.

March, James and Jan Olsen. 1989. *Rediscovering Institutions. The Organizational Basis of Politics*. New York: Free Press.

Marcou, Gérard. 2004. "Nouveaux cadres territoriaux et institutionnels de la gestion administrative en Europe centrale et orientale," in Violette Rey, L. Coudroy de Lille, and Emmanuelle Boulineau (eds.). *L'Élargissement de l'Union Européenne: réformes territoriales en Europe centrale et orientale*. Paris: L'Harmattan: 153–168.

Marie, Jean-Jacques and Balasz Nagy (eds.). 1966. *1956, Pologne–Hongrie, ou le Printemps en Octobre*. Paris: Études et Documentation internationales.

Mathijs, Erik, Gezja Blaas, and Tomas Drucha. 1999. "Organizational Form and Technical Efficiency of Czech and Slovak Farms." *Moct–Most* 9: 331–344.

Maurel, Marie-Claude. 1998. *Les paysans contre l'Etat*. Paris: L'Harmattan.

McDermott Gerald. A. 1997. "Renegotiating the Ties That Bind: The Limits of Privatisation in the Czech Republic," in Gernot Grabher and David Stark (eds.). *Restructuring Networks in Post-socialism*. Oxford: Oxford University Press: 70–106.

McFaul, Michael. 2002. "The Fourth Wave of Democracy and Dictatorship. Non-cooperative Transition in the Post-Communist World." *World Politics* 54 (4): 212–244.

McMaster, Irene and Martin Ferry. 2005. "Implementing Structural Funds in Polish and Czech Regions: Convergence, Variations, Empowerment?' *Regional and Federal Studies* 15 (1) (March): 19–39.

McMenamin, Ian. 2004. "Parties, Promiscuity and Politicization: Business-Political Networks in Poland." *European Journal of Political Research* 43: 657–676.

Merkel, Wolfgang. 1994a. "Die Konsolidierung postautoritär und posttotalitär Demokratien: Ein Beitrag zur theorieorientierten Transformationsforschung," in Wolfgang Merkel (ed.). *Von der Revolution zur Transformation*. Vol. 3. Opladen: Leske und Budrich: 39–61.

———. 1994b. *Systemwechsel. Theorien, Ansätze und Konzeptionen*. Vol. 1. Opladen: Leske und Budrich.

———. 2000. *Zivilgesellschaft und Transformation* 5. Opladen: Leske und Budrich.

Meuschel, Sigrid. 1992. *Legitimation und Parteiherrschaft, Zum Paradox vom Stabilität und Revolution in der DDR*. Frankfurt am Main: Surkhamp.

Michel, Patrick. 1988. *La société retrouvée—Politique et religion dans l'Europe soviétisée*. Paris: Fayard.

Mihaly. 1985. "Industry and Foreign Capital," in M.C. Kasers and E.A. Radice (eds.). *Economic History of Eastern Europe, 1919–1975*. Oxford: Clarendon Press.

Miller, Leland Rhett. 2003. "Land Restitution in Post-Communist Bulgaria." *Post-Communist Economies* 15 (1): 75–89.

Miłosz, Czesław. 1986. *Histoire de la littérature polonaise*. Paris: Fayard.

Mink, Georges and Jean-Charles Szurek. 1994. "1989: une révolution sociale? Acteurs, structures et représentations à l'Est." *Revue d'Etudes Comparatives Est/Ouest* 25 (4): 5–228.

MIRE. 1997. *Comparer les systèmes de protection sociale en Europe du Sud* (Rencontres et Recherches). Vol. 3. Rencontres de Florence, Ministry of Labor.

Mises, Ludwig von. 1981. *Socialism: An Economic and Social Analysis*. Sixth Edition. Indianapolis: Liberty Fund.

Misztal, Barbara. 1999. "How Not to Deal with the Past: Lustration in Poland." *Archives Européennes de sociologie* 48 (3): 31–55.

Mlynář, Zdenek, Wlodziemierz Brus, and Pierre Kende. 1982. "Processus de 'normalisation' en Europe centrale soviétisée." *Les crises des systèmes de type soviétique.* Étude n° 1. Index: Cologne.

Morjé Howard, Marc. 2003. *The Weakness of Civil Society in Post-Communist Europe.* Cambridge: Cambridge University Press.

Morlino, Leonardo. 2000. "L'architecture constitutionnelle et politique démocratique en Europe de l'Est." *Revue française de Sciences Politiques* 50 (3): 698–712.

Myant, Martin. 2003a. "Civil Society and Political Parties in the Czech Republic," in Simon Smith (ed.). *Communities and Post-Communist Transformation. Czechoslovakia, Czech Republic and Slovakia.* London: Routledge.

———. 2003b. *The Rise and Fall of Czech Capitalism: Economic Development in the Czech Republic since 1989.* Cheltenham: Edward Elgar.

Neuman, Laszlo. 2000. "Decentralised Collective Bargaining in Hungary." *International Journal of Comparative Labour Law and Industrial Relations* 16: 113–128.

Nikolov, Jovo. 1997. "Crime and Corruption after Communism. Organized Crime in Bulgaria." *East European Constitutional Review* 6 (4) (Fall): 80–84.

North, Douglas C. 1994. "Economic Performance through Time." *American Economic Review* (June): 359–368.

Nove, Alec. 1961. *The Soviet Economy: An Introduction.* London: George Allen and Unwin.

O'Donnell, Guillermo and Philippe Schmitter. 1986. *Transition from Authoritarian Rules: Prospects for Democracy.* Baltimore: Johns Hopkins University Press.

O'Donnell, Clara M. and Richard G. Whitman. "Das Phantom-Zuckerbrot. Die Rekonstructionfehler der ENP." *Osteuropa* 57 (2–3): 95–104.

O'Dwyer, Connor. 2006. "Reforming Regional Governance in East Central Europe: Europeanization or Domestic Politics as Usual?" *East European Politics and Societies* 20 (2): 219–253.

OECD. 2004. *Economic Survey Poland n°8.*

———. 2006. *Business Clusters. Promoting Enterprises in Central Europe.* LEED. www.oecd.org.

———. 2007. *Competitive Regional Clusters. National Policy Approaches.*

———. 2008. *Poland, Territorial Review.*

Offe, Claus. 1996. *Varieties of Transition. The East European and East German Experience.* Cambridge: Polity Press.

Olearius, Axel J. 2006. "Zwischen Empowerment und Instrumentalisierung: Nichtstaatliche Akteure der Umweltpolitik während des Beitrittsprozesses," in Amelie Kutter and Vera Trappmann (eds.). *Das Erbe des Beitritts. Europäisierung in Mittel- und Os Europa.* Baden-Baden: Nomos: 339–358.

Orenstein, Mitchell A. 2000. *Out of the Red. Building Capitalism and Democracy in Post-Communist Europe.* Ann Arbor: University of Michigan Press.

Orenstein, Mitchell A. and Martine R. Haas. 2002. *Globalization and the Development of Welfare States in Post-Communist Europe.* International Security Program. Belfer Center for Science and International Affairs.

Orenstein, Mitchell A. and Michael Rutkowski (eds.). 2003. *Pension Reform in Europe: Process and Progress.* Washington DC: World Bank: 47–78.

Palier, Bruno and Yves Surel. 2007. *L'Europe en action, l'européanisation dans une perspective comparée.* Paris: L'Harmattan.

Papadimitriou, Dimitris and David Phinemore. 2003. "Les jumelages institutionnels: les leçons du cas roumain." *Revue d'Etudes Comparatives Est Ouest* 34 (3): 37–64.

Parsons, Talcott. 1966. *Societies: Evolutionary and Comparative Perspectives.* Englewood Cliffs NJ: Prentice Hall.

Pavlinek, Petr. 2002. "The Role of Foreign Direct Investment in the Privatisation and Restructuring of the Czech Motor Industry." *Post-Communist Economies* 14 (3): 363.

Perron, Catherine. 2004. *Les Pionniers de la démocratie. Elites politiques locales tchèques et est-allemandes. 1989–1998.* Paris: PUF.

Pirker, Theo, Maria Rainer Lepsius, Rainer Weinert, and Hermann H. Hertle. 1995. *Der Plan als Befehl und Fiktion. Wirtschaftsführung in der DDR.* Opladen: Westdeutscher Verlag.

Plasser, Fritz, Peter Ulam, and Harald Waldrauch. 1997. *Politischer Kulturwandel in Ost mitteleuropa: Theorie und empirische demokratische Konsolidierung.* Leke and Budrich: Opladen.

Polanyi, Karl. 1944. *The Great Transformation: The Political and Economic Origins of Our Time.* Boston: Beacon Press.

Pollack, Detlev. 2002. "Religion und Politik in den postkommunjistischen Staaten Ostmittel- und Osteuropas." *Aus Politik und Zeitgeschichte* B 42–43: 15–22.

Pomian, Krzysztof. *Pologne, défi à l'impossible.* Paris: Editions ouvrières. 1983.

Portet, Stéphane. 2005. "Poland: Circumventing the Law or Fully Deregulating?" in D. Vaughan-Whitehead (ed.). *Working Employment Conditions in New Members States.* Geneva: ILO: 273–337.

Potusek, Martin. 2004. "Accession and Social Policy: The Case of the Czech Republic." *Journal of European Social Policy* 14 (3): 253–266.

Pouliquen, Alain. 2000. *Compétitivité et revenus agricoles dans les secteurs agro-alimentaires des Peco, implications avant et après adhésion pour les marchés et les politiques de l'UE.* Rapport UE.

Pridham, T. 1994. *Democratization in Eastern Europe. Domestic and International Perspectives.* London and New York: Routledge.

Pryor, Frederic. 1993. *The Red and the Green, the Rise and Fall of Collectivized Agricultures in Marxist Regimes.* Princeton NJ: Princeton University Press.

Przeworski, Adam. 1991. *Democracy and the Market, Political and Economic Reforms in Eastern Europe and Latin America.* New York: Cambridge University Press.

Putnam, Robert. 2002. *Democracies in Flux: The Evolution of Social Capital in Contemporary Society.* New York: Oxford University Press.

Radaelli, Claudio. 2001. "The Domestic Impact of European Union Public Policy: Notes on Concepts, Methods, and the Challenge of Empirical Research." *Politique européenne* 5: 107–142.

Ragaru, Nadège. 2005. *Apprivoiser les transformations post–communistes en Bulgarie: la fabrique du politique (1989–2004).* Doctoral thesis, 2 vols.

———. 2007. "*Multigroup*: une trajectoire entrepreneuriale dans la construction du capitalisme bulgare," in Gilles Favarel-Garrigues and Jean-Louis Briquet (eds.). *Sociologie des entreprises criminelles.* Paris: Presses de Sciences Po.

Renooy, Piete, Staffon Ivarson, Olga van der Wusten, and Remco Meijer. 2004. *Undeclared Work in an Enlarged Union. An Analysis of Undeclared Work: An In–Depth Study of Specific Items.* Final Report. European Commission. DG Employment and Social Affairs.

Rey, Violette, L. 1996. *Les nouvelles campagnes de l'Europe Centrale et Orientale.* Paris: CNRS.

Rey, Violette, L., Coudroy de Lille, and Emmanuelle Boulineau. 2004. *L'Élargissement de l'Union Européenne: réformes territoriales en Europe centrale et orientale.* Paris: L'Harmattan.

Reynaud, Jean-Daniel, Catherine Paradeise, and Jean Saglio. 1988. *Le système des relations professionnelles.* Paris: CNRS.

Rieger, Elmar. 2004. "Wohlfahrt für Bauern? Die Osterweiterung der Agrarpolitik." *Osteuropa* 54 (5–6): 296–315.

Ringlod, Dena. "Social Policy in Post-Communist Europe. Legacies and Transition," in Linda J. Cook, Mitchell A. Orenstein, and Marilyn Rueschmeyer (eds.). 1999. *Left Parties and Social Policy in Post-Communist Europe.* Boulder: Westview Press: 11–46.

Roland, Gérard. 2000. *Transition and Economics: Politics, Markets, and Firms.* Cambridge MA: MIT Press.

Rollet, Henry. 1984. *La Pologne au XXe siècle.* Paris: Pedone.

Roszkowski, Wojcieh. 1995. *Land Reforms in East Central Europe after World War II.* Warsaw: ISP-PAN.

Rueschemeyer, Dietrich, Evelyn Stephen, and John D. Stephens. 1992. *Capitalism, Development and Democracy.* Oxford: Polity Press.

Rupnik, Jacques. 1979. "Dissent in Poland, 1968–1978: The End of Revisionism and the Rebirth of Civil Society," in Rudolf L. Tokes (ed.). *Opposition in Eastern Europe.* London: Macmillan: 60–111.

———. 2008. "De l'antipolitique à la crise de la démocratie: que reste-t-il de l'héritage de la dissidence?" in Christian Lequesne and Monika MacDonagh-Pajerova (eds.). *La citoyenneté démocratique dans l'Europe des vingt-sept.* Paris: L'Harmattan: 101–125.

Rusin, Philippe. 2007. "Économie politique de la transition polonaise," in Bafoil (ed.). *La Pologne:* 281–302.

Rychard, Andrzej. 1993. *Reforms, Adaptation and Breakthrough.* Warsaw: IFIS-Pan.

Rys, Vladimir. 2000. "Transition Countries of Central Europe Entering the European Union: Some Social Protection Issues." *International Social Security Review* 54 (2–3): 177–189.

Saurugger S. and Yves Surel. 2006. "L'européanisation comme processus de transfert de politique publique." *Revue Internationale de Politique Comparée* 13 (2): 179–211.

Schimmelfenning, Frank. 2005. "Strategic Calculations and International Socialization: Memberships, Incentives, Party Constellations, and Sustained Compliance in Central and Eastern Europe." *International Organization* 59 (Fall): 827–860.

Schimmelfenning, Frank, Stefan Engert, and Heiko Knobel. 2006. *International Socialisation in Europe. European Organisations, Political Conditionality and Democratic Change.* Basingstoke UK: Palgrave Macmillan.

Schimmelfenning, Frank and Ulrich Sedelmeier. 2005. *Conceptualizing the Europeanization of Eastern and Central Europe.* Ithaca NY: Cornell University Press.

Schmid Josef, Löbler Franck, and Tieman Heinrich. 1994. Probleme der Einheit. Organisationsstrukturen und Probleme von Parteien und Verbänden, Berichte aus der neuen Ländern. Metropolis Verlag.

Schoeneman, Richard. 2005. "Captains or Pirates? State Business Relations in Post-Communist Poland." *East European Politics and Society* 19 (1): 40–75.

Schülpetz A. 2004. "Policy Transfer and Pre-accession. Europeanizaiton of Czech Employment Policy." *WZB-Paper.* SP III. 2004–201E.

Sedelmeier, Ulrich. 2005. "Eastern Enlargement: Towards a European EU?" in Helen Wallace and William Wallace (eds.). *Policy-Making in the European Union.* Fifth Edition. Oxford: Oxford University Press: 402–428.

Sedik, David J., Fock Karin, and Dudwick Nora. 2007. "Land Reform and Farm Restructuring in Transition Countries: The Experience of Bulgaria, Moldova, Azerbaijan, and Kazakhstan." World Bank Report.

Seibel, Wolfgang. 1994. "Das Zentralistische Erbe, die institutionnelle Entwicklung der Treuhandanstalt und die Nachhaltigkeit ihrer Auswirkungen auf die bundesstaatlichen Verfassungstrukturen." *Aus Politik und Zeitgeschichte* B 43–44/94 October 28: 3–13.

Sgard, Jérôme. 1999. "Crise financière, inflation et Currency Board en Bulgarie (1991–1998). Leçons d'une transition indisciplinée." *Revue d'Etudes Comparatives Est Ouest* 30 (2–3): 215–235.

Sissenich, Beate. "The Transfer of EU Social Policy to Poland and Hungary," in Frank Schimmelpfennig and Ulrich Sedelmeier (eds.). 2005. *The Europeanization of Central and Eastern Europe.* Ithaca NY: Cornell University Press: 156–177.

Skalnik Leff, Carol. 1999. "Democratization and Disintegration in Multinational States. The Break-Up of the Communist Federations." *World Politics* 51 (2): 205–235.

Smith, Simon. (ed.). 2003. *Local Communities and Post-Communist Transformation. Czechoslovakia, Czech Republic and Slovakia.* London: Routledge.

Smolar, Alexander. 1996. "Civil Society after Communism: From Opposition to Atomization." *Journal of Democracy* 1: 24–38.

Sozialstaat. WZB Jahrbuch 2004. 107–139.

Staniszkis, Jadwiga. 1991. *The Dynamics of Breakthrough in Eastern Europe: The Polish Experience.* Berkeley: University of California Press.

Stark, David. 1990. "Privatization in Hungary: From Plan to Market or from Plan to Clan." *East European Politics and Societies* 4 (3): 351–392.

———. 1992. "From System Identity to Organizational Diversity: Analyzing Social Change in Eastern Europe." *Contemporary Sociology* 21: 299–304.

———. 1996. "Recombinant Property in Eastern European Capitalism." *American Journal of Sociology* 4: 993–1027.

Stark, David and Gernot Grabbher. 1997. *Restructuring Networks in Post-Socialism: Legacies, Linkages, Localities.* London: Oxford University Press.

Stark, David and Laszlo Bruszt. 1998. *Postsocialist Pathways. Transforming Politics and Property in East Central Europe.* Cambridge: Cambridge University Press.

Stark, David and Victor Nee (eds.). 1989. *Remaking the Economic Institutions of Socialism: China and Eastern Europe*. Stanford: Stanford University Press.

Starosta, Pawel, Krzysztof Gorlach, and Imre Kovach (eds.). 1999. *Rural Societies under Communism and Beyond*. Lodz: University of Lodz.

Sterbling, Anton. 2003. "Eliten in Sudosteuropea, Rolle, Kontinuitäten, Brüche." *Aus Politik und Zeitgeschichte* B10–11: 10–17.

Stiglitz, Joseph E. 2002. *Globalization and Its Discontents*. London: Allen Lane.

Streith, Michael. 2005. *Dynamiques paysannes en Mecklenburg, survie d'un savoir-faire*. Münster: LIT Verlag.

Sugar, Peter. 1984. "Continuity and Change in Eastern Europe. Authoritarism, Autocracy, Fascism and Communism." *East European Quarterly*: 1–23.

Surdej, Alexander. 2005. "Political Corruption in Post-Communist Poland." *Forschungstelle Osteuropa Bremen* 65: 5–20.

Swain, Nigel. 1999. "Agricultural Restitution and Cooperative Transformation in the Czech Republic, Hungary and Slovakia." *Europe-Asia Studies* 51 (7): 1199–1219.

Szczerbiak, Alex. 2002. "Dealing with the Communist Past or the Politics of the Present. Lustration in Post-Communist Poland." *Europe-Asia Studies* 54 (4): 553–572.

Szelenyi, Ivan, E. 1988. *Social Entrepreneurs. Embourgeoisement in Rural Hungary*. Madison: University of Wisconsin Press.

Szelenyi, Ivan, E. and Szonja Szelenyi. 1995. "Circulation or Reproduction of Elites during the Post-Communist Transformation of Eastern Europe." *Theory and Society* 24: 613–628.

Szelenyi, Ivan, E. Wnuk Lipinski, and D. Treiman (eds.). 1995. "Circulation and Reproduction of Elites during the Post-Communist Transformation of East-Europe." *Theory and Society* 24 (5).

Tas, Rona Anton. 1997. *The Great Surprise of the Small Transformation: The Demise of Communism and the Rise of the Private Sector in Hungary*. Ann Arbor: University of Michigan Press.

Tatur, Melanie, Rainer Deppe, Helmut Dubiel, and Ulrich Rödel. 1991. *Demokratischer Umbruch in Osteuropa*. Frankfurt am Main: Suhrkamp.

Thaa, Winfried. 1996. *Die Wiedergeburt des Politischen: Zivilgesellschaft und Legitimationskonfilkt in den Revolutionen von 1989*. Habilitation im Fach Politikwissenschaft an der Universität Tübingen.

Tismaneanu, Vladimir. 2000. *Between Past and Future. The Revolutions of 1989 and Their Aftermath*. Budapest: Central University Press.

Tokes, Rudolf (ed.). 1977. *Opposition in Eastern Europe*. Oxford: Macmillan.

Tomka, Béla. 2004. "Wohlfahrtsstaatliche Entwicklung in Ostmitteleuropa and das europäische Sozialmodell, 1945–1990," in Hartmut Kaelbe and Günther Schmidt (eds.). *Das europäische Modell. Aud dem Weg zum transnationalen*. WZB Jahrbuch: 107–139.

Toole, James. 2007. "The Historical Foundations of Party Politics in Post-Communist East Central Europe." *Europe-Asia Studies* 59 (4): 541–566.

Touraine, Alain, François Dubet, Michel Wiewiorka, and Jan Strzelecki. 1983. *Solidarity. Poland 1980–81*. Cambridge: Cambridge University Press.

Tübke, Alexander. 2003. "Patterns of Industrial Change in the Post-Communist EU Candidate Countries." *Post-Communist Economies* 15 (2): 181–207.

Tulmets, Elsa. 2006. "L'adaptation de la méthode ouverte de coopération à la politique de l'élargissment de l'UE." *Politique européenne* 16.

United Nations Economic Commission for Europe. 1998. *Economic Survey of Europe*. Geneva.

———. 1999. *Economic Survey of Europe*. Geneva.

———. 2003. *Economic Survey of Europe*. Geneva.

———. 2004. "Poverty in Eastern Europe and in the CIS." *Economic Survey of Europe* 1: 163–176.

Uvalic, Milica and Daniel Vaughan-Whitehead (eds.). 1996. *Privatization Surprises in Transition Economies, Employee-Ownership in Central and Eastern Europe*. Cheltenham: Edward Elgar.

Vachudova, Milena Anna. 2005. *Europe Undivided. Democracy, Leverage and Integration after Communism*. Oxford: Oxford University Press.

Vajdova, Zdenka. 2003. "Local Community Transformation. The Czech Republic 1990–2000," in Simon Smith (ed.). *Local Communities in Contemporary Eastern Europe*. London: Routledge.

Vaughan-Whitehead, Daniel. 2003. *EU Enlargement versus Social Europe? The Uncertain Future of the European Social Model*. Cheltenham. Edward Elgar.

Vaughan-Whitehead, Daniel. 2005. *Working Employment Conditions in New Member States*. Geneva: ILO.

Vecernik, Jan and Petr Mateju. 1999. *Ten Years of Rebuilding Capitalism: Czech Society after 1989*. Prague: Academia.

Verdury, Katherine. 1999. "What Was Communism and What Comes Next," in Tismaneanu, *Between Past and Future*: 63–85.

Vortman, Heinz. 1989. "Die soziale Sicherheit in der DDR," in Werner Weidenfeld and Hartmut Zimmermann (eds.). *Deutschland Handbuch. Eine doppelte Bilanz 1949–1989*. Bundeszentrale für politische Bildung: 326–341.

Voskamp, Ulrich and V. Wittke. 1991. "Aus Modernisierungsblokkaden werden Abwärtspiralen. Zur Reorganization von Betrieben und Kombinaten der ehemaligen DDR." *Göttingen SFU Mitteilungen* (December): 12–30.

Voslenski, M. 1980. *La Nomenklatura, les privilégiés en URSS*. Paris: Belfond.

Wädekin, Klaus Eugen. 1977. "The Place of Agriculture in the European Communist Economies: A Statistical Essay." *Soviet Studies* 29 (August): 238–254.

Waele, Jean Michel De (ed.). 2004. *Partis politiques et démocraties en Europe centrale et orientale*. Brussels: Éditions de l'Université de Bruxelles.

Wasilewski, Jacek. 2000. "Polish Post-Transitional Elites," in Janina Frentzel-Zagorska and Jacek Wasilewski (eds.). *The Second Generation of Democratic Elites*. Warsaw: IPS: 197–216.

Weber, Max. 1978. *Economy and Society*. Berkeley: University of California Press.

———. 1994. "Socialism." *Political Writings*. Cambridge: Cambridge University Press.

———. 2004. "Introduction to the Economic Ethics of World Religions," in Sam Whimster (ed.). *The Essential Weber. A Reader*. London/New York: Routledge.

Werth, Nicolas. 2007. *La terreur et le désarroi. Staline et son système*. Paris: Perrin.

Westley-Scott, James. 2002. "Crossborder Governance in the Baltic Sea Region." *Regional and Federal Studies* 12 (4): 135–153.

White, Stephen, Judy Batt, and Paul G. Lewis (eds.). 2003. *Developments in Central and Eastern European Politics*. Basingstoke: Palgrave.

Wiesenthal, Wiener (ed.). 1995. *Einheit als Interessenpolitik. Studien zur sektoralen Transformation Ostdeutschland*. Frankfurt am Main: Campus Verlag.

Wild, Gérard. 2002. "Economie de la Transition: le dossier," in D. Colas (ed.). *L'Europe post-communiste*. Paris: PUF: 257–389.

Winiecki, Jan. 2004. "Determinants of Catching Up or Falling Behind: Interaction of Formal and Informal Institutions." *Post-Communist Economies* 16 (2): 137–152.

Wollmann, Hellmut. 1996. "Institutionenbildung in Ostdeutschland: Rezeption, Eigenentwicklung oder Innvation," in Andreas Eisen and Helmut Wollmann (eds.). *Institutionenbildung in Ostdeutschland. Zwischer exoegener Steuerung und Eigendynamik*. Opladen: Leske und Budrich.

———. 1997. "Institution Building, and Decentralization in Formerly Socialist Countries: The Cases of Poland, Hungary, and East Germany." *Environment and Planning, Government and Policy* 15: 463–480.

Womack, J.P., D.T. Jones, and D. Roose. 1990. *The Machine That Changed the World*. New York: Rawson Associates.

Woolfson, Charles. 2006. "Working Environment and 'Soft Law' in the Post-Communist New Member States." *Journal of Common Market Studies* 44 (1): 195–215.

World Bank. 2001. *Making Transition Work for Everyone, Poverty and Inequality in Europe and in Central Asia*. Washington DC: World Bank.

Yoder, Jennifer. 2003. "Decentralization and Regionalization after Communism, Administrative and Territorial Reforms in Poland and the Czech Republic." *Europe-Asia Studies* 55 (2): 263–286.

———. 2007. "Leading the Way to Regionalization in Post-Communist Europe. An Examination of the Process and Outcomes of Regional Reforms in Poland." *East European Politics and Societies* 21 (3): 424–446.

Zaleski, Eugène. 1980. *Stalinist Planning for Economic Growth, 1933–1952*. Chapel Hill NC: University of North Carolina Press.

Zapf, Wolfgang. 1994a. "Die Transformation in der ehemaligen DDR und die soziologische Theorie der Modernisierung." *Berliner Journal für Soziologie* 3: 295–305.

————. 1994b. *Modernisierung, Wohlfahrtentwicklung und Transformation.* Berlin: Editions Sigma.

Zaremba, Marcin. 2007. *"Pologne 1956–1980. Le socialisme du Bigos,"* in F. Bafoil (ed.). *La Pologne*: 198–222.

Zarycki, Tomasz. 2000. "Politics in the Periphery: Political Cleavages in Poland Interpreted in their Historical and International Context." *Europe-Asia Studies* 52 (5): 851–873.

Zecchini, Salvatore (ed.). 1997. *Lessons from the Economic Transition, Central and Eastern Europe in the 90s.* Dordrecht/Boston: Kluwer Academic.

Ziblatt, Daniel and Nick Biziouras. 2002. "Communist Successor Parties in East Central Europe," in Andras Bozoki and John T. Ishiyama (eds.). *The Communist Successor Parties of Central and Eastern Europe.* Armonk NY: M.E. Sharp: 287–302.

Zielonka, Jan and Alex Pravda (eds.). 2003. *Democratic Consolidation in Eastern Europe.* Vol. 1: *Institutional Engineering.* Vol. 2: *Institutional and Transnational Factors.* Oxford: Oxford University Press.

Zimmer, Annette and Eckhart Priller (eds.). 2004. *Future of Civil Society, Making Central European Nonprofit-Organizations Work.* Wiesbaden: VS Verlag für Sozialwissenschaften.

INDEX